The Methuen Drama Book of
Trans Plays Volume 3

The Methuen Drama Book of Trans Plays Volume 3

Young Adult Edition

The Interrobangers
Magic Girl! . . . And Her Demons
t4t
The Brunch Crowd
The More the Man
Man and Moon
Caeneus
Unfair Advantage
Tides

Edited and introduced by
LEANNA KEYES, LINDSEY MANTOAN, AND
ANGELA FARR SCHILLER

methuen | drama

LONDON • NEW YORK • OXFORD • NEW DELHI • SYDNEY

METHUEN DRAMA
Bloomsbury Publishing Plc, 50 Bedford Square, London, WC1B 3DP, UK
Bloomsbury Publishing Inc, 1359 Broadway, New York, NY 10018, USA
Bloomsbury Publishing Ireland, 29 Earlsfort Terrace, Dublin 2, D02 AY28, Ireland

BLOOMSBURY, METHUEN DRAMA and the Methuen Drama logo are trademarks of
Bloomsbury Publishing Plc

First published in Great Britain 2026

Contents

List of Illustrations

Acknowledgements

We are so grateful to Dom O'Hanlon for his support and guidance on this series of books, and for saying yes when we asked for a third volume. Mark Jones ushered this volume through production with grace and generosity. Merv Honeywood patiently and diligently went through this proofing process with us and we appreciate his care and attentiveness. Alan White gifted us with their beautiful insights, artistry, and contributions. Our gratitude goes to our families, who helped make the space for us to work on this project. And, as always, we thank the artists and scholars whose work comprises this volume—thank you for sharing your genius and creativity with us.

Licensing

The Interrobangers: For licensing information, contact M Sloth Levine at slothlevine@gmail.com

Magic Girl! . . . And Her Demons: For licensing information, contact Charlotte Snow at charlottesnow1789@gmail.com

t4t: For licensing information, contact Jessica Scott at jessvscottwrites@gmail.com

The Brunch Crowd: For licensing information, contact Dillon Yruegas at dillonyruegas@gmail.com

The More The Man: For licensing information, contact Jameson P. Murray at YesIndeedMedia@gmail.com

Man and Moon: For licensing information, contact Siena Marilyn at siena.marilyn@gmail.com

Caeneus: For licensing information, contact Samuel Achilles at samuel.achilles.e@gmail.com

Unfair Advantage: For licensing information, contact Tyler Rocio Ecoña at tylerecona@gmail.com

Tides: For licensing information, contact Eliana Rubin at elianashirarubin@gmail.com

Play Synopses

The Interrobangers by M Sloth Levine

Four groovy teens and a dog search the woods in their van outside the small town of Foggy Bluffs. When a dark figure from Zodiac DuMaurier's past is found dead, he must team up with his estranged childhood friends for one last mystery. They explore drugs, queerness, and the fear that men in rubber masks are scarier than monsters after all. The four question the world they know, looking into the parts of their history they would rather avoid.

Magic Girl! . . . And Her Demons by Charlotte Snow

Nox, a young impoverished and ignored girl, summons the son of Satan to make a bet: her soul for "super magic powers" to fix her life. The twist? She can only keep her soul and her newfound magic if she can go six days without murdering someone. Easier said than done when those six days are filled with a doubtful partner, her school's jealous popular girl, and the literal demons infesting her mind. Will she become the magic girl she's always dreamed of being, or will she be damned by her worst impulses?

t4t by Jessica Scott

Lily is a trans woman in a rough place in life. She's shut-in aside from going to her miserable job and spends the rest of her time wallowing in self-hatred spewed at her by her inner monologues. After her roommate, the one person she hasn't managed to push away, encourages her to try dating again, she makes the t4t connection of her dreams. The kind of connection that will fix her . . . right?

The Brunch Crowd by Dillon Yruegas

Always wanted to know how transgender people of color go about their daily lives? Spoiler alert: they don't just talk about hormones, surgery, or anything else that The Cis seem to be so obsessed about; they go to brunch and drink too many mimosas, just like you! In *The Brunch Crowd*, follow the lives of four twenty-something queer trans friends who often meet at their favorite Mexican brunch spot in rapidly gentrifying Austin, Texas.

The More The Man by Jameson P. Murray

A young Black trans man (King) hastily moves back home to New Orleans, while harboring a secret from his mother. He dreams of the kind of man his father is whilst he's confronted with the reality from his grandfather. King tries to maintain relationships with the women in his life while succumbing to the idea of manhood around him when he is pushed to reveal harsh truths about his transition, masculinity, and love.

Man and Moon by Siena Marilyn

A story about unlikely friends—Aaron, a transitioning man, meets Luna, a twelve-year-old girl with a deep passion for outer space, in the waiting room of a hospital's Oncology Unit. Together they learn how to wait, each navigating their own changing bodies and lives as they fit within the context of space and time.

Caeneus by Samuel Achilles

Taking place in an atemporal Ancient Greece and loosely based on a myth from Ovid's *Metamorphoses*, *Caeneus* turns this largely forgotten transgender male mythological figure into a hero. After his gender is transformed by the god Poseidon, Caeneus undertakes a sea voyage and attempts to make sense of his transformation, romance, family, and home.

Unfair Advantage by Tyler Rocio Ecoña

When Mia Jonas made history as the first trans girl on a woman's collegiate swim team, she expected backlash. What she didn't expect was for the NCAA to tweak participation guidelines after every race she won. But when the rules backfire on other participants, Mia finds herself in the midst of a larger struggle, begging the question: what does being a "real woman" actually entail?

Tides by Eliana Rubin

Tides explores an America where being queer and trans is outlawed. Its three parts do their best to contain the fires ignited by the people that live within it; however, much like our America, they refuse to be quiet. *Tides* examines the nuances of life through specifically queer and trans lenses and asks: What happens when people break curfew? What happens when elected officials follow through on their promises? What happens when queer and trans people are allowed to thrive?

Biographies

Ryan Adelsheim (they/them) is an interdisciplinary scholar of American performance, trans studies, and queer archives and Assistant Professor in the Department of Theatre Arts at the University of Iowa. Their current research focuses on aesthetics of unfinishedness in queer and trans theater, dance, and performance. An active artistic collaborator, recent credits include dramaturg for New Harmony Project, co-adaptor for *Affinity* based on the novel by Sarah Waters with director Alex Keegan, and dramaturg and researcher for *soldiergirls* by Emil Weinstein and Emily Johnson-Erday. Ryan received their doctorate and MFA in Dramaturgy & Dramatic Criticism from the David Geffen School of Drama at Yale University, and their writing has appeared in *Theater* magazine, *Performance Response Journal*, and in Routledge's *Dramaturgy and History* anthology.

Joshua Bastian Cole-Kurz (he/him) holds a Ph.D. in Performing and Media Arts from Cornell University and is currently a Visiting Assistant Professor in Gender, Sexuality, and Intersectional Justice at Hobart and William Smith Colleges. He formerly led the LGBTQ+ Resource Center at HWS and has taught at Quinnipiac University, Cornell, SUNY Plattsburgh, and CUNY. In addition to contributing to Volumes 2 and 3 of *The Methuen Drama Book of Trans Plays*, his work appears in *TSQ: Trans Studies Quarterly*, *Somatechnics*, *New Review of Film and Television Studies*, *Jump Cut*, *HowlRound*, *Fifty Key Figures in Queer US Theatre*, and more. He created the Killjoys LisT in 2014, and with over twenty-five years in the trans performance scene, he has performed on stage and screen.

Tyler Rocio Ecoña (they/them) is a Peruvian-American trans lesbian playwright, performer, and dramaturg based in Lenapehoking, aka Philadelphia. Their writing explores bilingual dialogues, intersectional realities, and Indigiqueer joy through magical realism and hope beyond margin. Ecoña has been a resident at the Kennedy Center's Playwright Discovery Competition, a Silver Medal recipient at the Scholastic Art & Writing Awards, and a Season Apprentice at InterAct Theatre Company. Their work has been featured by Philadelphia Theatre Company, Temple University's Institute on Disabilities, FringeArts, Philly Women's Theatre Festival, Azukafest & more. They are also the editor-in-chief of *Qhariwarmikuna*, a multilingual literary magazine of queer, trans, and 2Spirit Andean art; @qhariwarmikuna. BFA: The University of the Arts. @tyleriito

Sebastián Eddowes-Vargas (he/they) is a Peruvian playwright, scholar, dramaturg and educator, author of plays as *Nunca Estaremos en Broadway* (with Rodrigo Y. Sandoval); *Debut* (with Caro Black Tam); *Hasta que Choque el Hueso* (with Mario Zanatta); *El Rancho de los Niños Perdidos*; *Una Historia de (Poli)amor*; *Can The Peruvian Speak?* Their plays have been presented in Belgium, Brazil, Costa Rica, Ecuador, Perú, UK and USA, receiving recognition from IberEscena, Global Latin American Voices, Shakespeare is Dead, The Workshop Theater, Yale Summer Cabaret, Teatro La Plaza, Microteatro Lima, Municipalidad de Lima, among others. He is a DFA candidate at the David Geffen School of Drama at Yale with the dissertation *Post-National Dramaturgies of the Americas, or, The Nation Fails*, and a Lecturer at Boston University.

Angela M. Farr Schiller, Ph.D., (she/her) is an Emmy Award ® winning director and a multiple award-winning dramaturg, educator, and scholar. Her published projects include *The Methuen Drama Book of Trans Plays vol. 1* (Blooomsbury), shortlisted for a national Lambda Literary Award, and *Troubling Traditions: Canonicity, Theatre, and Performance in the U.S.* (Routledge)), recipient of the Association of Theatre in Higher Education (ATHE) national award for Outstanding Edited Volume, as well as an essay featured in the international journal *Modern Drama* entitled "Touching Back While Black: Self-Defense and the Politics of Black U.S. Citizenship in Paul Green's *In Abraham's Bosom*". She served as the historical fashion consultant for the national touring exhibit *Clothes Story*. Her work is ultimately rooted in revealing the ways that performance can be utilized as a meaningful tool for critical thinking, social justice, and the development of empathy and compassion for the human experience. Website: angelaschiller.com

Eric M. Glover (he/him) is an Associate Professor Adjunct at David Geffen School of Drama at Yale University, where he practices dramaturgy and dramatic criticism.

Stephanie Hsu is faculty in English and American Studies at Pace University in New York. Originally from Atlanta, Georgia, Hsu is the coeditor of *My Race is My Gender: Portraits of Nonbinary People of Color* (Rutgers UP, 2024), an editorial collective member for the Q+Public book series, and a recipient of the 2020 Community Catalyst Award from the National Queer Asian/Pacific Islander Alliance.

Caitlin A. Kane (they/she) is an Assistant Professor of Theatre History and Dramatic Criticism at Kent State University where they serve as the Theatre Studies area head and the chair of Kent State United Faculty Association's LGBTQIA2S+ advocacy committee. As an artist-scholar, their research and creative practice center on feminist, queer, and trans approaches to staging history that illuminate contemporary socio-political issues. Alongside Erin Stoneking, Kane is co-editor of *Dramaturgy and History: Staging the Archive* (Routledge) and a forthcoming symposium in *Theatre and Performance Notes and Counternotes* entitled "Dramaturgical Interventions into Contested Histories." Their scholarship has been published in *Theatre Topics, The Journal of American Drama and Theatre, The Journal of Dramatic Theory and Criticism,* and *The Scholar as Human.*

Leanna Keyes (she/her) is a co-editor on this anthology and also published her play *Doctor Voynich and Her Children* in the first volume. She's a multi-hyphenate theater professional: playwright, lighting, video, audio, and more. Through her company, Transcend Streaming, she served as the Director of Photography for a hybrid production of *The Orchard* starring Mikhail Baryshnikov and Jessica Hecht, and has worked on many other off-Broadway productions. As an artist, she's most interested in the intimate messy lives of queer and trans people past, present, and future. leannakeyes.com

Fig Lefevre (they/them) is a playwright, dramaturg, director, educator, intimacy choreographer, and artist whose work focuses on transness & queerness, theater as a tool for social change, and consent-based practices. Fig is also deeply invested in drag, the *Scream* movies, and the color pink. They currently serve as an instructor of theater at Holyoke Community College, and have previously taught at the University of Massachusetts, Westfield State University, and Keene State College. Recent projects include a traveling applied theater workshop called the Trans Naming Ritual, developing a play about motherhood & cannibalism (*Mother*), and intimacy choreographing across Western Mass. Recent publications include chapters in *The Palgrave Handbook of Queer and Trans Feminisms in Contemporary Performance, Beyond Binaries: Trans Identities in Contemporary Culture,* and *Troubling Traditions: Canonicity, Theatre, and Performance in the US.* www.figlefevre.com

M Sloth Levine (they/them) is a playwright, director, and designer in New York City. Their plays are sour gummy worms, written for gothic dollhouses made out of velvet, petrified wood, slime, celluloid, gold leaf, gelatin, and citric acid. *The Interrobangers* premiered in Boston in 2024 with Company One Theatre and The Theatre Offensive. *At Hotel MacGuffin* was the 2021 Parity Development Award recipient from Parity Productions. Sloth's plays have been developed at thousands of coffee shops around the country, Roundabout Theater Company, Company One, Theatre [Untitled], Sparkhaven Theatre, Central Square Theatre, Tufts University, University of Massachusetts Amherst, and University of Wisconsin Madison.

Lindsey Mantoan (she/her) is the Ronni Lacroute Chair in Theatre Arts and an Associate Professor at Linfield University. Her latest book project (Oxford UP, forthcoming) researches the way musicals set in high schools frame adolescence as a laboratory for personal and communal experimentation. She is the author of *War as Performance: Conflict in Iraq and Political Theatricality* (Palgrave 2018) and co-editor of *Troubling Traditions: Canonicity, Theatre, and Performance in the US* (Routledge 2022, winner of the 2024 Editing Award from the Association for Theatre in Higher Education) and *The Methuen Drama Book of Trans Plays* (Bloomsbury 2021, shortlisted for a Lambda Literary Award), among others. She is an occasional contributor to CNN.com, a director, and an intimacy director.

Samuel Achilles (he/him) is a New England-based playwright, fiction writer, and archivist who seeks to tell expansive queer and trans stories inspired by mythology and history. His work has been produced with Theater Between Addresses, Hampshire College, Eggtooth Productions, Fresh Ink Theatre, and Auburn University. He holds a BA in Playwriting and History from Hampshire College, and owes the success of this play to the wonderful collaborators and mentors he met there.

Siena Marilyn (they/he/she) is a bi-racial, queer playwright, poet, and actor. They graduated from CSUF's BFA Acting program and Chicago Dramatists' Russ Tutterow Fellowship. *Man and Moon* was produced by NNPN's Rolling World Premiere at Good Company Theatre, 16th Street Theater, and Oregon Contemporary Theatre, followed by Moxie Theatre. SDSU included the script in its MFA Theatre program on gender identity education. *The Empty Space* premiered at the University of Wales, Trinity Saint David, and later at Rollins College. *Inosculation* ran at the Hollywood Fringe Festival with Sacred Fools Theater. *Say NO to One Paseo* was presented by Company of Angels and Euphoria Theatre Company. Learn more at gayforplays.com and @tadasiena Biggest thanks to Chris and their mom for their love and support!

Jameson P. Murray (he/him) is a Black, trans writer, director, and comedian based in Los Angeles. His multi-hyphenates have earned him awards for writing, directing, theatre and film. When he's not rollerskating behind Kenan in *Good Burger 2*, he can be found performing stand-up in Los Angeles or writing on films like *A Movie Named*

Sucka (Kids in the Spotlight, Inc). Murray has also written screenplays and stageplays for Fresh Ink Theatre, The Theater Offensive, and Yes Indeed! Media. As a proud New Orleans native, Murray trained at New Orleans Center for Creative Arts (NOCCA) and Comedy Uprising before graduating and receiving a Classical Acting certificate from the London Academy of Music & Dramatic Arts (LAMDA) and a BFA from Boston University (BU). Follow his journey @jaypaydro.

Jo Michael Rezes (they/them) is a Boston-based educator, director, and Elliot Norton Award-winning (and Berkshire Theatre Critics Award-nominated) actor dedicated to new trans plays with fabulously grotesque aesthetics. Their TEDTalk, *A Playful Exploration of Gender Performance*, is available online. Jo has held teaching positions at Boston College, Emerson College, and Harvard University, and is the Curriculum Developer for The Theater Offensive. They have forthcoming chapters in *Queers at the Table* (Arsenal Pulp Press) and *Milestones in Queer US Theatre* (Routledge), and a monograph in development called *Fractals: Nonbinary Acting Methods*. Rezes is a Vassar alum and Ph.D. Candidate at Tufts University. Learn more: JMRezes.com.

Eliana Rubin (she/her) is a queer and trans artist and educator currently based in New York City. She aims for her work to help people better understand themselves, each other, and the world we all live in. She received her Master of Educational Leadership from Hebrew Union College - Jewish Institute of Religion, with her work focusing on uplifting marginalized communities within the larger Jewish population. BFA: NYU / Tisch (ETW). She will never say no to a bag of movie theater popcorn. elianashirarubin.com

kt shorb (they/them; BM-Oberlin, MA & PhD-UT Austin) is a director, scholar, and assistant professor of theater and dance at Macalester College. They were the Social Science Research Council Arts Research with Communities of Color Fellow with Theater Mu, 2023-24. Their article on reappropriation and reparative creativity appears in the *Journal of American Drama and Theatre*. Forthcoming writing includes articles in *Theatre History Studies* and an anthology with Routledge on directing and ensemble creation. They also write for *American Theatre* and *HowlRound*. kt is currently the Vice President for the Consortium of Asian American Theaters & Artists, the only national service organization for theatre artists of the Asian and Pacific Islander diaspora.

Charlotte Snow (she/her) is a Boston based actor, director, dramaturg, costume designer, and . . . PLAYWRIGHT! She has worked in a variety of roles with Deadword Theatre Company, Moonbox Productions, Lyric Stage, Boston Playwright's Theatre, Fresh Ink Theatre, and Central Square Theatre. Her plays have been produced by TC Squared, What If? Queer Creator Collaborative, Wild Hare Studios, Fork and Shoe Theatre Co-Op, The Dramashop, and the Orlando Fringe Festival. Accessible through her New Play Exchange profile, the following are available to read: *Horseplay (Played By Medusa The Horse)*, *Hades And The One Year Winter*, *Missing Mercy*, *HOOKED*, *Unicorns Forever*, *The Lost Queen Returns*, and *The Found Queen Departs*. Charlotte would like to thank her found family, friends, mentors, therapist, and partner for their uplifting love and support.

Dillon Yruegas (he/él) is a queer trans mixed coahuiltecan/xicano theatremaker from his ancestral lands in Central Texas. He holds both a BFA in Theatre and a BA in Spanish from Texas State University. On stage, off stage, and online, he has collaborated with theatre companies and cultural institutions across Turtle Island. He is a steering committee member of the Latinx Theatre Commons. Recently, he was the HowlRound Theatre Commons fellow and a selected playwright for Breaking the Binary Festival, SolFest, Texas State University's Black + Latino Playwrights Celebration, Company One Theatre's PlayLab, TransTheatreFest at the University of Wisconsin-Madison, and the Boston Theatre Marathon.

Jessica Scott (she/her) is a playwright and screenwriter currently studying to get her MFA in Writing for Screen and Television at USC. In her work, she likes to tear deep into what it means to continually forge and reforge an identity, and all the joys and terrors that come with facing that daunting task of growth. She would like to thank the professors, mentors, friends, and family (both blood and chosen) that have helped her immeasurably along the way.

Introduction

Leanna Keyes, Lindsey Mantoan, and Angela Farr Schiller

Art, in times like *these*?

Laptop and cell phone notifications buzzing on a continuous loop. (*Bing*) Diversity, Equity, and Inclusion banned in US schools and universities. (*Bing*) The US and UK governments only recognize two genders. (*Bing*) US issues widespread mass deportations. The leading edge that informs each new notification that comes across our screens (*Bing*) . . . cruelty. We are reminded of history's echoes. (*Bing*) We are reminded of the deeply hypocritical and profoundly self-serving cruelty of Roy Cohen in *Angels In America*. The twisting overt cruelty of The Mayor in *Fucking A*. Or the manipulative, power-hungry, narcissistic cruelty of Heather Chandler in *Heathers the Musical*. (*Bing*) They don't learn. (*Bing*) Art reminds us of who we can become if we aren't careful.

Art has played a significant role in every major social movement since this colony started narrating itself as a nation-state. In times when we have been too scared to face each other as fellow human beings, art *also* reminds us of who we *can* be. Offering both forms of resistance and a means of processing collective trauma in deeply dark times— whether political, social, environmental, or existential—art is a powerful tool for articulating resistance, offering hope, and challenging dominant narratives. Performance provides frameworks for understanding the urgency of storytelling as essential not only for bearing witness to injustice but also for cultivating new ways of thinking about the world as it is and as it can be. While always slyly whispering the question . . . *what* else *could this be?*

Dreaming about this particular collection of plays, with its focus on stories about the curious and often mysterious time of young adulthood, we are again reminded that for those of us who inhabit marginalized bodies and communities, especially as people of color and members of the LGBTQIA+ community, art is an essential mode of survival in hostile environments. (*Bing*) Thank you, playwrights like Basil Kreimendahl, Kit Yan, Taylor Mac, Sylvan Oswald, Petrona Xemi Tapepechul, Olivia Dufault, Lady Dane Figueroa Edidi, Shakina Nayfack and the brilliant playwrights across all three of our volumes. In times of darkness, where the violence of systemic racism, trans- and homophobia, and misogyny seems pervasive, your art offers us an avenue for expressing pain and loss while simultaneously dancing flirtatiously side by side with ideas of possibility beyond our wildest (*Bing*) imaginations.

Additionally, art provides a space where joy and resistance are not mutually exclusive but rather deeply intertwined. (*Bing*) That said, beyond resistance and critique, in times where the murky waves of politics and history lap a little too closely under our chins, barely treading water, art offers a balm for healing and hope. (*Bing*) Thank you, arts organizations like The Kilroys, Angel Rose Artist Collective, and Breaking the Binary Theater. Because trauma, particularly racial, gendered, and colonial trauma, often leaves us feeling disconnected from ourselves and from each other. (*Bing*) We are not alone.

As a peak behind the curtain: the playwrights and editors struggled with this volume's subtitle of "Young Adult Edition," because "Young Adult" is a term with a lot of connotations, many of them even contradictory. Some people hear "theater for young adults" and think "plays intended to be performed for middle schoolers," and other people hear "plays about people under 40." This book takes seriously the adult part of "young *adult*." Here's what we mean, as one playwright put it in our brainstorming session: "These are the plays we wish we'd had when we were young adults." Whether they're about pre-teens, high schoolers, college kids, or twenty-somethings, these plays have content that will help growing minds grasp their possibilities and be prepared for the vast experiences that lay ahead. They also speak to people past the young adult years—because trans adolescence happens at many ages.

Adolescence and young adulthood are full, often fraught times. (*Bing*) Bodies change, styles shift, sexual awakenings occur, independence grows, prefrontal cortexes develop. Sometimes pronouns change. (Sometimes not). As acne rolls in, then fades away, romances bloom and kids become young adults who move out and start to navigate professional worlds. The changes of these years are embodied, emotional, interpersonal, and, increasingly, political.

This dynamic time period has been overwhelmingly targeted by anti-trans legislation and sentiment, leaving a lot of trans youth feeling isolated and vulnerable. (*Bing*) From attempts to intervene in youth sports, pediatricians' offices, and even parent-child relationships, the radical right has put trans youth on the front lines of their culture war. This time of discovery and exploration deserves support and recognition, not to be transformed into a political talking point. Toward that end, this third volume in the *Methuen Drama Book of Trans Plays* series focuses on stories about adolescence, high school and college, and the young adult years.

In the opening to *Methuen Drama Book of Trans Plays,* vol. 2, Leanna Keyes argues in her Preface, "Trans theatre is a key to a locked door [. . .] inviting you to open that door and take a look. You might poke your head through, have a pleasant time, and close it again. But some people who look through the door realize that they like it so much on the other side that they walk through the door and throw away the key" (2025: xi–xvi). Sometimes we just need to be able to come inside those sacred hush harbors that art provides as a place of tender refuge—being welcomed in and feeling seen. (*Bing*) Theater offers a radical opportunity to break away and envision a world where our humanity is deeply and lovingly affirmed.

In times such as these . . . (*Bing*) (*Bing*) (*Bing*) buzzing in the darkness, we're reminded of the words of scholar bell hooks, when she writes that "[w]e are transformed, individually, collectively, as we make radical creative space which affirms and sustains our subjectivity, which gives us a new location from which to articulate our sense of the world." (1989: 23) In this case art—and the plays and introductions offered in this anthology—are essential not only for surviving dark times but for creating new possibilities for freedom and dare we say . . . hope. Our goals here include amplifying the playful, experimental tone of these years, to remind all of us that being goofy is an essential part of being human. We're also invested in exploring the gravity of these life phases and their lasting impacts on shaping individuals and communities.

We've divided the nine plays collected in this book into three thematic parts. As has become standard practice for us in creating these volumes, we've paired each play with an introduction that situates the play in the broader landscape of trans theater, critical theory, dramatic history, and contemporary art. Part 1: Exploring the Dark Places, includes three plays that differ tonally and in terms of genre, but that take characters and audiences into the depths of forests, hell, and the human psyche, both literally and metaphorically. M Sloth Levine's *The Interrobangers* confronts the challenges of adolescence with echoes of the classic animated series *Scooby-Doo*. Dismantling the harmful trope of trans characters as aliens, this playful script uses humor and heart to reveal the deeply human contours of friendship, community, and getting lost in the woods. In *Magic Girl! . . . and Her Demons* by Charlotte Snow, a teenager tries to escape her rural town first through dance, and then through a deal with a demon. Discovering that perhaps hell is where queer people go to find acceptance and the best parties, this light-hearted riff on *Faust* asks if it's possible to sell your soul, attain high school popularity, and still get the girl in the end. A deep dive into the mental struggles of young adulthood, Jess Scott's *t4t* grapples with inner demons. The play unflinchingly showcases the way self-doubt and anger can debilitate a person, and the process of climbing out of the darkness.

For Part Two, we take a "Dance Break," because an important way to both process and recover from darkness is moving our bodies to music and rhythm. All three plays in this section contain dance and/or movement, although each deploys this aesthetic choice to different effect. Dillon Yruegas's *Brunch Crowd* queers a common rom-com trope of four friends meeting for brunch and gossiping. Here, our queer and trans heroes are all artists of color in their twenties, figuring out what they want for their future—against the backdrop of a gentrifying Austin, TX—and their relationship to community. In Jameson P. Murray's *The More The Man*, we move from Austin to New Orleans to follow a protagonist as he explores what kind of man he wants to be. Tension about sexuality, talking about feelings, and relationships motivate this story about self discovery and the ways our families shape us. The final play in Part Two, *Man and Moon* by Siena Marilyn, sees two strangers meeting in the waiting room of a breast cancer treatment center. Despite an age gap, the two connect over questions about mothers, astronomy, gummy worms, and music in a beautifully rendered meditation on what makes us us.

Part Three takes us to the sea with three plays that use water in literal and symbolic ways. Samuel Achilles' *Caeneus* adapts an ancient Greek, and often overlooked, story of the titular character as he travels across the sea on the Argo with Jason, Medea, and the Argonauts. Exploring romance, family, and the comedy and disappointment that comes with meeting our heroes, *Caeneus* theatricalizes both the epic and the personal aspects of adventures. In *Unfair Advantage* by Tyler Rocio Ecoña, NCAA sports take center stage. With scenes in the pool, locker room, and dining room, this play examines the very politicized issue of trans athletics, personalizing the ways in which arbitrary rules can punish a range of athletes and spread strife within families. The final play, *Tides* by Eliana Rubin, envisions a future that seems more likely with the passage of more and more anti-queer legislation. Told in three parts, the play imagines changing waves of political sentiment and asks what it might take to interrupt cycles of violence.

We are completing work on this third volume in the series against fraught political and cultural landscapes, and we look to the future with trepidation and hope. We look to the young and young adults around us, and we want to protect them, inspire them, and foster their journey into adulthood through art. More than anything, we want trans youth and young adults to know that we see you and that trans theatre includes you.

References

hooks, bell. 1989. "Choosing the Margin as a Space of Radical Openness." *The Journal of Cinema and Media*. No. 36: 15–23.

Keyes, Leanna, et al., editors. 2021. *The Methuen Drama Book of Trans Plays*. Methuen Drama

Part 1: Exploring the Dark Places

Notes on Playing (with Monsters) in the Fog: Mysteries of Queer Adolescence in M Sloth Levine's *The Interrobangers*

Jo Michael Rezes

Teenagers smoke weed in a van. Childhood friends turned high school acquaintances strain to reconnect in the woods they once called home, or rather, used as a playground. The yet-to-be-named Interrobangers tell stories of mysteries once solved together: a ghost haunting the Old Sherman Factory, a burglar dressed as a goblin—*men in masks*. Whether clouded by weed or veiled by the fog that "makes everything so spooky" (15), our heroes ignore that which lurks in the trees around them. Sensing the fog as protection, they open their hearts. With smoke filling their lungs, they open their minds. At the end of this scene, dozens of red eyes of the Things in the Woods will appear in the trees, shaking them from their stupor. But for now, they are safe. In the van, in time suspended, in the Greywoods Forrest of Foggy Bluffs, New York, the Interrobangers try to recall, Frankenstein-together, the events (and monsters) of their past when they were "just little babes" (21).

"Remember when we'd go play in the woods and come back all covered in mud and our parents would be so—?"

A pause. The scene threatens to unsuture itself.

But the actor playing Zodiac has not called for a line. A cue is missed; the sound of "a car pulling up" misfires. I dart my eyes to our stage manager who nonchalantly points at the disruption with a knowing smirk: wafting clouds tumble onto the stage. Our two-story trees constructed from clothing-on-hangers are now lost to moody blues and purples. The dense fog consumes the cast, dressed in their distinct, cartoonish color palettes. Undergraduate actors titter together as a backstage machine whirs and moans: "*Too much fog.*"

Queer Pedagogies of the Fog

Fog is a swirling atmospheric trickster. A staple in gothic horror and science fiction—of shrouded mysteries, lurking dangers, and misshapen figures. In its fluidity, fog obscures binaries, refuses clarity, and creates space for ambiguity. Fog doesn't just hide—it redefines landscapes and bodies, blurring the lines between what is real and imagined, what is known and unknowable. It is no coincidence that fog often signals a narrative rupture, a portal into the uncanny, where the rules of the world no longer apply. Within M Sloth Levine's works, I see *pedagogies of the fog* materialize as queer methods for embodying trans and nonbinary characters; young artists can embrace *opacity* on stage (and in rehearsal), transcending politics of representation and legibility, while playing in the foggy aesthetics which constitute "trans plays."

Within this play, fog is as much a character ("the fog is important") as it is a setting. In this 1970s-nostalgic, Gothic cartoon of a smalltown, fog represents a space of uncertainty and the supernatural. And it was here, in the miasma of M Sloth Levine's writing, that my student-actors learned the most about the power of art and the monsters of their (characters') past. Playing in the fog offers opportunities for "queer pedagogy," allowing teachers to "create monsters of their students," encouraging them to learn through acts of failure, "getting lost" in the mist (Halberstam 2011: 20, 24). I see a pedagogy of the fog which recognizes that "[c]lassrooms, colleges, campuses may not have been built to cultivate queerness . . . but they have in rare and beautiful occasions incubated queer performances, often through the risky pedagogies of women, queer, and trans people" (Montez and Khubchandani 2020: x), and "trans plays" like M Sloth Levine's offer space for covert triangulations of queerness, pedagogy, and performance to take shape—even if only in monstrous silhouette.

Fog has loomed as both a setting and a symbol for queer horrors in Gothic literature and film. Spanning nearly a century—from the shadow-drenched streets of Victorian London in the *Strange Case of Dr. Jekyll and Mr. Hyde,* the 1886 novella by Robert Louis Stevenson, to the eerie coastal mist of John Carpenter's *The Fog* (1980), fog acts as an agent of both transformation and duplicity. These symbolic meanings originated from paranoias around the Industrial Revolution where the "deceptive nature of blurry fog . . . fuels the feelings of suspicion and mistrust among the city dwellers, because one can no longer perceive another person's true nature" (Maryam and Tay 2018). In H.G. Wells's *The War of the Worlds* (1898), fog becomes synonymous with the transformative power of alien invasion, terraforming the Earth into an unrecognizable nightmare. In *The Interrobangers*, extra-terrestrials serve as only one possible explanation for the traumas our heroes face in Foggy Bluffs, despite the town's propensity to supernatural tourism like Roswell, New Mexico. In Scene Five, the fogginess of the woods and the weed smoke swirl, as interpersonal truths and judgments tumble out of characters. Unable to hold in the stinging memory of Zodiac's kidnapping, Hank coughs up a deep hit, spilling the metaphorical bong water: "But if you're just trying to like, make it easier by saying it was aliens, but like, it definitely wasn't aliens and at least you could stop pretending around us?" (43). A tense fight ensues about the existence of alien abduction versus an alleged adult predator, Mr. Jenkins. In the fog and smoke of the Greywoods Forrest, highly logical Luna even begins to move beyond their scientific method with, "I don't know that I am ready to believe in aliens, but I'd like to help you" (44). Like in many gothic-inspired tales, fog drapes overs streets, forests, and relationships, unspooling repressed emotions.

For transgender actors, fog offers opportunities to overcome traumas of outsider recognition. There is safety in queer pettifogging—embodying abject characterization as a predator, villain, or harbinger of disease: from hiding in the proverbial closet to skulking amidst a bone-chilling mist. Acting in one of Levine's play-worlds offers rare opportunities for trans and nonbinary actors to embody monsters safely. Just as light bends between droplets in fog, character development becomes an atomic process of connection and refraction. This enables queer and trans figures to emerge—sometimes as monsters, yes, but also as survivors, antiheros, and agents of change. Zac Blas writes about the aesthetics of opacity, and the ways that "queer darkness is the refusal to cohere, to become legible . . . a minoritarian refusal, a *fog of illegibility*, an opaque being, a nonidentifiable collective presence" (2022: 177–181). Levine's scripts shield transgender actors from prying eyes, like the fog shelters cryptids from the flash of paranormal investigator's camera. Here, they can all transform on their terms—sprouting wings, growing fangs, and practicing howls in the glow of a moonlit dressing room.

I first considered the pedagogical possibilities of fog in the works of M Sloth Levine when originating the role of Count Orlok in *Nosferatu, The Vampyr*—a production postponed indefinitely due to COVID-19. The piece was exhumed for Zoom livestream audiences as a staged reading-cum-metatheatrical-horror-sleepover via HowlRound. TV in May 2020. Before plague quarantined our rehearsals, a black-box studio at Chelsea Theatre Works (Chelsea, MA) became a ballroom where I gilded the Nosferatu's glittering cloaks with my trauma and hid comfortably behind a mask (of the Red Death). Like all of Levine's characters, Nosferatu is connected to past trans representation: "Levine's characters are not archetypes, but their lives *are* affected by queer history ... Its ghostly detritus manifests as trauma" (Hyman 2020). I knew (dramaturgically) that my character's trauma was grounded in a history of ancestors deemed too monstrous to live. From within a haze of anachronisms and allusions, I found the haunted fragments needed to build my character. As theatre historian Mia Levenson writes, "Rezes-as-Orlok ... reveals that one of their light sources was their phone. This moment requires the audience to consider the queer performer in front of them, the monster they embodied" (2022, 45). Reclaiming monsters becomes a method for queer actors to perform transness in theatre beyond the politics of representation. Levine's queer horror challenges cisgender audiences to endure a queer opacity: transpoetic language which defies legibility in traditional dramatic criticism and characters which only exist under the cover of night. These foggy play-worlds are not sanitized through *cislation*, defined as "the translating of seemingly illegible (i.e., not understandable) genders for cis recognition" (Jourian and Nicolazzo 2019). Rather, characters negotiate queerness on their own terms. Levine writes, in final stage directions of *Nosferatu: the Vampyr*, that if caught in the houselights, in full view of the cisgender gaze, monsters begin "to burn from the inside out ... claw[ing] at their own permanence until it begins to rip" (2020). Like an early-morning mist torn apart by daybreak, Levine's characters are never quite here to stay—yet have always been.

Getting Lost and Unmasking Our Monsters in (the Woods of) Rehearsal

With trans plays like *The Interrobangers*, not only can we offer roles to trans and nonbinary actors, but also opportunities for them to play outside of the boundaries of their bodies, gender presentations, and perceptible realities—all in the safety (and mystery) of the fog. In their final monologue, Luna reflects on the intersection of queerness, magic, and monstrosity: "I'm learning there's a, an interplay. Between being queer and believing in magic. In monsters, aliens, ghosts. I'm real. I'm not a girl and I'm not a boy ... I live in, I am in, this in-between space" (76). Nonbinary theory is discovered in the Greywoods Forest—in the fog of a rehearsal room. When I directed the collegiate premier production of *The Interrobangers* at Tufts University in the Fall of 2022, I embraced Jack Halberstam notes in *The Queer Art of Failure* which state that "failing, losing, forgetting, unmaking, undoing, unbecoming" (3) can offer more creative, cooperative modes of existence. Luna wrestles with their nonbinary identity, inhabiting an "in-between space" between monster and human, resonating with Susan Stryker's field-shattering declaration: "Like the monster, I am too often perceived as less than fully human due to the means of my embodiment . . . I am a transsexual, and therefore I am a monster" (1994: 238-40). Reclamation of monstrosity allows Luna to transcend imposed definitions. The monstrous is not a site of fear but a space of possibility. Luna challenges the idea that "everything we know is built on the facts of gender" (76) reframing them as mutable constructions. Levine even aesthetically roots *The Interrobangers* in cartoon worlds like *Scooby-Doo,* highlighting Halberstam's celebration of "cartoonish qualities" of queerness—a performance mode which rejects rigid forms of adulthood.

The fog in *The Interrobangers* disrupts the linear pathways of logic, offering space for Luna to reflect on the "interplay" of queerness and belief in magic. Fog provides a pedagogical opportunity for theatre directors, paradoxically guiding actors towards "getting lost," a method of dramaturgical inquiry. Luna meanders from feeling like a monster ("a goblin inhabiting a human body") to unmasking why bad people hide behind costumes ("They dress up like horrors to scare people away or feel powerful") (76). These revelations echo Stryker's avowal that "monsters, like angels, functioned as messengers," embodiments of profound truths hidden beneath social constructs (2024: 137). As the Tufts production's dramaturg, Sam McQuaid, wrote in their program note: monsters "are mirrors of ourselves, but they are also reflections of the other . . . monsters are reflections of what we impose onto them, of what we want them to embody in a given moment." Within trans plays, directors and educators can encourage young actors to "unmask" their own "monsters:" trauma and preconceived notions of identity, power, and failure. Aligning with Levine's stage directions that insist the fog "shouldn't be one single thing" (14) student actors in *The Interrobangers* can find pieces of themselves in their characters, in the monsters, in the fog beyond binary conceptions. Ultimately, Luna's monologue becomes an invitation to those on and off stage to shine a flashlight on monstrosity: "if I exist, then who is to say that some monsters aren't just costumes?" (77). Levine's play asks us to lose our way and discover new ways of seeing (batteries included) within the mask of the fog.

Nostalgia is a gift rarely granted to queer and trans people—especially to those embracing their inner monsters. *The Interrobangers* presents queer youth an opportunity to reclaim memories lost to trauma. We must "allow [young actors] to get lost in order for them to experience confusion and then find their own way out or back or around" (Halberstam 1994: 14). I believe that collaboration in the fog allows adolescent characters (and actors) to move safely, and on their own terms, into young adulthood. Acts of mystery which lie beyond can be first rehearsed in the world of Foggy Bluffs. At the end of this play, friends walk out of the woods, hand in hand, and M Sloth Levine implores us to dream of prequels, sequels, and fanfictions.

The Interrobangers offers actors the chance to transform into the iconic *Scooby-Doo* gang we watched on Saturday mornings, the siblings who let us play dress-up with their hand-me-downs, the friends with whom we fought monsters-under-the-bed, or even the playmates we lost along the way. We are asked by M Sloth Levine to (mis)remember the magic of our childhood, or else watch it transform behind a haze of time. Despite the omniscience of monsters, ghosts, and extra-terrestrials, *memories* haunt this play-world most of all. But with the Interrobangers playing tricks and setting traps at our side, we are safe to explore the inner folds and dark woods of our past. The next time you see a character venturing into the fog or fading away beyond the static of a television set, do not just think of it as a horror trope. Consider it a queer opportunity—an unsolved mystery, a chance to get lost, or a brave step into the unknown.

References

Blas, Zach. 2022. "Queer Darkness." In *Studies into Darkness: The Perils and Promise of Freedom of Speech*, edited by Carin Kuoni, 173–90. Amherst College Press.

Halberstam, Jack. 2011. *The Queer Art of Failure*. Durham, NC: Duke University Press.

M Sloth Levine. 2020. *Nosferatu, The Vampyr* with Original Music by Alissa Voth, May 1, video, HowlRound Theatre Commons. https://youtu.be/NtB4COXCV9Q.

Hyman, Chloe. 2020. "Specters of Queer Trauma in Nosferatu, the Vampyr" *HowlRound*, August 4.

Jourian, T.J., and Z. Nicolazzo. 2019. "Not Another Gender Binary: A Call for Complexity Over Cis-Readability." *Medium*, June 4.

Levenson, Mia. 2022. "Exterminating the Phantom: Nativist Constructions of Contagion and Monsters in Nineteenth-Century New York City." In *Monsters in Performance: Essays on the Aesthetics of Disqualification*, edited by Michael Chemers and Analola Santana, 25–40. London: Routledge.

Maryam, Hanna, and Terry Tay. "Glossary of the Gothic: Fog." *e-Publications@Marquette*. Accessed January 3, 2025.

McQuaid, "Beasts, Bogeymen, and the Role of the Monster in Queer and Trans Stories."

Montez, Noe, and Kareem Khubchandani. 2020. "A Note from the Editors: Queer Pedagogy in Theatre and Performance." *Theatre Topics*, vol. 30, no. 2: ix–xvii.

Stryker, Susan. 1994. "My Words to Victor Frankenstein Above the Village of Chamounix: Performing Transgender Rage." *GLQ: A Journal of Lesbian and Gay Studies* 1, no. 3: 237–54.

When Monsters Speak: A Susan Stryker Reader. 2024. McKenzie Wark, ed. Duke University Press.

The Interrobangers

M Sloth Levine

1.1 "The Foggy Bluffs Monster," 2017 - Illustration by M Sloth Levine.

@mslothlevine

mslothlevine.com

The Interrobangers received its world premiere at Company One Theatre, Boston, 2024. Artistic Director, Shawn LaCount; Production Director, Josh Glenn-Kayden; Dramaturgs, afrikah selah and Regine Vital.

Characters & Doubling

Zodiac DuMaurier – Late teens, identifies as cis (for now.) Not necessarily white, but he has white parents.

Hank Mason – Late teens, white cis man.

Luna Takamoto – Late teens, trans masc *sansei,* or third generation Japanese immigrant.

Dani Bundy – Late teens, Black cis woman.

Tess Mason/Bettie Roswell – Tess is in her early 50s, Bettie in her mid-60s. Black, cis.

Nathan Hobart/Mr. Dahl – Nathan is a middle-aged white man. Mr. Dahl seems perhaps inhuman.

Sheriff Craig/Guy at The Jackalope – Could be anybody, if you think about it.

Hoover DuMaurier – A dog, sort of like a German Shepherd. Hoover should be realized in multiple mediums throughout the play, such as life-size puppets, shadow puppets, projections, or real dogs. The *idea* of Hoover should transcend the ways he's physicalized on stage.

Casting Policy

White characters may be cast with people of color at the discretion of the director and consent of the actors. Please allow this to alter the way you perform the character and build the world of the play. Non-white characters will not be cast with white actors under any circumstances.

Zodiac could be played by the right cis actor. Luna may not be played by a cis actor.

Setting

It is and it isn't the 1970s, the 1990s, the early 2000s, and right now.

Notes

The Things In The Woods should be puppets, projections, fog, sounds, lights, rubber masks. But they shouldn't be one single thing. They also don't need to be convincing, or expensive.

The fog is important.

Prologue

Through the pitch dark, the crackle of walkie talkies. We hear the kids over the radio waves:

Hank   The fog makes everything so spooky.

Luna   Stay focused, Hank. Do you have eyes on the ghost?

Dani   Excuse me, I do. About to engage.

Zodiac   Like, why are Dani and I always the bait?

Hank   Eyes on the prize, Zodiac!

Luna   Everybody, focus!

Dani   Luna, are you ready?

Luna   Yes. Are you?

Zodiac   Here he comes. And . . .

Static.

Hank   Run! Run! Run!

Zodiac   Shit, he's gonna get us!

Dani   Luna, pull the rope!

Luna   Careful!

The lines go dead. A thump and the rush of a rope running through pulleys.

The bank of the Little Green River in Foggy Bluffs, NY. The Greywoods Forest surrounds.

A glowing green ghost, dressed in old exterminators' coveralls and gas mask, struggles against the rope tying him up. The fog clears and four kids approach. It becomes apparent this is a man in a costume.

Hank   We got him!

Luna   Another mystery in the books!

Dani   Time to see if we were right about this ghost.

Zodiac   Be careful!

Luna *walks over to the ghost, and pulls off his gas mask.*

Luna   The Exterminator's Ghost is really . . . .

A white man.

All   Nathan Hobart!

Luna   I knew it!

Hank   I didn't.

Zodiac   Like, can someone explain?

Luna   It's simple, Zodiac—

Nathan   I should have known you fucking brats would get in the way. I'm the only one who deserves the deed to that factory.

Police sirens. A car door slams.

Hank   I called my mom.

Tess   Hank? Is that you, kids?

Tess *and* **Sheriff Craig** *enter.*

Tess   You have got to stop getting involved in these police investigations. You're twelve!

Hank   We did it mom! We proved it was Nathan Hobart haunting the old Sherman Factory all along!

Craig   They did apprehend the suspect, Tess.

Tess   Don't encourage them, Craig. Get this guy in handcuffs.

Luna *unties* **Nathan**, **Craig** *quickly locks him in cuffs.*

Nathan   I woulda gotten away with it if you fuckers woulda just minded your business.

Dani   You shouldn't have made it so interesting. If there's a monster, we're going to unmask it.

Luna   It's always just a bad man trying to get away with something.

Tess   Hank said he's got some evidence That's going to put you under for real estate fraud and manslaughter for the death of Kimberley McKay.

Luna   It's all here!

Luna *gives* **Tess** *a Ziplock with the incriminating evidence.*

Craig   You should get these kids home.

Hank   I'll undo the ghost trap.

Tess   Walter, will you help my bonehead son?

Zodiac   No one calls me Walter anymore, Ms. Mason.

Tess   Okay, Zodiac, if you want to keep calling me to crime scenes it's Mayor Mason.

Zodiac   Deal.

Dani   We're writing a story on this case for the school paper. May I record?

Craig   Just stand back, okay?

Craig *reads him his rights.* **Luna** *and* **Dani** *watch,* **Dani** *taking notes on her texting phone.* **Hank** *dissembles the trap.* **Craig** *writes a report. Fog creeps in.*

Zodiac *hears a noise. He turns towards the woods.* **Hank** *is nearby.*

Zodiac   Hank, did you hear that?

Hank   No. Help me with the cables.

Another noise, and this time **Zodiac** *sees something.*

Zodiac   Do you see that?

Hank   See what?

Zodiac   It looked like a dog. Like when you shine a light in a dog's eyes. Or when a photo develops weird. Red.

Hank   It was probably a coyote. There isn't actually any monsters in there.

Hank *coils cables, which leads him back towards the group. Sheriff* **Craig** *leads* **Nathan Hobart** *offstage.*

Zodiac *sees the eyes again. He approaches. His gaze tracks upwards.*

Zodiac   Oh, it's you! Hey, wait up.

Zodiac *walks into the woods.*

Tess   It's a school night. What am I supposed to tell your parents?

Luna   We solved another murder?

Tess   I'm driving you all home. Hank's mine, Danielle I know you're out by the country club, Luna, you're on . . .?

Luna   Hannah Avenue, we live above our store.

Tess   That's right. Walter?

Dani   He's down the block from me.

Tess   Where'd he go?

Hank   He was right there helping me a minute ago. He saw a dog.

Dani   This isn't funny, it's time to go home!

Luna   Zodiac?

Tess   Walter, come on, time to go.

Hank   Where'd he go?

They stand looking into the woods. They see nothing. They hear nothing.

Hank *pushes his walkie talkie.*

Hank   Come in, Zodiac. I repeat, come in Zodiac.

His walkie lies on the ground. **Hank***'s voice comes through the night on a minuscule lag.*

Hank *looks to his mom. The kids look at each other. Darkness.*

A dog barking. Distorted news stories fly through the airwaves. "FOGGY BLUFFS CHILD GONE MISSING" "2 WEEKS—THE SEARCH FOR WALTER DUMAURIER CONTINUES" "ABDUCTED CHILD FOUND" "AN ARREST HAS BEEN MADE" "KIDNAPPING TRIAL DRAGS ON" The silhouette of the Foggy Bluffs Monster is sort of visible holding something that may be **Zodiac***. "ELIAS JENKINS— NOT GUILTY." . . .*

Several years later, **Tess** *is doing paperwork in her office.* **Craig** *comes in.*

Tess   Knocking, Craig.

Craig   The new community service paperwork is ready for approval, and I wanted to remind you about that meeting next Friday?

Tess   Thanks. And can you get those reports in this week instead of next?

Craig   Yeah, um, also, Jay said Walter DuMaurier's on his class roster for the new school year.

Tess   He moved back?

Craig   Thought you'd want to know. We never closed the file.

Tess   I haven't seen him since the trial. I worry about that kid.

Craig   Do you think he still . . . says it was aliens?

Tess   I don't know. I still feel bad all these years later.

Craig   If he woulda just said Jenkins, we'd have that guy in prison.

Tess   I'm sure it's hard, being a kid and having to talk about something like that happening to you.

Craig   He was so adamant that we were wrong. He always said, from the second we found him outside the bunker in those woods, he said it was aliens.

Tess   God knows why he'd want to come back here.

Craig   That kid's cracked in the head.

Tess   Craig I swear to god. Just, close the door on your way out.

Craig *leaves,* **Tess** *pauses for a second, pulls out a file from her desk and picks up her phone.*

One

The bank of the Little Green River. **Zodiac**, *now 18, enters. He's holding a folded piece of paper, and puts it into his pocket. On the outer side of his arm is a stylized interrobang tattoo.*

Zodiac   Hoover? C'mere, boy.

A big dog that might be a German Shepherd trots in. **Hoover** *scans the perimeter, making a circle around* **Zodiac**.

Zodiac   We're fine, Hoov. Don't need to worry. Like, relax, man.

Zodiac *packs a bowl and lights up.*

Zodiac   See, it's fine here.

Hoover, *convinced that there's no immediate danger, joins* **Zodiac**.

Zodiac   There's nothing wrong with this place. Want a hit?

Hoover *is a dog.*

Zodiac   Nah, you're a dog.

Zodiac *takes a hit. He looks at the piece of paper again.* **Hoover** *looks at it too, like he's reading it.*

Zodiac   Yeah. I guess he's looking for them too.

Hoover *hears a sound. His ears perk up. He stands, looking at the woods.*

Zodiac   What do you hear? What's out there?

Zodiac *looks into the woods in the same direction as* **Hoover**. *He can't see anything.*

Zodiac   Oh, man.

From the road, enters **Dani**.

Dani   Zodiac?

Zodiac *whips around.* **Hoover** *barely budges.*

Zodiac   Dani?

Dani   Zodiac!

They hug.

Zodiac   How you doin', dude?

Dani   I'm so excited to see you! How are you?

Hoover *quietly darts into the woods.*

Zodiac   I'm just lettin' it happen, you know? Wanna join me?

Dani   Thanks.

She sits, he offers her the piece.

Zodiac   Wanna hit?

Dani   No thanks. I don't really . . .

Zodiac   I'm sorry dude, I'll put it away. I didn't mean to—

Dani   No it's okay, I just shouldn't.

Zodiac   That's what they want you to think.

Dani   I just like . . . probably shouldn't. I'm the class president and have to like, organize assemblies sometimes. About not doing it.

Zodiac   You're the president? Oh man, I have been gone for so long.

Dani   I've been class president since 9th grade. Class President, Editor of the School Paper, and Speech & Debate Captain.

Zodiac   President Danielle Bundy. Sorry, I don't wanna like, jeopardize your position . . .

Dani   Don't put it away on account of me, it's not like anyone's watching.

Zodiac   Okay.

He takes another hit.

Dani   So are you like, back for good?

Zodiac   Yeah.

He looks over the river.

Dani   That's it?

Zodiac   Well I mean, I got kicked out of boarding school again, and my grandpa didn't want to pay for another library, so.

Dani   So you're doing senior year?

Zodiac   Next week at Foggy Bluffs High, yep. Crazy how things work out.

Dani   I honestly didn't think we'd see you again.

Zodiac   That wouldn't be the first time.

Dani *looks at him.*

Zodiac   Sorry. You guys probably don't like joking about it.

Dani   I didn't think there was much to joke about . . .

Zodiac   I guess it's been a while since I saw you.

Dani   Where did Hoover go? Wasn't he just here?

Zodiac   Probably just wandered off. I hope he doesn't jump into the river.

Dani   The river is so gross.

Zodiac   Always has been. Remember when The Gill Goblin kept showing up and stealing people's stuff down at the beach?

Dani   It wasn't a real goblin. Just a petty burglar.

Zodiac   Those were the days. Simple times. We were just little babes.

Dani   That was fourth grade we started that. Wow. Solving mysteries, uncovering truths.

Zodiac   You still see those guys?

Dani   I mean, I definitely see them. I was trying to get Hank to run for class secretary, he'd get the votes. Luna doesn't talk to me much. They got like, I dunno. They're non-binary now. There was a whole thing last year.

Zodiac   Oh cool. What are they up to?

Dani   We don't talk much, but we're in a lot of the same AP's. Just different friend groups.

The fog begins rolling in.

Zodiac   We should get together sometime. The four of us. And Hoover, when I find him.

Dani   Maybe, yeah.

Zodiac   Wait so what are you doing at the river?

Dani   It's a good place for self-reflection.

Zodiac   That's important.

Dani   I'd heard you were back in town too.

Zodiac   From who?

Dani   Hank's mom called my mom.

Zodiac   Why does she care?

Dani   I mean it was a really big case and the mayor's office took a lot of flak for it . . .

Zodiac   Oh. Of course. They're keeping an eye on me.

Dani   'Cause it's like, technically still an open case.

Zodiac   That's what they say. There's always someone in the corners. Just in case they come back.

Dani   You still think?

Zodiac   I *know.* The aliens took me and brought me back two weeks later, and the government wants to know why.

Dani   I would want to know. If I thought I'd been abducted by aliens.

Zodiac   The truth, as they say, is out there.

Dani   Probably. But, um, why did they arrest Mr. Jenkins?

Zodiac   'Cause they found me near his property. That's it. He happened to live in the woods.

Dani   It's just, not that unbelievable is it? I mean, old creeps kidnapping kids and like, you know, it's not uncommon.

Zodiac   Yeah, but that didn't happen to me.

Dani   It does happen a lot though.

Zodiac   I know and That's terrible. But That's completely different.

Dani   I'm sorry I brought it up. I'm glad you're back.

Zodiac   Really?

Dani   Of course. I think about you a lot.

Zodiac   Hoover isn't usually gone this long. He better not have gone swimming.

Dani   I should head home. It's getting real foggy. Let's get lunch sometime!

Zodiac   Oh I'm hungry. Is that pizza place still open? We should go there.

Dani   It's a vegan diner now.

Zodiac   Even better. I'm vegetarian.

Dani   I'll text the whole gang. Gimme your phone, I'll put my number in.

He hands her his phone and scans the bank for signs of **Hoover**.

Zodiac   Hoover? Where you at, Hoover?

He spots him down the river.

Zodiac   Come here, boy! Time to head home! He looks all wet. Shiny.

Dani   That's not water. He looks slimy.

Hoover *jumps into the water and swims down to them.*

Zodiac   Aw, buddy, don't jump in the water. He's gonna stink so bad.

Dani   That's rough. Let's get together soon, before school starts? Bring Hoover. If he's clean.

Dani *gives him a quick hug and leaves.*

Zodiac   Bye, President Dani.

Hoover *steps out of the river.*

Zodiac   Whatever you got into, it's washed off now. Gross dog.

Hoover *nudges* **Zodiac** *to leave.*

Zodiac   Yeah, let's go home. This place is giving me the creeps.

Hoover *looks at him as if he's hurt.*

Zodiac   I mean yeah, we did meet here. So yeah, That's a good thing about it.

Zodiac *hears himself, age 12, the night of the abduction.*

Zodiac   Oh, it's you. Hey, wait up. Hey, slow down. Wait for me.

A dog steps out from under the brush.

Zodiac   Oh. There *is* a dog. I thought it was him.

Zodiac *looks past the dog.*

Zodiac   I know you're there too. When'd you get a dog?

Zodiac *goes to touch the dog. The dog turns and goes deeper into the woods.*

Zodiac   Where are you going? Wait up! I'm coming!

Zodiac, *age 12, continues deeper, following the dog and the unseen.*

Back into now.

Hoover *pulls* **Zodiac** *away from the woods.*

Two

The Jackalope. It's a vegan diner both crunchy granola and atomic retro. **Luna Takamoto** *sits at the counter, reading and eating a vegan hotdog.* **Dani** *walks in.*

Dani   Hey, Luna!

Luna   Dani? Uh, hi.

Dani   How are you?

Luna   Reading.

Um.

Dani   What are you reading?

Luna   It's about these Cold War scientists who did experiments on animals to make the perfect space traveler.

Dani   Oh That's awesome.

Luna   But one of them was a woman and her work was stolen from her and then her partner was accused of being gay so they chemically castrated him and by that time America already got to the moon.

Dani   That's a bummer. So, did you hear Zodiac is back?

Luna   In Foggy Bluffs?

Dani   Yeah, he's gonna do senior year here. I saw him yesterday, down by the river. Yeah, the spot.

Luna   Okay, nice to see you, Dani.

Dani   Can I sit?

Luna *goes back to reading.* **Dani** *sits and calls to the guy at the counter.*

Dani   Hey, can I order a coconut milkshake? Luna, do you want a milkshake?

Luna   What are you doing here?

Dani   I like vegan food. I was vegan last spring.

Luna   But you're not anymore?

Dani   It was just for prom.

Luna   Right.

Dani   I totally understand why people do it, but I'm anemic so I had to stop. Plus who can give up chicken nuggets?

Luna   Chicken farms are like one of the worst as far as animal cruelty goes.

Dani   I feel bad about that.

Luna   It's pretty horrific. There's documentaries online where you can see them huddled up in cages covered in their own blood and feces.

Dani   So, I was talking to Zodiac, and I thought it would be a great idea to get the gang back together! I texted Hank, but I didn't have your number anymore, so.

Luna   You want to hang out?

Dani   We used to be best friends, and Zodiac is back, so like, it could be cool to see him again.

Luna   I guess.

Dani   Great! He'll be here soon. Hank hasn't texted me back yet.

Luna   We're hanging out *now*?

Guy   Here's the shake.

Luna   So now that Zodiac is back in Foggy Bluffs you want to hang out?

Dani   Mm, coconutty. What are you talking about?

Luna   We haven't talked in like, years.

Dani   That's not true, we did that Suffragette project last year in APUSH.

Luna   And you only talked to Rita the whole time. You didn't say anything when I left the school paper, so why should we pretend now that Zodiac is back?

Dani   I'm sorry for whatever you think happened, but he hasn't been in town for this long since the thing happened and I think it'd be nice if we could give him a little support.

Luna   It's been five years, I think he's going to be okay. It's not like he was hurt.

Dani   Not physically, but we don't know what, what kind of like, psychological scars he has. It would be nice for him to have some friends, don't you think? You know what people say about him.

Luna   I know what they say about me too.

Dani   Then why wouldn't you want to help him out?

Luna   I haven't seen him in a while.

Dani   And just so you know, I don't let people say stuff about you around me. Even if we don't hang out anymore, I don't let people say stuff around me. I always make them use your pronouns.

Luna   Golly, that makes me feel so wonderful.

Hank *walks in.*

Dani   Hank! I'm glad you came!

Hank   Of course, anything for you. Hey Luna

Luna   Hi Hank.

Hank   I thought Zodiac unfollowed me, so I was kinda surprised he wanted to hang out.

Dani   I don't think he's on social media. He's like, very zen now.

Luna   Is he Buddhist?

Dani   I don't know.

Luna   Then zen isn't the right word.

Dani   Okay, he smokes a lot of . . . weed. Yeah. And he has a tattoo.

Luna   It's probably an anxiety thing. He always needed to chill.

Hank   I used to bribe him to go into haunted houses and stuff.

Zodiac *enters,* **Hoover** *trots behind him and begins sniffing around the counter,* **Dani** *pets him.*

Zodiac   Greetings earthlings. Lol. Hey everyone.

Hank   It's him! And Hoover!

Luna   Hi, Zodiac.

Zodiac   Luna! Oh my god, dude! I like your new hair!

Zodiac *gives* **Luna** *a giant bear hug.*

Luna   Thanks! It's good to see you.

Zodiac   Hey Hank!

Zodiac *goes to hug him, but* **Hank** *goes for a handshake, then realizes* **Zodiac** *was gonna hug him, but* **Zodiac** *has already adjusted and starts to shake, but* **Hank** *wants to keep it cool so now he's shifted to a high five. They just kinda hit hands.*

Hank   Nice to hello.

Zodiac   Yeah, cool!

Hank   This is Hoover still.

Zodiac   Yeah, he's big!

Hank   Hi buddy, you remember me?

Hoover *jumps up on* **Hank** *with his front paws, licking his face.*

Dani   I guess he does.

The guy notices that there's a dog in his restaurant.

Guy   Uh, I don't think you can have a dog in here.

Hoover *looks at him sideways.*

Zodiac   Hoover's not a dog, he's family.

Guy   Please don't get me fired.

Zodiac   He's a service dog, actually.

Luna   Shouldn't he be wearing a vest?

Zodiac   Dogs don't wear clothes, Luna. Not natural.

Guy   Ok, just like, don't make a mess or my manager is gonna be pissed.

Dani   Hey, guy, how about three veggie burgers? My treat you guys. Luna, you want anything else?

Luna   I'm good.

Guy *writes it down and goes.*

Zodiac   So what is up? What's been going on? Dani's like, school president right?

Hank   Best one we've ever had. I started football. New season starts soon. Foggy Bluffs Fangs!

Dani   Go Fangs!

Zodiac   The mascot is a fang? That's rad.

Dani   It's actually a wolf, but they're called the fangs.

Zodiac   Right right right. I remember. It's like a werewolf right?

Hank   I guess yeah.

Zodiac   I wonder how actual werewolves feel about that.

The others laugh.

Zodiac   I mean, yeah it's funny, but it's probably hurtful to the werewolves.

Luna   It's better than when we were the Foggy Bluffs Braves.

Dani   The mascot was literally an Indigenous man with an ax.

Zodiac   I mean for sure, but the werewolves *are* more likely to seek revenge through violent means.

Hank   Yeah, me and the boys could fight 'em off.

Zodiac   Probably not. Werewolves are really strong. You have to outsmart them.

Dani   Good thing they're not real.

Zodiac   Yes they are.

It hangs in the air.

Luna   OH, you believe that.

Hank   I think it's mostly they just wanted a mascot that references town history. You know, the Foggy Bluffs Monster and all the suburban legends.

Zodiac   But the Foggy Bluffs Monster isn't a werewolf, it's an alien.

Dani   I thought the Monster was the ghost of that colonial woman with the dead baby?

Hank   I heard it was like, a prehistoric lizard-ape that lived in the woods?

Luna   The Foggy Bluffs Monster is just a superstition. Any time something bad happens in Foggy Bluffs they find a way to make it about a monster.

Zodiac   There's a lot of theories, but the Foggy Bluffs Monster is an extraterrestrial. There's more than one, probably.

Luna   This kind of stuff, it just isn't real.

Zodiac   I've been doing a bunch of reading about cryptozoology and I think there's a lot out in the world that we don't know about.

Guy   Veggie burgers up.

Dani   Hank, what are you working on at the garage?

Hank   I'm fixing up this old van that was dropped off a few weeks ago.

Zodiac   You can fix car?

Hank   Yeah, I took auto-shop twice just for fun.

Dani   It's a van?

Hank   Yeah, like one of those cool 70's ones. I'm gonna put shag carpet in the back.

Luna   Wasn't the whole thing of catching monsters that it was always just bad people doing bad things?

Zodiac   Look, I know it's been a while, and like, my brain is kind of weird. But, there's a lot of things about the world people don't understand! Things . . . people disappear. And reappear. Stories of ghosts and monsters have to come from somewhere.

Luna   But there's just so much proof against it, like lemme google Foggy Bluffs Monster and I'll show you.

They pull out their phone to prove him wrong.

Zodiac   Trust me, I've googled it before. I was abducted in a UFO, I've done googling.

Luna   Look, when you search Foggy Bluffs . . . Oh my god.

Hoover *eats a burger off the table.*

Dani   What's up?

Luna   Um.

Hank   Who died?

Luna *hands their phone to* **Zodiac.**

Zodiac   Oh.

Dani   Somebody say something, please!

Luna   The news today . . .

Zodiac   Elias Jenkins is dead. Mr. Jenkins.

Hoover *looks up.*

Hank   How? What happened?

Zodiac   He was found in the woods, this morning. Apparently it was like. Torn apart. Saying it was probably a bear attack.

Luna   There aren't any bears in the Greywoods.

Zodiac   It wasn't a bear. I know it wasn't. It was the monster. It must have been. He got too close, Jenkins was looking for it—

Dani   How do you know he was looking for it?

Zodiac   He told me. He sent me this, he left it for me in my mailbox.

Zodiac *takes out that piece of paper, slides it down the counter.*

Luna   This is just a Wikipedia article about the Foggy Bluffs Monster.

Zodiac   He didn't communicate directly. But he was telling me, he found something about the monster. Something that must have proved it was real. To prove he was innocent.

Dani   How long have you been pen pals with Mr. Jenkins?

Zodiac   We're not pen pals, it only happened a couple times. I think it was after the trial. I left this letter, telling him what really happened, how I knew he didn't do anything to me, even if everyone else believed it.

Hank   Why would you do that?

Zodiac   Because he was innocent. He was framed.

Hank   He was an insane pedophile.

Zodiac   Don't just say that! They blamed him for something awful, because no one wants to admit that there are parts of the universe that are so unknown they frighten our unconscious mind.

Dani   Like, he's just, gone? There's no, there's. I thought. One day.

Luna   Me too.

Hank   Why would he give you that article in particular?

Zodiac   To show me that they're connected. The aliens and the Foggy Bluffs Monster. Maybe the same thing.

Luna   It doesn't add up. Why would he be sending Zodiac messages? To get arrested again? And then he's killed? I don't know what, but there's something missing.

Hank   If they're saying it's a bear attack. . . . Craig's probably not looking into it. You can't arrest a bear.

Dani   That's not surprising. When has the Sheriff's department ever gotten anything right? I think we should do some investigating of our own. Find out the truth.

Luna   If Mr. Jenkins gets killed, brutally, the night after he sends Zodiac a message. Something is going on.

Dani   You mean, you want us to solve a mystery?

Luna   I mean That's sort of strong language that, I dunno, minimizes a potential murder but, I guess yeah.

Zodiac   I don't know. What's there to find out, other than maybe getting us killed too?

Luna   To find out what happened to Mr. Jenkins. If he's innocent, then an innocent man is dead. If there's something else— why now?

Dani   Before the whole thing happened, he worked at the school. None of us remember talking to him. He was there, but like, just there.

Hank   Zodiac, don't you want to know? To find proof?

Zodiac   What do you think, Hoover? Is it time to go alien hunting?

Hoover *paces, nervous.*

Zodiac   I'm nervous too, Hoov. What happens when we find the aliens, or, they find us? They find me again?

Dani   We're not gonna know unless it happens.

Zodiac *looks at the phone again.*

Zodiac   Where do we start?

Luna   Well, I think we have to find out what Mr. Jenkins was up to last night. And with this research he was sending you.

Dani   I have a friend, she knows a lot about the Foggy Bluffs Monster. She might be able to help us.

Hank   Let's talk to her.

Dani   She owns that thrift shop on Hannah Avenue, do you know it?

Luna   Roswell's? Of course, it's down the street from the store.

Hank   I'll drive.

Three

Roswell's Thrift 'n Find. Several racks of clothes, an area with shabby furniture and a shag carpet. At the counter are boxes of alien print tchotchkes and 'sasquatch crossing' signs.

An older hippie woman sits behind it, knitting a dog sweater. **Dani** *pokes her head in.*

Dani   Hi Bettie!

Bettie   Dani! How are we today?

Dani   I brought some friends. Is it okay if we bring a dog in here?

Zodiac *squeezes next to her.*

Zodiac   He's a service dog.

Bettie   Come on in.

Dani   Thanks!

Dani *opens the door for* **Luna**, **Hank**, *and* **Hoover**.

Bettie   Welcome! I thought today might bring some new spirits to my life.

Dani   This is Zodiac, Hank Mason,

Luna   Luna Takamoto.

Zodiac   And this is Hoover. Say hi, Hoover!

Hoover *barks.*

Bettie   Hello buddy! Can I give him a treat?

Zodiac   He's always hungry.

Bettie *reaches behind the counter and pulls out a dog treat.*

Bettie   He do tricks?

Zodiac   I mean, kinda. If he feels like it. He's pretty lazy. Sit.

Hoover *looks* **Zodiac** *in the eye.*

Zodiac   Yeah, I know, bud. Do it for the food.

Hoover *sits.*

Bettie   He's smart. That's better than obedient.

Zodiac   He had to go through training to come to boarding school with me. He takes care of me.

Bettie *reaches out with the snack in her hand.* **Hoover** *bounds over and licks it up in one bite.*

Bettie   Good boy! I see why you call him Hoover. And I like your name, Zodiac! How did you get it?

Zodiac   When I was little I was like, super into astrology. I'm an Aquarius. So they called me Zodiac.

Bettie   I'm an Aquarius as well.

Dani   We used to give each other code names when we went on missions. I was Saturn and Hank was Jupiter.

Zodiac   When I went to boarding school, all the guys thought I was named after the serial killer. Which was great, 'cause they left me alone.

Dani   These are the friends I was telling you about, the ones I solved mysteries with.

Bettie   I realized after, I was there when you saved the movie theatre from the vampire!

Luna   It was just Rhys Lanchester trying to lower property values so he could buy cheap.

Mr. Dahl *walks past the shop. He looks in the window, but no one notices.*

Bettie   It's an honor to have local heroes in the shop. I'm Bettie Roswell.

Luna   Thanks for having us.

Bettie   Dani's friends are my friends.

Hank   That's really sweet Mrs. Roswell.

Dani   We're actually here to ask you about the Foggy Bluffs Monster.

Bettie   Oh?

Dani   We're trying to learn more about it.

Bettie   It's mostly a way to make money now, t-shirts and stuff. But Foggy Bluffs has always been plagued by stories of creatures, and some think it all comes back to The Monster.

Zodiac   I think I saw it once. What do you think it is?

Bettie   Well how much do you know about it?

Hank   I don't really remember the story.

Luna   It's just an urban legend. It's an owl as seen by hippies on hallucinogens.

Bettie   Well, my friend, I saw it.

Zodiac   What happened?

Bettie   It was just a passing look. It didn't stick around for long. Not much to tell, other than I saw it.

Zodiac   I think maybe the Foggy Bluffs Monster is one of the aliens who abducted me.

Bettie   You've been abducted?

Zodiac   You remember the DuMaurier Kidnapping, a few years ago?

Bettie   Of course, it was the only thing in the Gazette for a year.

Zodiac   Yeah that was me, only I wasn't kidnapped, I was abducted.

Bettie   What happened?

Zodiac   My memories are grainy. I remember experiments, there was some sort of computer that let me speak to Hoover. Hoover asked them to let us go. He got us out, I think. They opened the metal doors, and I couldn't move or see, but I heard the sound. And Hoover pulled me out. I don't always remember all of it, but I remember red eyes.

Hoover *sits proudly on the couch.*

Bettie   Dani, you never told me you knew an abductee.

Dani   It never really came up.

Bettie   You know . . . I don't usually tell people this, so please don't share it, but I feel like I can trust you kids. You're special. But . . . I was also abducted.

Zodiac   You were abducted?

Bettie   Yes. Long before you. I haven't said that out loud in a good while. I'm so honored to finally meet someone else who understands.

Zodiac   See, guys? I told you it was real. I told you the monster abducted me. What happened to you? What was it like?

Bettie   Wait one minute. Lemme find the VHS. Back when it happened, I tried to tell everyone. Some folks even believed me, and made this to get our story out.

Bettie *rummages around for a VHS tape.*

Bettie   Watch this.

She puts it in the TV/VHS player she has hanging over the counter. Grainy VHS footage of Foggy Bluffs pours from the screen. **Bruce** *and* **Beth's** *voices are recordings of original testimony, played by* **Dani** *and* **Hank**. *The narrator is a discount Vincent Price.*

Narrator   In the small town of Foggy Bluffs, NY, not much was said to happen. But in-between the rolling mists and scenic forests lurks a secret few admit to believe in. One dim October night, a young married couple was driving along the banks of the Little Green River. To protect their identities, let's call them— Bruce and Beth Frank. The newlyweds were arriving back in town from their honeymoon. Late at night, the famous fog filled the roads. Around 11:23PM, Bruce Frank reported seeing something in his rearview mirror.

Bruce   I thought, it must have been a deer. You see deer all the time.

Narrator   Then, a large shape zoomed by Beth on the passenger side. Suddenly, about 100 feet in front of the car, two giant red eyes shone out at them, like fiery orbs.

Beth   They must have been 10 feet off the ground at least,

Narrator   Slamming the brakes, Bruce and Beth faced what would become known in the years to come as the Foggy Bluffs Monster.

Beth   It stared at us. It definitely stared. You could feel it, thinking, taking us in.

Bruce   At first I thought it must have been an owl. I told myself the fog was throwing off my depth perception. But no owl is that big.

Narrator   An amateur sketch artist, Bruce Frank produced this impression of the Monster.

A rudimentary drawing of the Foggy Bluffs Beast is seen.

Narrator   After a harrowing standoff, the Foggy Bluffs Beast seemed to pulse its eyes at them.

Beth   Next thing we remember, it's morning. We're driving down the road, a couple miles south of where we were. No fog, no monster. We didn't know what to do, so we went home.

Bruce   I'd have thought I dreamed the whole thing, if it weren't for Beth saying she saw it too. That, and the scorch mark on the side of the car.

Beth   That night was the first of the dreams. Originally, it was just images. But soon I began to remember more and more about what happened, in blurry ways.

Bruce   I didn't have the dreams. I never really remembered my dreams, but she does.

Beth   We were taken somewhere by the monster, somewhere where I felt lighter. Sometimes Bruce was with me, and sometimes I would turn my head and he wasn't. I remember experiments. I remember there were more than one. I remember them showing me things, visions from the future.

Narrator   The Franks reported their experience to local police, and other than a few items in the local papers, little came of it. But, more and more sightings were reported in the following years. What is the Foggy Bluffs Monster? An alien? A demon? A ghost? Although you can find its visage printed on many a t-shirt or tourist trap souvenir lunchbox, the residents of Foggy Bluffs, New York know that something dangerous lurks in the woods by the river.

Fade to black on Bruce **Frank***'s illustration. Credits roll.*

Luna   That was the most ludicrous documentary I've ever seen.

Bettie   A little sensationalized maybe, doesn't mean it didn't happen. Wandering the woods at night, you might catch a glimpse of those big red eyes like I did.

Zodiac   Yeah, I remember eyes. Like I was being measured. Or judged. For some purpose.

Luna   Do you have any books about it?

Bettie   The best one is "Creature in the Fog." Anything else is just ripping it off of this one. It comes with a DVD of the documentary too.

Luna   I'll buy it.

Zodiac   Have you ever seen it since? I can feel it watching me, sometimes. But it doesn't reveal itself.

Bettie   Don't go running towards danger. They're guarding something in those woods. There must be things they don't want you to see, or else the monster wouldn't have kept showing up.

Hank   Why don't we go for a drive in my van? Down to the bluffs?

Dani   Great idea, Hank. We can look for the monster.

Bettie   Be careful. Take that dog with you, there's power in numbers.

Zodiac   Let's just hang out for a bit, before we go chasing after the monster, you know? Make sure we know what we're getting into.

Luna   I agree, I'd like to get my hands on any official records of the case too. For some perspective.

Dani   Gotta find clues.

Bettie   Why don't you kids take a look around. Anything with a green sticker is 20% off today.

Zodiac *and* **Hank** *wander off to the men's clothing,* **Luna** *spins a display of enamel and button pins shaped like cryptids and emblazoned with phrases like "I Want To Believe" and "Bush Did 9/11."*

Bettie   How are you liking those cards, dear? Are they teaching you?

Dani   They're so beautiful. I carry them with me everywhere now!

Dani *pulls a deck of tarot cards out of a designer makeup bag.*

Bettie   I thought you'd like them.

Luna   You read tarot? I thought you were a skeptic.

Bettie   We all contain multitudes, my dear. Reality is a kaleidoscope.

Dani   Tarot aren't magic. They just tell you what you are already thinking about, but might not be ready to admit.

Luna   Then how do they tell the future?

Dani   They don't. But it can help you make decisions. For self-reflecting.

Luna   Will you do a reading for me some time?

Dani   I'm not great yet. I still use a guidebook.

Luna   That's okay. You don't have to do it now.

Bettie   Everything will be seen in time.

Luna *wanders over towards* **Zodiac** *and* **Hank***.*

Bettie   That's the Hank you were telling me about?

Dani   I don't know what you mean, Bettie.

Zodiac *is trying to get* **Hank** *to buy a floral sweater.*

Zodiac   I like the flowers. You should try it on, Hank.

Hank   Oh, I don't think it's really my style.

Zodiac   I think you'd look nice in flowers.

Hank   I dunno, it's not really very manly, you know?

Zodiac   Who cares about manly? Try this scarf.

He wraps an ascot around **Hank's** *neck.*

Zodiac   You look cool! Nice and soft.

Hank *looks in a mirror.*

Hank   Soft.

Luna   That's a good thing.

Hank   Okay.

Zodiac   You should get it!

Hank   I don't know what I'd wear it with.

Zodiac   With this! This outfit!

Hank   I don't know, I don't think I'm gonna buy anything today.

Zodiac   Then I'll buy it for you. It's a gift! A welcome back gift. Welcome back, me.

Hank   You don't have to do that. That's really nice.

Zodiac   I just think you should have it!

Dani   What do you think of this necklace, Hank?

Hank   It's nice! Everything looks nice on you.

Zodiac   Let's grab a pizza before we head out. I'm starving.

Bettie   Come back any time. Will that be all?

She begins to cash them out.

Four

Outside Flatwoods Pizza. **Hank** *is on the phone,* **Hoover** *resting his head on his lap. He takes off the ascot as he's talking.*

Hank   Hey mom.
. . .
Work was fine. I don't have practice tonight, but I'm not gonna be home for dinner.
. . .
I'm with Dani, we're getting pizza.
. . .
We were talking about student council and stuff at Rita's birthday last month and just kinda remembered why we used to be friends.
. . .
Maybe, I dunno, like she's always been awesome, but idk. You're being embarrassing! Luna's here too anyway, so.
. . .
No, just us.

Hoover *lifts his head.* **Hank** *gives him a nudge.*

Hank   Ok, gotta go, love you mom!

The rest come outside with two pizzas and drinks. **Dani** *has a bag with pepperoni in it.*

Zodiac   Hoover, don't worry, Dani got your favorite. An entire stick of pepperoni.

Hoover *bounces over to lick the bottom of the paper bag.*

Zodiac   Say thank you!

Hoover *expresses thanks to* **Dani**. *It's getting late, and a little foggy.*

Dani   You're welcome, Hoover.

Zodiac   It's so weird, how this town. It's like everything is mostly the same, yet not at all. Like, it's an oil painting and I remember a cartoon.

Luna   It's just a normal town. You'll get bored of it soon.

Dani   Your mom still hovering?

Hank   She's just so nosy like she has to know every single thing I'm doing every minute.

Zodiac *sees someone across the street. He falls silent.*

Dani   You can chill, don't worry about her. You think I'd let you get into too much trouble?

They notice **Zodiac** *looking far off.* **Hoover** *jumps up and begins circling* **Zodiac**.

Luna   What's up? What are you looking at?

Zodiac   I think. It was nothing. Just a. No, I'm good. It's okay, Hoov.

Hank   Ok, I parked over here.

Hank, **Luna**, *and* **Dani** *walk away.*

Zodiac   That was Mr. Dahl, right?

Hoover *absolutely wasn't paying attention.*

Zodiac   Pay attention, dude.

A small grey man in sunglasses is across the street, staring.

Zodiac   Um. Mr. Dahl? That you? You real?

A streetlamp flickers. Cars pass. The sound of flapping wings. **Mr. Dahl** *is gone.*

Zodiac   No, it wouldn't be.

Hoover *pulls him away to follow the gang, he leaves.*

Zodiac, *aged 12, follows a dog. The dog stops in front of an old metal door angled out of the ground, like some sort of bomb shelter or something.*

Mr. Dahl, *a small grey man in sunglasses, steps out of the trees.*

Zodiac   Mr. Dahl, is this your dog?

Mr. Dahl   It is a dog.

Zodiac   Mr. Dahl, I want to see what you look like.

Mr. Dahl   You've seen me.

Zodiac   The real you. I know you look different.

Mr. Dahl   What could you mean?

Zodiac   When I'm not looking. When you're looking at me. When your eyes look red.

Mr. Dahl   Will you come with me?

Zodiac   Where will we go?

Mr. Dahl   Nowhere difficult, but very far away.

Zodiac   And you'll tell me who you are?

Mr. Dahl   Yes.

Zodiac   And will you take me back here?

Mr. Dahl   Yes.

Zodiac   Can I tell my friends goodbye?

Mr. Dahl   You don't want them to be jealous of you, do you? You're a special boy. Only you get to come with me.

Zodiac   How long will we be gone?

Mr. Dahl   We don't have time.

Zodiac   Can the dog come too?

Mr. Dahl   It is useless.

A pause for calculation.

Mr. Dahl   The dog can come too. Come here, Walter.

Zodiac   I want to say goodbye to my friends.

Mr. Dahl*'s red eyes spread a vibrant pink, then green, and wash over* **Zodiac** *and the dog. Impossibly long fingers reach down for* **Zodiac***. And then darkness.*

Five

In **Hank's** *van. It's not really decorated, but drives just fine.* **Hoover** *munches pepperoni.*

Dani   Zodiac, as we continue the investigation, can you lay out exactly what you know to be true? So we're all on the same page?

Zodiac   Can we eat first? It's been a long day.

Hank   Yeah, I'm starving too. We didn't get pepperoni for the humans did we?

Luna   Just the dog, sorry. One vegan pizza, and one veggie deluxe with extra cheese.

Dani   Maybe Hoover will share with you.

Hank   Gross.

They start eating. **Zodiac** *is a little shaky.*

Luna   Are you okay, Zodiac?

Zodiac   Yeah, I'm fine.

Dani   Oh my god I love cheese.

Zodiac   Actually, do y'all mind if I pack a bowl?

Hank   A pizza bowl?

Zodiac   Smoke some weed. My nerves are a little, like, ?

Everyone looks to **Hank***.*

Hank   Uh, yeah. I'll pop a window. Let's just get a little music going.

He pops a window and plays some groovy throwback music. **Zodiac** *unzips his backpack and begins his smoking ritual. He grabs his piece, decides it's too small, and pulls out a small bong. He shows* **Hank** *what he's doing.* **Luna** *inspects the smaller piece, looking through the glass.*

Hank   When did you start smoking weed?

Zodiac   Is that not like, common here?

Luna   I don't think so. At least, I've never been offered before.

Zodiac   That's wild. Boarding school is like, based on weed.

Hank   What's it like?

Zodiac   It's the best. Like, your mind gets sort of, soft. But like not in a scary way. In a wide way. And you just like, I dunno man. It's fun.

Hank   I'd try some time.

Zodiac   I've got plenty if you wanna share! You guys all want some?

Dani   Um, I don't know.

Zodiac   It's completely natural.

Luna   I've heard it's got some health benefits. People use it to treat epilepsy.

Dani   I don't have epilepsy.

Zodiac   You're already a step ahead!

Luna   The system vilifies a lot things that are actually good for us, so sometimes the stuff we're not supposed to do is what we're exactly supposed to do. Did that make sense?

Dani   I'm just not someone who does things I'm not supposed to for the sake of doing it.

Luna   You used to be.

Zodiac   If you really don't wanna we don't have to.

Luna   She's nervous.

Zodiac   Well the weed will make you not nervous. Win-win.

Dani   You guys go ahead. I don't know if I'm going to.

Zodiac   Gnarly.

Dani *sits back, petting* **Hoover**. *She sways to the music.*

Zodiac   This thing would be great with like, some pillows. And a lava lamp.

Zodiac *takes the first hit.*

Zodiac   Who's next?

Luna   Me!

Zodiac   Here you go. You need me to show you how to—?

Luna *was watching, and perfectly mimics his actions to rip the bong. They're a little cautious. They exhale.*

Zodiac   Nice.

Luna   I'm a quick study. Hank?

Hank *looks at the bong and lighter in his hands.*

Zodiac   You need help?

Hank   Just a little.

Zodiac   Okay, I'll light it for you. Put your mouth here, and inhale smooth, and when I say go, suck in really deep, like breathe it into your ass, okay?

Hank *nods.*

Zodiac   Okay, 1, 2, go. breathe.

Hank *inhales a gigantic hit. He immediately starts coughing.*

Zodiac   That was a little ambitious. Dani, pass me his soda.

Dani   Is he going to be okay?

Zodiac   Yeah, he'll be fine. You want a hit?

Hank *gulps down the soda, still coughing.*

Dani   I'm okay.

Zodiac *takes another hit. So does* **Luna**. **Dani** *shuffles her tarot deck and pulls cards for herself.*

Luna   I don't feel anything yet.

Zodiac   You gotta let it seep into you. Right Hoover? You wanna hit?

Hoover *wags his tail.*

Zodiac   Nah, I'm kidding, you're a dog. One time he ate a bunch of my edibles. It was like he was seeing ghosts everywhere. It was really funny.

Hoover *rolls over.*

Zodiac   I'm sorry, you're right. That was insensitive. I'm sure it was very scary.

Zodiac *whispers to* **Hank**.

Zodiac   It was really funny.

Hank   If you were a crypto or whatever, which one would you be?

Zodiac   Gotcha fast, huh bud?

Luna   He means cryptid.

Hank   I know.

Zodiac   I'd be . . . hm. Well like, probably . . . Sasquatch.

Hank   Not an alien?

Zodiac   I mean, no. I'm more, something from Earth. As much as I love space. I'm something furry, and lonely, in the woods. If I was an alien they wouldn't have chosen to study me.

Luna   I think I could be extraterrestrial. Like one of the little Greys, scurrying around but still like "I come in peace."

Zodiac   Or a fairy. Unless you believe that fairies are just aliens. Which, could be true.

Hank   Whoa?

Luna   Yeah, say more about that.

Zodiac   You're really smart. And in like, a way that is sort of intimidating. In a good way! And you're queer, which like, puts you in-between worlds.

Luna   I never thought about it like that.

Dani   I think I'd be a mermaid.

Hank   That's not a crypto.

Dani   Yes it is a cryptID. I love the water.

Zodiac   You're a Cancer so that makes sense.

Dani   And I love beauty and stuff, but not in a vain way. Like, art and glamour. Makeup is art! I'm also tough and scaly.

Hank   Ew.

Dani   Metaphorically! And I would be one of those classical mermaids, like Sirens. The scary ones. Like, who sing beautiful songs and lure men to their deaths. Mermaids are scary!

Zodiac   I wish I could lure men to their deaths with my voice.

Dani   Can I try some of the pot?

Zodiac   Yeah.

Dani   Will you help me too?

Zodiac   O'course. Here you go.

Dani *takes a small hit, with* **Zodiac's** *help.* **Zodiac** *looks to* **Hank**.

Zodiac   What about you, Hank? Cryptid.

Hank   Um, like, I think a ghost.

Zodiac   Interesting.

Hank *is absentmindedly tying the ascot around his neck.*

Hank   Because like, ghosts can be invisible. And they exist past when they should. Like they're stuck going around even though they should be gone.

Dani *takes another hit and coughs a bunch.*

Luna   Do you feel that way?

Hank   No, I'm done coughing.

Zodiac   Ha ha.

Luna   No I mean, like you're supposed to be gone?

Hank   Doesn't everyone, sometimes? And like, some ghosts throw furniture and stuff, and I'd love to be able to get away with that.

Dani   I would love to throw stuff.

Zodiac *gently takes the bong from her.*

Dani   Not right now ob-vi-ous-ly. But like. Sometimes just, in the middle of Chemistry? Just like. Chuck an Erlenmeyer. Right out the window. Or into the window. So it smashes.

Luna   You don't have to be so dramatic about it.

Dani   Aren't you get sick of it? We're always trying to be the smartest most correct person all the time and I'm just? I never want to see another report card!!

Luna   But it's not about grades for the sake of grades. If our parents want us to get into the best schools, which is why we met in Science Quest to begin with, we can use that to go wherever we want after. The status isn't the important part, it's how we can use it.

Zodiac   It really all doesn't matter.

Dani   But, like at the same time it so does.

Zodiac   If you're unhappy in the system, you can get out. There's nothing keeping you there except your own fear.

Luna   You guys are like, really winning at high school right now, by the traditional value system. But you don't seem to be enjoying it very much. Like Hank, I don't want you gone. I don't like hearing you say that. But if you feel stuck going around and around, find something new.

Zodiac   There's more important things to worry about than school.

Hank   Like, like, what, like, um, looking at the moon?

Zodiac   I think that was a jab, but yes, the moon is very beautiful. Luna gets it.

Luna   Yeah I love her. Moon's great. Moon's a lesbian.

Hank   Are the aliens from the moon?

Dani   Hank don't be rude.

Zodiac   That's not rude to ask questions.

Luna   There are no aliens on the Moon. The Moon can't support life.

Zodiac   That's true too. Though you can't rule out sublunar life, 100%.

Hank   'Cause there's no such thing as aliens, right?

Dani   Hank, can you pass me a slice? I'm hungry.

Zodiac   Hank, I know your mom says one thing, but it was aliens. I was abducted. Not kidnapped.

Hank   It was Mr. Jenkins, dude, like I'm so sorry it happened, but it was a long time ago. I'm sorry, and like, I'm sorry we kind of stopped talking to you a little bit. But if you're just trying to like, make it easier by saying it was aliens, but like, it definitely wasn't aliens and at least you could stop pretending around us?

Music, hollow.

Zodiac   They couldn't convict Mr. Jenkins because he didn't do it. I know they say he kidnapped me and, and, and, molested me, or, whatever, but he, he didn't. That's why he didn't go to jail. He didn't touch me, he was just a scapegoat. Aliens are real, and we've been influenced by them throughout history. Bettie Roswell just confirmed it! And it wasn't a long time ago. It was six years ago.

Hank   A bear killed Mr. Jenkins.

Dani   Or something like a bear.

Zodiac   Like the Foggy Bluffs Monster.

Hank   Why wouldn't it be a bear?

Luna   I'd like to help you. Find the answers.

Zodiac   Really?

Luna   Yes. I don't know that I am ready to believe in aliens, but I'd like to help you.

Hank   You're not gonna find anything satisfactory. Your prime witness is gone. Unless you talk to his ghost, and ghosts aren't real.

Zodiac   That's just, another conversation.

Dani   I've seen a ghost.

Luna   Twist.

Hank   What?

Dani   When my grandpa died. I was in class when he died, and I didn't find out until later. But I saw him outside my classroom. He waved to me. And blew me a kiss.

Zodiac   Wow.

Dani   I thought it was kind of weird, because he hadn't done that before, but he was on the school board, so he came around sometimes. I was taking a test so I didn't wave back. Later I found out he had a heart attack that morning.

Zodiac   He came to say goodbye.

Dani   I think so. I never told anyone that.

Zodiac   That's beautiful. Thank you. See? Things like this happen.

Dani   I think when people matter to you, something ties you together.

Zodiac   Like us. Running into each other, at the river yesterday.

Dani   I've known you longer than anyone other than my family.

Zodiac   Remember when we'd go play in the woods and come back all covered in mud and our parents would be so mad?

Sounds of a car pulling up outside.

Zodiac   What is that?

Dani   Oh fuck. We jinxed it. Our parents found out. They're gonna be so mad.

Zodiac   Put everything back in the backpack, quick.

Hank   This'll be fine, I'm the Mayor's son.

From outside:

Tess   Henry Welles Mason what do you think you're doing? Come on, kid.

Hank   Oh shit, it's my mom.

Hank *scrambles out of the van,* **Hoover** *with him. The doors swing open onto the foggy night.*

Tess   A patrol car saw you kids from the road. You're lucky Craig knows your van or he wouldn't have called me.

Hank   Sorry mom.

Tess   What dog is this? And why are you wearing that scarf?

Zodiac   That's Hoover, Ms. Mayor.

Tess   Walter?

Zodiac   Zodiac. Hi.

Tess   Sorry Zodiac. Oh. Hi Luna.

Luna   Hello.

Tess *sniffs the air.* **Tess** *peeks into the van.*

Tess   Hello Danielle.

Dani (*cowering inside*)   Hello Ms. Mason.

Tess   Hank, I'll say this. I didn't expect to find you smoking weed in a van by the river. With your middle school science club. You constantly find new ways to surprise me.

Zodiac   We weren't smoking, I swear. Hoover just smells bad.

Hank   Mom, we were just—

Tess   Don't tell me you're solving crimes again. Didn't end so well last time.

Hank   What if we were? We're older now, we're gonna be fine.

Tess   You're lucky you're my son or the cops would have stopped you, so. Don't give me sass, Hank.

Hank   Am I in trouble?

Tess *looks him in the eyes.*

Tess   Just, don't make trouble, ok? If you're gonna be delinquents, don't do it so close to the road?

Hank   Yes, mom.

Tess   No, wait, don't you go into the woods there might be bears.

Zodiac   We heard.

Tess   You should all just go home. Actually, no, I don't want you driving.

Hank   We'll just chill here for a while and then I'll drive everyone home as soon as I can. Nothing weird, just sitting in a van.

Tess   Don't stay out all night.

Hank   Yes, mom.

Tess   That's Mayor Mom to you.

Tess *leaves.*

Hank   Oh my god.

Zodiac   That was lucky.

Dani   I hope she doesn't tell my mom. Please don't let her tell my mom. I'm going to be dead.

Luna   I'd say we got out of that in the best possible way.

A snap from the woods. Then, a really big snap.

Dani   Did you hear that?

Hank   Probably just a. Deer?

Dani   Let's go see.

Dani *ventures into the woods.*

Luna   Where are you going? Careful!

Zodiac   Like, don't get too close!

They follow her.

Hank   Guys!

Hank *looks at* **Hoover**.

Hank   Well I'm not staying here alone.

Zodiac   What was that?

Hank *locks the van and runs after them.* **Hoover** *tries to open the van. He's a dog, so it doesn't work. He looks around, then follows the gang.*

They walk through the underbrush.

Dani   I think I see something, up there.

Zodiac   I don't—

Luna   Oh my god.

In the dark, two dim red eyes turn to face them. **Hank** *and* **Hoover** *catch up to them.*

Hank   Hey, you guys—

Luna   Shhh.

Hank *sees the beast.*

Zodiac   The Foggy Bluffs Monster.

The shape solidifies slightly. It threatens to become something they can see. Then, its red eyes turn and it goes into the woods.

Dani   Don't let it get away!

She bolts after it.

Zodiac   Wait! No!

Luna   Dani, wait!

Hank   Dani!

All of them follow her.
They run through the woods.
They get separated.

Angles topple. Stars burst through the leaves. Dirt falls. Wood and earth storms and brews around them.

Red eyes appear from everywhere.

Hank *runs.*
Hank *runs out of the woods and head first into the side of his van.*

Hank   How'd I get turned around? I was running in a straight line.

Dani *runs.*
She sees a figure, 10 feet tall. She turns, red eyes glowing, tears streaming down her face.
A woman in white.
The woman screams.
Dani *runs.*

Branches.

Luna *runs.*
They see the eyes. Blinking. Red eyes. Sometimes in pairs. Sometimes only a single, red dot. Blinking.

They run past a tree.
A small grey man in a suit reaches out and grabs them.
Luna *starts to scream, he covers their mouth. Raises one finger to his own mouth.*
A silence.
Luna *reaches up to his sunglasses and pulls them away. His eyes glow, red.*
Luna *rips themself away from the man and runs.*

Branches.

Zodiac *runs.*
Zodiac *hears a scream.*
Zodiac *runs towards the scream.*
He stops, disoriented by fog.

Zodiac   Hoover?? Where are you?

He turns. The small man in sunglasses looks at him from far away.
The man waves, and circles away around a tree.
Zodiac *runs away.*
He hears **Luna** *start to scream before they're stifled.*
Zodiac *trips on yellow police tape. He lands on the metal doors of the shelter. Blood is caked onto the doors. Little white flags dot the ground.*

Jenkins was killed here.
Zodiac *was found here.*

Zodiac   Shit.

A monster steps out of the woods, 10 feet tall.

Maybe furry, maybe feathered. Nothing on its face but those big red eyes. Small, clawlike hands. A thin body, no legs visible. Maybe a dress. From behind, two large appendages.
Perhaps wings. Perhaps arms.
The monster moves closer.
Zodiac *is frozen.*
A green light begins.
Zodiac *hears* **Hoover** *howling.*
Zodiac *sprints towards* **Hoover**.

Hoover *runs through the woods at night. Just the woods.*

Dani *runs.* **Luna** *runs.* **Zodiac** *runs.*
They run out of the woods, onto the side of the road.

Dani   I saw it.

Zodiac   Me too.

Luna   It's not a monster.

Dani   It's a ghost.

Luna   It's a man.

Zodiac   It's the monster. It's the alien. Somehow we ended up at the bunker–we were back there again–all three of us–

Two lights shine on them, low, through the fog.

Zodiac   There it is!

The van breaks through the fog. It's just headlights.

Dani   It's Hank.

Hank *parks and gets out of the car.*

Hank Where have you guys been? I've been driving around for like half an hour.

Dani We saw it, the Foggy Bluffs Monster.

Hank All of you?

Zodiac You've gotta believe us.

Luna There was someone in those woods with us. Trying to scare us, or something. He grabbed me.

Hank Did he hurt you?

Dani It was a woman.

Luna I was grabbed by a man. He tried to tell me something, but I ran.

Zodiac No, it was exactly like the Franks said in the movie. Tall.

Dani Tall, and a woman. She was crying, her eyes were red from crying.

Hank You all sound crazy.

Zodiac Hoover? Hoover, where are you?

Dani I'm sure he's right behind you? Hoover!

Zodiac I don't want to call the monster to us.

Hank Hoover!

Zodiac What if the monster got him?

Dani She wouldn't hurt a dog. She's sad.

Hank I'm sure he's fine.

Zodiac No, I need to know. I need him, he needs me. I have to find him.

Hank You're not going back in there.

Zodiac No, he can't be alone in there, he's not safe.

Luna Don't go in there, Zodiac, we have to get out of here.

Zodiac Hoover! Come! Hoover!

A rustling in the woods again.

Luna Oh no.

Hank Guys, let's please go.

Hoover *walks out of the bush. So casually.*

Zodiac Hoover, what the ever-loving fuck! Don't do that! I can't lose you.

Hank Let's go. Everyone into the van.

Six

Zodiac *is in the front next to* **Hank**. **Hoover** *stands in-between the seats.* **Dani** *in the back.* **Luna** *is dropped off.*

Luna   Good night. Will you guys text me you got home safe?

Hank   For sure. I've got your number.

Dani   I'll start a group chat.

They drive off.

Dani   So, I think, I think we will get a good night's sleep. And get together again tomorrow, now that we know there's something in those woods. We're closer. We just have to be more careful.

Hank *pulls up to* **Dani's**.

Zodiac   'Night Dani.

Dani   You know, even though this was like, terrifying, I sort of had a wonderful time. Being with you all again. 'Night Hank.

She gets out of the van.

Hank   'Night, Dani.

Hank *watches her walk up her driveway, then starts the van to drive* **Zodiac** *home.*

Hank   I'm sorry for like, going at you before.

Zodiac   It's weird to see you turned into this like, aggro jock guy. Like the whole, letterman jacket, in the running for Homecoming King.

Hank   I didn't mean to, it just, it happens. You changed a lot too, it's not a bad thing.

Zodiac   I'm used to being the weird kid. Really, I'm okay with it. But I used to think about being in Foggy Bluffs, or being here before it all happened, as like, a good time. Having all of you as friends, exploring the woods and raiding the library, it was like the last time I had friends.

Hank   Now you're back though—

Zodiac   Maybe I'm just. I'm really cynical about most stuff and I was holding on to the idea of you guys.

Hank   Oh.

Zodiac   You're not used to people being this frank are you? I'm trying to embrace radical honesty.

Hank   I just like haven't talked *about* being friends with anyone in a while. The guys on the team, we're friends but we don't talk about it.

Zodiac   What do you talk about?

Hank   I dunno.

Hank *pulls into* **Zodiac**'s *driveway and parks.* **Zodiac** *doesn't move.*

Hank   When we were talking about what sort of cryptid we would be. I said ghost then, but I think I'm a Swamp Monster. Like, a big, dripping, green amphibian. I'm like, fine swimming underwater, I can breathe here. But I also want to live on land. That part of me feels just, scary, and unappealing. Not to me, but like, people would be scared. And I just want to be normal and go to school and like, be alive, but my gills freak everyone out.

Zodiac   I mean, I really like Swamp Monsters.

Hank   We should keep hanging out. All four of us. And Hoover.

Hoover *sticks his head up.*

Zodiac   Dani seems determined to find the monster again.

Hank   Are you?

Zodiac   If it means hanging out again.

Hank   I'd like it.

Zodiac   You wanna keep hanging out with him, Hoov?

Hoover *licks* **Hank's** *face.*

Zodiac   That's a yes.

Hank   We're going to need more on Jenkins. I think I've got an idea. You free tomorrow?

Zodiac   Yeah, I don't do anything. Bye!

As **Hank** *drives away, red eyes watch* **Zodiac** *and* **Hoover** *walk inside.*

Seven

Town Hall. **Luna** *and* **Zodiac** *are standing out by the back door.* **Hoover** *paces.* **Dani** *is on speaker from* **Zodiac**'s *phone.*

Dani   Last night was really crazy in a fun way but I do just want us all to remember I am in fact Class President and that means I will not be breaking into Town Hall and stealing any kinds of files so I appreciate you letting me sit this one out. I'm heading to Roswell's to see what Bettie knows about ghosts. I'm rooting for you. Foggy Bluffs Fangs!

Luna & Zodiac   Go Fangs.

Dani *hangs up.*

Zodiac   Are we really doing this?

Luna   Be gay do crimes I guess.

Hank *opens the back door for them.*

Hank   Be quiet, don't get caught. I've got her distracted in the front room.

Hank *disappears again and runs back to his mom.*

Zodiac   Wait here, Hoov.

Luna *and* **Zodiac** *slip inside,* **Hoover** *follows them.*

Zodiac   No, wait outside.

Sheriff Craig *is meandering around the office making coffee*

Luna   Shh! Oh no. The Sheriff is in.

Hank *and* **Tess** *can be heard out front as* **Tess** *takes a smoke break.* **Luna**, **Zodiac**, *and* **Hoover** *crawl and roll down the hall and between desks to avoid* **Craig**.

Craig *goes into the bathroom. They get to the door of* **Tess'** *office. It's locked. They look to* **Hank**. *He's grabbed the keys and holds them behind his back so they can see.*

Luna   He has her keys, but how are we supposed to get them?

Zodiac   Dude, no.

Hoover *creeps over behind* **Tess**. **Hank** *notices and moves so* **Tess** *has to turn away from the dog.*

Craig *flushes.* **Luna** *realizes they're in plain view of the bathroom. They pull* **Zodiac** *to the floor, with only a piece of furniture between the two of them and* **Craig** *coming out of the bathroom.*

He opens the door, and **Luna** *tosses a stapler at a stack of papers on his desk. The papers go everywhere.* **Hank** *takes the opportunity and tosses the keys to* **Hoover**.

Tess   Sheriff, what is going on back there?

Craig   A stack of files fell again.

Hank   Hey Mom, I just wanted to say I'm really sorry about last night, I didn't mean to make you worried.

Tess   It's the last place I expected you to be. I didn't even know you did drugs!

Hank   I don't!

Tess   And with that group, you can see why I would be surprised, I haven't had to worry about you with that crowd in a while. The four of you together are trouble.

Hank   Dani and Luna are like the smartest kids at FBH.

Tess   I don't want you hanging out with Zodiac, especially in the woods, it can't be good for you, and can't be good for him. It's all a mess. You can kiss SUNY Norville goodbye if you start up with whatever bullshit I let you do in middle school, and also doing drugs? Not to mention football goes out the window if you're smoking and destroying your lungs, do not look at me like that I am your mother.

Tess *hears the crash and turns around.* **Hoover** *narrowly dodges her gaze.*

Tess   If you did your paperwork on time the stacks wouldn't get so high and topple off your desk.

Craig   If you'd approve the new budget we wouldn't have to share an office.

Tess   Don't get me started, Craig.

Hank   But I was saying—

Tess *turns back.* **Hoover** *slowly, carefully gets back to* **Zodiac** *and* **Luna**, *who unlock the door and slip inside.*

Hank   Oh I forgot, can you take a look at the van? 'Cause I'm not sure if the tire is flat or not.

Tess   You work in an auto-shop.

Hank   Ok but I want you to see it.

Tess   Fine.

Inside her office. Some files and a computer on her desk, and a filing cabinet next to it.

Zodiac   Guard the door, Hoov.

Luna   It's gotta be in the cabinet.

They each unlock a drawer and start looking through. **Zodiac** *breaks the silence.*

Zodiac   So, you got a new gender.

Luna   Do you want to talk about this right now?

Zodiac   You were the first person to tell me they were gay. I thought you'd keep me updated.

Luna   You disappeared, you can't get mad at me for not telling you about everything in my life.

Zodiac   What? 'Cause I get abducted, suddenly I don't deserve to know you?

Luna   I don't mean that. Afterward. You disappeared. You stopped coming to Science Quest, you transferred schools—

Zodiac   My parents made me talk to all these specialists and we were in and out of court, it was hard to focus on stuff.

Luna   I'm not saying it wasn't hard for you. I just had a hard time too. It felt like you came back, but I didn't get my friend back.

Zodiac   I'm back now. Dani and Hank sincerely care about the Homecoming Dance and that can't be the only energy I surround myself with.

Luna   Oh god. I can't believe them.

Zodiac   I mean, they have fun with all that school spirit stuff, but I just.

Luna   I shudder. Somehow they got more normal. I just got weirder.

Zodiac   I don't think they're all that normal.

Luna   Well they aren't trans. And they weren't sent to the principal's office once a week for being a disturbance when other people were harassing me last year.

Zodiac   I didn't know that. I'm sorry. Does your family know?

Luna   My parents aren't terrible about it. When I told them I'm not a girl, they said "okay" and then mom brought me a bowl of sliced apples and we haven't talked about it since. I don't think my grandma even realizes what trans is. She hates my hair, but I know she still loves me.

Zodiac   I do too. Always will.

Luna   You're gay too right?

Zodiac   Huh? Oh. Um. Yeah.

Luna   Okay. I thought so.

Zodiac   I never really, like, came out. 'Cause of the whole, I don't know, Mr. Jenkins thing. Everyone thought I was anyway. Well, I wasn't even really kidnapped by him anyway. I don't think aliens have a concept of gender anyway, so like is it even gay if like, what if I'm not a boy? I don't know, there's too much going on in my brain. Can we get out of Town Hall?

Luna   Yeah . . . I don't think you're lying about aliens, but I also don't know that I believe in aliens, but I know something touched me last night. And I believe this mystery isn't going to end at Jenkins. I think he—

Tess *is heard trying the door.*

Tess   Dammit, I locked my keys in my office again. Craig where did you put the spare? Because I need my spare! Don't give me all that again.

She walks away.

Luna   Shit. We gotta get out of here.

Zodiac   How? She's right outside.

Luna   And we didn't get your file.

Hank *appears in the window over the desk, waving frantically. He can't really be heard through the glass and has to jump to be seen.*

Hank   My mom! Is coming! Back! Inside!

Luna   The window!

Zodiac   Are you crazy?

Luna *climbs up onto the desk to open the window.*

Luna   Hank gimme a hand!

They flip through the window with a thud. **Zodiac** *follows, much less confident. He somehow twists himself backwards and lowers himself out the window, face towards the desk. He sees something and hesitates.*

Luna   Come on!

Zodiac   My file! It's been on her desk the whole time!

Hank *pulls* **Zodiac** *through the window. The door is about to open.* **Hoover** *leaps across the office, grabs the file in his teeth, jumps onto the desk and through the window.* **Tess** *opens the door.*

Tess   I swear to god I never do any actual work.

She sits at her desk.

Elsewhere, **Luna***,* **Zodiac***,* **Hank***, and* **Hoover** *with the file in his mouth, zoom into the van.*

Hank   Okay, Luna you take those files and start going through them. I'm gonna swing by Roswell's to pick up Dani.

Zodiac   I gotta go home and get my bong. That was crazy. Luna, will you come with me?

Luna   Let's all meet up at Pterodact Hill tonight. Remember, where we stopped that hang-glider from crashing Founder's Day?

A breeze blows in a little fog and **Tess** *realizes the window is open, then the door opens.*

Tess   What can I help you with?

Mr. Dahl   Hello again, Mayor.

Tess   Have a seat.

Mr. Dahl   I cannot stay long. I've been sent from the higher ups, as we like to say. I have to advise you, close the investigation into the death of Elias Jenkins.

Tess   The bear attack? Park Rangers have been notified and are on the search for a bear that might have wandered down from upstate.

Mr. Dahl   We both know there are no bears in the Greywoods Forest.

Tess   I don't know if you've seen the crime scene photos, but nothing less than a bear, maybe a wolf, could have done that to a human body.

Mr. Dahl   Regardless, it is in the best interest of Foggy Bluffs if the matter was ignored.

Tess   I remember the last time you came in. When you told us to stop investigating Jenkins after he abducted the DuMaurier kid. I can't just ignore this again. That's not how this works.

Mr. Dahl   In this case, it will be. It is strongly advised that any criminal investigation connected to Elias Jenkins be allowed to die with him. It's in the past. Foggy Bluffs will stay a calm, quiet town hiding in the mist and you can continue to organize raffles and build parking lots. But you will not look at things you have been told are too dangerous for the public. We wouldn't want any disruptions to the future of this town, of your son's future.

Tess   Are you trying to threaten me?

Mr. Dahl   Goodbye Mayor. I trust this will remain secret.

He closes the door. She is dumbstruck. She looks at her desk, realizes the file is missing.

Tess   The bastard stole my file.

She runs outside, but he's absolutely gone. It's hard to see in the foggy afternoon. She steps into the parking lot towards a figure who may be him. She sees a woman in white, looking for her children.

Tess   Ma'am? Can I help you?

The Woman in White fades and **Tess** *sees* **Dani**.

Dani   Mayor Mason?

Tess   Oh! I didn't recognize you. You gotta be careful walking out in the fog, you can't see who else is out here. I thought you were hanging out with Hank?

Dani   I'm meeting him over at Roswell's.

Tess   That lady is something else. I'd be careful of spending too much time around her.

Dani   We're just getting some stuff for his van.

Tess   It's nice to see you and Hank hanging out again. You're a good influence on him.

Dani   Thanks?

Tess   Is everything ok?

Dani   Yeah it's just. It's kind of frustrating to always have to be a good influence. Like I always have to be better than everyone else.

Tess   Ah. I know the feeling. The pressure to be perfect can crush you. Don't let it. Don't throw away what you've got going.

Dani   I promise I didn't smoke anything last night.

Tess   I won't tell. Just don't get distracted from what's important. You're a leader. Be safe out there Danielle.

Dani   Bye Mayor Mason.

Tess   That's Mayor Mom to you too.

Tess gives her a hug and **Dani** *continues on to Roswell's.*

Eight

Dani *and* **Hank** *in Roswell's.* **Bettie** *is in the back.* **Dani** *shuffles her tarot cards.*

Hank   And Hoover was like, superhuman, it was crazy. Well not human, he's a dog. Sometimes I forget. But he was jumping up on shit and like, it was incredible, and they totally pulled it off.

Dani   As Class President I cannot condone it but as your friend it was way badass of you.

Hank   What do you think about this stuff I picked out? I like the orange shag carpet, and the green pillows.

Dani   It's giving carrot, but it's that retro vibe you're going for.

Hank   I just like, I want Zodiac to think it's a cool van. He's a different kind of cool, you know?

Dani   Yeah. Do you feel it too? Around him?

Hank   Feel what?

Dani   I feel like I realized we both got kind of boring, didn't we? Compared to Zo, or compared to before. I'm thinking about like. Who we were and who I thought I was gonna be and whoever I actually became.

Hank   Yeah, but look at us today. We haven't pulled off a heist like that in years. And we're like, getting closer, I think. To figuring out what happened.

Dani   I'm gonna do a quick reading, sorry, I'm just kinda ?, sorry.

Hank   No sorry.

Dani *shuffles and pulls the top three cards.* **Bettie** *comes out with a lava lamp.*

Bettie   I found it! I knew I had one somewhere.

Hank   Hell yeah, this is gonna be so groovy.

Bettie   You kids having fun tonight?

Hank   Yeah, we're meeting up with Zodiac and Luna, to go through some of the case files.

Bettle   Case files?

Hank   We got Zodiac's file from my mom's office.

Dani   Mind you, That's Mayor Mason. It was a whole heist thing.

Bettie   I think it's a felony.

Hank   It is?

Bettie   No more of this, I don't want to know anything!

She begins ringing up **Hank**'s *purchase.*

Hank   What's your reading say?

Dani   Nine of Swords, The Moon, and The Lovers. So the Nine is Anxiety. That makes sense.

Hank   The crimes, yeah.

Dani   And then The Moon is illusion, like, hidden feelings and subconscious dreams.

Hank   Oh. Sure. And then The . . . Lovers . . .

Dani   A powerful match is going to be made. It doesn't *have* to be romantic.

Bettie   If you ask me, something unspoken has to manifest. If you want to dispel the Swords and become the Lovers.

Hank   This stuff is wacky.

Dani   I just don't know how I can connect all this Zodiac/Jenkins stuff to all the other weird Foggy Bluffs weirdness. What do you know about the ghost of Avarice White?

Bettie   It's a ghost story about a colonial woman. Don't know much more. Hauntings aren't my thing.

Dani   Darn.

Bettie   But I know I've got a book here somewhere that has the story.

Hank   I'm gonna go start loading up the van.

Hank *hauls his stuff outside and* **Bettie** *finds a coffee table book called "Strange Days Upstate."*

Dani   Do you think the cards said I'm in love with him?

Bettie   Are you?

Dani   I don't know. Maybe. He's obviously like. The guy of the town. I just don't think he likes me back?

Bettie   Which would be stupid of him. You're the coolest girl in Foggy Bluffs.

Dani   That's dumb, that doesn't actually mean anything. I'm not. I'm just ah I don't know. He's waiting in the van. There's too much going on. Ahh. I should focus on Zodiac. Thank you for the book.

Bettie   Don't do anything I wouldn't do! But also remember, I'd do a lot!

Dani *gives her some money.* **Bettie**'s *phone rings. She picks it up.*

Bettie   Hello? Roswell's Thrift 'n' Find . . .

Dani *leaves. A sound comes from the phone, familiar to anyone who has come across the Foggy Bluffs Monster.*

Bettie   You've called the right place, I've got a bunch of Foggy Bluffs Monster merchandise. You know I don't tell people this often but I've actually seen it, I'll tell you all about it when you stop by the shop . . .

Roswell's fades into the fog as **Hank** *and* **Dani** *drive away.*

Nine

Pterodact Hill. The van is parked where they can see the town below them as the sun sets.

Zodiac *plays fetch with* **Hoover**, *while* **Luna** *takes a hit from the bong.* **Hank** *sets up the new van interior.* **Dani** *is reading.*

Zodiac   Do you think dogs get sick of playing fetch? It's kind of demeaning.

Luna   Hoover seems fine with the situation.

Zodiac   It'd be nice to have something so simple bring you so much joy.

Luna   You're playing fetch too.

Zodiac   Oh true, I am. Wild.

Hank   I think it's done. Take a look.

Zodiac   Can't, gotta throw this ball for my dog.

Luna   Lemme see lemme see.

Hank *helps them into the van.*

Luna   Oh, it's cozy. I like the carpet. I hope you washed it.

Hank   Uh. Dani, tell me what you think!

Dani *is stuck to the book.*

Dani   Luna, have you heard this story before? About Avarice White?

Zodiac   She was married to Ephraim White—

Luna   The founder of Foggy Bluffs.

Dani   Yeah, she tried to leave him after their son died of some pox. She fell in love with this Indigenous man. His name is not printed in this book, of course. She tried to leave Old Fogg; but Ephraim White accused her of witchcraft and had her hanged.

Luna   What the fuck! Why is there a statue of him in front of the school?

Dani   You know why. But listen. After she died, Ephraim started seeing her at night in the woods and shit. This is from his journal. "In the deepest effluvium of the wood,

I hear a cry as coarse and wrenching as the baying of hounds. I see her, Avarice, looking for our buried child, her eyes scarlet from weeping."

Zodiac   I don't get it.

Dani   She's the monster! Scarlet eyes! I saw her in the woods, she's a woman wronged, stuck in this fucking shithole town.

Hank   It's not that bad a town.

Zodiac   It's a pretty bad town.

Dani   I'd want revenge if my baby died and my husband killed me. All she wanted was to be happy.

Luna   Hauntings aren't real, there's always explanations. Like carbon monoxide poisoning.

Dani   But the eyes!

Luna   The red eyes. Why are their eyes always red?

Zodiac   Oh, 'cause I'm usually stoned.

Dani   Zodiac, don't you think maybe the thing you've seen in the woods could have actually been the ghost of Avarice White?

Zodiac   But that doesn't explain going missing for two weeks. Ghosts don't abduct people.

Dani   Maybe, you reminded her of the child she lost? That's a ghost thing.

Luna   To bring us back to the more recent past— I've begun reading through this Jenkins file. There's a lot in here, but I don't have one clear motive for who might want to kill him.

Dani   I mean, I wanted him dead. Everyone did. He couldn't go anywhere without nasty looks and whispering. Half the restaurants in town wouldn't serve him.

Zodiac   Really?

Dani   Do you know how mad people were, about you being taken?

Zodiac   I guess that makes sense.

Luna   I found in the files, I was sort of expecting it actually but. It looks like Jenkins was in the military, and moved to Foggy Bluffs to work in a government laboratory.

Hank   You think Jenkins worked with the *government* to kidnap Zodiac?

Luna   The US government isn't above kidnapping their own citizens, ask my grandparents about internment.

Dani   Well then what's the laboratory?

Luna   I'm trying to find out. I've been following a subset of UFO conspiracy theorists I've found on the Dark Net,

Hank   Where?

Luna   Reddit. They say abductions are happening, with experiments and memory wipes, but it's not aliens. They think it's government agencies using Americans as test subjects, and they cover it up, or allow the alien stories to discredit their victims.

Zodiac   Is that what you think happened to me?

Luna   I don't know what I think anymore.

Zodiac   Do you think the laboratory was in the bunker? It was empty when they found me.

Luna   I don't know. I haven't found another reference to any kind of government lab in Foggy Bluffs. At all. Ever. But that doesn't mean it doesn't exist. I'll keep looking. I'm gonna take these home.

Hank   I don't know, no one can find those, Luna. It's like, top secret stuff.

Luna   I hid my binders in my room for like two years before I came out. No one's gonna find anything.

They put the files into their backpack.

Dani   Don't go, we're having such a good time!

Luna   It's just that it's getting dark and-I don't really want to be so near the woods after how it went yesterday. I'll let you know what I find.

Luna *leaves.*

Dani   So what do you guys wanna do? We should try to find out more about this ghost, I think.

Hank   I think we should split up. Dani, can you find out more about people seeing things in Foggy Bluffs? Maybe the answer is in our past.

Zodiac   Maybe the answer is in the past. That's so poetic.

Dani   Good thinking. Based on this story, it sounds like people have been seeing things in this area for a long, long time. I'll go to the library.

Hank   Great idea. And you and me, Zodiac, we should see, um, we should—

Zodiac   We should have a stakeout. Look for the signs of spacecraft. We're bound to see it coming down from up here.

Dani   If you see anything, call me immediately okay? I'll come right back.

Zodiac   You want a hit before you go?

Dani   No thanks. Gotta stay clear-headed for this.

Zodiac   I just don't want you to stress about this so much.

Dani   "I ain't afraid of no ghosts!"

Zodiac   I appreciate it. But you don't have to do it for my sake.

Dani   Yes I do. I'm gonna figure this out. Bye boys.

She turns and goes. **Zodiac** *looks at* **Hank**.

Zodiac   Bi boys.

Hank   You sure all this mystery stuff isn't bumming you out?

Zodiac   I'll be fine. I'm kinda cold though.

Hank   Wanna get in the van? I haven't hit the bong yet.

Zodiac   yeahyeahyeah.

They get in the van, **Zodiac** *prompts* **Hoover** *up, and he curls up in the corner.* **Hank** *hits the bong.* **Zodiac** *watches the lava lamp goob around.*

Hank   What's your tattoo?

Zodiac   It's an interrobang.

Hank   It looks like a question mark.

Zodiac   Yeah, it's a question mark mixed with an exclamation point.

Hank   It's pretty cool.

Zodiac   Thanks. It's pretty important to me.

Hank   'Cause you like grammar?

Zodiac   Well— yes. But it's more than a reference to English. It's like— it's two things. It's an exclamation point. It's excitement! It's happiness, and fear, and anger. It's standing up and feeling more than you're supposed to be feeling. It means action! But it's also a question mark. It's asking. It's wanting to know more. It's not accepting that what's in front of you is everything there is to know. But it's also confusion. An interrobang is it's own emotion. It's its own action. It's not knowing, and being excited about not knowing. It's about being electric and curious at the same time. It's anxiety. It's worry.

Hank   Anxiety doesn't sound too nice.

Zodiac   It's not! It's terrible! So I put it on my body. Because I'm always feeling it anyway, so why not try to remind myself of all the good things it can be?

Hank   That's really cool. It looks so . . . cool too.

Hank *almost touches the tattoo, until he realizes he's really close to* **Zodiac**. *He pulls his hand away.*

Zodiac   You can touch it.

Hank   Okay.

Hank *touches it.*

Zodiac   It's just skin.

Hank   Yeah.

Zodiac   What?

Hank   What?

Zodiac   You just, what are you thinking about?

Hank   Um. You're so smart. That's cool.

Zodiac   It's just a tattoo. I can't build a car.

Hank   It's just a van.

Zodiac   Yeah but it's a good van. It's like, more than a van. It's a real banger.

Hank   An interrobanger.

Zodiac   You should call it The Interrobanger.

Hank   Dude, That's exactly it.

Zodiac   You gotta christen it.

Hank   How do I do that.

Zodiac   We'll make a toast.

Hank   I don't have any wine.

Zodiac   Okay, I'm gonna pack another bowl.

Zodiac *shuffles over to the bong. He starts packing it.* **Hank** *sits and looks at his hands.*

Hank   I'm glad you came back.

Zodiac   How much more are you gonna smoke? I could do like, another full one. But you gotta drive?

Hank   We could sleep in the van if we have to and drive back in the morning. I don't have to be home tonight.

Zodiac   Me neither. I'll pack a full one.

Hank   The Interrobanger. I like it. I've never named a car before.

Zodiac   Really? I name everything.

Hank   Like a toothbrush? Did you name your toothbrush?

Zodiac   Maybe not everything. But stuff with a personality. Like my bong is Malachite, because it looks like the malachite stone. Or my fridge at home is Bev, because she actually takes care of me and Bev is like, the name of a woman who would probably feed you. And Hoover's named after the head of the FBI because he's smart but also like, mysterious, and probably gay. And he eats like a vacuum.

Hoover *sticks his head up.*

Zodiac   Yes, you. You're a gay dog.

Hoover *rolls over and falls back asleep.*

Hank   Like, I don't know. It never occurred to me.

Zodiac   Well, we have to name The Interrobanger even more now. Because you made this thing. And we can paint it!

Hank   We should ask Dani to design it, she's really good.

Zodiac   She could paint the words "The Interrobanger" on the side. And like a big interrobang. Okay, here we go.

Zodiac *has the bong and lighter ready. He shuffles over to* **Hank**.

Hank   Careful, don't spill the water.

Zodiac   Eh, it's kinda baptismal.

Hank   How do we do this?

Zodiac   Okay, so— we gotta like, imbibe the van with the name. Using the smoke.

Hank   You should make a speech.

Zodiac   Ok, is it cool if I invoke a god? I was thinking Trivia.

Hank   There's a god of trivia?

Zodiac   Yeah, she's in charge of like mysteries and ghosts and stuff. It feels apt.

Hank   Yeah That's apt. For an interrobang.

Zodiac   Yeah That's what I thought.

Hank   Go for it.

Zodiac   Okay, so—O Trivia, Goddess of Ghosts and Crossroads. Take this dank weed as an offering, as we dedicate this van to you.

Out of the fog, the woman in white emerges. She listens from the other side of the van door.

Zodiac   May The Interrobanger always take the right turn at the crossroads. Not like, only turning right, but like take the one That's right for the journey. May it protect us from ghosts, but also like I'd like to see some ghosts too.

Hank   But like, don't haunt the van.

Zodiac   Yeah, don't haunt it, just like, use your magic to make it more interesting. So we always feel like . . .? . . . like we're doing something cool and mysterious. So I dub thee, The Interrobanger.

Hank   That was beautiful.

Zodiac   Before we do the last part, say some words. About like, the name and your hopes for the van.

Hank   I . . . Miss Trivia, please make this the coolest van in the world and make it take us somewhere awesome. Don't make us stay in Foggy Bluffs, but bring us on adventures. Be a van that can carry friends and host good times. And like, prevent us from getting flat tires in the middle of nowhere. And just, take us somewhere where we can be as cool as the van will be. I dub thee, The Interrobanger.

The woman returns to the fog.

Zodiac   Okay, now we're gonna use the smoke to finalize it. Take a hit, and when you exhale, say 'Interrobanger' and just blow it right in my mouth.

Hank *makes a face.*

Zodiac   No, trust me it's gotta be personal. And it like, mixes our souls with the van. Plus, recycling, I'm running out of weed. 'Interrobanger.'

Zodiac *sits face to face with* **Hank**. *He takes a hit and then exhales.*

Hank   Inteeerrobangeeeerrrr.

Zodiac *inhales the smoke.* **Hank** *doesn't say anything, but watches* **Zodiac** *inhale. They sit face to face.*

Zodiac   Iiiiiinteroobangeeeer.

Hank *inhales some of it again. He breathes it out. They look at each other through the smoke.*

Zodiac *kisses* **Hank**.

Zodiac   So now your van has a name.

Hank   What just.

Zodiac   Was that okay? It felt like the right way to end it.

Hank   Yeah it's okay.

Zodiac   I know you're not gay or anything, it just felt like the, like the ancient way to name a van.

Hank   Hm.

Zodiac   What?

Hank   I kinda liked it.

Zodiac   Me too.

Hank   Do you kiss boys a lot?

Zodiac   Just a couple guys when I went to boarding school. Have you ever kissed a guy before?

Hank   No.

Zodiac   That's okay.

Hank   I mean, I'm not sure I'm gay.

Zodiac   Okay.

Hank   Can I hit the bong again.

Zodiac   Yeah.

Zodiac *hands the bong to* **Hank***, and their hands touch, a little.* **Hank** *takes a big hit.*

Zodiac   Careful.

Hank   I wanna be really high right now.

Zodiac   Okay.

Hank *takes a big hit. He exhales and stares into space.* **Zodiac** *takes the bong and takes another hit.* **Hank** *doesn't say anything.*

Hank   Do you wanna try that again?

Zodiac   Yeah.

They kiss again. **Hoover** *wakes up. He begins barking.*

Hank   Woah!

Zodiac   Dude, come on. Calm down!

Hoover *is fully up and pacing. He almost knocks over the bong.*

Zodiac   I'm gonna let him out, I think he's gotta go.

Hank   Okay.

Zodiac   Don't worry, I'll be back.

Hank   Okay.

Zodiac   Don't worry.

Hank *smiles sheepishly.* **Zodiac** *gives him another kiss and gets out of the van.* **Zodiac** *is too high and distracted to see that* **Hoover** *is staring at* **Mr. Dahl***.*

Zodiac   What? Go bathroom or whatever.

Hoover *barks at* **Mr. Dahl** *behind* **Zodiac***.*

Zodiac   Hey, I'm allowed to kiss people. You don't own me.

Hoover *steps towards* **Mr. Dahl***.* **Hoover** *bares his teeth. The sound of flapping wings.*

Zodiac   Yes, and I don't own you. You're just also a dog, and you have to understand that.

Mr. Dahl *disappears.* **Hoover** *relaxes.* **Hoover** *goes to pee on a bush.*

Zodiac   Yeah, I know Dani likes him. Can we not think about that right now?

Hoover *comes back.*

Zodiac   At least be happy for me!

Hoover *nuzzles* **Zodiac**.

Zodiac   Thank you buddy. Let's forget monster hunting for one night.

Ten

Luna *combs through the Jenkins file. They search the internet. They travel down rabbit holes through fractured galaxies of conspiracies, monsters, and legends. There are red herrings and dead ends. There are blueprints and documents with redacted information. The Zapruder film. Maps of Foggy Bluffs. The words "Project: BARGHEST" show up and slip away. Footage of UFOs and alien autopsies and security footage of men in black permeates. News reports of sightings show up throughout.*

At the same time, this maelstrom of the strange functions as an obstacle course, through which runs a dog. A scientist, alike but not identical to **Mr. Dahl**, *measures the dog under red light. The dog is designated Useless and sent away.*

Luna *halts at an old photograph of a young Black woman and a young white man.* **Luna** *takes this photograph and leaves.*

Luna *texts the group chat.*

Luna   Hey you guys, look at this pic I found.

Zodiac   Who is that?

Hank   That can't be who I think it is.

Dani   More like who it's *not*.

Roswell's Thrift 'n Find. **Bettie** *arranges Nessie plushies.* **Dani** *leads in* **Luna**, **Hank**, *and* **Zodiac**. **Hoover** *stays by Zo's side.*

Bettie   Back again? This is the third day in a row.

Dani   We have some more questions.

Zodiac   She's gonna have an explanation.

Bettie   I do not want to discuss anything in that file that you are not supposed to have, which I am not supposed to know about.

Dani   You're the only adult who's been honest with us.

Luna   And you're the only one we know who's been abducted.

Zodiac   Right?

Dani   Right?

Bettie   Yes, but the aliens operate on a high vibration, it's not so easy to parse—

Dani   Come on!

Zodiac   No, she's right, there's different levels—

Dani   Zo, please—

Bettie   Let's all calm down. What is this about?

Luna   I found the original Bluffs Gazette article about the case from the documentary. "Locals Cry Alien Abduction." The real Beth and Bruce Roswell are right here— and That's a picture of someone else.

They hand her a newspaper clipping.

Dani   That documentary isn't about you. You lied to us. You were never abducted.

Zodiac   Tell them they're wrong. Tell them it was you.

Bettie   No, they're right.

Zodiac   No, you were abducted.

Bettie   I wasn't. I'm sorry, kid.

Zodiac   You said it was real.

Dani   Why would you tell us you were?

Bettie   It sells t-shirts. That's what my store is for. People come to Foggy Bluffs for scary stories, and I sell the merchandise. They buy more when it's coming from an actual abductee. The real Beth and Bruce died a couple years back, so I just started saying it. No harm done.

Dani   Is your name even Bettie Roswell?

Bettie   My name is Bettie . . . *Cottingley*.

Hank   So Zodiac is the only one who's seen the aliens?

Bettie   I'm sorry.

Zodiac   But the movie is real. You didn't make that up.

Bettie   Beth and Bruce told people they saw aliens. But you can't take it so seriously.

Zodiac *heads back to the door.*

Dani   Wait, don't go!

Zodiac   You all think I'm crazy. C'mon Hoover.

Hoover *hesitates before going outside.*

Hank   We don't think you're crazy!

Zodiac   Just leave me alone. Don't follow me.

The door slams.

Hank   I'll handle it.

Hank *leaves.*

Bettie   I'm sorry, I didn't mean to— I didn't mean to upset you all so much.

Dani   You said when you gave me my cards, "these will help you be honest with yourself." But you're just another bad guy in a mask.

Bettie   There is truth in these things, tucked in-between the pretend. But it's not flesh or stone.

Luna   But Zodiac is literal. Something literally happened to him. Something is literally going on in the woods. There have to be knowable explanations. In this article, it says Bruce Roswell worked in "laboratory maintenance." And before Elias Jenkins worked at the high school, he also worked at a lab somewhere in Foggy Bluffs. But now it's gone, like something vanished it away.

The Interrobanger starts up and drives away.

Bettie   I don't know anything about labs.

Luna   The labs and Jenkins and and and something else—the government, or something that can disappear and reappear, but it goes so far back, and there's so many pieces that don't make sense, the alien element almost fills it in–

Bettie   A few days ago you were the skeptic.

Dani   Or it's something much older That's been poisoning those woods since this place was named Foggy Bluffs. We're built on land stolen by a man who killed his own wife. It's not coming down from the sky it's rising up from the ground. Avarice White's been trying to warn us, I've seen her. I swear.

Bettie   People see what they want to see. Suggestion is very powerful.

Luna   There's something real out there, with fingers that grabbed me, and I don't know what arm they're attached to.

Bettie   Something grabbed you?

Luna   I keep expecting us to make some kind of breakthrough, like I'm going to solve some puzzle and we'll be pointed in the right direction.

Bettie   I'm sorry I lied to you kids. I really am. I'm just running a business. You need to stop looking at all these things, whatever that Jenkins really did or what he's involved with I don't know, but stop doing this to yourselves.

Dani   I'm not going to just cover my eyes and pretend this isn't happening.

Luna   Ignoring it just makes it worse. We should go. She's not going to help us.

Dani   She never did.

They leave the shop.

Luna   The van is gone.

Dani   Where did they go?

Zodiac *storms along the edge of Foggy Bluffs and the Greywoods.*

Mr. Dahl *watches* **Zodiac**. **Hoover** *sees him first. He bristles.* **Zodiac** *notices* **Hoover**.

Zodiac   What's up— Oh.

Mr. Dahl *stares.*

Zodiac   Why don't you just reach out and take me off this planet again? Why leave me like this? Tell me what you want. Tell me why this is happening. Say something!

Mr. Dahl *doesn't speak.* **Mr. Dahl** *takes one step forward.* **Hoover** *erupts into a fury, howling and barking and gnashing his fangs. Nobody has seen this before. He tries to leap at* **Mr. Dahl**. **Zodiac** *grabs him by the neck, the collar, to try and stop him.* **Hoover** *pulls* **Zodiac** *a few feet before stopping.*

The lights of the Interrobanger flash over **Zodiac** *and* **Hoover** *as* **Hank** *pulls up. The sound of flapping wings.* **Mr. Dahl** *is gone.*

Hoover *calms down. Returns to normal.* **Zodiac** *pets him.* **Hoover** *licks his hands.*

Hank   How did you get away from Roswell's so fast? I've been driving all over town looking for you.

Zodiac *doesn't say anything.* **Hank** *sits down next to him.* **Hoover** *growls a little bit, but* **Zodiac** *gives him a pat on the head and he lays down again.*

Zodiac   Did you see that?

Hank   See what?

Zodiac *stares at the spot where* **Mr. Dahl** *stood.*

Dani *and* **Luna** *outside Roswell's.*

Luna   I'm sure they'll call us back as soon as they can. Maybe Hoover ran off again.

Dani   I shouldn't have let him run away. Last time I looked the wrong way I let him get taken.

Luna   What? You never let anything happen to Zodiac.

Dani   If I'd been paying attention, I could have done something.

Luna   No you couldn't. It's not your fault, Dani.

Dani   If I'd kept my eye on him. If I'd been on top of it. I could have seen what was going on.

Luna   We were just kids.

Dani I don't know how to keep everything in order.

Luna I don't know if That's possible anymore.

Dani I looked away from you too. I shouldn't have.

Luna It's ok.

Dani No it isn't.

Luna It isn't. But you didn't know how to help me.

Dani That's no excuse.

Luna I really missed you.

Dani I missed you too.

Who's gonna cry first?

Luna We're not gonna cry about this, it's embarrassing. My grandma is making gyoza, do you want to come over?

Dani Yeah I really do.

Luna It's a 50-50 she remembered I'm vegan so let's see how it goes.

Dani I'll tell the boys.

Dani *pulls out her phone as they leave.*

Hank *and* **Zodiac** *on the edge of the woods.*

Hank Was it the monster? What did you see?

Zodiac He was right in front of us. The Interrobanger's lights scared him off.

Hank I guess I was just looking at you.

Zodiac Hoover saw him. Didn't you see him freak out?

Hank I really did not notice anything that weird. Is it the monster? Should we go?

Zodiac It was so solid. I could hear him breathing. And you're saying it wasn't there?

Hank I'm just saying I didn't see it. Not that it wasn't there.

Zodiac It's really hard to remember something true when everyone else tells you otherwise.

Hank I'm not telling you otherwise.

Zodiac When everyone says you're crazy, it's hard not to consider that they might be right. And it sits like an owl in my head, this thought that I've got it backwards, and I'm refusing to remember something. That other version of things, the one where Jenkins was there, I've had to carve every *if* of it into my head so that I can remember what it's not. People have pitied it into me, this horrible other version of myself, made

me think about who that person is, so much that he exists in me anyway. Sometimes I don't actually really always know what happened.
I just . . . what if it's not?

Hank   Aliens?

Zodiac   Everyone says I made it all up, aliens aren't real, it was that man, but I don't, I don't want to, I don't want it to be him. He's just a man, and now he's dead and I don't know if it was him.

Hank   You've always said aliens.

Zodiac   But everyone else thinks it was like . . . Everyone thinks it was Mr. Jenkins. I don't even remember seeing him that night.

Hank   What do you remember?

Zodiac   I remember the things he told me, about how big the universe is, and how much there is I don't know and how much I'll never be able to know. If it was him, why do I remember the alien so well? Why did he tell me a different name?

Hank   Who told you his name?

Zodiac   I'm not supposed to tell you about him.

Hank   You're not supposed to?

Zodiac   Maybe I invented it.

No, he was there. It doesn't make sense for Jenkins to be there. I remember everything they did to me. Us. Me and Hoover. Hoover convinced them to let us go. And it wasn't Jenkins, over in the corner it wasn't him. But if that version is wrong, who was it, what happened to me?

Hank   Let's slow down, Zo, you don't have to figure this out right now.

Zodiac   But we've dug out all these pieces and they have to turn into something.

Hank   How about we go meet back up with those two nerds? We can smoke a little and they'll walk us through it, or we just hang out, or you and I could just hang out, if you want.

Zodiac   I think I want to be alone tonight.

Hank   Oh. Okay. I'm sorry.

Zodiac   You didn't do anything wrong. I just don't want this to be all your guys's problem. I'll be fine. Don't worry. Just gotta figure some stuff out.

Hank   Ok. Hoover, if you need back up, lemme know.

Hoover *licks* **Hank**.

Zodiac   Why don't we go to the Jackalope tomorrow? I'll meet you guys there. Don't worry. I just need some fresh air tonight.

Hank   I'll see you tomorrow. Make yourself useful, Hoov.

Hank *drives off.* **Zodiac** *looks at* **Hoover**.

Zodiac   Let's go for a walk. I need to see something.

Zodiac *and* **Hoover** *walk through the woods.*

The fog rolls in thickly between the trees.

They get to the clearing around the bunker.

Hoover *sniffs the ground up to the door.*

Zodiac *walks up behind him looking down at it.*

Zodiac   Where did we go, Hoover?

Hoover *paws at the door.*

Eleven

The next day. A booth in the back of The Jackalope. **Luna** *is catching* **Hank** *up.*

Luna   So we ended up cleaning up the kitchen for my grandma and then Dani got my parents to sponsor a float in the homecoming parade. It was wild.

Hank   What's next for the case?

Luna   Have you heard from Zodiac?

Hank   No, and I'm worried he's mad at me and I'm not loving it.

Luna   Ohhh.

Hank   What.

Luna   I see.

Hank   See what? You don't see anything. You have glasses. Shut up.

Luna   I can't say I never saw it coming.

Hank   Shut up!

Luna   Whatever you say . . .

Hank   Just because you're so gay doesn't mean everyone else is.

Luna   Listen, I'm vividly aware that there are not a lot of us in this town.

Hank   Okay.

Luna   I always say, you can't always tell who's gay, but you can always tell who's definitely gay.

Hank   I've had girlfriends. I like girls.

Luna   Ok, bisexual.

Hank   I know! Stop!

Luna   Ok I'm gonna drop it, but like. If there was a girl here who would feasibly date me? Like if I could have a high school girlfriend? I wouldn't want to turn that down.

Hank   Please don't tell Dani about this.

Luna   And . . . you know she—

Hank   Yeah I know she has a crush on me That's what I'm talking about. She should at least . . . I dunno.

Luna   Of course not. I wouldn't.

She walks in.

Dani   Is Zodiac here yet?

Luna   No, I thought he'd be coming with you.

Hank   He didn't say anything in the group chat.

Dani   I rang his doorbell and his parents said they thought he went out this morning and hasn't been home.

Hank   The Bettie thing really shook him.

Dani   Tell me about it.

Hank   He was talking about his abduction in like, a different way. He seemed scared of it this time.

Luna   So where is he? Should we call his parents?

Dani   They seemed kind of annoyed that I was there.

Hank   My mom says they weren't much help during the investigation.

Luna   They're shitty.

Dani   I'm worried about him, you know? What if he's not okay?

Hank   Is there something we can do?

Dani   I'm worried I pushed him too much, investigating the abduction. Maybe it was a bad idea. I don't know. I was just excited, with him back.

Luna   He seemed fine.

Dani   Can we make sure he's not alone?

Hank   I'll text him again, remind him we're all hanging out and we can pick him up.

Dani   Can we not just sit around and get high tonight?

Luna   We should watch an old movie or something.

Dani   That sounds like fun.

Hank   He's not responding. Where is he?

Dani   Let's not panic. I know where we could check.

They pile into The Interrobanger.

They find **Zodiac** *sitting on the bank of the river.*

Luna   Hey Zodiac!

Zodiac   Oh, hi.

Hank   Where've you been?

Zodiac   Great question.

Dani   Wanna go for a walk?

Zodiac   No, I can't.

Dani   It's okay, we can sit. Is it okay if we sit with you?

Zodiac   Yes please. You can all stay.

They all sit. **Hank** *sits next to* **Zodiac**.

Luna   I mean, it's almost green, but it's still a nice river.

Dani   Yeah. The river is nice. I'm glad we saved it that one time.

Hank   Zodiac, what are you thinking about?

Zodiac   I don't know. My brain.

Hank   Tell me what's happening.

Zodiac   It feels like it's flying apart. Floating. Like, all the molecules are just drifting in different directions.

Dani   Yikes.

Zodiac   I'm not having fun.

Hank   How can we help?

Zodiac   It feels like I'm not here. Like when you're looking through binoculars and you suddenly become aware of the sides of the lenses. And you're not holding them right up to your eyes. But you can still kind of see through the glass. I think it's the aliens. Sometimes when they check in on me. They push me out of the way a little bit. You know, I think they just wanted to study human beings. And for some reason they chose me. But they chose wrong. Because I'm not a human being. I'm just not quite there. And it's their fault. Maybe I was a human being until they decided to look at me. If they didn't do this, I could, I could probably just. Be alive. And not feel like I was trapped inside of this.

Luna   Well we're here. When you come back.

They sit together. It gets a little darker. **Dani** *gets cold, puts on her sweater.* **Zodiac** *leans over, onto* **Hank**'s *shoulder.* **Dani** *looks up. Looks around. Something is wrong.*

Dani   Zodiac, where's Hoover?

Zodiac *deflates into* **Hank***.* **Hank** *holds him.* **Luna** *moves over to them.*

Luna   Zo, breathe. Where's Hoover?

Zodiac   He's gone.

Dani   What? What do you mean?

Zodiac   They came back for him.

Hank   What? Who?

Zodiac   He left with them.

Dani   What happened?

Zodiac   Last night. We went for a walk. We went back there, to the woods, to the bunker.

Luna   Why would you go there?

Zodiac   I don't know. I had to see it again. And Mr. Dahl was there. He took him back, he took Hoover back with him.

Dani   I'm so serious, I would kill for you, who is Mr. Dahl?

Zodiac   He's their, like, secretary or something. Or emissary.

Hank   Is this the man you met, before?

Zodiac   He won't talk to me this time. He just walked out of the lights between the trees, and he spoke some other language or something, and Hoover just walked away with him. And then I was sitting here.

Luna   We should get you to your parents.

Zodiac   They won't do anything. And I'm fine.

Dani   You just said all your molecules were falling apart.

Zodiac   Well That's fine. I just want to be with you guys.

Hank *hugs him tighter.* **Dani** *understands.*

Luna   I believe you.

Dani   Luna?

Luna   I'm learning there's a, an interplay. Between being queer and believing in magic. In monsters, aliens, ghosts. I'm real. I'm not a girl and I'm not a boy. People don't believe that. But I live in, I am in, this in-between space. Everything we know is built on the facts of gender. But I am my own proof that those facts mean nothing unless you want them to. It's a secret I get to keep to myself. But I feel like I'm a goblin inhabiting a human body. And sometimes that starts to hurt, and sometimes the world feels like it's falling apart. I'm the opposite of those crazy people in rubber costumes. They dress up like horrors to scare people away or feel powerful, but underneath it's always a human committing a crime. I'm a human, but not in the same way. Or maybe exactly the same way. But I know that there is more to being a human than being a boy or girl, or straight or just gay. And That's a kind of magic. So if I exist, then who is to say that some monsters aren't just costumes? Maybe all the way through, there are animals that aren't human, that aren't strictly flesh and blood.

Zodiac I don't feel real.

Hank You're real. Look. This is real! Right?

Hank *pushes up* **Zodiac**'s *sleeve and traces the interrobang.*

Hank A question and an exclamation point. That's real.

Dani I feel more real with you guys. We've got all these parts of ourselves. These pieces. Maybe . . . clues? To our selves? And it's like. I think this is what you were saying, Luna. Or what I think I realized is— I don't feel like my pieces all fit together with each other, actually. But I feel like I fit with you guys. It doesn't make sense to me.

Zodiac Well That's the question mark part of it. It doesn't really make sense.

Dani We can make sense of it. Eventually. I really believe that. Even if I can't see the answers right in front of me.

Luna And That's going to have to be okay for now.

Dani *takes* **Luna***s hand.* **Hank** *touches* **Luna**.

Luna I mean, like, science is still important. I just want to make sure everyone knows I didn't stop believing in science.

Zodiac Yes.

Hank Just, Zodiac, we're all here now. All of us, we're feeling the fear of the question and the excitement of not knowing. Right with you.

Dani We're not going anywhere. We're gonna help you figure this out, get Hoover back. We're still a team, remember?

Zodiac Science Quest Corp. went bankrupt.

Hank We don't need them, Dani's the one who brought us together.

Luna We can be our own team. The Interrobang Team!

Hank The Interrobangers?

Dani That sounds dirty.

Zodiac Hch. I'm cold.

Dani Let's go. We can look for Hoover. He escaped from them once, he can do it again.

Zodiac Yeah. Let's go.

Epilogue

The Foggy Bluffs Monster stalks through the woods. We can't see what it's stalking. The Interrobangers walk through the woods with flashlights and dog treats.

Luna   These woods are creepy.

Hank   It's the fog.

Zodiac   And the looming threat of aliens and monsters.

Dani   Or ghosts.

Hank   Or just the fog.

Zodiac   What if we don't find him?

Hank   If he's out there, we'll find him.

Zodiac   Sure. I believe you.

*He takes **Hank**'s hand. The Interrobangers walk out of the woods.*

*The Foggy Bluffs Monster turns and spots **Hoover**.*

A sound—a metal door opens.

And then closes.

End of play.

Faustian Utopia: Jouissance and Cruel Optimism in Charlotte Snow's *Magic Girl*

kt shorb

Rooted in the story of *Faust*, with a healthy dose of fantasy, magic, and camp, Charlotte Snow's *Magic Girl . . . and Her Demons: A Faustian Breakup Tragicomedy Surrounded by Hell's Loudest Bacchanal* is irreverent, spectacular, and thoughtful. Steeped in the hallmarks of genre theatre, the break-neck tale of a high school trans girl selling her soul to a queer demon in return for magical powers demands a close reading for deeper understanding. While *Magic Girl* intentionally does not take itself seriously, the structure, tropes, and ideas laid out over the course of the play are all serious concepts. Through depictions of queer/trans *jouissance* and cruel optimism, *Magic Girl* engages in utopic world-making that reveals many issues trans and queer youth face with deft juxtaposition of classical literature, pop culture, and teenage angst.

Magic Girl engages in an aesthetic maximalism (magic, dance party aesthetics, overlapping theatrical mirrors, etc.) while leaving room for a wide-range of producing companies to mount the work on varied budgets. Anchored in openly-interpretable "moments of magic," the play invites potential creators to embrace how theatre itself is magical, while challenging them to catalogue and execute as many stage magic tricks as possible. Meanwhile, the story and structure revel in a kind of equanimity—recognizing and centering the precarious existence of many trans youth in the heartland while also grounding the resilience of the trans and queer characters in a process of radical self-acceptance, connection, and resistance.

Tracing the canonical journey of many incarnations of Faust, the primary character, trans girl Nox, seeks magical powers inspired by her favorite comic book character. In a bet with her "bestie," trans/queer-coded demon Jez, Nox wagers she can avoid murdering someone for six days in exchange for keeping the magical powers endowed to her by Lucy (short for Lucifer), the sexually-voracious campy monarch of Hell. Gwen, Nox's closeted lesbian beloved raised in a fundamentalist-Christian family, plays an analog to Faust's Gretchen/Marguerite—encountering ambivalence over Nox's hellish powers and the change in Nox's personality it brings. Meanwhile, the multiple Faustian enemies distill into one character, the perfectly beautiful trans girl ballerina, Courtney. Snow makes multiple references to the Faustian theatrical mirror, including opening the entire play with a ballet sequence from Gounod's opera, *Faust*.

Faust's story has much staying power because of the seemingly universal desire underneath it. From *Little Shop of Horrors*, to *Oh God, You Devil* to *Mean Girls*, the idea that possessing (supernatural) powers will eradicate the adversity of life is a very human wish, rooted in both hope and delusion. For Nox, becoming Magic Girl is a way to escape transphobia, the inability to pay ballet tuition, the melancholy of an addict mother, bad grades, and the shackles of fundamentalism inflicted upon her queer romance. While the original Faust's hubris leads to contemplations of power, evil, piety, heaven, and hell, Nox's tale shifts toward ideas of the promise of acceptance and the ways magic impedes true change.

This relationship between the magic and damnation/loss becomes what Lauren Berlant describes as cruel optimism. "Cruel optimism exists when something you desire is actually an obstacle to your flourishing" (Berlant 2011: 1). Berlant goes further to say cruel optimism is "a relation of attachment to compromised conditions of possibility whose realization is discovered either to be *im*possible, sheer fantasy, or *too* possible, and toxic" (italics in original, Berlant 2011: 24). Crucial to understanding cruel optimism is delving deeply into the ambivalence of attachment/desire and the multiplicities of that attachment. Berlant's writing shows an ambivalence with desire for "the good life," as she puts it, and the ways that aspirations toward ease and comfort attach to neoliberalist institutions that are complicit in the hegemonic problems of normativity.

Magic Girl shows many versions of the elusive "good life" and its ambivalence. Early in the play, Nox and Courtney embody the trans teen girl's version of this ambivalence. Nox asks Courtney about using her "platform" as popular winter formal queen to be a "voice for the voiceless," to which Courtney replies "That's not really my thing. I just want to be like everyone else and also liked by everyone else" (109). Nox presses that Courtney is beloved by all while shaming and urging Courtney to disclose her trans identity. Courtney rebuffs she's "already had enough" encounters with transphobia. Just as Nox begins to ask if staying closeted is due to Courtney's boyfriend, the conversation shifts to teen love triangle drama. As this conversation plays out in front of Gwen, the Demon Chorus of Fear, Hatred, and Shame all smell ambivalence rise from Nox. Nox struggles with wanting to both become Courtney while also wanting Courtney to be more than what she is. Courtney's strategy to escape transphobia is to remain closeted about her identity, thereby living a popular (cis)girl life. She does not wish to transform the social structures that brought her the misery of "boys ask[ing her] out on a dare and girls who sit behind [her], cutting [her] hair with scissors" (109).

Nox, however, has more social analysis than Courtney. In the back-and-forth Scene Two between Nox and Gwen, they joke about how COVID vaccines, homophobia, and critical race theory mingle with far-right political affinities in their Wyoming town. Rambunctious and light-hearted at first, this joking leads to conflict with Gwen about religion and hell. A dismayed Nox in a moment of desperation summons her demon friend to ask for magical powers. Although Nox possesses the analytical skills to realize she is in a political and social structure that leads to her life of ostracism in Winstonrock, WY, she still fixates on ways she can attain the "good life." Her visions of magic show a vindication of carnage in her imagination, saying that, "If a door is locked, you don't pick the lock then thank the door for being closed. You disintegrate the door" (93). Nox's next line, "It shouldn't have been locked in the first place," points to a possibility of true liberation, but instead inspires more revenge. Gaining magic is justification toward the seemingly-minor risk of making a bet with a demon. The incremental shifts from optimism to harmful existence characterize specifically what enables cruel optimism.

Aside from Nox's choice to summon magic, Nox already navigates cruel optimism through her not-so-magical relationships. Her obsession with her inability to match Courtney's grace in dance class while also dodging tuition payments pushes Nox further into debt. Aside from the contentious theological conflict over heaven and hell with Gwen, Nox seems unable to hear the mundanely grounded yet completely vital needs and asks of Gwen. As is so often the case in allegorical narratives, the crux of the interpersonal conflict lies not in access to magical intervention but in deeds completely within the protagonist's power to enact before the story begins. It is precisely the attachment to the "good life" that leads Nox to toxic acts and attitudes.

The arrival of Jez, demon spawn of Lucy, shifts the construct of this world, however. Jez's flamboyant speech and affect undermine expectation about hell and damnation. In *Magic Girl*, hell is a "more inclusive" (98) place than heaven, where the queers party non-stop, participating in orgies where queer historical figures take up residence and bored demons host knitting pentagrams. Despite this hedonistic hell, Jez wants to rekindle his romance with angel Gabriel, leading to his willingness to participate in Nox's proposed bet. Jez, Lucy, and the demons of Fear, Hate, and Shame, all speak with "bent wrist" lilt (86), channeling club kid patois. Even as Fear, Hate, and Shame embody a familiar and deep self-hatred, the rhetorical and characteristic moves of these beings signals a version of queer *jouissance.*

After many before her, Kathryn Bond Stockton discusses the difficulty of defining *jouissance* alongside its very necessity as a theoretical framing in queer studies. Stockton's exploration of *jouissance* begins with ideas of bliss, which she calls "a quintessential queer accouterment. It's hedonistic and wedded to pain. It's clearly buoyant, yet it is dark. It's provocatively sexy, intimate, scandalous, and bodily, while it's evasive of capture and speech" (Stockton: 2017:102). *Jouissance*, then, as applied through a queer psychoanalytic lens, is "a means of naming explosive, infinite, unsolvable desire (not the imagined serenity of plenitude), which requires us to reconceive relationships around such oddities as caressing lack, embracing shame, and flirting with the cutting force of beauty" (Stockton 2017: 102). *Magic Girl* engages with this conflicting affect with its cattiness, in-jokes, the seamless references to damnation and drag queens. The trans- and non-binary-coded characters speak with an explosive sense of glee while also challenging normative binary notions of good and evil, pleasure and pain, even life and death. Much like Nox's summoning of Jez, *jouissance* bears a nonchalant resistance that necessitates and springs forth from a seemingly casual disavowal of the fundamental tenets of normativity. While the acts of anti-normative resistance seem almost banal, the effects and affects of *jouissance* are always dramatic. Through the lens of queer *jouissance*, it becomes inevitable that the solution for fraught queer teen romance leads to the ultimate taboo of forming a pact with a devil. Gleeful hijinks ensue.

While the personified demons of Fear, Hate, and Shame show a very serious side of many trans (and queer) experiences of maturation, youth, and identity, their dialogue teeters between caricature of demonosity and affectionate chiding. Rather than spark fear or insight horror, they throw shade. Their embodiments of thoughts that go through a young trans/queer mind feel too close to real self-hatred in an uncomfortable and reflexive way, yet they scream hilarious one-liners that demand a sense of cartharsis. Lucy, the monarch of hell, presents as avuncular (referring to Jez as "M'boy" multiple times), sexually irresistible, sensitive, and nurturing. Jez is emo yet powerful. The personification demons are themselves insecure and meek. Trading continuous insults along the spectrum of a "read" with Nox, cutting words can feel buoyant and loving.

Magic Girl engages in a queer utopic world-making. As José Esteban Muñoz states, "Queerness is essentially about the rejection of a here and now and an insistence on potentiality or concrete possibility for another world" (Muñoz 2009: 1). Rather than grapple with the Enlightenment quandary of good vs. evil, *Magic Girl* rewrites the frames of what Muñoz calls "anticipatory illumination of art, which can be characterized as the process of identifying certain properties that can be detected in representational practices helping us to see the not-yet-conscious" (Muñoz 2009: 4). Why not embrace a possibility that "hell" is actually the place where the outcasts and interesting people reside, where trans and queer people find community and fun? Snow's heaven means ostracism and isolation but hell means belonging. Hell is a resource for this isolated trans girl, and in *Magic Girl*, it is a space of benevolence, if ambivalent. To turn one's back on heaven in a Judeo-Christian U.S. context is the ultimate rejection of social reality, yet it carries out the important queer theoretical work of simply asking, "what else is there?"

It is, perhaps, theoretical folly to engage with ideas of *jouissance* alongside utopia, when these schools of thought tend to be in conflict with one another. For Lee Edelman, *jouissance* is a kind of relinquishing of hope, a way to embrace abjection as a mode of turning away from normality and therefore the normative move to plan futures (Edelman 2004: 5). *Jouissance* is aggressively in the present. Utopia and queerness, however, is "not yet here" (Muñoz 2009: 1). *Magic Girl* illustrates our particular historical moment around trans narratives where both the danger and explosive precarity of trans existence in the United States the now necessitates expression through ambivalent modes that cannot help but imagine a different future that Muñoz argues we cannot yet touch. Snow engages with these temporalities explicitly by writing a Nox who travels back in time to change the now and a Lucy who takes on cosmic bureaucratic administrative work keeping timelines consistent for the "Time Traveler's Contingencies Contingent" in exchange for more "cosmic space needed to expand hell" (113). This classic "if only" trope, alongside the prosaic framing of time, shows both Edelman's turn away from planning futures along with Muñoz's expansive future-casting. Time is both oddly boring but also easily manipulated.

While Dorrine Kondo uses the term "reparative creativity" to engage with ideas of race and racemaking, her framing of world-making in a minoritarian context can be useful with queer theory and queer texts (Kondo 2018: 32). Kondo's assertion that creativity and creative processes can unmake and remake race opens the possibility for forging and finding the queer utopic worlds that Muñoz name. She states that creativity "offers a way to remake worlds counter to the affective violence of minoritarian life." She further describes how reparative creativity can revisit "histories of affective violence" that can address the complexities of facing that violence and its effects while also imagining something else (Kondo 2018: 212). Rather than indulge a move toward normativity or assimilation, *Magic Girl* re-envisions the narrative structures that have been historically used to persecute trans and queer people. Instead of a sense of "if only," Snow's script humorously asks, "what if?"

Ultimately, in addition to Snow's multiple narrative and theoretical turns, perhaps the most important intervention of *Magic Girl* is that it provides space for a trans girl to live through a (magical, fantastical) story of teenage angst and coming of age without the trappings of coming out or transition that characterize earlier works in the field. Nox is allowed to "just" be a teenager—to be awkward, self-involved, preoccupied, distracted by and distracted in love, to want "the good life," but make multiple mistakes along the way. *Magic Girl* is neither tragedy nor complete comedy. No character serves as a villain yet the main character arcs do not fit neatly into standard tropes. The narrative concludes in a somewhat sober but guardedly hopeful way. Indeed, Snow addresses the forces of cruel optimism, *jouissance*, and even utopic world-making by grounding the end back in a "real"-seeming world. Magic, it turns out, does not actually assuage the deepest of our attachments. The ebullience with which we encounter the world may, in fact, be fueled by what ails us. While the end is not "happy" in the normative way, where the hero gets the girl, its depiction of connectedness in the acknowledged presence of long-term harm explores how reparation can begin. The equanimity with which Nox/Audrey and Esther decide to "figure it out together" (137) perhaps signals the true utopic move of Snow's script. Having endured much and despite not really understanding one another, they commit, ultimately, to the togetherness of community and the imperfection of figuring it out.

References

Berlant, Lauren. 2011. *Cruel Optimism*. Durham: Duke University Press.

Edelman, Lee. 2004. *No Future: Queer Theory and the Death Drive*. Durham: Duke University Press.

Kondo, Dorinne. 2018. *Worldmaking: Race, Performance, and the Work of Creativity*. Durham: Duke University Press.

Muñoz, José Esteban. 2009. *Cruising Utopia: The Then and There of Queer Futurity*. New York: New York University Press.

Stockton, Kathryn Bond. 2017. "*Jouissance:* The Gash of Bliss." In *Clinical Encounters in Sexuality: Psychoanalytic Practice & Queer Theory*, eds. Giffney, Noreen and Eve Watson. Earth, Milky Way: Punctum Books.

Magic Girl ! . . . And Her Demons

Charlotte Snow

Characters

Nox 17, trans girl. A loner seeking a life of love and worship from all the worst places.
Jez Old as hell, a demon boy who looks 19. A charismatic schemer chasing the impossible.
Gwen 17, cis girl. An incredibly gracious soul slowly discovering her limits.
Courtney 19, trans girl. The forever "It Girl" earnestly loving what life offers her, the best!
Lucy Only reads as Fabulous. Reigning monarch of Hell who rules with a bent wrist.
Fear Personification demon. A hellion that is both afraid and fear itself.
Hate Personification demon. A hellion that is both hated and hateful.
Shame Personification demon. A hellion that is both shamed and shaming.
Esther 38 – 48, cis woman. Hit rock bottom and is always changing, but that's not her fault.

Casting policy

Nox and Courtney must be played by trans-feminine actors.

Lucy, Jez, Fear, Hate, and Shame are trans and queer coded and ideally cast accordingly. At the same time, gender and sexuality are fluid . . . like blood!
So, if you can't find any trans or queer actors, look again, and then cast the most demonic person.

You've my unholy blessing to alter Lucy and Jez's pronouns to fit the actor's identity, if desired.

The brief roles of Madame, Gabriel, and Lou can be split among the actors.
The role of Esther is best doubled with Lucy, but please prioritize actor comfortability.

Lastly, and certainly not least, diversity in all forms is expected, not just encouraged.

Setting

October in Winstonrock, Wyoming.
It's one of those small mountain towns that's a bizarre blend of the 80s, 90s, and early 2000s.

It's also October in Hell, which is neon lights, kinesthetic, and the campiest realm imaginable, daaaaaaaaaaaaaaaaaaaaaaaaaaaaaaaaaaaaaaaaaaaaaaaaaaaaaaaaaaaaaaaaaaaaaaaaaaa aaaaaaaaaaaaaaarling.

Only a few items of furniture make up either world so transitions can flow quickly and freely.

A Note on Magic

Stage magic is as vital to this narrative as dance is to ballet. Please note, it's not expected for a production of *Magic Girl! . . . And Her Demons* have a goliath budget. Quite the opposite, as I have written the magic to be performed utilizing theatricality over spectacle. The Demon Chorus is also encouraged, whenever possible, to assist in performing moments of magic.

A "moment of magic" is one isolated trick or illusion. (Example: A magician's wand transforms into a bouquet of flowers.) A "series of moments of magic" are "moments of magic" that flow into each other. (Example: A magician's wand transforms into a bouquet of flowers, the flowers squirt water, and the bouquet disappears.)

I have written the magic to be purposefully open-ended, hoping to inspire collaboration between every member of the production. In the end, what else is more magical for theatre-makers than the sharing of time, space, and collaborative creative expression?

Special Thanks

To every soul who has shaped a performance of this play, "Thank you with my full essence."
To every soul who has served as inspiration, "I am as eternally grateful as I am sorry."
To every soul who has been told the lie "if you want to be loved you have to sell your soul," this is for you.

Act One

Scene One

A spotlight on **Nox** *and* **Courtney**, *two dancers of varying talent, finishing their duet as the last notes of Charles Gounod's Waltz from Faust bombastically resound. When they land their final poses,* **Nox** *lights up at the sound of an imagined wild applause.* **Courtney** *is used it. Lights rise to reveal reality, a worn-out dance studio with* **Madame** *wildly applauding.*

Madame   Encore! Encore! You see Courtney Cooper's performance? Her extensions, alignment, turnout, the absolute golden standard. You captured the essence of Marguerite: split between knowing the danger you're in, yet lustfully tempted by the demon Mephistopheles! Brava, brava!

Courtney   Thank you, Madame.

Nox   What about me, Madame?

Madame   Eh, oui, eh, bravo, what is your name, it's now . . . Eh—

Courtney   Nox. **Her** name is Nox, N.O.X.

Madame   Eh, oui, merci, like the door! Your performance was only mediocre, Knock Knock. Your feet sickled, your arms flopping, your shoulders tense, and your battements are still too low. Far too low. I've seen more grace from a newborn horse! I like your faces though, your faces are funny. Class dismissed!

Nox *and* **Courtney** *perform a révérence.* **Nox** *and* **Courtney** *cross to the corner and put their civilian clothes over their dancewear.*

Courtney   Hey girl, don't worry about Madame, she's so old school. Like, what is she even doing teaching in Wyoming. You're just . . . new school.

Nox   Um, uh, thanks, Courtney Cooper! You really are just the BEST!

Courtney   Oh no, not at all . . . but thank you. And don't worry your gorgeous little head, you are so graceful. Don't give it a second thought. Between us dolls, if ballet was easy, they'd let cis girls do it.

Nox   Um, it is mostly done by . . .

The epitome of an un-cool car horn honks from outside the studio.

Courtney   That's me, exit stage left! My boyfriend, Kyle, and his boys are picking me up today . . . IN HIS NEW FORD FIESTA! EEEEEEEEEEEEEEEEEEY!

Courtney *scampers out of the dance studio.*

Madame   A word with you, Knock Knock. Where is your tuition?

Nox   . . . OOOOOOOOH the tuition money! I left it at home again, I'm so–

Madame I've let you go two years without paying your tuition. When have I ever been unsympathetic to your financial situation? But now I think you'll never pay.

Nox If I were to ask for an extension–

Madame I'll give you this courtesy, you have until tomorrow morning's dance lesson to get me only one month's worth of tuition! This is possible, oui? . . . Now run along, I have another class in five.

Thunder claps and rain pours.

Scene Two

Outside of this barren bedroom, the storm rages. Inside there's a bookshelf containing comic books and graphic novels, a closed door located on either side of the room, and a bed cover crumpled in a corner. **Nox** *darts about her room frantically as* **Gwen** *cooly paces, reviewing her homework packet. The two are on different planets.*

Nox I'm nothing if I can't learn from Courtney Cooper! Courtney Cooper makes being a girl look as easy as being a boy! Courtney Cooper's got it all figured out; "her morning routine," "her ballerina gracefulness," "cutesy little voice," "infinite supply of girl-clothes," "having a boyfriend," "NYC Juilliard dreams," "being winter formal queen for the past two consecutive years!" I know boys who call me slurs and pretend to gag when they see me and then turn around and vote for her as winter formal queen! I'm telling you, when high school's over, she's gonna triple pirouette into the sunset of New York while I'm gonna be stuck in this goddamn, godforsaken, assbackwards town! It's just . . . my pronouns are she but not her, because I'll never be Courtney CoopHER!

Gwen *puts her homework down and hugs* **Nox**.

Gwen Baby, darling, sweetie, wonderbunny, it'll all be fine. Courtney has been dancing since she was three and socially transitioning since she was five. You've been–

Nox My happiness peaked in kindergarten. This month it was pay for dance lessons or the electrical bill.

Gwen Is there anything I can help? My parents / would be happy to–

Nox / Are fascist bigots who think we could've won Vietnam?

Gwen They contain multitudes. I know if I asked them, they'd be willing to help out with–

Nox Not taking your family's money, Gwen. I can't.

Gwen We don't think of you as another charity that needs a donation. We really–

Nox Let's drop it, okay? I have a source. Dance lessons or no dance lessons, I'm good.

Gwen   A source, what sort of source!? Is it a drug thing? Or a sex thing? Or a sex drug thing? Sorry, stupid question. You don't have to answer that, I'm just worried. Are you safe? Do you need–

Nox   IS THIS A STUDY SESSION OR A GAME OF TWENTY QUESTIONS?! Like, Jesus Christ, can I help you study? . . . I'm a cunt . . . I'm a cunt with no cunt . . .

Gwen   No you're not. That was on me, I'm just—I really am sorry, Nox.

Nox   Me too. Sometimes, I swear, my blood flows quicker than–*(abruptly soothing.)* It doesn't matter, it doesn't. What matters is keeping up your four-point-oh GPA! Let's study!

Gwen   "Let's study!" *(pretending to be on the phone.)* Hello, Police, my girlfriend's been captured and replaced by her evil twin!

Nox   There's no saving my GPA. So it's my newfound mission to make sure you're Valid Victorian.

Gwen   You mean, valedictorian?

Nox   Yeah, her too! And as you probably guessed, I haven't paid for heating in a bit. So let's bundle up!

Nox *and* **Gwen** *wrap the blanket around each other. They lock eyes and lean in to kiss. The Vocatoris Libri, a disturbingly old leather-bound book with many stains, appears in the room in a moment of magic.*

Gwen   WHAT'S THAT!? WHAT THE ABSOLUTE FU–FUNNEL CAKE IS THAT?

Nox   It's the Vocatoris Libri! I found it in the attic when I was six. It's really cool because whenever I lose it, it just sort of—poof—appears! It's written in Latin, so I've been practicing on *Duolingo*–

Gwen   Okay, but what is it actually?

Nox   It's my childhood diary. I thought it was metal but now I wish it was fuzzy, pink, and had a lock.

Nox *slides spellbook behind the bookshelf.*

Nox *(to the book)*   Stay, stay, staaaaaay! Good book. *(to* **Gwen**.*)* All done. Now let me hold you! I haven't gotten to play with your hair all day.

Gwen *concedes, resting her head on* **Nox**'s *lap as* **Nox** *runs her hand through* **Gwen**'s *hair.* **Nox**'s *mother,* **Esther**, *staggers into the room.*

Esther   HEY, YOU TWOOOOOO, can you keep it down, okay? Shhhhhhhut it! For once, I'm just tryin—to have a good night but it's TOO LOUD!

Nox   Uh, yes, uh, I will. It was my fault. I'll be quieter.

Esther   Your father was loud, it's in your blood. Wanted a kid sooo bad but when one finally pops outta me, buh-bye! What a charmer.

Gwen   I'm sorry, it was me. I got startled. I promise I'll make less noise, Ms. Beauregard.

Esther (*to* **Gwen**)   No, no, please call me Esther. I'm cool. Ms. Beauregard was my mom and she was a drunk! (*to* **Nox**.) Watch yourself, kid. Don't be loud, don't be a charmer, don't be like your father.

Nox *and* **Gwen** *watch* **Esther** *finally exit.*

Nox (*calling off to* **Esther** *as she exits*)   Think I got that last part covered . . . I thought she was getting better but . . . I don't want to talk about it.

Gwen   Okay, yeah, totally . . . But you are a charmer!

Nox   I love it when you flirt with me. (*sitting back down.*) Now where were we?

Gwen *resumes resting her head in* **Nox**'s *lap.*

Nox   That's right, my little sheepheart. Back to studying and look where we are! It's Mr. Sexton's problematic word problems!

Gwen   Aaaaaaw, he's the reason for us. It's so cute that we were the only two people in class that laughed at him and not with him. And then we fell in love in detention! . . . That's actually the worst meet-cute ever.

Nox   Yes, but it's our meet-cute. Mr. Sexton would spontaneously combust if he knew his classroom was a breeding ground for lesbian yearning.

Gwen   What do you think he'd hate more: us, or critical race theory?

Nox   OOOH, critical race theory, for sure. He would just think we haven't found "the right man." Alright, let's do this. "If five thousand, three hundred, and forty-six children are vaccinated, and thirty-seven percent of them will be infected with autism, how many of these children's lives will be ruined by the Covid-19 cure?" Your turn!

Gwen *can't help but laugh and join in.*

Gwen   Wow, he almost makes the American education system bearable. "If you turn to page fifteen in your packet, you will see a map of our godly town of Winstonrock, Wyoming. The map is color coded by political affiliation. Determine the area of each color and calculate if the town will vote republican or socialist!"

Gwen *flips open her packet to reveal a map of the county covered in red with one tiny blue box inside it.* **Nox** *doubles over in laughter.*

Gwen   The answer is . . . ONE PERCENT! (*a Bernie Sanders impression.*) "The one-percenters of Winstonrock, Wyoming are socialists!"

Nox   Sooooo true, so true. "If heaven is three thousand feet into the air, and Jesus can descend at the speed of sixty-five miles per hour from the stairway to heaven, how long would it take for our Lord and Savior, Jesus H. Christ, to arrive and rapture the true believers and smite the homosexuals straight to the fiery depths of hell where they belong?"

Nox *erupts into laughter and* **Gwen** *shrinks.*

Nox (*caricature of an evangelical minister*)   God's on the prowl to smite anyone with a bent wrist! You wear a carabiner? HELLFIRE! You watch Drag Race All Stars? PREPARE TO BE SMOTE! You're sexually liberated and respect for your partner? I'M MAKING A WHOLE NEW LEVEL OF HELL JUST FOR YOU! (*bawling.*) C'mon, Gwen, this is comedy gold!

By this point, **Gwen** *is fighting back tears.* **Nox** *almost immediately stops laughing.*

Gwen   I miss my brother so much. I don't know if he's safe, or alive, or what's happening anymore. They don't let him answer my texts or letters. My parents keep throwing money at this military school and it's like, why? He's never going to get "better" because nothing was wrong with him in the first place! Imagine if they found out about . . . I don't know what would happen to us.

Nox   I'm sorry that I . . . that I forgot.

Gwen   You always forget . . . But how could I be so foolish, you're the only one with any real problems.

Nox   I never thought that!

Gwen   Then what do you think?

Nox   I think about a lot of things! I think about money, bills, getting my mom back into recovery, not failing school, my dance lessons, Courtney Cooper!

Gwen   What about me, Nox? Please. If you love me, tell me that Jesus won't damn us to hell.

Nox   I'll do you one better. For the past two years, I've used dark magic to conjure the son of Satan. He likes to do me little favors because he's a weirdo and we bond over our shitty parents. I'll summon him and he'll tell us that Jesus doesn't damn gay people. He's a reliable source.

Gwen   I . . . see you tomorrow, I guess.

Nox   Come on, Gwen! Gwen! What do you want from me? I'm already trying to be perfect!

Gwen *grabs her homework and leaves.* **Nox** *screams and then represses it, going to her bookshelf and picking out a graphic novel titled "MAGIC GIRL!" with a witchy superhero on the cover.* **Nox** *reads a few pages and paces about, carrying the graphic novel.*

Nox   In issue three of Hunter Zora's run on *Magic Girl*, Magic Girl faces . . . The High Castle of Wizards. "If you don't open the council to all magic users, I will retrieve The Axe of Fire and burn this castle all the way down to the nether-pits." End of issue five, The High Castle is reduced to ash. I wish I could do that . . . Sure, everyone around her thought she was on a quest to destroy the planet but . . . it was just the castle . . . and it was for the right reasons. It was worth it in the end. If a door is locked, you don't pick the lock and then thank the door for being shut on your face. You disintegrate the door. It shouldn't have been locked in the first place.

From under the bookshelf, The Vocatoris Libri slides to **Nox**, *already open.* **Nox** *reads it aloud and the more she does, the more the storm outside rages. A series of moments of magic occurs; lights flicker as silhouettes scamper across the room, sounds of laughter and crying are heard, horrifying chaos, etc. It's a transcendent experience, slashing the veil between Earth and Hell.*

Nox   "Omne gaudium coeleste abrenuntio ad lucra terrena delectanda. Anima mea in sinu infantis iacet. Spero iniquam pactionem facere, spem omnem salutis despicere. Nullus spiritus damnationem evasit in introitu daemonis. Ipse nunc surgat nobis dictatus, Jezestfiliuscaprae!"

Scene Three

In a moment of magic a portal from hell appears, playing club music. **Jez** *crawls from the portal, trying to be creepy.*

Jez   Hello, best friend.

Nox   Drop the act. I've read fanfic scarier than you.

Jez *picks up the book, opens to an illustration of a monstrous demon, and holds it to his face.*

Jez   Unbelievable, they never get my cheekbones right.

Nox   Focus, Jez, I have to say something important. You always look out for my best interest and give me . . . the money I need, no questions asked. Everything is piling up now. Just to cover the bare minimum I need a lot more than—

Jez   "A lot more?" You know that's out of the realm of "favor" and borders on "making a deal with me."

Nox   Right, but I don't want to try an unwinnable game. I'm not an idiot or a narcissist. So instead of a deal, I want to make a bet. I want super magic powers, the ones from this graphic novel.

Nox *shows* **Jez** *the graphic novel. In a moment of magic* **Jez** *receives a vision. It's never fun.*

Jez   It's back! The future is at my feet! I taste blood . . . hear screaming and see you falling to the ground and . . . the vision's slipping! It's all gone . . . No can do, toots. When a human gets magic, it ends with bloodshed at the end of the week. The vision didn't end with rainbows and kittens.

Nox   Magic Girl doesn't kill anyone and I'm just like her!

Jez   Sure you are, toots. So what are these hypothetical terms of the bet, best friend?

Nox   If I can go a week—

Jez   Nah, Sundays give me a rash. Six days.

Nox   If I can go six days being a hero and not kill anyone, I win the bet and keep my super magic powers forever. And if I lose the bet . . . you can have my soul.

Jez   Ooooooh? . . . (*like it's a wrong answer on a gameshow.*) THAT'S BORING! I got hundreds of those? What am I gonna do with one more? Use it as a paperweight? No. If I win, I get to take your place as a human!

Nox   WHAT!?

Jez   You heard me right, dollface. If I win the bet, I'd become human and you'd live in Hell for eternity. Oh, don't look so blue. You humans get everything about Hell all topsy-turvy. What's your source again? A two-thousand-year-old book that's been translated from an ancient language and edited for hundreds of years to fulfill political agendas? Yeah, that's reeeally reliable. Just because the everlasting damnation scene wasn't for me, doesn't mean it won't be for you, dollface! Your human mind can't fathom Hell's endless supply of drugs, booze, lube, and poppers. If that's a little too much, there's a bunch of demons who've started a knitting pentagram, it's very popular. Also, there's no such thing as a bad night of sleep in Hell, mainly because no one sleeps . . . But hey, that also means no alarm clocks, so that's a win! We've got all the best artists in an eternal residency. I'm talking: Freddy Mercury, Gertrude Stein, Ma Rainey, Shakespeare, Frida Kahlo! It's like doing a high school play without the tenor boys you have a crush on but then find out they're super problematic. Always the tenors. Also, you like punk rock, right? Good, because there's tons of screaming in Hell! Everyone just wants to scream about HOW GREAT HELL IS ALL THE TIME! YAAAAAAAAAS!" . . . Okay, I lied, the screaming is from the Island of Elephant Dildos.

Nox   Uuuuhhhh—

Jez   You're hesitant? You're hesitant. Hey, I get it, sweet cheeks. In case this bet goes tragically wrong for you, you'd really miss earth. I mean, on earth you have . . . NOTHING! I don't need to see the future to know you've got nothing to lose, babycakes. Being in high school is supposed to be the best time of your life, and whatcha doing with it? NOTHING!

Nox   Go suck a pitchfork and die!

Jez   I could make all of your wildest dreams come true. I'm like Oprah, with a few less cars.

Nox   So what are you hiding under the chairs, Oprah? What aren't you telling me?

Jez   All cards on the table, huh? We can play it that way. I used to live in Heaven when my old man was God's favorite cousin, but then he had the bright idea to revolt. Next thing you know, Daddy Dearest becomes God's cousin eternally removed and we all get cast out of heaven, banished to Hell. So, we bedazzled the hell out of Hell. I know it's a stereotype but all of us REALLY do love interior decorating! So what else were we gonna do? I'll always love my little interdimensional hub of debauchery, but I'm still banned from Heaven and I miss Gabriel . . . I thought I could turn them to our side but . . . they turned away from me. They miss me too though, because they're the one who gives me these angelic visions! They're always trying to tell me something. The two of us used to be a part of something cosmic, doing good and important work. So I understand why they couldn't give that up. My grand plan: become human, live a morally good life, die, go to heaven, and spend eternity with them continuing our work . . . That's my eon's long life story. (*Extending his hand.*) We making this bet or what?

Nox   Six days of not killing anyone? I can manage that!

Nox *shakes* **Jez**'s *in a tranquil moment of mutual admiration.* **Jez** *suddenly takes* **Nox**'s *hand, and in a moment of magic, puts it in his mouth, biting her fingers. Blood drips from* **Jez**'s *mouth.* **Nox** *retracts her hand, screaming.*

Nox   AAAAAAAAAAAAAAAAAAH!! YOU BIT MY HAND, YOU LITTLE FREAK!

Jez *performs a moment of magic, producing a cartoonishly long contract, and unrolling it.*

Jez   The handshake didn't mean squat. You have to sign a demon contract in blood or else it's useless. Look, we've also got a lot of lawyers in Hell and we need to give them something to do. We tried to invite them to one of our parties but we found them guilty of killing the vibe, your honor. Oh hey, your fingers are dripping buckets, you should sign at the bottom.

The contract is signed. A moment of magic occurs and **Nox** *is consumed with magic.*

Nox   I feel . . . STRONG! I FEEL . . . POWERFUL! I AM MAGIC GIRL!

Jez   There's a legal clause we'll go over in the morning. You look tired, you should sleep.

Nox   I AM NOT SLEEPY! I AM MAGIC GIRL, THE MOST POWERFUL HUMAN TO–

Jez *performs a moment of magic,* **Nox** *suddenly falls asleep on the floor.*

Jez   Screaming? Check. Blood? Check. Falling to the ground? Check.

Scene Four

There's a moment of magic where **Fear, Hate,** *and* **Shame** (*the* **Demon Chorus**) *enter out of a portal from Hell. The* **Demon Chorus** *isn't a hivemind per se, rather a creepily in sync polycule.*

Demon Chorus   HAVE YOU DONE IT?

Jez (*turning around, startled*)   MISSIONARY POSITION IN HOBBY LOBBY! Sorry, you just about scared me straight. Fear, Hate, and Shame, you really do creep up when it's least expected, don't you?

Demon Chorus   YOU! YOU'RE SO DUMB WE SHOULD CALL YOU IGNORANCE. YOUR PLAN WILL NEVER WORK.

Fear   YOU'RE TOO COMFORTABLE.

Hate   YOU'RE TOO FAR GONE.

Shame   YOU'RE TOO MUCH LIKE YOUR FATHER.

Demon Chorus   THE APPLE OF WISDOM DOESN'T FALL FAR FROM THE TREE.

Jez   You still have to help me! You've signed your names in your contractually-obligated blood! (*Reading from the bloody contract.*) "In addition to gaining magic, the warlock will also be bound to the personifications of Fear, Hate, and Shame for the duration of the bet. If the signer of the contract feels anything but fear, hate, and shame, the responsibilities of the personifications shall be terminated." So quit sitting on my shoulders and let's do the binding ritual before my dad—

Lucy *enters, wearing something akin to a silk robe over fishnets, from the portal in a moment of magic. Have your own take on* **Lucy** *and his entrance but make Tim Curry quake in his stiletto boots.*

Demon Chorus   ALL HAIL LUCIFER!

Lucy   Call me Lucy, you hellions. And bow away from me, I wanna see those dirty bottoms of my dirty bottoms.

The **Demon Chorus** *bow to* **Lucy** *by shaking ass.*

Demon Chorus   ALL HAIL LUCY!

Lucy (*to the* **Demon Chorus**)   Zaddy says rise. (*to* **Jez**.) Sorry I'm late. I just got back from a threesome with Zeus and Princess Diana from the timeline where she came out as Pan-sex-u-al instead of getting into that car crash she called a marriage. WOOF!

Jez   Dad, I don't want to hear about your sex life!

Lucy   M'BOY JUST TEMPTED HIS FIRST HUMAN, AND A GIRL NO LESS! / Shaking things up!

Jez   I've tempted girls before, pops. / It's just that men are more likely to give away their souls than—

Lucy (*outstretching his arms*)   Give me a hug, m'boy. Any moment now, any moment.

Lucy *eventually runs to* **Jez**, *bear hugging him.*

Lucy   Let's take this party home!

Demon Chorus   ALL HAIL LUCY!

Lucy *performs a moment of magic and instantaneously everyone including the sleeping* **Nox** *are in Hell. It's revelry incarnate. Loud house music plays, sweaty bodies dancing, lights blaring, various substances and people are being done in corners.* **Lucy** *immediately parties and audience members should be invited onstage to dance.* **Jez**'s *lines are drowned out by the music.*

Jez   Hey, pops! I'm not really in the mood to party. I've actually . . . it's hard to say to you. It's important though. It's actually about this soul I just tempted. It's all in the contract, if you just . . . Can you please stop throwing your ass back? You always want to do this when I have something serious to say. Like, remember two thousand years ago when I told you I was attracted to more femme people and you threw a Burning Man Burning Men Party instead of actually talking to me? Remember that? . . . I said do you even remember that? Can you even hear me or are you purposefully ignoring me? Dad? DAD, I WANT TO BECOME A HUMAN!

A literal record scratch, the music drops dead. Any audience members onstage are ushered to their seats by the **Demon Chorus***. Complete silence.* **Lucy** *and* **Jez** *lock eyes.* **Nox** *starts to rise.*

Nox (*barely awake*)   Who was playing the muuuusic? Where am—

Without breaking eye contact, **Jez** *performs a moment of magic and* **Nox** *falls right back to sleep.*

Jez   It's all in the contract, old man.

Jez *hands* **Lucy** *the contract, which* **Lucy** *speedreads.*

Lucy   You didn't make a deal, you made a bet!? And it's signed in ir-re-voc-a-ble human blood! FOR MY COUSIN'S SAKE, WHAT HAVE YOU DONE? Just to undo this, you know the kind of paperwork I'll have to go through? And with those . . . oh no . . . You just killed the vibe of the party. Are you coming out to me as a lawyer!?

Jez   UG GROSS, DAD! It's not that, it's just—I love this place, but I'm not a kid anymore. I want to move out of the house!

Demon Chorus   OOOOOOOOOH, DAMN!

Lucy   Are you blaming me for losing the revolt? It's not my fault God saw it coming. Omnipotence is a real bitch!

Jez   Can't you just admit that, deep down, there's a part of you that misses Heaven?

Demon Chorus (*to* **Lucy**)   IS THERE?

Lucy   Being with you is all the heaven I need. And not at all, I showed my cousin my authentic self. I suggested we make Heaven inclusive to more people. I tried to forge a new era in Heaven's history. But NOOOOO! All of our names got blacklisted in the Lamb's Book of Life! Even if you do end up becoming human and dying, Gabriel couldn't even see your name under the many slashes of red ink. Then you wouldn't even be sent back to Hell, oooh nooo, you'd wind up in purgatory. Surrounded by nothing but white walls, an endless supply of paperclips, and bleedin' Catholics! Even I wouldn't be able to get you out of that sticky situation, and I'm the king of sticky situations!

Jez   I don't think that's true, pops! I get these visions from Gabriel, leading me to them, they need me. I mean, they're not even out to God yet.

Lucy   And then what? You spend your eternity being closeted? No one deserves that. Especially you. Hell, I remade Hell for you, Jez. I remade it so you'd know loneliness and rejection and . . . and you . . . WANT TO LEAVE ALL OF US BEHIND?! Someone, open a portal! I'm too distraught!

The **Demon Chorus** *opens a portal in a moment of magic.*

Lucy   I love you, m'boy, and I always will. No matter where you go, or who you are, you'll always be my demon semen. Now if you excuse me, I'm off to get pity-fucked by Cthulu.

Lucy *tearfully exits through the portal. The party resumes.*

Jez (*to the* **Demon Chorus**)   LET'S GET HER HOME. WE'LL DO THE RITUAL THERE!

In a moment of magic, the **Demon Chorus** *and* **Jez** *step through a portal to* **Nox**'s *bedroom.*

Jez   Oh my God, oh my God, oh my God! I made my pops cry! Who does that!?! Please, Gabriel, my cherub . . . I need a vision! AAAAAAAH! I smell . . . plums. I hear . . . sopranos, and I feel . . . Your face in my hand? It's gonna work, one day I'll be in Heaven! (*Discovering the* **Demon Chorus**.) You. You three, get over here now! You need to be bound to . . . my best friend.

Jez *bends over the still asleep* **NOX**, *kissing her forehead.*

Jez   I'm sorry it had to be you. (*to the* **Demon Chorus**.) Let the ritual begin.

The **Demon Chorus** *sign their names in blood on the contract. Then they perform a moment of magic to bond with* **Nox**. **Jez**, *not being able to look at* **Nox**, *leaves. Late night turns to morning.*

Scene Five

The **Demon Chorus** *performs a terrifying series of moments of magic to awaken* **Nox**.

Fear   MAGIC / GIRL!

Hate   MAGIC / GIRL!

Shame   MAGIC / GIRL!

Demon Chorus   MAGIC GIRL! MAGIC GIRL! GOOD MORNING, MAGIC GIRL!

Nox *awakens to find* **Fear**, **Hate**, *and* **Shame** *looming over her.*

Fear   WHAT ARE THESE VOICES? AM I LOSING IT? WILL I BE TAKEN AWAY?

Hate   I OWE MADAME TOO MUCH MONEY! I HOPE SHE GETS LUNG CANCER AND WE DANCE EN POINTE OVER HER GRAVE!

Shame   EVERY MORNING I WAKE UP HOLLOW, PATHETIC, DESERVING OF LONELINESS.

Nox   WHO EVEN ARE YOU?

Fear   WHO?

Hate   WHO?

Shame   WHO?

Demon Chorus   WHO ARE WE? WE ARE THE MICROPHONE OF YOUR THOUGHTS, / MAGIC GIRL!

Fear (*chanted*)   / I HAVE TO GO. I HAVE TO RUN. I HAVE TO HIDE. I HAVE TO DODGE. / I HAVE TO MOVE!

Hate (*chanted*)   / DRINK THEIR BLOOD. DANCE IN BLOOD. BATHE IN BLOOD. SWIM IN BLOOD. RED LIQUID, / RED LIQUID!

Shame (*chanted*)   / MISPLACE. DISGRACE. MISTAKE. DEBASE. ERASE. DISTASTE. REPLACE. EFFACE. FORSAKE.

In a moment of magic, **Nox**'s *voice overpowers the* **Demon Chorus**.

Nox   JEZ! JEEEEEZ! WHERE ARE YOU AND WHAT HAVE YOU DONE!?

Demon Chorus   WAH, WAH, WAAAH! I'M MAGIC GIRL AND I CALL DEMONIC ENTITIES FOR HELP!

Jez *appears in a moment of magic.*

Jez   HAPPY DAY ONE OUT OF SIX!

Nox   You want to tell me why I'm getting visited by the genderfluid three stooges?

Jez (*to the* **Demon Chorus**)   Oh hey, how's it going, friends? Don't worry, dollface, they can't read your mind, they're just really good guessers. See, toots, when you signed on the contract in blood, you accepted your magical ability to be unlocked . . . AND for my friends to tag along.

Nox   Dumb, dumber, and dumbest?

Jez   Fear, Hate, and Shame. You did read the contract, right?

Demon Chorus   YOU CAN'T READ YOURSELF OUT OF A PAPER BAG, LET ALONE A LEGALLY-BINDING CONTRACT THAT HOLDS DOMINION OVER YOUR IMMORTAL SOUL!

Nox   PSH-YEAH, I read the contract . . . No DUH!

Jez   Then you must know that we are the only ones who can see or hear our friends. So don't open your big mouth to the wrong person; or you'll be strapped to a table waiting for a lobotomy!

Nox   YOU TRICKED ME!

Demon Chorus   YOU TRICKED YOURSELF, MAGIC GIRL! YOU HUMANS ARE FUN.

All of a sudden, **Nox**'s *ringtone blares before she answers the phone.* **Gwen***, on her phone, steps on the other side of the stage.*

Nox   Hello?

Gwen   Hey, wonderbunny, I'm sorry about last night. I feel awful about . . . I mean, I handled things so–

Nox   No, I'm sorry, sheepheart. You mean the world to me and I made you feel less important than . . . stupid things like Courtney Cooper.

Demon Chorus (*to* **Jez***, secretly*)   COURTNEY COOPER. Use her!

Gwen   I'm so glad things between us are getting better. How did your dance lesson go?

Nox   What time is it?

Gwen   Uh, seven forty-five.

Nox   MY DANCE LESSON! I'M LATE! I've got to go, love you, bye!

Fear   WHAT IF YOU'RE TOO LATE TO PAY YOUR TUITION? WHAT IF YOU CAN'T BE NEAR COURTNEY COOPER EVER AGAIN?

Hate   YOU MIGHT AS WELL TAKE THE RIBBONS OUT OF YOUR POINTE SHOES AND HANG YOURSELF FROM A BALLET BARRE!

Shame   THE REASON YOU DON'T HAVE MONEY IS BECAUSE YOU'RE LAZY, STUPID, AND UNLOVABLE.

Demon Chorus   COURTNEY COOPER IS EVERYTHING YOU DREAM TO BE AND EVERYTHING YOU'LL NEVER BE.

Nox   I'M SO SCREWED!

Jez   Hey, best friend, I know you're not used to rolling for psychic damage, but let me remind you . . . . you've got "super magic powers." Here's what you gotta do, doll; time travel a few minutes before your lesson and then, bada-bing bada-boom, you're early!

Nox   The first rule from comic books, time travel is a big no-go. One wrong step and my parents never meet. Or I get stuck in a time loop. Or my entire existence gets rebooted and a shitty universe becomes the main universe! Who do you think you're talking to, a fake fan?

Jez   Your lesson was twenty-seven minutes ago, you'll be fine . . . And the more you use your powers now, the easier it'll be for me to win later.

Nox   Can't wait to time travel to a reality where I didn't see you today.

Demon Chorus   YOU CAN'T GET US OUT OF YOUR HEAD. WE'LL BE RIGHT BESIDE YOU.

Nox   Bye loser.

Nox *performs a moment of magic and she and the* **Demon Chorus** *time travel to a few minutes before the lesson starts. As the world shifts . . .*

Demon Chorus (*a repeated half-whisper*)   Time travel! Time travel! Time travel! Time travel! Time travel! Time travel! Time travel! Time travel! Time travel! Time travel! Time travel!

Scene Six

Nox *and the* **Demon Chorus** *are now outside the dance studio. On the other side of the stage is the interior of the dance studio where* **Courtney** *superbly rehearses.*

Nox   I DID IT! I TIME-TRAVELED, TIME-TRAVELED, TIME-TRAVELED! Just like Magic Girl in "Hours of Tomorrow's Yesterdays!" I'm gonna KILL THIS DANCE LESSON!

Demon Chorus   DANCE LESSON?

Fear   WHAT IF YOU FORGET EVERY STEP? WHAT IF MADAME SCREAMS AT YOU? WHAT IF YOU LAND ON SOMETHING WRONG AND YOUR NECK SNAPS?

Hate   IF I HEAR THAT MY BATTEMENTS TO BE HIGHER ONE MORE TIME, I WILL RIP OFF MADAME'S LEGS AND THROW THEM IN THE RECYCLING BIN!

Shame   YOU, BALLET? WHY EVEN TRY AN ART FORM THAT WILL NEVER EMBRACE YOU? YOU'LL NEVER BE LIKE COURTNEY COOPER.

Demon Chorus   MAGIC GIRL CAN'T DANCE! MAGIC GIRL CAN'T DANCE! MAGIC GIRL CAN'T DANCE!

Nox *takes a deep breath and enters.* **NOX** *and the* **Demon Chorus** *watch* **Courtney** *in awe.*

Fear   COURTNEY COOPER IS THE BARYSHNIKOV OF WYOMING!

Hate   COURTNEY COOPER IS THE DANCING QUEEN, YOUNG AND SWEET!

Shame   COURTNEY COOPER IS THE BEST THING SINCE SLICED HEAD OF JOHN THE BAPTIST!

Demon Chorus   TALK TO COURTNEY COOPER! PLEASE, PLEASE, PLEASE, PLEASE, PLEASE–

Nox   I CAN'T JUST TALK TO HER!

Courtney *is frightened and thrown out of the dance.*

Courtney   Shizzlesticks! Hey, Nox, how are you?! (*Stopping the music.*) Everything okay, girliepop?

Demon Chorus   YES, NOW THAT YOU'RE HERE.

Nox (*to the* **Demon Chorus**)   SHUT UP, SHUT UP, SHUT UP!

Courtney   Excuse me?

Nox   My bad, today has been awful! My mind is just . . . scattered. I thought this was my solo lesson with Madame? Or is it another full class day, or—

Courtney   No, I just finished my solo lesson, Madame took her smoke break early, and then you arrived.

Nox   Right, uh, sorry, yes. Your dancing is incredible . . . and you're so pretty. I was wondering if–

Courtney   Oh, you're so sweet. I actually have a boyfriend and I'm not interested in—

Nox   That's not what I was going to ask.

Demon Chorus   ASK IF SHE KNOWS OUR NAMES!

Nox   I was asking if you wanted to have a girls' night tomorrow after school? It'd be at my place with me and Gwen, she's my giiiiir–best friend!

Courtney   Oh, uh, YEAH! Sounds fun, girlie, let's do it!

Courtney *is barraged by phone notifications.*

Courtney   Calendar reminders? Boo! Love to chat but gotta run. I have to make the morning announcements, inject estrogen into my bloodstream, post flyers for my winter formal queen campaign, and then take lunch with MY BOYFRIEND, if he's not with his boys! LATERZ!

Nox   WAIT! BEFORE YOU GO, What's your number?

Courtney *hands* **Nox** *a business card.*

Nox   You have a business card?

Demon Chorus   SO PROFESSIONAL!

Courtney   Laminated, eggshell white, Montserrat font, 91-degree angles. They're having me audition for colleges in New York, getting my name out there.

Nox   So cool! How's that going?

Courtney   I'm gonna miss my mom and dad, but I can't wait to get out of this dumpster fire of a town. See ya!

Courtney *starts to leave.*

Demon Chorus   DON'T LET HER ESCAPE!

Nox   Have you read the *Magic Girl* graphic novel series?

Demon Chorus   SHE SAID THE UNSPEAKABLE! IT'S TOO PAINFUL TO WATCH! AVERT YOUR EYES!

Courtney (*completely unphased, even a little interested*)   No, I haven't.

Nox   You should! . . . If you get the chance. See you tomorrow night, buckaroo!

Courtney   Fun! See ya then, gorgeous!

Courtney *exits the stage, practically skipping.*

Nox   Buckaroo?

Demon Chorus   THERE IS NO ONE IN HELL LIKE COURTNEY COOPER!

Fear   HER SMILE BEGUILES ALL DOUBT!

Hate   HER VOICE DESTROYS ALL ANGER!

Shame   HER PRESENCE CLEANSES ALL HURT!

Demon Chorus   WHY CAN'T WE BE HER INNER DEMONS?

Nox   Why are you obsessed with her?!

Courtney *re-enters with a flyer in hand, a headshot reading "Vote For CourtME Cooper!"*

Demon Chorus   WHY ARE YOU?

Courtney   Me again, teehee, just thought I'd give you this! Figured I could count on your vote but flyering never hurts . . . Laterz!

Courtney *exits the stage right as* **Madame** *enters.*

Madame   Knock Knock, will you tell me you don't have the money or are we ready to dance?

In a moment of magic, **Nox** *conjures a thick stack of dollar bills.* **Madame**'s *jaw is on the floor. In another moment of magic,* **Nox** *conjures a second thicker stack.*

Nox   I want this room named after me. Not Knock Knock. Nox. N. O. X.

Blackout.

Scene Seven

Continuing from the previous scene, **Courtney** *is texting furiously by the door to the studio. In a moment of magic, a portal from Hell opens and* **Jez** *steps out of it, making a flashy entrance that goes unnoticed by* **Courtney**.

Jez (*to the audience*)   Huh, kids this century.

Courtney (*trying for a phone call*)   Hey sweetie, I thought you were going to pick me up today from my . . . Voicemail. He better not be with his boys, if he's with his—

Jez   You must be Courtney Cooper. Long time fan, first time interactor. Let me guess, you're "gifted and talented," set lofty goals, consider yourself different from the rest.

Courtney   I'm sorry, who are you?

Jez   Just someone in the same boat . . . I also happen to be your fairy godfather.

Courtney   Okay, I have a boyfriend and he'll be here any minute now to—

Jez   No he won't.

Jez *performs a moment of magic and time freezes.*

Courtney   Why is everything so still?

Jez   I froze time. Now you won't be late. You're welcome, dollface.

Courtney   Magic . . . A flare for the dramatic . . . I guess you really are my fairy godfather!

Jez   Trust me, I'm a fairy in more ways than one. And thankfully I've flown down in the nick of time. Listen closely, Cinderelly. You can't trust Nox.

Courtney   . . . Okay? Why? I've been her dance partner for three months. She's weird, yeah, but she's nice if not a little socially anxious.

Jez   Have you ever wondered why she's that way around you . . . and nobody else?

Courtney   Weeeeeell, I do think she was flirting with me earlier.

Jez   It's not that she wants to be with you, she wants to be you. I even think she wants to steal your crown as winter formal queen.

Courtney   But . . . But I just handed her a flyer!? I can't believe she–I handed her A FLYER!? Don't get me wrong, she's nice. One day, she may even be pleasing to the eye, but I've won for the past two years and this is my senior year. Okay, so when I was a freshman, I went to a school in a different district. Someone discovered that I . . . It was homecoming season, and I got randomly nominated for homecoming queen. Amazing, right? I thought so, but then flash-forward to the night of the dance. They call my name, I go onstage, and before I even start my acceptance speech these boys in the rafters pour a bucket of spiders on me. Arachnids everywhere, but mostly in my strapless mermaid dress. So, I tell you this story because I've endured prejudice, transphobia, and eighty-seven spider bites. So, when I transferred to Winstonrock High, I CHOSE to run for Winter Formal Queen. The student body voted for me because after all of that, I could endure . . . and I got really hot. Could she persist like I have? Could she build an immunity to necrotic AND cytotoxic venoms? I don't think so. She's not ready. At least not yet . . . What's wrong with you?

A moment of magic has occurred during the tail-end of **Courtney**'s *monologue.* **Jez** *is in the middle of a vision.*

Jez   I'm just getting a . . . fairy vision! I hear you crying . . . inconsolably. I feel something . . . squishy, soft . . . a mattress, your bed. I smell . . . Ice cream? Somebody has a breakup in your future. In the next few days, your boyfriend . . . won't be yours.

Courtney   Do you think my boyfriend's having an affair with Nox!?

Jez   . . . YES!

Courtney   Is my boyfriend a chaser!? No, he's always been so loyal, kind, and my biggest fan . . . but lately he's been spending so much time with his boys. I don't know what to do, fairy godfather! What are you doing?

Jez *performs a moment of magic and time resumes.*

Jez Time had to be unfrozen. Now, here's what you gotta do, Toots. Go to her house, confront her, be aggressive, and do whatever you gotta do to make sure the love of your life stays in your life!

Courtney   You are so right, good plan. I am going to—WAIT! How did you know that Nox invited me to her house!?

Jez   . . . Fairy magic.

Courtney (*after staring into* **Jez**'s *soul*)   . . . That makes sense. Thank you for telling me the truth. Nox will face the wrath of Courtney Cooper!

Courtney *exits.* **Jez** *stands in a spotlight.*

Jez   Day one out of six is over. We're now in the middle of day two.

Scene Eight

The lights rise in **Nox**'s *room, revealing* **Nox** *and* **Gwen** *playing a game of tag.* **Nox** *chases* **Gwen** *and the* **Demon Chorus** *chases* **Nox**. **Gwen** *shrieks each time* **Nox** *gets close to her.*

Demon Chorus   ENJOY THIS FLEETING MOMENT OF HAPPINESS, SHE WON'T LOVE YOU FOREVER!

Fear   WHAT HAPPENS IF YOU GET MARRIED AND SLOWLY GROW TO RESENT EACH OTHER LIKE A STRAIGHT COUPLE?

Hate   SHE'LL DISCOVER YOU'RE A PATHETIC LEECH WHO CRAVES ATTENTION!

Shame   IF YOU CAN'T LOVE YOURSELF, HOW THE HELL ARE YOU GOING TO LOVE SOMEONE ELSE?

Demon Chorus   GWEN WILL FOREVER BE OUT OF YOUR GRASP!

Nox *tags* **Gwen** *and* **Gwen** *falls down, exhausted.*

Gwen   You win, you win!

Demon Chorus   FOR NOW.

Nox   You're so pretty when you're exhausted.

Gwen   Then I must be pretty all the time, wonderbunny.

Nox You are . . . Is it okay if Courtney Cooper comes to hang out soon? Because . . . she is. Is that okay?

Demon Chorus IT ISN'T.

Gwen Yeah, it's fine. I just . . . I didn't think I'd have to do more hiding today. Unless you told her were–

Nox I said we were besties! I see what you mean and . . . I'm sorry . . . that you can't be out yet. That sucks.

Gwen Thanks. But hey, you've always wanted to learn tips and tricks from Courtney, right? This is great . . . Is there anything else that I should know about?

Demon Chorus I WIELD DEMON MAGIC FROM A DEAL I MADE WITH THE SON OF SATAN AND NOW I HEAR VOICES IN MY HEAD TELLING ME TO DO BAD THINGS.

Nox No, that's it.

All of a sudden **Esther** *enters, incredibly cheerful but dead behind the eyes. She dresses like, and has the composure of, a cartoon nineteen-fifties housewife.* **Esther** *extends a tray of warm cookies.*

Esther Knock-ety knock knock! You girls must be hungry after all that running. Would you like some freshly-baked cookies?

Nox *gets cookies for her and* **Gwen**.

Nox Thanks, Mom! OH, right, uh, my mom is in recovery aaaaand has been watching reruns.

Esther I love you, honeynut! Uh, you two are just so darling together. Have you two ever thought about going steady? Oh silly me! I shouldn't be prying like this! Teehee! Tootles, girls!

Esther *exits.*

Nox Recovery looks different for everyone.

The doorbell rings. **Courtney***'s voice is heard after the actual doorbell ring.*

Courtney Cooper (*offstage*) DING DONG!

Demon Chorus COURTNEY COOPER! **THE** COURTNEY COOPER!

The **Demon Chorus** *face each other and squeal as they jump up and down before exiting.* **Nox** *almost leaves then turns around.*

Nox Could you straighten out the cover for me? Thanks, love you, sheepheart!

Nox *blows a kiss towards* **Gwen** *and then exits.* **Gwen** *reluctantly begins to straighten out the cover on the floor. In a moment of magic the Vocatoris Libri falls out of the unwrapped covers.* **Gwen** *jumps away from it, becomes tempted, and then opens it up to read it.*

Gwen   Oh my Heavens! . . . Is that a demon? No! It can't be– She did say she was besties with the son of Satan!? No, that's absurd! But why else would she say she could summon demons if she wasn't telling me the–

Gwen *hears* **Nox** *offstage and hides the book.*

Nox (*offstage*)   So that was the kitchen, slash entryway, slash living room.

Nox *reenters, leading* **Courtney** *into her room.*

Nox   This is my room and this is my . . . bestest friend Gwen.

Gwen   Hey! Nice to meet you, I've heard **a lot** of really good things.

Courtney (*to* **Gwen**)   Hi, me too. (*to* **Nox**.) So this is your room? Where are the chairs? Or your bed? . . . Where's all the furniture?

Demon Chorus   YOUR MOM SOLD THE FURNITURE FOR A—

Nox   WHY DON'T YOU DO ME A FAVOR AND **SHUT UP** FOR ONE GODDAMN MINUTE! . . . (*to* **Courtney**, *a sorority girl impression.*) Shut up, girl, you're so pretty. So pretty, Goddamnit.

Courtney   Thank you? And I like your room, totes honest. It's giving minimalism! I'd even say, serving.

Demon Chorus   COURTNEY COOPER DOESN'T APPROVE OF YOUR INTERIOR DECORATION.

Nox   Let's do nails! You've got to try the Magnifique Midnight Minute!

Nox *goes to one of the bookshelves to retrieve a bottle of nail polish. Both* **Gwen** *and* **Courtney** *begrudgingly sit down as* **Nox** *gently pushes the bottle towards* **Courtney**.

Courtney   Cute. But I prefer my signature, my boyfriend goes craaazy for it. Perhaps you've heard of—

Courtney *reveals a pink nail polish bottle from her purse.*

Courtney & Demon Chorus   PROUD CEO WHO OWNS A FORTUNE 500 AND ALSO A VULVA!

Fear   WHAT IS WRONG WITH YOU, MAGIC GIRL!?

Hate   HOW COULD YOU CHOOSE SUCH A GAUDY COLOR AS SILVER!?

Shame   YOU'LL NEVER BE AS WELL-ADJUSTED AS COURTNEY COOPER.

Demon Chorus   TOO BAD, TOO BAD, SO SAD!

Gwen   Well, that's okay, Nox! We can use the same—

Nox   It's all yours. I'm not really in the mood to appeal to the male gaze.

Gwen, *embarrassed, takes the nail polish.* **Courtney** *and* **Gwen** *paint as* **Nox** *plots.*

Nox   So, Courtney, you're gonna go to college next year. Exciting. Are you going to join the debate team, or student government, or a literary magazine?

Courtney   I'll probably be too focused on dance to do anything frivolous.

Gwen   . . . that's great?

Nox   What about using your platform? You could be a hero, a voice for the voiceless?

Courtney   That's not really my thing. I just want to be like everyone else and also liked by everyone else.

Demon Chorus (*sniffing the air around* **Nox**)   WHAT'S THAT SMELL? IS IT . . . AMBIVALENCE?

Nox   Mmmmhmm?

Demon Chorus   Mmmmmmmhmmmmmm!

Gwen (*to* **Courtney**)   Mmmmhmmm! (*to* **Nox**.) Mmmmhmmmm!

Courtney   Mmmhmmm.

Nox (*to* **Courtney**)   Fascinating. That's a lofty goal, to be liked by everybody, becoming the ultimate people pleaser. No, I see it, it makes sense for someone like you. I mean, I guess that's why you've been clinging to being winter formal queen year after year after year? Because it defines your worth?

Gwen   WHO ELSE WANTS SNACKS?!!

Nox   You could mean so much more to so many more people!

Courtney   I'm sorry, are you wanting me to come out to the school? No thanks. I've already had enough boys ask me out on a dare and girls who sit behind me cut my hair with scissors.

Nox   Okay, but now you're THE Courtney Cooper. Everyone loves you and would love you no matter what! Do you want that part of you hidden forever? Really? Wait . . . is your boyfriend making you keep it a secret? Because, if he is, that's so—

Courtney (*rushing to her feet*)   Enough "girl talk," okay?! I know you had sex with my boyfriend!

Nox & Gwen & Demon Chorus   WHAT!?

Demon Chorus   HOW DARE YOU DO THAT TO COURTNEY COOPER!

Courtney   You don't breathe half as delicately as me. Your outfits aren't as slay girl-boss werk as mine. You don't even speak with a coy sultry tone or walk with a sophisticated lightness half as well as me!

Demon Chorus   WHAT DID COURTNEY COOPER EVER DO TO YOU?

Nox   I never did that, Gwen. I swear, I never—

Courtney   You're a liar, we both know you did the hanky panky with KYLE!

Gwen   Let's all slow down and take a deep breath. Nox couldn't have done this, right? I mean, this whole thing is ridiculous! Nox couldn't have laid with a man because Nox is not attracted to—

Courtney (*to* **Gwen**)   You want to know what's actually ridiculous? It's ridiculous that a sophisticated man like my boyfriend, KYLE JENKINS, would choose you over me! Your under-eye circles are so deep you look like a sleep-deprived racoon on meth. Your hair is so flat and sad it should be on antidepressants. Your fingernails are so short that you . . . you can probably do everyday tasks easier than me, BUT I'M BETTER AT EVERYTHING ELSE! You know, I used to really admire you and I'd have been overjoyed to be an older-sister figure to you, especially because of your situation. I'm pretty sure we're the only two trans girls in Winstonrock. EVER! But nooooooo, instead of waiting for me to give, you decide to take! You take . . . you take away the one person who . . . who knows the real me!

Demon Chorus (*physically comforting* **Courtney**)   IT'S OKAY, COURTNEY COOPER, (*sung*) "YOU'RE IN THE ARMS OF THE DEEEMONS!"

Nox *performs a moment of magic and makes the* **Demon Chorus** *physically restrain* **Courtney**, *sending her in deep pain.*

Courtney   Wha-What are you doing to me?

Demon Chorus   WE DON'T HAVE CONTROL! PLEASE FORGIVE US COURTNEY COOPER!

Nox   I AM NOT YOUR LITTLE FREAK FRIEND TO BE MOCKED OR PITIED BECAUSE I REFUSE TO BE YOUR TYPE OF GIRL. I DON'T NEED TO CONFORM TO YOUR RIDICULOUSLY RIGID BEAUTY STANDARDS TO BE SEEN AS NOT A BOY. I AM MAGIC GIRL, AND MY ENEMIES WILL KNOW THAT I'M A GIRL BECAUSE EVERY GIRL IS MAGIC. I WILL TRANSFORM THIS WORLD FOR THE BETTER!

Gwen   NOX, WHAT ARE YOU DOING?

Nox (*to* **Courtney**)   I COULD OBLITERATE YOUR MEMORY AND REINCARNATE YOU INTO THE LITTLE BITCH EVERYONE THINKS YOU ARE.

Nox *performs another moment of magic and the* **Demon Chorus** *torture* **Courtney** *again.*

Courtney   NO-NO! PLEASE. DON'T.

Demon Chorus   WE'RE SO SORRY, WE'RE YOUR BIGGEST FANS!

Gwen   YOU CAN'T DO THIS! YOU CAN'T JUST—

Nox   ACTUALLY I CAN, I AM THE MOST POWERFUL BEING IN THE MULTIVERSE!

Gwen   NOX, THIS ISN'T YOU! You wouldn't do this, this is the work of Satan's child! Yeah, you're weird, incredibly weird—

Nox *performs another moment of magic and* **Courtney** *is sent into even more pain.*

Gwen   But you're not magically-torture-your-enemy kind of weird! You are kind, and you're a lot of things, and you're ultimately good. You helped me realize that I love girls, ever since you first stared into my eyes. Everyday you help me love the fact that I love girls, just by being the girl I love. And you're so SO patient with me . . . majority of the time. We've only been dating for a year but, in the best possible way, it's felt like ten. You can try to convince me all you want but we both know that all you want is to be loved. Well, all you've got to do is be your wonderful self. It worked on me, and it'd work on anyone you'd want. The one thing you can't do though, is lash out at Courtney . . . Okay? . . . Nox, I've tried to be nice here but . . . Here we go, I'm not going to ask you. You are going to let go of Courtney. Now.

Nox *hesitates then performs a moment of magic. The* **Demon Chorus** *releases* **Courtney**.

Demon Chorus (*to each other*)   WHAT HAVE WE DONE?

Courtney   Ohmygosh, ohmygosh, ohmygosh! You're going to pay for that. Because I'm making a call-out post about you stealing my boyfriend, KYLE FITZGERALD JENKINS! . . . Give me a second. (*angrily typing.*) Boyfriend not blow-queen. Stupid autocorrect. (*holding up her phone.*) Look at this! Know what this is? A phone? WRONG! This is your dirty little secret about you and my boyfriend, KYLE FITZGERALD JENKINS THE THIRD, being spread to my 92 followers!

Courtney *clicks a button on the phone and a notification sound is heard.*

Courtney   That's right, ninety-two!

Courtney *tries to open the door by pushing it.*

Courtney   Ohmygosh, did you lock the doors? Are you going to go full *Carrie* on me? Dear God, not again! You're gonna kill me, aren't you? At least let my skeleton look snatched! HEY, SOMEONE GET ME OUT OF HERE!! Ohmygosh, how do you open this door!?

Gwen   You pull it, the door. You pull the door to open it.

Courtney   Thank you. No, FRICK YOU! (*to* **Nox**.) AND FRICK YOU MOST OF ALL! And FRICK THIS GOSH-FORSAKEN FURNITURELESS ROOM! And I don't curse, because it's unladylike, but you're a cu . . . a cun . . . You're an Immanuel KANT!

Courtney *officially leaves, terrified.*

Nox   You are what you eat, amiright or am I right?

Demon Chorus   A SHINING LIGHT HAS LEFT THIS ROOM IN DARKNESS. COURTNEY COOPER IS ANGELIC.

Nox   I'm sorry, Gwen. I felt thousands of burning coals in my stomach and—

Gwen   You're going to hurt me too, aren't you?

Nox   What? No.

Gwen   Are you going to make me come out to my parents? Because, I'm sorry, I love you but I just–I can't do that for—

Nox   I would never hurt you like that.

Nox *reaches out towards* **Gwen**, *who backs away.* **Gwen** *tries to run out of the room. In a moment of magic,* **Nox** *anchors* **Gwen***'s feet to the ground.*

Nox   I'm so sorry, sheepheart. I can't let you go yet. You don't understand—

Gwen   Oh, I understand perfectly! You're filled with evil, possessed by the devil, corrupted by sin. You let Satan into your heart and he took it! How could you do this foolishness?

Nox   No, no, NO! It's not like that, it's more complicated than that. I have these demons in my head, literal demons! They get me so . . . VOLATILE that I–bear with me, I know it sounds insane.

Demon Chorus (*to each other*)   ARE WE THE BAD GUYS? MAYBE WE'RE THE PROBLEM?

Gwen   We all get negative thoughts, but we have to grow from them and turn them into . . . not this. Now can you let me go?

Nox   Can you promise you won't run away?

Gwen   I won't, wonderbunny, I promise. I overreacted before. I love you, and nothing will change that. Eventually though, I will have to walk out of this room.

Nox *nods and in a moment of magic, releases* **Gwen**. **Nox** *breaks down and* **Gwen** *holds her.*

Gwen   Hey, I've got you, I've got you, wonderbunny. I'm sorry, I also let my voices get the best of me. You're not the devil, you're not sinful. You are magic and we're safe in this room, just you and me. We can be ourselves here, messy and disgusting as we may be. Here's what I need you to do, not right now but . . . soon. You have got to . . . you've— you need to figure out how you'll use your powers without giving into and . . . being bullied by these demons. If you keep going down this path, I will have to . . . let's not focus on that right now, okay? I really don't want us to . . . I just can't love a person who hurts people on purpose. I can't and I shouldn't have to. I don't have to, actually, and it'd be pretty messed up if I was . . . cursed to be okay with it. You know that, right?

Nox   I know. I'm gonna get better. I promise, I really do know. I'm so–

Nox *cries. In a moment of magic, the lights short-circuit with her sobs. When* **Nox** *wails there's a–*

Blackout.

Scene Nine

Lights rise in Hell, during the afternoon. This region of Hell is less sex-club, more drag brunch. A gay anthem plays in the background. **Lucy** *sits at a table sipping a rainbow martini and eating from a freshly peeled banana. A rainbow martini and unpeeled banana sit on the other end of the table.* **Jez** *finally enters.*

Lucy   You're late, m'boy. You're late for boozy brunch! . . . I sacrifice so much for you and you don't even . . . I've caved. I've finally joined the Time Traveler's Contingencies Contingent. Somebody's gotta make sure those cosmically slippery rat-bastards aren't destroying the fabric of space time.

Jez   Okay, I'm sorry, pops, that you . . . got a desk job? But why? And why are you telling—

Lucy   Eat your banana, m'boy! Please. I know it's your favorite.

Jez *un-peels his banana and eats it as* **Lucy** *stares.*

Jez (*after a beat*)   I've lost my appetite. Am I missing something? You're acting weirdER than usual.

Lucy   I took this job as a trade-off. I help regulate the proper flow of time and, in return, I get the cosmic space needed to expand Hell. For you. You miss Heaven, that's fine, sure why not, BUT you're going to be Duke of this new territory. Meaning, you can turn it into whatever your baffling little heart desires. You don't . . . you don't even . . . (*an outburst, gesturing to the space*) YOU DON'T EVEN HAVE TO MATCH THE THEMING! You want everything in your Dukedom made out of cumulus clouds? Fine. You want harps, and halos, and a children's choirs singing Latin? Just say the word, but please don't leave me.

Jez   I'm sorry, old man. I really am, but my mind has been made for decades. I love Gabriel with my whole essence and—

Lucy   Love wins. I know, I know. Just know that I am working very hard to put this banana and rainbow martini on the table.

Jez   Thanks, pops, I know . . . You've gotta know that someday, sometime, I will leave Hell forever and you can't stop me. You just can't if you really love me. You know that right? . . . If you're curious, I could show you the progress of the bet? Gabriel would give me a vision and I could . . . Gabriel has been so sweet these past few days, he really is an ang—

Lucy   I don't want to see it . . . Alright, you can show me. I love watching straight people suffer!

Jez   Actually the girl is a . . . everyone involved, actually, is . . . one of us.

Lucy   M'boy, where did I go wrong? Because the Demon Semen I raised would never hurt our own . . . Just show me.

Jez (*calling to Gabriel upwards*)   Alright, Gabriel, c'mon. Please show my old man all the hard work I've done to get our stars crossed again. Pleeeeease?

In a series of moments of magic, **Jez** *gets a vision and then expands it outward. It's as if the insides of his head are being projected outward.* **Nox** *and* **Courtney** *appear as ghost-like entities.*

Jez   Here they are . . . Nox has decided to hurt Courtney Cooper where she hurts the most, her morning routine. Here's day three of the bet.

Courtney *stares ahead as a diddy, something bouncy like Scott Jopin's "Maple Leaf Rag," or any other upbeat up-tempo song, is heard.* **Nox** *appears behind the oblivious* **Courtney***. The following is a movement piece:* **Nox** *begins to mess with* **Courtney***, playing with her hair, rolling up her sleeves, giving her devil horns, giving wet willies and noogies, drawing a moustache on her face, tripping her on banana peels, various silly Looney-Tunes-esque practical jokes, etc.*

Jez   Day four of the bet.

Nox*'s antics become unnerving and biting, causing the song to become more sinister.* **Nox** *ruins* **Courtney***'s makeup, locks her door, undoes her hair, dishevels her clothes, creates a chill in the room, makes the lights flicker and the walls ooze, turns her room into a haunted one, etc.*

Jez   Earlier this morning, day five of the bet.

The song is now unrecognizable as **Nox** *twists and pulls* **Courtney***'s hair, replaces her screams with silence, short-circuits the lights, distresses her clothes to appear ratty, disappears her furniture, knocks objects off shelves, distorts her makeup to look like a clown's, makes* **Courtney** *hit herself, hits* **Courtney** *herself, turns her life into something that feels like it's ripped out of The Exorcist, etc. The vision ends with the music fading into nothingness.* **Nox** *and* **Courtney** *disappear under shadows.*

Jez   So . . . what do you think?

Lucy   If you don't have anything nice to say . . . How are Fear, Hate, and Shame taking all this?

Jez   Those hellions. They're nothing but vile, remorseless parasites completely fixated on Nox.

In a moment of magic, The **Demon Chorus** *enters in despair from a portal leading to earth.*

Demon Chorus   JEZ, WE DON'T WANT TO DO IT ANYMORE!

Fear   WE TRAVELED TO EARTH AND LEARNED WE'RE NOT JUST ABSTRACT CONCEPTS!

Hate   WE HURT HUMANS AND PUT THEM THROUGH INEXPLICABLE SUFFERING!

Shame   WE WANT TO BE A CATALYST FOR POSITIVE CHANGE!

Demon Chorus   OUR EXISTENCE IS MISERABLE AND NO ONE SHOULD FEEL US!

Jez   You know these personifications, always in their feelings. A moment please?

Jez *huddles the* **Demon Chorus** *as if they were a football team.*

Lucy   It's not too late to, I don't know, stay in hell with me.

Demon Chorus   WE HAVE NEWS TO TELL YOU!

Fear   EVEN WITH OUR COMBINED FORCES—

Hate   GWEN, THE HUMAN THAT NOX LOVES—

Shame   ALWAYS DE-ESCALATES NOX'S VIOLENT TENDENCIES!

Demon Chorus   SHE'LL NEVER KILL SOMEONE! OUR EFFORTS ARE FUTILE!

Jez   Hey, going soft will not put wings on my back. Now go back to earth, commit Nox to sin, and party like it's thirteen-ninety-nine! I don't care if you don't want to do it, do it, or there'll be—

Demon Chorus   HELL TO PAY. WE KNOW, WE KNOW!

The **Demon Chorus** *exits through the portal.*

Lucy   When I say "be gay and do crime," I don't mean crimes against humanity! You don't need to be doing this nonsense with Fear, Hate, and Shame. That human already has so much going on.

Jez   Maybe you're right. Maybe she's already about to see red and all she needs is that extra little temptation.

Lucy   How can you accuse me of being a bad listener, when I don't even think you're actually hearing–

Jez   The only way I can guarantee her first drop of blood, is if I go back to earth as . . . a fly on the wall!

In a moment of magic **Jez** *turns into a fly and flies away.* **Lucy** *takes a large sip of his drink.*

Lucy   I remember turning into a fly. Puberty's the worst.

Scene Ten

In Winstonrock High's cafeteria, **Nox** *carries a tray full of food as she hears the whispers from other teenagers, who are unseen. She tries to make contact with them, but it's clear she's become a pariah. The sounds of everyone whispering about her are pervasive.* **Nox** *sits at a table alone, until the* **Demon Chorus** *enters, surrounding* **Nox***.*

Demon Chorus   DID YOU MISS US? WE MISSED YOU!

Fear   I MISSED YOUR OCEAN-LIKE EYES.

Hate   I MISSED YOUR SPICY TAKES.

Shame   I MISSED YOUR PETULANT RELENTLESSNESS.

Demon Chorus   WE'RE SORRY WE WERE SO MEAN BEFORE. IT WAS IN OUR CONTRACT!

Gwen *enters unnoticed by* **Nox**.

Nox   If you want to help me out so much, maybe you should just leave!

Gwen   I've been starting to think the same thing.

Jez, *as a fly, flies into the cafeteria and remains unnoticed as he watches.*

Nox   Gwen! Gwen. I . . . I've missed you.

Gwen   I miss you, Nox, with all my being but . . . I know you've been going full Linda Blair on Courtney.

Nox   Courtney is this elitist, empty, plastic, American Dream of a trans girl. She makes us look awful. I'm doing her a favor, trying to wake her up. If she started acting more human and less Barbie, then the rest of us won't be held to such an impossible standard. And I could meet the high bar Courtney made up if I wanted, and look like I sold my soul to Teen Vogue. I shouldn't have to, though. So that's why what I'm doing is feminist! It's what Magic Girl would do!

Gwen   No one is making you . . . What you're doing is petty, just call it what it is.

Nox   She cyberbullied me, Gwen! To her ninety-two followers! And now I'm persona non grata!

Gwen   You already were, remember!? I was your only friend, okay? Your biggest fan, your supposed "love of your life," or at least I believed I was . . . before Kyle.

Nox   Really! You believe Courtney's propaganda? That I'd seduce Kyle Fitzgerald Jenkins?

Gwen   Maybe you did, maybe you didn't! I don't know what to believe anymore, okay? I just . . . Once upon a time, I believed you to be sweet and charming and an almost perfect girlfriend. It was just you and me versus this stupid town. Sure, it wasn't . . . I don't know, perfect or ideal? But you lead me to believe that we were happy enough together. And now . . . I don't know what you are, but I'm nowhere near happy. I'm miserable around you, but it's also unbearable without you . . . Look, you want to be loved, you want to be popular? Fine, I don't get it, but you get treated like a threat when you bring your demon powers to school. Everyone becomes afraid that you'll turn them into a frog to be dissected. Or explode their heads like it's Sloppy Joe Wednesday. Or freeze them in a time loop if they beat you at the Pacer Gram Fitness Test!

Nox   Gwen . . . I'm still learning how to use my—

Gwen   How are you like Magic Girl? Genuinely, how? You used to go on and on about how she'd go to these galaxy-ending lengths for her loved ones. What about me? I told you what I wanted three days ago, Nox! "Don't give into the demons and don't hurt anyone." And what have you done? . . . This is my free period. I'm driving to the park.

Gwen *exits with* **Nox** *in hot pursuit. The intercom turns on.* **Courtney** *re-enters the stage.*

Courtney   Good morning, Winstonrock Woodchucks! It's me, Courntey Cooper, doing the morning announcements . . . No. You know what? No. I'm going to talk about something REAL, and vulnerable. I need your votes for Winter Formal Queen, okay? I might not be the hottest girl at this school, I know that, but I'm also far from the ugliest. We can't all be Winstonrock nines and New York fours. But there's a girl who goes here who's a one out of ten. Both aesthetically and spiritually. Her name is Nox, she's that one emo kid who constantly smells like the storage room of a deli! The one who looks like an alligator skin purse because of her non-existent skin care routine. The one who causes earthquake drills in other countries, because she's always stomping around in those ugly clunky gay platform boots! She's been nothing but a big stinky bully, using her telekinesis, yes, telekinesis to knock me over. And we all know this school has a zero no-bully tolerance policy that is ALWAYS upheld! Bullying is a national problem like arms control, the electoral college, and lowrise jeans making a comeback. Here's the naked truth that none of you want to see: you don't know what it's like to over-achieve. Your dreams are simple, child-like, easily achieved. I've been dancing since before I was potty-trained so I could go to New York. Yet here I am, still in this tiny little poo-poo hole of a town AND a witch had intercourse with my boyfriend! So yeah, I didn't lead the pledge of allegiance or announce today's lunch specials, but I hope I opened your eyes to true injustice. Because maybe one day you'll blink and become a feral sleep-deprived girl with nothing left but the marbles she's losing while she does the morning announcements!? . . . And that's the morning announcements, let's go, Woodchucks.

The intercom turns off, a roar of laughter throughout this scene. **Courtney** *exits in tears.*

Nox   Oh my God! Won't you listen to that!? Look at that!? Feel that!? This is what I've been crying for, and searching for, and fighting for my whole life!

Demon Chorus   CAN'T YOU SEE THEY'RE LAUGHING AT COURTNEY! NOT LOVING YOU! WE WANT TO HELP YOU, MAGIC GIRL, WE CAN SAVE YOUR SOUL!

Nox   They don't love me? None of them love me? They will, this whole school will love me.

Jez *watches as a fly.* **Nox** *performs a series of moments of magic. The laughter is turned into a dedicated chanting of "**Nox**." Darkness swells with the volume of the chanting. A spotlight hits* **Nox***, she slowly begins to smile as the crowds' fervor builds. When her grin is at her largest and the sound is at its zenith—*

Blackout.

Act Two

Scene One

Lights rise on **Nox**'s *room, as* **Nox** *wallows.* **Jez***, still a fly, continues to spy in the corner of the room. The* **Demon Chorus** *performs moments of magic, trying to cheer up* **Nox***.*

Demon Chorus YOU ARE A GLISTENING COMET HURTLING THROUGH SPACE!

Nox I'm too pathetic to function.

Demon Chorus EVERYONE LOOKS AT YOU WITH AWE.

Nox Yeah, because I put a love spell on the whole school.

Demon Chorus EVERYONE LIKED YOU BEFORE YOU PUT THEM UNDER A SPELL.

Nox Nobody likes me. I don't even like me.

Demon Chorus EVERYONE WILL BE RELIEVED IF YOU LIFT THE ENCHANTMENT.

Nox If I undo the curse, everyone will know what happened and they'll hate me even more.

Demon Chorus YOU HAVE THE CHANCE TO RIGHT YOUR WRONGS.

Nox I am nothing like Magic Girl. I am nothing.

A knock on the door.

Nox Go away, Mother, I don't want cookies! I don't deserve cookies.

The door gets opened to reveal **Gwen***.*

Nox Hey, what brings you here?

Gwen I want my nail polish back, *The Magnifique Midnight Minute.* I loaned that nail polish to you on our second date. I was fine with it being lost until I saw it when you offered it to Courtney the other day. I almost took it then but I didn't want you to be mad at me . . . Where is it?

Nox *gets the nail polish from the bookshelf, and hands it to* **Gwen***.*

Gwen Thanks. I'm going to go now.

Nox You're not under the love spell?

Gwen A love spell, who did you put under a–

Nox I put a love spell on the entire school. Thankfully you must've left before I . . . I have a confession, Gwen. At the end of the date, I stole the nail polish. I would always forget to return it on our next dates so you could never get rid of me. So I guess, in a way, I already put you under a love spell, before . . . all this. I used to think that magic was everything and it could make my problems disappear. Turns out, it only makes them more obvious. I think . . . I'm really broken, beyond magic's power. You deserve to find a girl who isn't a trainwreck. You could move to a cottage together, paint each other's nails, bake rainbow strudel bread, own twenty-seven houseplants! You're the real magic girl in this relationship. So, you ought to be with someone who's just as magical. I've got a spell to lift.

In a series of moments of magic **Nox**, *with* **Fear**, **Hate**, *and* **Shame**, *breaks the love spell.*

Gwen   Wonderbunny, we both have things to work through. It's not just you who—

Nox   But it is mostly me. You could really break my soul, if you wanted. You know that? . . . I don't want you to . . . break up with me, but if you did, I wouldn't try to stop you. Or even blame you.

Gwen   You just lifted a spell, without me asking, that gave you . . . everything you've ever wanted. I believe you . . . and not just because I really want to. I think we're Gucci, cutie.

Nox   Soooooo . . . we're not done?

Gwen   Please, no! And . . . oh man, I was wondering if–would you be my date to the Winter Formal?

Nox   You mean . . . you want to be seen on my arm, slow dancing together, wearing those . . . those matching flower things? Aren't you—

Gwen   I am terrified, yes. But I'm not gonna be on this earth for a long time. So if I can't wear "matching flowers" with my girlfriend, then what am I even doing here? BUT I have one condition . . . I get the boutonniere and you wear the corsage.

Nox *and* **Gwen** *kiss. It's both passionate and domestic. A series of moments of magic occur, a lot of romantic sitcom tropes happen at once. Maybe it rains on the couple, there are fireworks, they float together, etc. As soon as* **Nox** *and* **Gwen** *softly break away from the kiss,* **Jez**, *still as a fly, performs a moment of magic that freezes time.*

Nox   Gwen? . . . Gwen?

Jez, *as a fly, flies around* **Nox**. **Nox** *swats at* **Jez**, *but he remains a fly throughout this scene.*

Nox   Ah! Jez!? Is that you?! What are you—

Jez   Time needed freezing and you needed a "come to Lucifer" chat. Before tomorrow's midnight, you will kill someone.

Nox   Are you giving me orders?

Jez   You're naive if you think . . . THIS (*flying around* **Gwen**.) will last.

Nox   I'm not killing anyone. You're just scared that if you're wrong about me, you're wrong about—

Jez   End of the day, you homo sapiens are still animals. You just haven't had your instincts kick in.

In a series of moments of magic **Jez** *unfreezes time and disappears.*

Gwen   What happened? I feel like something just happened?

Nox   I've got you. Miss Gwendolen Rose Sunday, I'll be better than ever. Everything will be perfect.

Blackout.

Scene Two

The lights rise and **Jez** *appears in* **Courtney***'s bedroom, in his usual form.* **Courtney** *lies face down on the floor, listening to moody breakup music, and eating from a carton of frozen yogurt.*

Jez   Hey, Courtney! You seem blue.

Courtney   Oh hello, Fairy Godfather. I am blue, that's why I'm listening to indie pop.

Jez   Well, scooch on over and let me join you, friendo.

Jez *performs a moment of magic, making a spoon for himself appear.* **Jez** *sits on the ground and* **Courtney** *rests against him as* **Jez** *eats her frozen yogurt.*

Courtney   Kyle broke up with me today. He kept telling me "I didn't do the sex thing with Nox." I didn't believe him and he . . . I could get over his cheating, and live happily ever after, but I can't stand that he lied to my face over and over again . . . I don't know what he wants from me!

Jez   I'm proud you've put on a brave face, especially since Nox started dating someone.

Courtney *wails, drops her head straight into the carton, and cries into her frozen yogurt.*

Courtney (*incoherent, muffled gibberish*)   You don't have to rub it in, I know she's dating Kyle.

Jez   Want to run that by me one more time?

Courtney *lifts her froyo covered face from the carton and stares intently at* **Jez**.

Courtney   "You don't have to rub it in, I know she's dating Kyle."

Jez   Hate to break it to ya, toots, but Nox never loved Kyle. She only pretended to do that to get back atcha. Now she's dating . . . Gwen!

Courtney   Oh . . . Nox is bisexual?

Jez   I know, I know, can't they just make up their mind. Oh wow, I just remembered this out of the blue. You should call this number!

Jez *performs a moment of magic and hands* **Courtney** *a phone.*

Jez   Gwen is keeping a big secret from her folks. Your parents love you, know that? And when you tell them difficult information they still love you, right? Gwen just needs that same reassurance from her folks, just a little push to come out of the glass closet, if you know what I mean!

Courtney   WHAT!? I'm not going to do that! No one deserves to be outed!

Jez   You didn't deserve your boyfriend breaking up with you, right? Remember, Nox stole him from you, she stole Kyle Fitzgerald Jenkins!

Courtney   The Third.

Jez   Exactly! Only the best of men have Roman numerals attached to their names.

Courtney   Obviously, but it still doesn't—

Jez   I can prove that calling that number will be a net benefit! Come on, Gabriel, I need a vision! Show it to me . . . NOW! . . . Aaaaaaaaany moment.

Courtney   It's not a net benefit, is it?

Jez pretends to have a vision.

Jez   It is! It's a . . . OOOOOOOH, oh, I got one, A FAIRY VISION! I see, I see . . . You as an adult, with a grown up, um . . . oh right, A GROWN UP KYLE FITZGERALD JENKINS THE THIRD! It's a rainy Sunday afternoon in New York, ooooooh! He bends down on one knee, and from his pocket he pulls out A . . . A . . . A MULTI-SEASONAL CONTRACT FROM LINCOLN CENTER! WAIT . . . OH NO, NO NO! Everything's becoming all DISTANT and FOGGY! If you don't act right now YOU'LL LOSE YOUR FUTURE FOREVER! BUT IF YOU CALL THIS NUMBER RIGHT NOW YOU CAN GET YOUR LINCOLN CENTER CONTRACT!

Courtney *slaps* **Jez.**

Courtney   GO TO Heee . . . Go to Heee . . . Go to H-E Double Metal Straws!

Jez   I'M A DEMON, I LIVE THERE! I'm not your fairy godfather! Fairies aren't real, you susceptible bitch!

Courtney   Get out of my room this instant!

Courtney *physically removes* **Jez.** *Maybe she ballet lifts him and sends him flying. Or a cartoonish shirt grab and push out of the room. Or a continual whack of a Teen Vogue magazine until he's gone. Have fun with it. Either way, he leaves.*

Scene Three

Flowing from the previous scene, the lights shift as a spotlight appears on **Jez.**

Jez   After that embarrassing incident I teleport from the scene of the crime. I need a place to be alone, somewhere serene and close to the slice of Heaven I remember. I appear at a barren strip of peninsula off the coast of Queensland, Australia.

The lights morph to sparkling blue as gentle tides roll.

Jez   Here the morning sun just now decided to rise and I stand opposite the Great Barrier. Gabriel took me to an island like this once.

Jez *sees* **Gabriel** *and, for the first time and only time, the audience sees* **Gabriel***. The two do a reuniting movement piece as* **Jez** *talks.*

Jez   They're what I'm fighting for and . . . I wish I had a choice. I have this perfect Get to Heaven scheme, but . . . my old man would hate it, the personifications can't know too much about it, and Courtney flat out refused . . . I have to be the one with bloody hands. But if I do it, it's a one-way trip to Heaven where I pry open the pearly gates and reunite with the love of my immortality. I must do it! It's not every day you enter a bet with a human that could skyrocket your soul to the divine happily-ever-after!

Jez *and* **Gabriel** *are the closest they've been in centuries.*

Jez   It's just so . . . evil.

Gabriel *breaks away from* **Jez** *and in a moment of magic* **Gabriel** *disappears. After losing them again,* **Jez** *makes the call . . . and it goes through.*

Jez   Hell-o, Ms. Sunday, sorry to bother you so late at night. I go to school with your daughter, Gwen. I thought it was my duty, as a servant of the Lord, to let you know that I saw her yesterday. She was kissing a girl . . . I think she even . . . when she left school, went to her. I'm sorry, I really shouldn't have . . . The brother was the same way too, huh? . . . Well, God bless you too.

Jez *hangs up, a beat.* **Jez** *performs a moment of magic.* **Demon Chorus** *stumbles through a portal from Hell.*

Jez   You three haven't been doing your job. I gave all of you second chances. That's six chances in total, the magic number!

Demon Chorus   WE WANT OUT OF THIS JOB!

Jez   Oh you'll get out, don't worry. Remember this?

In a moment of magic, **Jez** *conjures the contract and a quill.*

Jez   "If the signer of the contract feels anything but fear, hate, and shame, the responsibilities of the personifications shall be terminated." So thank you for your services, have fun in Hell forever!

In a moment of magic, **Jez** *makes a slash on the contract and a portal to hell appears. The Demon Chorus take a beat . . . before partying!*

Demon Chorus (*Adlibbing celebratory and relieved responses, such as . . .*)   It's over, thank Lucy's cousin eternally removed! / I hated this job! It had no benefits, no insurance, no PTO! / Does anyone have devil's food cake?

The **Demon Chorus** *are sent to hell.* **Jez** *is alone again.*

Jez (*to the audience*)   Why do I feel the most human when I feel the most guilty?

Blackout.

Scene Four

Lights rise in **Nox***'s room.* **Gwen** *is curled under the bed-cover.* **Nox** *is already awake, pumped with an unparalleled nervous but celebratory energy.* **Gwen** *slowly starts to wake up.*

Gwen   Nox? You're awake?

Nox   Today's the last day, day six out of six.

Gwen (*still waking up*)   Whaaaaaat?

Nox   The bet I made with the demon. I was promised I'd keep my super magic powers if I don't kill someone for six days straight. And I made it this far—didn't think I'd make it this far! Kidding. Mostly kidding. Who cares, I'm keeping my super magic powers forever!

Nox *performs a flagrant display of series of moments of magic. Suddenly, it hits* **Gwen**.

Gwen   My parents! I forgot to let them know that I'd be here—Oh God, I stayed the night! I gotta—

Gwen *takes out her phone and frantically makes a call*

Nox   Hey, my little worry-wart, things are gonna be—

Gwen (*on the phone*)   Hello, Father. I am so sorry! I forgot to tell you last night that Nox invited me to a sleepov—WHAT?! . . . THAT'S INSANE— . . . You're just gonna . . . I'm gone. I'm—NO, DAD, PLEASE, NO, NOT THAT, YOU KNOW I LOVE JESUS AND GOD AND— . . . Okay. Goodbye. I lov—

The unseen speaker hangs up on **Gwen**.

Nox   You're scaring me. What—

Gwen   My parents kicked me out. If I went home, they wouldn't let me through the front door. I have nowhere to live, to go, to—How could God do this to me?! Someone must have tipped them off but . . . we were so   QUIET! WHO WOULD'VE DONE SOMETHING LIKE—

Nox   I WISH I KNEW—

In a moment of magic, **Jez** *appears crawling and* **Gwen** *screams!*

Gwen   WHAT IS THAT!?

Nox   Hey, Jez, down, boy, boy! We're in the middle of a crisis.

Gwen   You know this thing? Is that the demon—

Jez I'm beyond sorry to say this but your folks will abandon you. I saw it all in a vision!

Gwen Visions? From God, your immortal enemy?

Jez Don't worry, there is a shred of hope. In my vision, you ended up safe, but it was close. Too close. So everyone needs to do exactly as I say. Courtney can be reasoned with, but—

Gwen WHAT IS HAPPENING? Why can't everything SLOW DOWN?

Nox Did you say "Courtney?" As in the—

Jez (*to* **Nox**) Courtney Cooper was the one who ratted you out to your parents. She was trying to get back at Nox for, well, everything. I originally reached out to her days ago because I thought she might help me win the bet but . . . she proved too much of a wildcard and now she's gone too far! We've got to talk some reason into her! (*to* **Gwen**.) If Courtney calls your folks again and says it was all a twisted prank, they'll take you back!

Gwen Okay! So if we need to get to her, let's go to her!

Jez YES buuuuuuuuuuuut not you. You can't come with. In my vision, you stayed behind. If one little thing changes from what I saw exactly, then what happened in the vision won't happen. Our top priority is to protect you.

Gwen Nox, I don't like this. This isn't right. Nothing feels safe! I just want to be held!

Nox Jez may be on top of my shit-list, but his visions are never wrong.

Gwen I'm so scared, Nox. Please! I don't trust him! I don't trust his vision! I don't trust anything about him! I need you here, I need you here to hold me! If you leave this house . . . it's over. No more second chances!

Nox I'll always love you. I hope to God this proves it.

Nox *kisses* **Gwen** *and then quickly leaves through the portal with* **Jez.** **Gwen** *is alone in silent shock and then brutal acceptance. Eventually, she leaves.*

Blackout.

Scene Five

Lights rise on **Courtney**'*s bedroom where she's sleeping in her bed.* **Nox** *and* **Jez** *watch her.*

Nox What did we do now in your vision?

Jez You woke her.

In a moment of magic **Nox** *amplifies her voice!*

Nox   RISE AND SHINE, COURTNEY COOPER!

Courtney *wakes up screaming.* **Lou** *is an offstage voice who calls out to her.*

Lou   HONEY, IS EVERYTHING OKAY?

Courtney *looks to* **Nox***, who slowly nods.*

Courtney   I'M ALL GOOD! I'M PRACTICING MY SCREAM FOR WHEN I'M CROWNED WINTER FORMAL QUEEN.

Lou   OKAY, JUST TRY TO SCREAM A LITTLE QUIETER.

Courtney   What are you doing here?

Nox   I'll be asking the questions. Did you know that Gwen's being disowned?

Courtney   WHAT? NO! DISOWNED?! WHAT HAPP—

Jez   Look at her trying to play dumb!

Nox   You called someone last night? Didn't you!?

Courtney   NO, I DIDN'T! I SWEAR ON MY GRANDMOTHER'S GRAVE!

Nox   Did you know that Gwen and I were dating?

Courtney   Only since last night.

Jez   A likely story, missy, a likely story!

Nox   People don't just figure out who's dating who and then out them to their fundy freak parents!

Courtney   Humans don't, but demons do! He was in my room last night, begging that I call Gwen's parents! There was this thinly veiled attempt to try to get me to out Gwen. He saw my perfect future, or whatever, in a fake vision.

Nox   . . . did he now? I think he used that same move on me.

Jez (*after some nervous laughter*)   I'm sensing a lot of judgment right now . . . and it's all very pointed towards me. So let's take this moment to de-escalate our—

Nox   If you're behind this, I'll douse you in an ocean of holy water. I'll make the sky rain a circle of salt around you forever. The power of Christ will compel and I'll shove a cross so far up your—

Courtney   Assuage her anger, Jez. She deserves to hear the truth.

Nox   So tell me truthfully, did you set this up?

Jez   Here's the Gooooo . . . the Gaaaaa . . . The God's honest truth is that Courtney Cooper is not . . . the victim! She's up to her ole' tricks.

Courtney   HE'S A LIAR!

Jez   Didn't she call you a liar, right after she falsely accused you of sleeping with her boyfriend?

Courtney   You didn't have sex with Kyle Fitzgerald Jenkins the Third?

Nox   COURTNEY COOPER, I AM A LESBIAN!

Courtney   . . . congratulations on coming out, it takes a lot of courage to be your—

Jez   She's changing the subject, toots! We all know Courtney Cooper won't stop till she gets on top again, even if she is a bottom! You've been the bane of her existence and it's been less than a week. I bet she even hated you from the moment you came out. There could only be one token trans girl in Wyoming, and she'll never let it be you. If you let her get away with this, Gwen will never forgive her, that is if you ever see Gwen again. This is nothing like how it played in my vision, so I bet Gwen is doomed to be a Bible-thumping housewife forever. My opinion, justice needs to be served and nothing hurts more than being played, best friend.

Jez *slightly pushes* **Nox** *to* **Courtney**. **Nox** *uses a series of moments of magic to kill* **Courtney**, *who screams all the way through her death.*

Courtney   Tell . . . Kyle . . . Fitz . . . Gerald . . . Jenkins . . . the Third . . . I'm sorry . . . and that I lo—

Courtney *succumbs to her own mortality.* **Nox** *and* **Jez** *sit in shock and despair.*

Lou (*still as an offstage voice*)   . . . SOUNDS GREAT, HONEY!

Jez   . . . I'm the winner. I actually . . . won!

Nox (*realization finally hitting*)   YOU LIED TO ME!

Nox *initiates a tussle with* **Jez**.

Nox   / YOU WERE MY BEST FRIEND AND YOU SCREW ME OVER LIKE THIS!

Jez   / AAAAH! STOP! OW, OW, OW! WHY ARE YOU—JESUS CHRIST, THAT—AAAAAAH!

Nox *performs a moment of magic and controls* **Jez**'s *body, making him choke himself.*

Jez   Two . . . in . . . one day? Pace yourself.

Nox *releases* **Jez** *from her hold.*

Nox   You're not going to heaven, dipshit! I'm no Bible-person, but I'm pretty sure heaven isn't for you. I think you committed some big no-nos. If you think you can be this much of a douchebag, I've got a world of news, you can. No one will stop you. But when it's all said and done for your waste of a life, Saint Michael, or Peter, or some other angel with a boring name will pull the lever and you'll fall right back to where you started. I'm a lot of things but at least I'm not a demon.

Jez (*chuckling*)   Half-truths are also half-lies. Isn't it odd that you could perform the spell to summon me in the first place? Did you think that spellbook was just bought in a garage sale? Don't you ever sit and wonder who exactly is dear old dad?

Nox   My mother always said that he was / a charmer.

Jez   / A charmer? Right on the money, best friend. Or should I say, sister? I may be a demon, but I started as an angel. You are part demon and part human, not an award-winning combination. You've gotta understand, my not cis sis, when our old man shoots his demon semen in humans, it creates dangerous offspring.

Nox   No. No, you're lying. That can't be me. I'm a good person! I'm a hero, I'm Magic Girl!

Jez (*looking to* **Courtney,** *then to* **Nox**)   There are no heroes, we created this bet together. I didn't have to write the contract and you didn't have to sign on the dotted line. So don't tell me I'm not going back to Heaven because I . . . I don't think they'll let me in after . . . all of this. Heaven wasn't built for Demons like us.

Nox   So, the bet? What do we do now?

Jez   Any moment now, our father will realize you lost the bet and drag us both to hell for a hearing.

Nox   What? No. This can't be the ending! There has to be a way to undo this? If comics taught me anything, it's that nobody stays dead forever. We could . . . um . . . we could time travel back to the very beginning of Courtney's dance lesson! Then we could convince her to return back to our time, right now. So it'll be as if she never died, right?

Jez   My old man just took a job at the Time Traveler's Contingencies Contingent. He'd see what we're doing and stop it before we've even done it . . . I don't know.

Nox   Look . . . I know you did all of this to get back to Gabriel. You're scared you'll lose them forever, but right now . . . right now we've lost Courtney. She had a whole life outside of ours. Her life would have been full of dancing and moving to New York and finding true love. We have to give that time back to her. We at least have to try. So what do you say? Are we going to do this as reformed-villains-turned-heroes?

Nox *extends her hand.* **Jez** *takes* **Nox**'*s hand.*

Jez   As good people in training.

Jez *takes* **Nox**'*s hand. A moment of magic occurs and* **Nox** *and* **Jez** *time travel back to the beginning of Act One Scene Six.*

Nox and Jez (*repeatedly chanted*)   Time travel! Time travel! Time travel! Time travel! Time travel! Time travel! Time travel! Time travel! Time travel! Time travel! Time travel! Time travel!

Scene Six

On the side of the stage is the door to the dance studio. **Courtney** *enters the dance studio, dressed in her dance attire.*

Courtney   This earlier bird is ready to get her Juilliard scholarship.

Courtney *plays the same classical music from Act One Scene Six.* **Courtney** *takes a deep breath and* **Nox** *and* **Jez** *burst into the studio.*

Courtney   CHEEZITS RICE! What is going on?

Nox *performs a moment of magic causing the music to stop.*

Nox   We're from the future, come with us if you want to live.

Courtney   Girl, what?

Jez   In a few days you're going to be murdered, but we can keep you safe.

Courtney   MURDER? Who's going to MURDER ME!?

A moment of magic occurs and **Lucy**'s *voice is distorted and disembodied.*

Lucy   HEEEEELL—o, You two little, ingrates! Rewinding the clock is clever, but I'm in charge of keeping the timelines straight! It's the only straight thing about me!

Courtney   OH MY GOD, WHAT IS—WHO IS HE?

Nox   Our dad, Lucifer! He's trying to drag us to Hell.

Jez   We have daddy issues.

Lucy   NOW THAT THE BET IS OVER, I'LL BE SENDING YOU TWO TO A HEARING IN SIX . . .

Jez   Don't worry, you'll sneak under his nose if you come with us!

In a moment of magic **Jez** *makes a portal appear.*

Lucy   FIVE!

Jez   This portal will send you to your bedroom in just a few days from now! One step through it and you're safe!

Courtney   That's a portal and you're a wizard and Satan is speaking to us? And someone murders me soon!? And why? Do I get hate-crimed? Does some psychopath see me and—Do they find my body in one piece?

Lucy   FOUR!

Jez   We'll answer those questions / as soon as you leave through the portal. You've got to trust us!

Courtney   / Oh my God. The room is longer. I can't feel myself breathe!

Nox *runs to* **Courtney** *and hugs her.*

Nox   It's the pressure. Take three seconds to give me a big inhale (*as* **Courtney** *breathes*) . . . and out on "three." Three.

Courtney *breathes out on* **Nox**'s *count.*

Lucy   THREE!

Nox   Two.

Lucy   TWO!

Nox   One.

Lucy   ONE!

In a kaleidoscope of lights, sounds, and darkness **Nox** *tightly holds* **Courtney** *in an embrace. Eventually* **Courtney** *eases into the hug, both of their eyes are closed. Around the three of them appears the vibrant backdrop of Hell.*

Scene Seven

Flowing from the end of the previous scene, **Nox** *releases from the hug. Both* **Nox** *and* **Courtney** *are unaware of their surroundings or that* **Lucy** *and The* **Demon Chorus** *have danced onto stage.*

Nox   Courtney, you don't know it, but I've done . . . vile and . . . damnable things to you. I left your relationship in shambles, made you the ass of every joke, I even ended you. For no good reason. I just wanted what I thought you had. I don't expect you to forgive me but I'm going to be infinitely sorry.

Courtney   . . . that's a lot to throw at me.

Lucy (*grinning*)   WELCOME TO HELL!

Courtney *screams like a final girl in a horror movie.*

Lucy   This kid has some pipes! I planned on doing a Judge Judy homage and all that jazz but . . . I think I just heard a confession. Somebody's not fighting the guilty allegations. Take a seat!

Lucy *performs a moment of magic and* **Nox** *and* **Jez** *are seated by the* **Demon Chorus** *who hum something akin to the Law and Order theme song.*

Nox   What is this, produced by Dick Wolf?

Lucy   Wait, I recognize that sass. (*to* **Nox**) Are you Esther's kid? Huh, small universe. Your mom, she was . . . a magic kinda girl. / AWOOGA AWOOGA! WOOF WOOF!

Demon Chorus   / (*adlibbed*) Her milkshakes bring all the demons to the yard! HUMMINAH HUMMINAH! Call me Rosemary's Baby, because I wanna be inside of her! Pitchfork me, mommy! Boi yoi yoing!

Lucy (*abruptly*)   How's she doing? Holding up well, I bet. She talks about me, right?

Nox   She became an alcoholic and we live on the edge of poverty.

Lucy   As I was saying, you confessed to murder. So, you're guilty and lost the bet. Whomp, whomp. But because you are my daughter, you little Princess of Hell nepo baby, I'll give you a choice.

Lucy *performs a moment of magic and a portal to earth appears.* **Gwen** *steps out of it.*

Nox   Gwen!

Gwen   Nox!

Nox   Whatever the choice is, it's Gwen! I choose her! (*to* **Gwen**.) I never chose you enough till now but it's you, all you, I'll always want you

Lucy   Aw, cute. Let's put a pin in that. Onto the winner of the bet: m'boy, Jez. You deserve your reward. I hereby permanently exchange your demonality for mortality.

Lucy *performs a moment of magic and* **Jez** *is turned into a human.*

Lucy   You're a real boy now, kiddo . . . You're welcome.

Lucy *kills* **Jez** *without using magic.*

Nox (*rushing to* **Jez**)   JEEEEEZ! WHY WOULD YOU DO THAT!? HE'S YOUR SON!?

Lucy   If you love 'em, you gotta let 'em go.

Nox   JEZ! WHY'D YOU KILL JEZ NOW? HIS WHOLE GOAL WAS TO LIVE LIFE AS A HUMAN, A GOOD HUMAN, AND THEN DIE! YOU JUST KILLED HIM BEFORE HE COULD EVER DO ANYTHING GOOD!

Lucy   But I thought he . . . Mmm he did tell me that. Maybe I . . . am a bad listener?

Nox   THERE HAS TO BE SOMETHING I CAN DO TO SAVE HIM! PLEASE!

Lucy   Oh, well I guess you can make your choice here. You could keep your girl, your magic, your life. OR you can save my favorite son. But you can only trade a soul for a soul. Them's the breaks, kid. If you still want a hero's ending, say these words: "Lucy, I want to make a deal: exchange Jez's life for mine." But be warned, there's no take-backsies. So what will it be?

Nox *crosses to* **Jez**, *considering her options.* **Nox** *bends over the body.*

Nox   Goodbye, best friend.

Nox *slowly walks towards the portal where* **Gwen** *stands, but* **Nox** *can't meet her gaze. After a moment of clarity,* **Nox** *charges to* **Lucy**.

Nox   Lucy. I want to make a deal, exchange Jez's life for mine. I want to die of exhaustion.

Lucy *performs a moment of magic and* **Nox** *dies from exhaustion.* **Gwen** *wails.*

Gwen   NOOOOOOOOOX!

Jez *suddenly rises, gasping for air.*

Lucy   JEZ! Welcome back, my magical and favorite son.

Jez (*genuinely touched*)   Pops, you . . . You killed me. I don't know what to say.

Lucy   For you, m'boy, I did it for you.

Gwen   LUCY—

Lucy   We're in the middle of something here?

Gwen   I don't know how to live if Nox isn't alive. I'd like to make a deal, Nox's life in exchange for mine.

Lucy   You've got to be—

Gwen   Suffocate me.

Lucy *performs a moment of magic and* **Gwen** *dies from suffocation.* **Nox** *suddenly rises, gasping for air.*

Nox   I was here and then . . . NOOOOOOOOOOOOOOOOOOO! GWEEEEEEN!

Lucy   Alright, there was a few wrinkles to iron out, but—

Courtney   Lucy!

Lucy   For my cousin's sake, don't you say it.

Courtney   I don't belong in this group or this time. They love each other so much and I could see them (*subtly cuing the two*) creating an endless loop of sacrifices for each other! (*to* **Lucy**) I don't want that, so I'm breaking this cycle. I'd like to make a deal, exchange Gwen's life for mine.

Lucy   You've got to be—

Courtney   Drowning.

Lucy *performs a moment of magic and* **Courtney** *drowns.* **Gwen** *suddenly rises, gasping for air.*

Lucy   Alright, is EVERYONE HAPPY?

Jez   Father.

Lucy *takes out his rainbow flask and downs it all.*

Lucy   WHAT!?

Jez   These kids haven't lived for even a quarter of their lives. I'm older than the earth itself. I'd like to make a deal, exchange Courtney's life for mine. Burn me alive.

Lucy *performs a moment of magic and* **Jez** *is burned alive.* **Courtney** *suddenly rises, gasping for air. What follows is a series of moments of magic, flowing montage-esque in and out of each other. Upbeat music plays.*

Nox   LUCY! SEVERE ALLERGIC REACTION TO PEANUTS!

Lucy *performs a moment of magic and* **Nox** *has a severe allergic reaction to peanuts.* **Jez** *suddenly rises, gasping for air.*

Gwen   LUCY! SWALLOWED BY AN ANACONDA!

Lucy *performs a moment of magic and* **Gwen** *is swallowed by an anaconda.* **Nox** *suddenly rises, gasping for air.*

Courtney   LUCY! STABBED IN THE BACK!

Lucy performs a moment of magic and **Courtney** is stabbed in the back. **Gwen** suddenly rises, gasping for air.

Jez   LUCY! STABBED IN THE FRONT!

Lucy *performs a moment of magic and* **Jez** *is stabbed in the front.* **Courtney** *suddenly rises, gasping for air.*

Nox   LUCY! PAPER CUT TO DEATH!

Lucy *performs a moment of magic,* **Nox** *is paper cut to death.* **Jez** *suddenly rises, gasping for air.*

Gwen   LUCY! STICKING A KNIFE IN THE TOASTER!

Lucy *performs a moment of magic and* **Gwen** *dies from sticking a knife in the toaster.* **Nox** *suddenly rises, gasping for air.*

Courtney   LUCY! CRUSHED BY A FALLING PIANO!

Lucy *performs a moment of magic and* **Courtney** *is crushed by a piano.* **Gwen** *suddenly rises, gasping for air.*

Jez   LUCY! CRUSHED BY A FALLING COPY OF *INFINITE JEST*!

Lucy *performs a moment of magic and* **Jez** *is crushed by Infinite Jest.* **Courtney** *suddenly rises, gasping for air.*

Nox   LUCY! SCARED TO DEATH!

Lucy *performs a moment of magic and* **Nox** *is scared to death.* **Jez** *suddenly rises, gasping for air.*

Gwen   LUCY! BORED TO DEATH.

Lucy *performs a moment of magic and* **Gwen** *is bored to death.* **Nox** *suddenly rises gasping for air.*

Courtney   LUCY! JUGGLING PORCUPINES!

Lucy *performs a moment of magic and* **Courtney** *dies from juggling Porcupines.* **Gwen** *suddenly rises, gasping for air.*

Jez   LUCY! GUILLOTINED BY THE BOURGEOISIE!

Lucy *performs a moment of magic and* **Jez** *gets guillotined by the bourgeoisie.* **Courtney** *suddenly rises, gasping for air.*

Nox   LUCY! FALLING DOWN FOURTEEN FLIGHTS OF STAIRS!

Lucy *performs a moment of magic and* **Nox** *falls down fourteen flights of stairs.* **Jez** *suddenly rises, gasping for air.*

Gwen   LUCY! NATURAL CAUSES!

Lucy *performs a moment of magic and* **Gwen** *dies of natural causes.* **Nox** *suddenly rises, gasping for air.*

Courtney   LUCY! BREASTFEEDING A SNAPPING TURTLE!

Lucy *performs a moment of magic and* **Courtney** *unsuccessfully breastfeeds a snapping turtle.* **Gwen** *suddenly rises, gasping for air.*

Jez   LUCY! TRAPPED INSIDE AN ANGRY 8-YEAR-OLD'S BIRTHDAY PINATA AND BEAT TO DEATH!

Lucy *performs a moment of magic and* **Jez** *is trapped inside an angry 8-year-old's pinata and is beaten to death.* **Courtney** *suddenly rises, gasping for air.*

Lucy   WAAAAAIIIIT! Did I just kill m'boy five times?

Demon Chorus   SIX TIMES, THE MAGIC NUMBER!

Lucy (*as the true demonic Prince of Darkness*)   THIS IS TOO SILLY! THIS IS FAR TOO SILLY!

In a moment of magic, **Lucy** *kills* **Nox**, **Gwen**, *and* **Courtney**. *All four are on the floor.*

Lucy (*clearing his throat*)   Whew . . . you could win *Drag Race* with all of these death drops.

Demon Chorus   IF EVERYONE'S ALIVE, IT MEANS LESS WORK AT THE TIME TRAVELER'S CONTINGENCIES CONTINGENT!

Fear   A LOT LESS OF MIDDLE MANAGEMENT!

Hate   FEWER PAPER JAMS!

Shame   FEWER CRYSTAL BALL MEETINGS THAT COULD'VE BEEN AN EMAIL!

Demon Chorus   LESS WORK AND MORE TIME FOR ZADDY TO COME OUT AND PLAY!

Lucy   Aaaaaaaah, okay! I know what you're doing but . . . Lucy-Wucy likey!

In a moment of magic **Lucy** *resurrects them.*

Lucy   You four, you can stop breathing so heavily! You sound like an orgy I had in '67. NOW GET UP AND LISTEN TO WHAT I HAVE TO SAY! I pronounce a new ruling! You can keep your magic, your humanity, your life, your whatever the hell you want. On one condition . . . for the rest of your churlish lives, you stay the hell away from me. For all that is unholy, I don't want to see you until you're dead! So please, walk through the portal back to earth, and kindly piss off.

Gwen *and* **Courtney** *exit through the portal.* **Nox** *watches* **Jez**, *"so this is my family now?"*

Jez Hey, pops? I love Gabriel but I'm not ready for Heaven yet. I just don't know how to be a good person right now. Do you think I could stay with you, in hell, as a demon?

Lucy Of course, n'boy.

Lucy *performs a moment of magic and* **Jez** *is a demon again.*

Lucy I promise I'll give you more space this go-round, I'll be less of a HELLicopter parent.

Jez I've missed your stupid dad jokes and stories of your sexual escapades!

Jez *hugs* **Lucy**. **Nox** *starts to leave through the portal.*

Lucy Not yet, m'girl, no, no, no. You still lost the bet. Your soul will one day be mine. And that day always comes sooner than you'd hope . . . Are you sure you couldn't swing by for a weekend? I just really dig your vibe and we have so much Daddy Daughter bonding to do!

Nox I'm good, thanks.

Lucy HEY . . . Maybe not today, maybe not tomorrow, but soon, and for the rest of eternity.

Jez Goodbye for now, sister.

Nox *walks through the portal back to earth.*

Scene Eight

Nox *and* **Gwen** *are in* **Nox**'s *room, the sun has just risen. Beside* **Gwen** *is a packed backpack, packed duffle bag, and large opened suitcase on the floor.* **Gwen** *folds some clothes and puts them into the suitcase.*

Gwen I still need to get my Mister Fluffykins. Saved him for last so he wouldn't get squished.

Nox *nods, opens a portal in a moment of magic, steps through it, and returns with a beloved plushie rabbit in hand. The portal disappears.* **Nox** *gives* **Gwen** *the rabbit who is fiercely hugged before being placed in the suitcase.* **Nox** *zips the suitcase.*

Gwen Thanks. And thank you, seriously, for letting me crash here these past couple of days.

Nox Yeah, of course! I wasn't going to send you home. I'm not . . . heartless . . . So, you're making it out of Winstonrock. Congratulations by the way. How are you feeling about going to the gay-paradise of Vermont?

Gwen Um, it's a change for sure. It's a pretty affirming place which is so different and amazing. My uncle is so gay, like GAY gay, like he was almost on *Project Runway* season four type gay. And we're working on getting my brother moved in with us, but that's a whole other process.

Nox   I can only imagine. At least Vermont is nice in the fall, and not a wasteland like it is here.

Gwen   Yeah, it's great but . . .

Nox   But?

Gwen   But I've been on the apps, messaging a guy. He lives in the area. Callum is really sweet. Actually, not really "bro-y" at all.

Nox   That's . . . Wow. Callum . . . Callum, I hardly know 'em!

Gwen   Hehe, yeah. I should get my ride to the airport.

Gwen *takes out her phone and orders a ride.*

Nox   Yeah. Of course . . . No. Can I say something, really quick? At the very start of everything you asked me to reassure you that gay people aren't in Hell. I should have held you and said, "no, of course they aren't, my little sheepheart." Turns out they are but it's a disco-themed, interdimensional, safe-haven, but I still should have said no at the time. I think you could still get into Heaven, if that's what you really want. You save every insect you find in my room, there isn't a single dog you've met who hasn't received scratches behind the ear, and it's always your mission to treat people like adults . . . even when they're acting like children. So you've got nothing to worry about, sheepheart. Just be your fabulous self, and that's—

A notification on **Gwen***'s phone.*

Gwen   Sorry, so sorry, my Uber driver just canceled . . . You were saying.

Nox   I'm just saying that hell isn't a wrong or bad place. You'd be accepted with open arms, you'd be celebrated all day every day, and . . . they'd love you for you down there, not because you follow the rules or . . . whatever. Some people might even say it's even the better option. I don't know, if you like Callum and you want him in your life, good. Great! I'm genuinely happy for you. If not, don't feel like you need him so the rest of your life and afterlife will be perfect. You shouldn't have to hide your queerness from God or anybody. You shouldn't stop yourself from being another girl's girlfriend, just because you also happen to be a girl. Gwen Sunday, it's a special thing to be loved by someone as great as you. I'm sorry that I wasn't that great in return.

Gwen   I think I still love you. I'm not sure I ever won't, but I have to try . . . Because I'm not sure you loved me as much as you said you did. When wasn't I by your side whenever you needed me? I'm genuinely asking, Nox. When? . . . I remember when you weren't by mine, distinctly. I literally had nowhere else to go except for wherever the wind blew me. And I will always love you more than the earth itself but that was unforgivable and I pray to God you never forget it . . . But God also knows I'd be lying if I said I was a perfect partner. I always saw you as this . . . dangerous thing that was so outside of my world that every time I was with you it felt like I was escaping mine. I feel like a fake gay because I just am constantly filled with this sinking feeling of dread and doubt . . . That's not easy for you to love. I hate myself, I think . . . And you don't deserve being around that when you're so effortlessly and boldly yourself. Why do I fall more and more in love with you with every goodbye?

Nox   There are a lot of things I regret about the past few days, but the one thing I'll never regret is wanting to dance with you at the winter formal.

Gwen   . . . I was really looking forward to it, too.

Nox *performs a moment of magic and a slow song plays.* **Nox** *offers a hand to* **Gwen**, *who almost takes it but hesitates.*

Gwen   I want to dance with you, but I don't want to be touched right now.

Nox *nods, scooting back a few feet, holding her arms out as if to hold* **Gwen**'s *waist.* **Gwen** *does the same, arms up as it rests on* **Nox**'s *shoulders. The two slow dance with a distance between them.* **Nox** *performs a moment of magic to make it feel like prom. Maybe there's a disco ball, or the lights dim, or* **Nox** *and* **Gwen** *suddenly wear matching flowers and prom dresses. Eventually* **Gwen** *changes her mind, and the two dance closely together. The two's eyes are locked as they sway . . . until* **Nox** *breaks away from the slow dance to do a flashy solo piece of her own, ignoring* **Gwen**. **Gwen** *watches* **Nox** *dance at first in anger, but then wonder. It dawns on* **Gwen** *that, as magical as* **Nox** *can be, those moments of magic aren't worth being* **Nox**'s *second love.* **Gwen** *gathers her bags, breathes it all in one last time, and then leaves. When* **Nox** *finally finishes her solo, she looks around to find an empty room.*

Nox   Gwen?

Nox *runs offstage searching and calling for her.*

Nox   GWEN? GWEN? GWEN!

Nox *re-enters her room alone, and crumples on the floor. She's absolutely broken down.*

Nox (*sobbing more than speaking*)   GWEN! PLEASE! I'M SO SORRY! I'LL DO IT ALL SO DIFFERENTLY. I WOULD. I WILL! I'LL GO BACK IN TIME

Nox *starts a moment of magic but is interrupted by* **Esther** *entering.*

Esther   Knock-ety knock knock! I heard music and screaming thought you might like a happy face breakfast. Would you like me to start that, honeynut?

Nox *performs a moment of magic and* **Esther** *becomes who she used to be before she met* **Lucy**.

Esther   Oh. Oh my–Aaaaaah, my head. (*looking down at herself*) Why am I wearing a girdle? (*Looking at* **Nox**.) Are you . . . Are you my kid? You've gotten older.

Nox   I am your kid, Mother . . . You've actually gotten younger.

Esther   What happened to your room? What happened to the bed, and the furniture, and . . .

Nox   I had to sell it. Way long ago. Everything.

Esther I'm sorry . . . I . . . I don't remember that, I'm sorry . . . I do remember what heartbreak looks like and, you, you look like it. You need a hug?

Nox No . . . I'm fine. But . . . can you stay this time? Please. I've missed having a mother.

Esther Of course I will. But you gotta know . . . I was scared then and I'm even more scared now that you're grown . . . Because I don't really know how to be a mother. Never been one.

Nox That's alright. I've never been a daughter.

Esther What's your name, kid?

Nox I was going by Nox, but I want to change it to Audrey.

Esther Audrey. Okay, Audrey. Let's start by getting you some furniture, mascara that won't run down your face, and some good food. Then maybe we can get me outta . . . whatever the hell this is. I don't know why . . . but I feel like I haven't been a good mother.

Audrey I haven't been a good person this week. Maybe we can figure it out together?

Audrey *extends her arms, trying to initiate a hug. Something she hasn't done in a long time with her mother.* **Esther** *gives a slight nod.* **Audrey** *hugs* **Esther** *who is taken aback but accepts it just as she does her kid.* **Esther** *strokes* **Audrey**'*s hair as* **Audrey** *cries into* **Esther**'*s shoulder. A little bit of sorrow, a little bit of joy.*

FADE OUT.

END OF PLAY.

"Bickering with the Bad and Banal: Staging t4t Interregnums"

Ryan Adelsheim

I was on the phone with a trans friend shortly before I drafted this introduction, agonizing about a new trans crush (well, we were sending voice notes back and forth instead of calling, a kind of digital distancing that seems apt for a discussion of Jessica Scott's *t4t*). As we cycled through this particular looping anxiety, my friend, also a talented playwright, reflected: "whenever we meet someone who we're really into who is trans, there are just so many flavors of what that person could be in our lives . . . are you my friend? Am I attracted to you? Do I want to be you? Are there parts of you that I admire because I want them in myself?" The inherent relationality and shared affect of these questions are helpful reminders that t4t relationships, both beautiful and agonizing, among friends, lovers, and long-time partners, are not static. I bring these familiar questions into conversation with Scott's *t4t*, a play which asks us to consider whose voices we hear when we are our worst selves, and what t4t connections, crushes, and their attendant complications, porous boundaries, and crossed lines do in our world. She asks: how do we care for each other? How do we recover, together, from our own worst moments, our breaks? When is an ameliorative t4t connection not enough? When can these connections be a site of potential transformation?

Scott's play follows Lily as she manages the economic and social forces that make transition challenging; she is at a moment of crisis in her own emotional growth as she grapples with past relationships and her current isolation. Scott dramatizes Lily's constant inner-narrative with two embodiments of her consciousness: Visceral and Cerebral, who are fully present and "visually distinct from every other character" (146). Together, they haunt every scene of the play, their running commentary the endless noise inside Lily's head. Sometimes, like when Lily is high with a date, their language slips out through her mouth, but primarily they bicker without acknowledgement from Lily or the other characters, an extroverted manifestation of her combative, often cruel, inner world. When Lily's caring gay roommate Brian convinces her to try the t4t setting on Grindr to find connection, she plunges into an infatuation with Ciel, a transmasc, polyamorous, non-binary art student. They open Lily's world, bringing her from a cycle of despair into one of the unpredictable highs of romance, luring her out of her apartment and into the world where she encounters Ciel's partner Jamie, and Jamie's partner Grace, who also happens to be Lily's ex-fiancé. The complex network of relationships and harm, delight and despair, pull Lily's otherwise unremarkable life into a noisy break where her internal forces battle for control, and she develops an enfolded rage at both those who love her and the systems of trans antagonism.

In their 2022 *TSQ: Transgender Studies Quarterly* special issue, "The t4t Issue," editors Cameron Awkward-Rich and Hil Malatino give a helpful overview of the origins of the term t4t:

> T4t means, most basically, trans-for-trans. The term arose in the context of early 2000s Craigslist personals, working to both sequester trans folks from the categories of "m" and "w" and enable some kind of us to find one another for

hookups. However, while the term is linked to Craigslist, the overlapping things that it presently names—trans separatist social forms, trans x trans erotics, trans practices of mutual aid and emotional support—have been most robustly theorized within trans literature and other forms of cultural production that both predate and outlast the Craigslist personal. [. . .] What is obvious from such writing—as well as the term's origin—is that t4t resists idealization. T4t sex, desire, erotics, and social practices are nothing if not fraught, animated by tension and contradiction, riven by complex forms of triggering and retraumatization. Practices of t4t love, desire, connection, and support are simultaneously imperative and deeply difficult to cultivate and maintain.

(Awkward-Rich and Malatino 2022: 2–3)

Awkward-Rich and Malatino, in this issue and in their independent work, characterize t4t spaces (real and imagined) as holding the potential for radical re-worlding while being subject to the social inequities and antagonisms that facilitate and heighten bad trans feelings. In Scott's play, many of the possible valences of this definition of t4t come to the fore. Brian's t4t suggestion, for example, rides on the well-meaning assumption that trans connection might offer Lily some relief, following Malatino's argument that: "The hope is that, in community with one another, insulated—however temporarily—from cissexist modes of perception, some significant healing might be possible" (Malatino 2019: 654). Lily finds both: she is first plunged into the complex world of cis chasers—an ensemble of "cis people, mostly men, who fetishize trans bodies[. . .] all creepy in their own unique way," rife with transmisogyny, until she finds Ciel, a port in the storm and a conduit to an encounter with her past (146). Lily also finds that she must rely on t4t friendship and practices of care to facilitate her own survival. The social and relational elements of a t4t encounter—the ones that excavate past trauma and triggers, that hum on the edges of desire and friendship—make for a complex affective and theatrical space.

Part of the sociality of t4t relationships insists on a negotiation with what Malatino, in his book *Side Affects: On Being Trans and Feeling Bad* (2022), has called the "trans affective commons" a circulating and banal negativity that is bound by the affects that arise "in the face of relentless encounters with disposability" (Malatino 2022: 10). Attending to, even centering, these bad feelings—among them fatigue, numbness, envy, rage, and burnout—makes the systemic disposability trans people face visible and draws our attention to the "more or less shared affective orientations and habituations to relentlessly quotidian, hydra-headed forms of transantagonism" (Malatino 2022: 11). Two components of this definition work to clarify a kind of sociality trans people experience: first, is the commonality of these bad trans feelings and the cleaving of trans affective ranges from the expected dysphoria (despair)/euphoria (joy) dialectic for the individual trans subject. Lily's bad feelings in Scott's *t4t*, for example, are familiar rather than sensational, her life circumstances and experiences of negativity predictable. Malatino's definition of bad trans feelings also points to the larger social forces that structure trans antagonisms. In her recent book *A Short History of Trans Misogyny* (2024), Jules Gill-Peterson historicizes trans misogyny and trans feminization as a vector of colonial forces and explains how trans misogyny can be operationalized for and by the violence of the state. She roots her definition partially in sociality: "At the interpersonal scale, trans misogyny testifies to the uncomfortable thickness of social bonds across hierarchies of gender, class, and race [. . .] It is felt as a fear of proximity. Trans femininity is too sociable, too connected to everyone—too exuberant about stigmatized femininity [. . .] But sociability can never be confined or blamed on one person in a relationship; it's impersonal, and it sticks to everyone" (Gill-Peterson 2024: 27). Gill-Peterson works with a social and political framework of trans femininity that reveals how its connective stigmatization touches everyone. By staging trans femininity within a queer network, *t4t* makes visible the personal negativity associated with surviving as a trans woman under American racial capitalism, the bad feelings, and the connective force of trans femininity to larger social structures and to each other.

In dramaturgy of trans work, we are only beginning to develop a tolerance for the staging of these bad trans feelings. Despite recent advances in trans theater developed explicitly for trans audiences, the mainstream appetite for "trans plays" allows for only a narrow sliver of narratives that circle around transphobia, untimely death, or alternately gender euphoria (see: Sylvan Oswald's recent essay "Towards A Trans Theater" for an eloquent rehearsal of some of the challenges facing trans writers). Often bad feelings are present, but they are sensationalized rather than banal, rendering trans characters flat or only consumed with their transness. Simultaneously, our rote desire and expectation for Aristotelian catharsis and relatable naturalism diminishes our tolerance for affective variance (Oswald 2024: 481). Scott tries to solve this tension with a version of narrative realism that allows the drama to live in the realm of the emotional and psychological, using her small chorus (Cerebral and Visceral) to externalize internal thought patterns. The inclusion of Malatino's bad trans feelings onstage might also ask for a kind of engagement with what Jacob Gallagher-Ross has coined the "theaters of the everyday." An aesthetic and democratic grouping that he suggests holds the "persistent imperative to look to the small, abject, and unnoticed aspects of daily life" (Gallagher-Ross 2018: 32). His study pays particular attention to the ways that queer work makes the everyday strange and pliable. When translated into a trans context, this everyday becomes a surprising representation of trans life that, as Kadji Amin has demanded in "Whither Trans Studies," focuses on the simple trans life being enough, to the ordinary and abject as worthy of our attention (Amin 2023: 56–57). Scott seems to answer this call, drawing our attention to Lily's life as worthy of stage space, as enough.

Cameron Awkward-Rich, in his book *The Terrible We: Thinking with Trans Maladjustment* (2022), sets out a framework for thinking with bad trans feelings that identifies trans life under racial capitalism as a kind of "stuckness, waiting, 'lag time,' and recurrent" as he thinks with a trans rage and maladjustment that is less "politically enabling" (Awkward-Rich 2022: 8). This stuckness is endemic to what Malatino has identified as a particular kind of trans time in the interregnum that holds "crucial and transformative movements between past and future, between the regime of what was and the promise of what might be. [. . .] It is a kind of nowness that shuttles transversally between different imaginaries of pasts and futures and remains malleable and differentially molded by these imaginaries"(Malatino 2022: 32). An experience of trans time is particularly challenging to stage—it demands a patience for the banal and a flexible relationship to time that requires technologies, like Jack Pryor's time slips, that allow "normative conceptions of time fail, or fall away, and the spectator or artist [to] experience an alternative, or queer, temporality" (Pryor 2017: 9). In Scott's *t4t,* we meet Lily amidst the swirl of these bad trans feelings, in a period of extended stuckness and interregnum; she has been repeatedly misgendered at work (Target) and has been drinking and smoking while barely leaving the apartment. She explodes at her roommate Brian, refusing the modicum of care she is offered: "Why try? You know I'm going to kill myself in a couple years at fucking best so why in the living hell are you wasting your energy on someone who won't be around long enough to use it? Are you really that fucking stupid?" (151). Lily experiences a flush of rage, one that pushes Brian away, and that mirrors, with her threat (or is it an expectation?) of suicide, what Malatino has theorized as a break. He works to untangle the various operations of rage in trans life, suggesting that "We feel rage and are transformed by rage whenever we sense, or are reminded that the networks we rely on for survival are inimical to such survival. This sense precipitates loneliness, the feeling of being ontologically adrift, unmoored, homeless; it also, for many of us, produces suicidality or precedes suicide" (Malatino 2022: 110). Lily's experience, the daily antagonism she feels and is unable to cope with, is part of what reveals the tension between the networks she needs and their threat—in this moment of rage, we momentarily slip into feeling her experience of the interregnum. Malatino goes on to examine the prevalence of suicide within trans populations, largely tied to the "interpersonal, institutional, and systemic forces of discrimination" we face, and the tenuous and dangerous possibilities that such breaks, sparked by rage, engender:

> Sometimes, a break is followed by a suicide; but often, a break is a moment that enables a more livable life to be realized. [. . .] Breaks scare us, and others, for that reason. But our survival is radically dependent on these others; what happens during and after a break depends on the communal uptake such breaks receive, how they are witnessed and understood.
>
> (Malatino 2022: 111)

Returning us to the tension of t4t survival, which here hinges on the need to be witnessed and embraced, informs the complicated relationality coursing through Scott's play. Though much of the conflict is between Cerebral, Visceral, and Lily's own actions, she is not the only trans person in this world, and her encounters with Ciel (who holds their own religious trauma) and Grace (Lily's ex who is also on their own path of repair and gender self-actualization) put into relief just how challenging t4t relationships are, how much baggage they hold, and how witnessing and understanding are their own affective and ameliorative practices. Malatino suggests that rage and its communal recovery teaches us about survival and endurance, and develops a resilience that is not about "bouncing back, or about moving forward, but rather a communal alchemical mutation of pain into possibility" that demands its own care network (Malatino 2022: 123). Scott dramatizes the internal experience of these bad feelings, the outward, or performed, sequential expressions of rage, the break of collapse, and the new possibilities opened by descent. The play ends with small moments of slow repair—allowing Brian to witness and care for her, an apology and a boundary with Grace, the suggestion of friendship with Ciel, the refusal of a drink—that reform and reimagine these t4t connections. Scott shows the potential t4t relations in all their manifestations: ex-fiancés go from screaming conflict to a quiet coexistence; a rushing crush and fling to friendship; conflicted roommates to family; the characterization of internal voices to other partygoers. Through *t4t*, Scott gives us an example of what staging the banal feelings of transition, a holding within a break, the quieting of a dangerous internal monologue, might have to offer the theater, how we can begin to slip away from sensationalized trans bodies and instead allow our stories of quiet resilience to be enough.

References

Amin, Kadji. 2023. "Whither Trans Studies?: A Field at a Crossroads." *TSQ: Transgender Studies Quarterly* 10 (1): 54–58. https://doi.org/10.1215/23289252-10273224.

Awkward-Rich, Cameron. 2022. *The Terrible We: Thinking with Trans Maladjustment*. Duke University Press.

Awkward-Rich, Cameron, and Hil Malatino. 2022. "Meanwhile, T4t." *TSQ: Transgender Studies Quarterly* 9 (1): 1–8. https://doi.org/10.1215/23289252-9475467.

Gallagher-Ross, Jacob. 2018. *Theaters of the Everyday: Aesthetic Democracy on the American Stage*. Northwestern University Press.

Gill-Peterson, Jules. 2024. *A Short History of Trans Misogyny*. New York: Verso.

Malatino, Hil. 2019. "Future Fatigue: Trans Intimacies and Trans Presents (or How to Survive the Interregnum)." *TSQ: Transgender Studies Quarterly* 6 (4): 635–58. https://doi.org/10.1215/23289252-7771796.

——. 2022. *Side Affects: On Being Trans and Feeling Bad*. Minneapolis: University of Minnesota Press.

Oswald, Sylvan. 2024. "Towards a Trans Theatre." In *The Methuen Drama Handbook of Gender and Theatre*, edited by Sean Metzger and Roberta Mock, 475–89. New York: Methuen Drama.

Pankratz, J.C. Personal Communication. December 27, 2024.

Pryor, Jack I. 2017. *Time Slips: Queer Temporalities, Contemporary Performance, and the Hole of History*. Northwestern University Press.

t4t

Jessica Scott

Cast of Characters

Lily:	24 years old, Target employee, trans woman.
Visceral:	Aspect of Lily's consciousness representing raw emotion, physicality, and instinct.
Cerebral:	Aspect of Lily's consciousness representing logic, reason, and knowledge.
Ciel:	(pronounced see-ell) 22 years old, transmasc nonbinary art student, self-described genderfuck.
Brian:	26 years old, Lily's roommate, average looking cis gay man.
Twink/Kylan:	20-something, guy Brian picked up at a club a while back, cis gay man. Waiter at Waffle House.
Grace:	24 years old, AFAB nonbinary person, was engaged to Lily pre-transition.
Jaime:	23 years old, trans man. Works out a lot. Partnered with Ciel and Grace.
Chasers:	Several cis people, mostly men, who fetishize trans bodies. Varying body types, all creepy in their own unique way. Some can be VO. Need at least 4-5, more would only help.

Casting Policy

Trans characters must be played by trans actors and cis characters by cis actors. **Cerebral** and **Visceral** could be anyone.

Setting

The sad side of a college town. August.

Note

Cerebral and Visceral are visually distinct from every other character. No character aside from Lily acknowledges them at all for the majority of the play.

Scene 1

Setting: **Lily's** *apartment. The apartment and the furniture in it are visibly cheap, but with effort clearly put in to make the most of the space. There is a couch with coffee table in front center stage facing downstage, and a small table with a few chairs with some wilting lilies in old liquor bottles. There is a lamp on one side of the couch, and there is a door on the right edge of the stage. A trans pride flag and a progress pride flag, each without the creases ironed out, hang vertically from the back wall.*

At Rise: *Keys are heard jingling a bit and unlocking a door as the lights come up.* **Lily** *enters through the door in a target uniform, looking beaten down by life. She stands just inside the door for a moment and a breath. As she closes the door,* **Cerebral** *and* **Visceral** *step through after her.*

Cerebral   It was the stubble that did it.

Visceral   Fucking obviously. Of course I'm going to get sir'd when I can't even put the minimum effort in to be a woman and shave.

Cerebral   This is why I need to wear a mask to work. There have only been 2 times that I've ever been clocked at work with one–

Visceral   Because my face should be covered up at all times to protect the general public. Fuck I need a smoke right now.

Cerebral   I shouldn't, I told Brian I'd quit.

Visceral   I need to burn this day out of my brain and I don't need him getting pissy about me drinking again.

Cerebral   I already bought them, may as well. I'm too broke to waste money.

Lily *lights a cigarette and starts to smoke.*

Visceral   Ughhhhhh, I needed this. Finally fucking feel something.

Cerebral   It won't last.

Visceral   Doesn't matter. Not empty now.

Cerebral   Yeah . . .

Beat. **Lily** *looks to* **Cerebral**

Lily   Why am I like this?

Cerebral   Trauma, mainly.

Visceral   Nah, that's bullshit. My parent's didn't fuck me up this much.

Cerebral   Being born wrong.

Visceral   Not just that. I'm a stupid hon who thinks it can convincingly skinwalk as a woman. Anyone that sees me knows exactly what I am and the ones that prop up my delusions and pretend to not be disgusted just don't want the statistics to get worse.

Silence hangs in the air as **Lily** *begins to visibly unravel. After the beginnings of a breakdown, a door is heard opening.*

Cerebral   Pull it together.

Visceral   Hide what you are.

Twink *enters.*

Twink (*smiley*)   Oh hey, you must be Lily. Brian said you wouldn't be back yet. I'm/

Visceral   \I don't care.

Lily   Hi. Yeah, I left early.

Twink   You doing alright hun?

Visceral   As I said, a hon.

Lily   I'm fine.

Twink   You sure? You look like you're going through it.

Lily   I'm ok. Thanks.

Twink   Well, alright, I got work to get to. Have a good night sweetheart.

Lily   You too.

Twink *leaves through the door.*

Lily   Thank god.

Visceral   I just can't deal with some fucking twink right now.

Beat. The door down the hall opens again.

Cerebral   Shit, gotta get rid of this or he won't leave me alone.

Lily *puts out and tosses the cigarette.* **Brian** *enters.*

Brian   Oh, you're home early. Didn't hear you come in.

Lily   It's fine. Have fun?

Brian   I mean, yeah. Did you see the ass on him?

Lily   Kinda, wasn't really paying attention to that.

Brian   Well, that thing was crazy enough that Damian made me chase him down across the dance floor to make sure at least one of us got his number.

Lily   Wish mine existed enough to get attention.

Brian   Hey, hormone stuff takes time, right? It'll happen.

Lily   I'm like a year and a half in already. Most changes should have already happened. I'm never gonna make it.

Brian   Jesus Lily, you need to stop with that talk. I can tell you from the neutral perspective of someone not into women that you're pretty. Doll yourself up and touch grass and you'd be drowning in it. That offer to introduce you to people is still open, you know.

Lily   No, no, it's alright. I don't think your type of crowd would really like me.

Cerebral   And I am empirically ugly and mannish. Lying to me doesn't help.

Beat.

Brian (*sniffs air*)   Were you smoking?

Cerebral   I should have thought of the smell.

Brian   C'mon girl, what happened?

Lily   Just . . . rough day.

Brian *sits with her.*

Brian   Wanna talk about it?

Visceral   No.

Cerebral   If I don't talk I'm going to do something stupid. Not again, I promised.

Visceral   As if my word means anything.

Lily   I don't know. Got misgendered a couple times today. Double shift. It's nothing, I'm just tired.

Visceral   Case in point.

Brian   I'm sorry about that. I know that things have been rough lately.

Visceral   Oh, you don't know fucking anything. You aren't in the most hated group on the fucking planet. You don't have a body doomed from birth and ruined by puberty. You don't have to save up thousands of dollars over the course of years to have a surgery that will finally let you feel like a person.
You don't hate every fiber of your being.
You actually have people who love you.

Brian   Do you want a hug?

Cerebral   It will make him feel better.

Lily *nods, they hug.*

Brian (*continuing to hold her*)   I don't know how else I can help you at this point. Are you still going to therapy?

Lily   Haven't in a bit. Can't find any cheap enough. My last one started wanting to talk about my "paraphilias" way too much for comfort.

The hug ends.

Brian   Gross. How do those people end up working in mental health?

Lily   He was right about me being AGP though–

Brian   Oh my god shut the fuck up about that! I hate that I even know what that is because of you.

Cerebral   Sorry for keeping you informed.

Brian   Do you think that maybe it's time you try to meet someone new? I mean it's been a long time since everything with Grace–

Visceral   When she broke me forever.

Brian   Like I get how hard it all is. Well, I don't know ALL of it, but I see it at least. You're hurting from isolating yourself so much. And at least in my experience and especially from everything I've seen of you since I moved in I think that . . .

Brian *continues to speak visually but it is not audible.*

Cerebral   Of course he would make this sort of suggestion, he has an easy time with dating. He's confident, a top, and not absolutely horrifying looking, so he's rolling in a sea of desperate twinks.

Visceral   Meanwhile I am vile, inside and out. Incapable of loving and being loved.

Brian   . . . so what do you think? I know how it sounds but are you up to give it a shot at least?

Cerebral   What did he say? I really don't need to show him how bad a friend I am right now.

Lily   Uh sure.

Brian   Ok. (*shows her his phone*) So yeah, look. Like 90% of this thing is horny dudes looking to catch a dick or 50 year-olds with a foot fetish, but there's a good amount of trans people on here too. You can put a t4t filter on to find the ones looking for other trans people.

Cerebral   Oh my god he's trying to get me on Grindr.

Lily   I'm not sure if this is–

Brian   Hey, you said you would at least give this a shot.

Cerebral   Fucking ADHD.

Lily   I don't know. I don't even really know other trans people other than the ones I used to talk with over Discord. Making a new connection sounds like a lot right now.

Brian   Listen, I keep hearing from Moss, Kai, Gwen, like every fucking trans person I know that t4t is the greatest shit ever. This is a way to meet people for that. Even if you don't date you might make a friend or two on there. Someone that might actually get you to fucking do something when you're not working other than spiraling and drinking yourself unconscious.

Visceral   A drink would be *really* good right about now.

Lily   I don't know what getting with another trans person would even do. I feel like I'd just make things worse for them and drag them down with me–

Brian   Oh just shut the fuck up. I want you to get better and I'm doing what I can to help out but at some point you have to be willing to help yourself. I don't fucking see you trying anything. If you don't then what the hell am I even doing?

Lily   Yeah. What are you doing? Why try? You know I'm going to kill myself in a couple years at fucking best so why in the living hell are you wasting your energy on someone who won't be around long enough to use it? Are you really that fucking stupid? If you are then what reason do I even have to listen to you? You can just go and be stupid and happy fucking your stupid little rave boys and be rid of the crazy tranny who is the only disruption to you getting to enjoy being a stupid, mediocre fucking faggot.

Beat.

Brian   Fuck it, do whatever the hell you want. It's your life. I'm sorry for giving a shit.

Brian *exits.* **Lily** *lights up another cigarette.*

Cerebral   He wants to keep me alive. He'd feel guilty if he didn't try.

Lights begin to dim.

Lily   Why does he pretend like he cares?

Cerebral   He's not pretending. He's trying his best.

The only visible light now is the cigarette.

Visceral   He won't anymore, not after that.

The cigarette goes out.

Visceral   Fuck it, where'd he hide that bottle?

Scene 2

Setting: *The inhospitable expanse that is Grindr. Set empty aside from the couch and coffee table facing downstage. Several hours later.*

At Rise: *Low light on* **Lily** *sitting on the couch, looking at her phone and sipping straight from a bottle of vodka. She has not and will not sleep tonight.* **Visceral** *and* **Cerebral** *sit on either side of her, watching.*

Lily   What kind of pictures are you supposed to put on one of these? Like are creeps gonna start recognizing me in public?

Cerebral   I should crop my face out of it.

Visceral   Yeah, there's a chance someone will find me attractive then.

Cerebral   Alright, now the bio. Needs to be well put together.

Lily   Looking to meet other trans people and see what happens, up for whatever, winky face.

Visceral   That's cringy as fuck, get rid of the winky face.

Lily   Ok, let's make it: up for whatever, exclamation point.

Visceral   Desperate.

Cerebral   Just do no punctuation and go. That's a neutral approach that won't hurt my chances.

Lily   Alright, done. Now to just filter by trans . . .

The sound of a foghorn blasts her back as the **Chasers** *begin to come in stampedes, shrouded in shadow. They're gone almost as soon as they arrive but they just keep coming rapid-fire.*

Chaser   I'd love to watch you shit and piss.

Chaser   Can you cuck me with my gf?

Chaser   I'm married and wanna keep things on the DL, can you host?

Chaser   I really really want to suck you off.

Chaser   I bet your cock's bigger than mine, take a look.

Chaser   I've been looking to meet other crossdressers in the area . . .

Chaser   Didn't I rape you before?

Chaser   I could transition if that's all you're looking for.

Chaser   I've been wanting to experiment with a transvestite . . .

Chaser   Please please please can I suck your toes goddess?

Chaser   You're such a good sissy slut, I bet your cute little cock is just dripp–

Lily   AAAAAHHHHHHH! FUCK!

Lily *drops the phone.*

Cerebral   What was I thinking? Those horny shits aren't going to read a bio.

Visceral   THAT'S what Brian thought would help me???

Lily   But on the other hand . . . people thought I was hot.

Visceral   So much attention!

Cerebral   Still though. So gross.

Visceral   Exactly what I deserve to feel.

Cerebral   Win-win?

Visceral   Win-win.

Lily *picks the phone back up and starts scrolling intently. A murmur of chaser-speak accelerates faster and faster, blurring into itself until it's entirely indiscernible what is being said. It slams to a stop as a spotlight suddenly illuminates* **Ciel.**

Ciel   Hey there sweets, what are you looking for on here?

Cerebral   That's. Um. I really like their sense of styl–

Visceral   I want them to do strange and terrible things to me.

Lily   Oh you know haha I'm good for just like whatever happens lol.

Visceral (*disdainfully*)   Smooth.

Cerebral   Pull up their profile. I need to know who this is.

Visceral   And how can I get them to like me.

Ciel   Ciel, genderfucked dykefag. Art bitch. Poly and partnered. Queers only, any chasers that message me will be castrated publicly.

Visceral   Woah they're . . . definitely not a normie.

Cerebral   I've never met anyone like this.

Ciel   You're cute. No worries if this is too much or like makes you uncomfortable but I can't sleep, just driving around right now and bored as fuck. Wanna go to waffle house?

Cerebral   I have an early shift tomorrow and it's already pretty lat–

Visceral   And this is too fucking rad, no way I'm missing out on this.

Lily   Damn yeah haha that'd be cool. I'm bored too.

Cerebral   Guess I'm calling out sick. At least it's not just depression again.

Ciel   Killer. I'll pick you up in like 10?

Lily   Sounds great!

Beat.

Visceral   Oh god I look like shit.

Lily   I need to change. Do I wear a dress?

Cerebral   No, it's fucking Waffle House. Let's just go with jeans and a hoodie, keep it simple.

Visceral   Hides the lack of tits too.

Lily   Yeah, it's perfect. Oh wait, I worked all day.

Lily *sniffs her armpit.*

Visceral   Yep, that's terrible.

Cerebral   Just need to wash up real quick, I got time befo–

Lily's *phone vibrates.*

Ciel   Hey sweets, I think I'm outside your place if you want to come on down.

Lily   Fuckfuckfuckfuck–

Cerebral   Throw on the hoodie, I can't make them wait–

Visceral   Love to make a disgusting first impression, don't I.

Cerebral   GO!

Lily *scrambles offstage.*

Scene 3

Setting: **Ciel's** *car, Jaxon. It's held together with duct tape and dreams but mostly works.*

At Rise: **Ciel** *lights and hits a joint in the driver's seat. After a moment,* **Visceral** *runs out, leading* **Lily** *to the car.* **Cerebral** *follows and hands off* **Lily's** *keys to her that she had forgotten.*

Lily   Hey, so sorry for taking so long to get down here.

Ciel   Girl, seriously? You're fine. Come on in, sorry it's such a mess. You can just throw that stuff in the back.

Cerebral   Ok good they're real.

Visceral   And hot.

Lily *sits.*

Ciel   It's kinda nice you took a bit. Gave me a sec to roll a joint. Want some? Best way to enjoy Waffle House.

Cerebral   Been a while since I smoked in a car . . .

Ciel   Lily? No pressure if you don't want to.

Lily   Um, yeah. I'll do a little. Just gotta be careful, going on E killed my tolerance.

Ciel   Oh yeah, I know that happens for some people.

They pass the joint and start driving.

Ciel   So, what matters to you?

Lily (*struggling through the smoke*)   Wait, what did you say?

Ciel   What do you care about? What moves you? What inspires you? Y'know, what matters?

Cerebral   What the hell do you even say to that?

Lily   I'm uh, not really sure. I like movies and games and stuff. Watch a lot of video essays. Otherwise I'm just kinda . . . living. Making it to the next paycheck.

Ciel   No, I totally get that. Capitalism is built to keep people like us trapped in a loop of exploitation and misery until we die.

Lily   Yeah, I guess that makes sense.

Ciel   My way of getting away from it all is rock climbing. There's a few nice trails around here, some fun bouldering spots, a decent gym downtown to practice at. It's like really important to me to find time to connect with nature and recenter myself. Part of why I settled down here.

Lily   I . . . should probably do something like that too. I don't really get out all that much.

Ciel   Yeah. Y'know, if things work out nicely I definitely wouldn't hate having a cute girl out on the trail with me.

Lily   Yeah. I'd really like that.

Ciel   Killer. We can figure out stuff for that later, we made it to the fight club.

Lily   Wait, what?

Visceral   Should've known, too good to be true, this is how I die, the weed was probably laced–

Ciel   Friends and I call Waffle House post 1 a.m. fight club. There's like a 50/50 shot you'll see some drunk dumbfucks brawling it out in there.

Lily   Ohh, that's funny.

Ciel   To be transparent, I have been that drunk dumbfuck on occasion.

Cerebral   It is genuinely concerning that they're hotter to me now that I know that.

Lily   Cool.

Ciel   C'mon, let's get in the ring. Want one more hit of this?

Lily *takes a massive hit from the joint, leaving her a coughing mess.* **Ciel** *puts the joint out, and pockets it. Meanwhile,* **Twink** *slides a table in front of them with menus and water glasses on them and moves upstage to take care of another customer. The car is now a booth.*

Cerebral   Welp. I fucked up. That was too much. Bye bye brain.

Cerebral *wanders around in the background looking closely at random objects.*

Ciel   Doing ok there?

Visceral   Woahhhhh hehehehe.

Lily *is wobbling.*

Ciel   Got a little too high?

Lily *floppily nods,* **Ciel** *smiles a bit.*

Ciel   Here, drink some water.

As **Lily** *drinks,* **Twink** *comes over.*

Twink   Hey darlings, anything I can get started for you? Wait, hold up a second. Lily, right? Didn't think I'd be seeing you again tonight.

Lily *accidentally waterboards herself with her drink.*

Lily   Mm yea no I didn't think so either.

Twink   Sorry I spooked ya sweetie, happens sometimes when you have too much. Y'all good to order?

Cerebral   How does he know I'm high? Can everyone tell??

Cerebral, *paranoid, gets really close hyperanalyzing everything* **Lily** *does and adjusts her to make her look more normal.*

Ciel   I think we need a sec.

Twink   No worries, not like there's much going on around here. Call me over when you're ready.

Twink *leaves the table.*

Ciel   Sorry, probably shoulda warned you that my stuff is pretty strong. Any like allergies or dietary things? This place has like the perfect high food, was thinking we could split something.

Lily   Nah, I'm good with whatever you wanna do.

Ciel   Killer, I'll get an order in. I promise, you'll love this shit.

Ciel *looks at* **Lily** *shifting uncomfortably as* **Cerebral** *continuously makes her readjust.*

Ciel   If things are too much you can lean on me if you want. More than fine by me.

Lily *leans on* **Ciel** *as they flag down* **Twink**. **Visceral** *faints dramatically.*

Twink   Know what you want loves?

Ciel   Can we get a scattered all the way with . . .

Ciel *and* **Twink** *continue to silently exchange words.*

Visceral (*still on the floor*)   This is it. I've peaked. This is what like musicians and poets and shit are talking about. This shoulder. I have ascended. I'm god. No getting better than this.

Ciel *absentmindedly begins to scritch* **Lily's** *head.* **Visceral** *sits up suddenly.*

Lily   Mmmm feels soo good.

Twink (*chuckling*)   I'll be back with that in a bit, try not to get too busy you two. You wouldn't believe the stuff I've had to clean out of these booths.

Twink *exits.*

Cerebral   Oh fuck I said that out loud.

Lily *sits up suddenly.*

Lily   I'm sorry that was so weird.

Ciel   Nothing to worry about, that was cute. You back in your body?

Lily   Yeah, I'm good. Thanks.

Cerebral *pulls* **Visceral** *up to their feet.*

Ciel   Nice. That guy was cool, he's coming to the show I'm playing at The Tube in a few weeks.

Lily   Oh . . . uh cool. What's that?

Ciel   The Tube's this dope venue in an abandoned storm drain. The acoustics are fucking insane, if you don't wear earplugs your ears might start bleeding.

Cerebral   And you'd almost certainly get tinnitus even with them. It must be–

Lily   –like a firing range . . . Um, ah sorry. You're in a band?

Ciel   Yeah! I do vocals for this all-trans punk group called The Mutilators. I usually write up the lyrics too but that gets shared around a bit sometimes.

Visceral   There is nothing about me that is remotely as cool as that.

Cerebral   I need to pretend to be interesting to prove I have any kind of value.

Lily   Wow, that's so cool. I love that kind of music.

Ciel   Really? Didn't peg you as the type but that's rad. You gotta show me the stuff you like sometime.

Visceral   Why would I lie about that? Of course they'd ask.

Lily   Yeah, yeah, for sure.

Cerebral   I guess I'll need to research punk music now.

Ciel   Well, if you're free at 9:30 on the 20th you can come see us play.

Lily   Oh yeah–

Cerebral   I need to play this interested, but not desperate.

Lily   Uh, I think that can probably work out for me. I think I have something with friends earlier but it should definitely be done by then.

Ciel   Killer, I'll send you the flyer.

Cerebral   Good thing they didn't call me on that.

Ciel   So, what are y'all getting up to?

Lily   Umm . . .

Twink *comes in with a plate of hashbrowns made unrecognizable by the unconscionable amount and number of toppings piled on.* **Visceral** *stands up.*

Visceral   Thank fuck.

Twink   Alright, here's your scattered, smothered, covered, chunked, topped, diced, peppered and capped with an extra fork. Anything else I can get for y'all?

Visceral   What the fuck? Is that even food?

Ciel   I think we're good?

Ciel *looks to* **Lily**, *she quickly nods.*

Ciel   Yeah, all good. Thank you so much.

Twink   Ok, take care, sweethearts.

Twink *flashes a smile, then a wink at* **Lily**, *then exits.*

Ciel   Wow, he has a really nice ass, doesn't he?

Lily   Yeah, yeah that thing is crazy . . . So, what exactly is this?

Ciel   Stoner ambrosia. Honestly it's better if you don't know what's in it and just take a bite.

Lily *cautiously tries a bite. The flavor makes her sit up straight as a spotlight hits the table with an angelic sound. All on stage pose as if in a baroque painting.*

Visceral   I knew not where flavor doth lie before this of all days. That such an enrichment upon the very soul would be begotten from the raw ferocity of taste borne from a house of waffle inspires emotion unyielding. A brutal reckoning upon my spirit as all understanding

Ciel   Good?

The scene returns to normal.

Lily   Um. Yeah. Really good. Wow.

Ciel   Fight club knows what they're doing.

Lily   I can tell.

She takes another bite.

Lily   How'd you find out about this stuff? Like that it's actually good.

Ciel   Oh, I mean it's kinda a weird story. I grew up Mormon in this shitty little town in Utah. Family used to all go to Waffle House every Sunday after sacrament, so I ended up trying everything on the menu eventually.

Lily   Oh wow, I can't imagine what that was like.

Ciel   It was rough. Pretty much everyone were total fuckheads but when it's all you've ever known it's hard to tell. Sorta always knew gender was all bullshit but took a while to like, figure that out, y'know?

Lily   Yeah, I definitely get that.

Ciel   The big thing that changed things was when this trans guy Max started going to my school. His parents moved out there to try to bully him back into the closet. Unfortunately for them, turns out there was another faggot in town. We found each other quick and wound up real close. He helped me figure myself out and was the only thing really keeping me sane out there.

Lily   That's so amazing. Are you two still close?

Ciel   In a way. He took a bunch of sleeping pills when we were 16. He, like, is still here in a sense. I feel him with me all the time. Both of us found our way out in the end.

Beat

Ciel   But yeah, anyway, the moment I turned 18 I had managed to figure something out with an ex-Mormon lesbian who helped me leave. I was so nervous and guilty I made myself sick, so I used that as an excuse to stay home from sacrament. Spent the morning loading up that lady's truck with all my stuff and had her drive me over to the Waffle House before we left. I walked over to my family's booth, told them I'm trans, and walked back out before they had a chance to say anything. My dad was yelling something, but I just got in the truck, got a ride out here, and never saw them again.

Lily   Holy shit. That's . . . a lot.

Ciel   Yeah, but I'm through it now. Took a really long time for me to stop feeling guilty about it all, to my family and to God. It's still hanging on to me a bit, but Max is stronger than that shit. Got on DIY T pretty much immediately, I've been kinda on and off it since. Figured out my gender was just like, queer as in fuck you, tranarchy, fucking piece of angry raw meat. Things are pretty good now. I'm a fagdyke out here rocking shit, making art, living life.

Lily   That's . . . really great. I'm glad you were able to get to a safe place and find yourself like that.

Visceral   I have no idea what half that shit meant. And the idea of stopping HRT even for a second is horrifying.

Cerebral   Not for me, for sure. Seems like it works for them, though.

Visceral   Sure does *bites bottom lip*

Ciel   Thanks. Sorry for blabbing on like that, haven't talked through that shit in a bit.

Lily   No, no worries. Thank you for sharing.

Ciel   Of course. Good to keep processing even 4 years out now. Do you want to share too?

Visceral   How can I go and tell them how much of a coward I am after hearing that. But also I'd be a total dick if I didn't now.

Cerebral   They're waiting. I have to say something. Just a little bit.

Lily   Yeah. So I took a while to figure things out. Not really any signs when I was younger, at least none that I recognized. Got bullied a lot though. I was depressed and way too online as a teenager when I started feeling gender stuff, joined the Marines to repress it. Got engaged and kept just hiding it. It all got too much, got discharged for mental health. Came out about a year after I got back to the states. My ex broke off the engagement, now I'm just on my own. Just trying to save up whatever cash I can get together. Either gonna put myself through school or get bottom surgery, I'm not sure yet. It'd be good to get a better job, it would help so damn much but I don't know if I'll even be able to handle doing classes with *that* still there.

Cerebral   That was not just a little bit.

Visceral   I ruined it. I shouldn't have gone into that.

Ciel   Damn, I'm really sorry. When you're stuck in spots like that it feels so hard to get away from it. Like it's always looming over you.

Lily   Yeah . . . tonight has made me really happy though. Like- it's been a bit crazy but . . . nice.

Ciel (*smiling*)   That's a good sign then. Wanna go back to yours and keep it going?

Visceral *starts breathing very loudly.* **Lily** *eeks out a nod.* **Twink** *swoops in to take away the food.*

Twink   Guess that apartment might be getting a double feature. You kids have fun.

Blackout. The sound of an old car desperately trying to start.

Ciel   C'mon Jaxon, you can do it old man.

The car keeps struggling.

Ciel   Sorry, he gets performance anxiety sometimes around pretty girls. I don't though, don't worry.

Lily   Ok wow um ah that's a really–

Visceral   Hot.

Ciel *chuckles, the engine starts.*

Scene 4

Setting: **Lily's** *apartment, same as she left it.*

At Rise: **Visceral** *is pacing frantically around* **Cerebral**.

Visceral   Oh god, how do I do this? It's been so long, I'm gonna fuck it up.

Cerebral   They're clearly into me, there's no other reason they'd be here.

Visceral   Or they're just pitying me.

Cerebral   At this point, I'll take it. Sexy pity is still sexy.

Visceral   Fuck

Cerebral   We're here.

The sound of keys. **Lily** *enters awkwardly leading* **Ciel** *inside.*

Lily   Sooo, this is it.

Ciel   Nice flags.

Beat. **Ciel** *notices the flowers.*

Ciel   Oh shit, I love these. Dead plants have always been an aesthetic thing for me. I have a few in my room. These are lilies, right? That's cute.

Cerebral   Don't–

Lily   They were from my ex. I don't know why I still have them.

Ciel   Ah. That's chill.

Visceral   Why do I have to ruin everything.

Ciel   So, do you wanna like sit down?

Lily   Yeah.

They go sit on the couch, not touching. **Ciel** *is looking at* **Lily** *while she stares straight forward. Awkward beat.*

Cerebral   What do I do?

Lily   So do you want me to put on a movie or something.

Ciel (*off guard*)   Oh. Yeah, sure if you want to.

Lily   So there's a bunch of different stuff I like that I think you might too and like they are really good at helping me get more comfortable when I'm stressed. Like one that I love is Ranma ½ even though it may not seem relaxing or anything because of the crazy violence and body horror, the trans rep is like amazing though and it always kinda bothers me that it's so niche like I get it's a 90's anime for a very particular audience but the physicality of everything in the movie combined with the really interesting characters and themes just like were a big deal for me for a long time when I was still closeted–

Visceral   Holy shit stop talk–

Lily   –and it really helped with reaffirming my identity in like a weird way when I got imposter syndrome about being trans because like the only other people I've heard of that really connect with it are also trans or just in some way gender non-conforming and it has this really interesting fanbase made out of queer people that's like its own queer space that's way different from any other places I've found online like there's this discord server that I used to use a lot but then I just kinda . . . stopped going . . .

Ciel   I loved that one, I'll have to rewatch it sometime.

Lily   Yeah . . .

Beat.

Ciel   Do you want to make out?

Lily/Visceral/Cerebral   Please.

Ciel *leans forward and starts to kiss* **Lily**. **Lily** *is tense but eventually relaxes into it.* **Ciel** *lifts their head up to look at* **Lily**.

Ciel   Is there anything that you wouldn't be comfortable with me doing?

Visceral (*gasping*)   Whatever you want. To do to me. Please.

Cerebral   Wait. No. My body is wrong. I almost forgot there. Fuck.

Lily   Um. I haven't . . . done anything with like, down there, and I don't know if that would–

Ciel   It's ok sweets. We don't have to do anything you don't want to. All good with me.

Lily *pulls* **Ciel** *into a kiss that she slides into a tight, shaky hug.*

Ciel   You ok?

Lily   Just . . . nobody's asked before . . . I was scared I was going to have to use . . .

Ciel   Aww darling. Of course.

The hug lasts for a beat. Eventually they pull away.

Ciel   I don't fuck with anyone who's shitty about consent in any way. You should make sure you don't either. I'm so sorry you've been hurt too. You deserve better.

Visceral *starts to interject but* **Cerebral** *shushes them.* **Lily** *nods and takes a moment to collect herself.*

Lily   Do you maybe want to go back to my room?

Ciel   Lead the way.

They both stand and kiss one more time before exiting. **Cerebral** *and* **Visceral** *follow but* **Cerebral** *lingers near the door for a moment.*

Cerebral   Huh, this is what being happy feels like.

Cerebral *exits. Lights out.*

Scene 5

Setting: *The next day(s).* **Lily's** *apartment. The same except some used plates sit on the coffee table and the vodka bottle is gone.*

At Rise: **Lily** *is just finishing letting* Ciel **out of the door of the apartment, riding a confidence high. She is in actual normal clothes now.** Cerebral *and* Visceral *are hiding behind the couch.* Lily *closes the door and turns and drifts towards center happily.* **Brian** *enters, barely regarding* **Lily** *and goes to get his keys off a hook.*

Lily   Hey, good morning.

Brian *pockets his keys and goes back to his room.*

Lily   Sorry if I woke you up at all, I didn't realize I could get that loud.

Brian *reenters with his backpack and walks straight past* **Lily**.

Lily   Grindr ended up pretty great, I didn't think it would work that . . .

Brian *exits out the door.*

Lily   . . . well.

Visceral *pops up from behind the couch.*

Visceral   What the hell's up with him?

Cerebral *pops up.*

Cerebral   I did call him a mediocre fucking faggot and drank his vodka last night.

Lily   Ughhh, don't want to deal with his shit. Too tired.

Visceral   He'll get over it.

Lily   Yeah, (*yawns*) he'll be fine.

Lily *flops onto the couch. She almost drops right into sleep, as this happens,* **Cerebral** *and* **Visceral** *slowly drop back into hiding. Suddenly her phone buzzes and they bolt back up,* **Lily** *fumbles to pull the phone out.*

Lily (*reading*)   "Last night was cool. Ur fun."

Lily *sits up smiling and starts to type a response. Upbeat punk music fades in (suggested: Unconditional Love by Against Me!) fades in. The lights dim into blackness before rising again as the sun rising and setting. This repeats several times with different scenes visible each "day".*

Lily *is sitting cross legged wearing headphones listening to the music, head bobbing.* **Cerebral** *is doing research on a laptop, explaining things to* **Lily**. **Visceral** *is attempting to dance in that way that someone who doesn't know the song and can't dance does.* **Brian** *walks unnoticed behind them from his room out the front door, giving an irritated head shake as he goes.*

Lily *is standing, taking a selfie for* **Ciel**. *She deletes and retakes it endlessly, always hating how she looks until the day ends.* **Visceral** *gags at each one,* **Cerebral** *keeps trying to fix her appearance.*

Lily *sits on the edge of the couch anxiously.* **Visceral** *has their ear pressed to the door,* **Cerebral** *is trying to calm* **Lily**. **Visceral** *suddenly jumps back and gestures to* *the door excitedly.* **Lily** *runs over and opens the door.* **Ciel** *steps through, pushing her back with a kiss. After the kiss,* **Ciel** *grabs Lily* **by the collar and pulls her back towards her room.** **Twink** *is leaving* **Brian's** *room and gives them a little wave as he passes them on his way out.* **Visceral** *beats them to the door,* **Cerebral** *starts to follow.*

Lily *is bringing a package to the coffee table. She puts the headphones back on, opens the package, and starts pulling out rock climbing gear.* **Cerebral** *inspects each item as she puts it on the table.* **Visceral** *rubs* **Lily's** *shoulders like a boxing coach.*

Lily *walks out of her room to where* **Cerebral** *and* **Visceral** *are. She holds two outfits you'd find by typing "punk outfit" into Amazon, comparing them. The music fades out.*

Lily   Hmm. What do I go with for tonight?

Visceral   I'd look dumb in both.

Lily   But I'd look even dumber if I was the only one not wearing punk clothes.

Cerebral   This is what people wear, I looked it up. Maybe I should ask Ciel . . .

Visceral   A chance to talk to them sounds nice.

Lily   I can't. I already texted them three times today and they haven't responded, so I'd look desperate if I sent any more.

Brian *enters through the door and walks towards his room.*

Cerebral   He'll know. He does this kinda stuff.

Lily   Hey Brian, which one of these do you think I could pull off better? This one orrr this one?

Brian   I don't know.

He tries to push past her, she blocks him.

Lily   C'mon, it's for a punk show and I don't know what I'm doing.

Brian   I don't care, will you let me past?

Lily   What the hell? God, you've been such an asshole lately.

Brian   Oh, I'm the asshole?

Lily   What?

Brian   You've been a total cunt all week. Before that too to be honest, but you got me to feel bad for you back then.

Lily   Seriously? So you get pissy with me as soon as I finally have something good going on in my life?

Brian (*deep breath*)   I'm glad you found someone that's making you happy. But that doesn't mean you get to be shitty to everyone else.

Lily I think you're just jealous.

Brian You think I'm jealous? Of your little fling? Fuck off.

Lily Yeah. Cause I'm basically dating like the coolest person ever, meanwhile all you've ever had going on is hookups from the club and that one Twink that comes by to get railed by you every once in a while.

Brian You don't even know his fucking name? We're dating, he was here like every day last week!

Lily How was I supposed to know that? Good for you?

Brian You're unbelievable.

Brian *blows past her to exit but stops at the door.*

Brian I'm starting to doubt you ever will, but I seriously hope you realize that you're the real reason your life is so bad. Not because you're trans or poor or anything else, but because you don't give a shit about anyone other than yourself.

Brian *exits out the door and slams it.*

Lily FUCK YOU! YOU DON'T KNOW ME!

Visceral I fucking hate men.

Scene 6

Setting: *The wooded exterior of The Tube, a storm drain turned crusty venue with lights and fog pouring out of it.*

At Rise: **Lily** *is recovering outside the venue, smoking and drinking a beer. There's a few finished bottles on the ground next to her. She's drunk. Noise music echoes out.* **Cerebral** *stands staring into the fog,* **Visceral** *is sharing the cigarette with her. After a bit,* **Twink** *passes by on his way into The Tube:*

Twink Hey doll, love the fit!

Lily Thanks. Just Amazon.

Visceral I look so stupid in this.

Twink Well you're rocking it! Having a good time?

Lily Yeah, I'm alright. I need a little bit of a break.

Twink OMG yeah it's so loud in there it shakes your whole body, I love it so much.

Cerebral I hate it when people say OMG out loud.

Lily It's kinda a lot though.

Twink So valid queen. I'm gonna go find Brian, you take care Lily!

Cerebral   Of course he'd be here.

Lily   You too, uhh–

Twink *enters The Tube, not hearing her.*

Lily   Whatever.

Visceral   It was fucked up of him to lie about me looking good.

Cerebral   That research was a waste of time. I really should have asked Ciel what to expect. There was no reason for me not to.

Visceral   They always know the right thing to do. They're so smart.

Cerebral   Their set was really good.

Lily   Fuck, they were so amazing. I need to see if their stuff is online anywhere, I neeeed that one song about pink and blue bombs on my playlist.

Cerebral   I'm glad I won't have to lie when I say that I loved it.

Visceral   And when they winked at me? Uggngmgmmgf.

Lily   I don't know how I didn't pass out. I almost did just from being around so many people. It feels like it's been years.

Visceral   I'm glad I could just focus on **Ciel**. And that there were drinks.

Lily *knocks back the rest of the beer and puts it next to the others. Beat.*

Cerebral   I don't know how long it takes to pack up but I'm starting to–

Ciel *enters dressed to throw bricks at cops and heads over by* **Lily**. **Lily** *plays it *really* cool.*

Ciel   Hey, cool you came.

Lily   Yeah, of course!

Ciel   Can I get some of that?

Lily   Oh, yeah, take the rest of it.

Ciel   Killer.

They drink in some much-needed nicotine.

Ciel   So, what'd ya think?

Lily   Oh my god you all were soo amazing.

She starts getting really touchy. **Ciel** *isn't exactly stopping her but isn't exactly engaging.*

Ciel (*distracted*)   Glad you liked it. Our drummer Annie got caught up in New Mexico so we had to find a backup real fast. He did alright, might do more gigs with him . . .

Lily   Yeah, that's so great . . .

Ciel finally meets her eyes and smiles. They kiss gently, then **Ciel** *puts their arm around her and pulls her close.*

Visceral   Finally.

After too short a moment of this, **Jaime** *enters and moves to* **Ciel***.*

Jaime   Hey! Did you go on yet? Car decided to start leaking oil, had to patch it.

Ciel   Ah, goddammit Jaxon. We just got off.

Ciel *pulls away from* **Lily** *and gives a quick peck to* **Jaime**)

Jaime   I'm sorry babe.

Ciel   Hey, it's alright babe. At least you made it in time to watch the Lightning Dykes set.

They remember **Lily**.

Ciel   Oh, and this is that girl I mentioned, Lily. Lily, this is my boyfriend Jaime and his partner Grace is . . .

Jaime   Bathroom.

Cerebral   That name still stings.

Visceral   Ugh, forget that bitch, Ciel really likes this guy? Didn't realize their standards were that low.

Cerebral   Like the poly stuff sounded ok when Ciel talked about it the other day but now that I'm face to face with it . . .

Visceral   I'm supposed to be Ciel's person. They're supposed to feel the same as me.

Cerebral   Gonna have to work extra hard to be more interesting.

Jaime   Hey there, glad to meet ya. I like your outfit.

Cerebral   Maybe not *that* hard.

Lily (*to* **Ciel**)   Thanks! So, who's that band you mentioned, the Lightning Dykes?

Jaime   Oh, they're great!

Visceral   I wasn't asking you.

Jaime   They use two basses which is really great sounding, especially in The Tube. I've been following them for a bit now, I was so pumped when I saw their tour came through here.

Ciel   Those girls were super nice too when I talked with them earlier. It was great we got to play an event they're headlining, hopefully can help with exposure.

Jaime   Hey, don't get too caught up in that. Remember what you said? You'd be happy even if it was just me as your only fan.

Ciel   Yeah, yeah. You're the best groupie I could ever ask for.

They just begin to kiss . . .

Lily   But like your stuff is so good you're like definitely gonna hit it big. Like this type of music isn't even really my thing but you got me hooked. And I mean like HOOKED.

Ciel   Thanks. Happy to hear it. (*they get a text*) Oh goddammit, one of the monitors is fucked. I gotta run and fix it.

Jaime   Alright, go do your thing. I'll meet you inside once Grace gets back.

Ciel   Killer, I'll see both of you in a bit.

Ciel *runs off.*

Cerebral   Guess I'm staying out here too. Damn.

Beat.

Jaime   So, what do you got going on. Like what's something you're looking forward to?

Visceral   You shutting the fuck up.

Lily   I mean, not really much. Might go rock climbing with Ciel Tuesday.

Jaime   Oh that's great! I can never keep up with them, not an endurance kinda guy. Need to get better with that, but it's just way more fun to get a lift in instead. Glad they got someone they can go hike with though!

Lily   Yeah.

Beat. Eventually, **Grace** *enters.*

Grace   Wow that line was crazy. Did I miss Ciel's band?

Cerebral   Oh my god. The hair is different but–

Jaime   We missed it before we got here. Still in time for the Lightning Dykes though!

Visceral   Why the FUCK is SHE here?

Grace   Oh yay!

Jaime   This is **Lily** by the way, **Ciel**'s been talking with her.

Lily   We've met.

Grace   We hav-? oh. Oh.

Lily   Jaime, do you mind if I talk with her a bit, catch up? We'll meet you inside.

Jaime   It's them.

Lily   What?

Grace   I use um, they/them now.

Visceral   The fucking audacity.

Lily   Ah, ok.

Jaime   This good with you Gracie?

Grace   Yeah, I've actually wanted to talk to her for a little while, it would be great to catch up. I'll see you inside.

Jaime   Alright, see ya bug.

Jaime *gives a little wave and heads inside. They wait until he's gone.*

Lily   What the absolute fuck?!

Grace   I know–

Lily   You know? Fuck you, you don't get to do this to me.

Grace   I know I hurt you–

Lily   You did way more than hurt me. I can't fucking trust anyone anymore!

Grace   I did. I'm sorry I hurt you. I've spent a while reflecting and figured out a lot about myself and everything that happened. I tried to reach out but you blocked me on everything.

Lily   Well it should be fucking obvious why. "I fell in love with a man." "Why can't you just admit you're gay." "No one will ever see you as a woman." I needed you. You were the only person I had when I was going through the hardest shit I've ever done. I thought you'd be the one person who would be there, you're bisexual for fucks sake.

Grace   I actually go by pan now–

Lily   I don't fucking care.

Grace   Yeah, sorry. Not important. Look, I was young and stupid–

Lily   Two years ago?

Grace   I just wanted to say I'm sorry, I understand if you don't want to accept it.

Lily   No. You don't get to fucking do that. You can't just say that kind of shit to me, abandon me in a time that I thought I wasn't gonna make it through, and then show up to this concert with music I know you don't like involved in some poly bullshit, pretending that you have ANYTHING in common with people like me. You acted like my transition was so *fucking hard for you* and now you're a fucking theyfab? You're a piece of shit Grace.

Grace   That's too far Danny– shit, Lily.

Lily   Oh, you fucking would. You can't hurt me anymore, bitch!

Grace   I'm not trying to hurt you–

Lily   Fuck you. You don't deserve shit.

Grace   You're drunk again, please stop.

Lily   You can cut the bullshit out, I know you. You're a cishet lying about being queer for woke points whenever it's fucking convenient for you. Anyone who believes you is a fucking idiot.

Grace   You know, there's other reasons why I left you.

Ciel *enters and approaches the pair.*

Grace   You may have transitioned, but you haven't changed much at all.

Grace *walks off into The Tube as* **Ciel** *reaches* **Lily**.

Ciel   Hey, what the hell was that?

Lily   I had to talk some shit out with that cunt.

Ciel   Do you know Grace?

Lily   Yeah, I was engaged to her.

Ciel   Them.

Lily   Sure, I was engaged to "*them*".

Ciel   What the fuck's your problem?

Lily   Grace is a fucking sociopath. They played up this sob story to everyone we knew to make sure I was left with nobody when I finally came out.

Ciel   Look, I'm not saying you have to like them, but you can't be starting shit. I've heard they grew up conservative and I'm sorry if they hurt you, but lots of us have pasts we're not proud of. You used to be in the Marines fighting for oil for fucks sake.

Lily   I was at a goddamn desk.

Ciel   Still advancing imperialism. But you've moved on. Grace has too. Please just keep it chill.

Lily   I "moved on" because I tried to kill myself!

Beat.

Ciel   I'm sorry–

Lily   It's whatever. I just don't believe they're any different.

Jaime *enters fuming, followed* by **Grace**.

Jaime   You need to leave. Now.

Lily   No, I wanna hear the Lightning Dykes. **Ciel**, c'mon let's go inside.

Ciel   Jaime, what happened?

Jaime   She said Grace was faking being queer for "woke points". Who are you, Tucker Carlson?

Lily   I just told the truth.

Jaime   Gatekeeping my partner's gender is not fucking ok. Either she leaves or we do.

Ciel   I just- ughhhh.

Ciel starts to panic, but calms themselves.

Ciel   Lily, I think you need to go.

Lily   Ciel–

Ciel   Please. I don't need any more fucking queer drama in my life. I can't deal with this right now.

Beat.

Lily   Fine.

Cerebral *starts to lead* **Lily** *out, then* **Visceral** *yanks her back to stop and face* **Jaime**)

Lily   I hope she fucking ruins your life too!

Jaime *is about to go after her but* **Grace** *pulls him back inside.* **Cerebral** *ushers* **Lily** *and* **Visceral** *offstage.* **Ciel** *stays for a moment.*

Ciel   Godfucking damn it.

Ciel *goes inside. Lights out.*

Scene 6

Setting: *Later that night.* **Lily's** *apartment.*

At Rise: **Lily** *is sitting on the couch taking shots that* **Visceral** *pours her.* **Cerebral** *is doing whatever they can to not puke.*

Lily   Fuck Grace.

Visceral   Yes! Fuck that bitch.

Lily   She just HAD to show up to ruin my life again. I finally had something good going.

Cerebral   They now.

Lily/Visceral   Oh, shut the fuck up.

Beat. **Lily** *drinks.*

Cerebral   One more and I'm past the point of no return.

Lily   That's the idea. I'm done thinking. I'm done feeling.

Visceral   I'm done living.

Lily   What?

Cerebral   Don't act surprised. I have been for a long time now.

Lily   Not anymore, I transitioned, that was supposed to fix me.

Visceral   The pain is still there, that disgustingly masculine rage.

Cerebral   The only difference is estrogen made me able to cry now.

Lily   Ciel, they were supposed to fix me.

Cerebral   Twenty-three sent texts, zero received.

Visceral   They're not coming back to me, it's over.

Cerebral   I'm alone.

Visceral   As I deserve to be. How could I be so cruel to think otherwise?

Cerebral   I am made of pain. Inflicting myself on others like I do is causing conscious harm. That is what defines true evil.

Visceral   I will never stop hurting, myself or others.

Lily   Unless I go away. Forever.

Cerebral   Anything short of that is just another act of cruelty upon the world.

Cerebral *hands* **Lily** *a kitchen knife. She pauses, then takes it. She freezes. Behind her,* **Visceral** **guides the blade to her wrist. The door opens,** **Brian** *and* **Twink** *enter feeling each other up until they see.*

Brian   Lily?

Twink   Hey sweetheart. Do you think you can give that to me?

Twink *slowly approaches.* **Visceral** *holds in place.* **Lily** *peels their hand off her with great effort and hands* **Twink** *the knife. He and* **Brian** *exchange a look,* **Twink** *takes the knife offstage.* **Brian** *sits by* **Lily**.

Brian   Hey. Look at me. What's going on?

Lily   I'm a terrible person.

Brian   Yeah.

Lily   I just . . . yeah?

Brian   Yeah. You are.

Twink *enters.*

Twink   Brian, I don't know if–

Brian   Trust me.

Twink *sits by them, eyeing* **Brian**.

Brian   You don't have to be one though. I've seen it. Otherwise I wouldn't bother talking to you.

Cerebral/Visceral No, I'm worthless–/I'm a piece of shit–

Brian Stop the self-pity, it doesn't help anything.

Lily, **Cerebral**, *and* **Visceral** *are shocked that he heard.*

Brian What happened tonight?

Lily Grace was at the show, sh-they're metamours or whatever with Ciel.

Twink Sorry, who's–

Brian Her ex, the one I told you about.

Twink Ohhh. Wait, her ex is that Grace? Like Jaime's partner . . . oh tea.

Lily How do you know Grace?

Twink Jaime and I dated for a bit last year but we're besties now. I met Grace at Jaime's birthday- that was so lit by the way, I was in this cunty lil fit with–

Brian Kylan.

Twink/Kylan Sorry.

Cerebral Oh, that's your name.

Beat.

Brian So . . . Grace. Let me guess, you were drunk and loud and shitty?

Visceral She deserved it for what she did! I-I . . .

Lily I was. They tried to apologize. I didn't want to hear it. I just . . . I just . . .

Lily *attempts to stammer out more before falling into a weepy hug with* **Brian**. *He takes a breath before holding her.*

Brian There it is. I gotcha. Let it out.

Lily *blasts raw emotion into* **Brian's** *shoulder.* **Kylan** *slinks away, mouthing to* **Brian** *that he'll see him later and exits. Eventually,* **Lily** *looks up.*

Lily I'm sorry.

Brian For what?

Lily For everything. For taking you for granted. For being shitty to you when you were nice to me. For you having to know me.

Brian No, no. I'm glad I know you. You're just in a really fucking bad place right now.

Lily I feel like I always will be.

Brian You won't. You'll get through this.

Lily How? Everything always just gets worse.

Brian Do you want it to get better?

Visceral   No, I want to be worse. I want to milk every good feeling I can get out of life until I totally destroy myself. There's no other way for me.

Brian   Why not try? If you're going to be dead soon anyway, why not see if you can make a life that's worth living. Because that's not something that just happens to you or that someone can give to you. It takes effort, day in and day out. It's fucking hard. But you're an out trans woman. You know you can do hard things or you wouldn't be here now. You put so much work into becoming yourself, why not make sure that self is someone fucking worth being? Someone worth loving? I'm so fucking tired of being around you when you don't try. Move out if you're going to stay the same so I don't end up having to clean blood off my couch.

Lily *stares at* **Brian**. *Lights out.*

Scene 6

Setting: *A few months later. A small house party.*

At Rise: *COMPANY besides* **Lily**, **Brian**, *and* **Kylan** *are clustered about talking with solo cups as punk music plays.* **Cerebral** *and* **Visceral** *are dressed like normal partygoers and mingling too.* **Lily**, **Brian**, *and* **Kylan** *enter to the edge of the stage.* **Lily** *is wearing makeup and a good outfit.*

Lily   Fuck, I'm scared. Is this a good idea?

Kylan   You need to get out bae. We can't babysit you everywhere. Spread your wings, leave the nest!

Brian   Remember, I'm buying you Taco Bell if you stay and talk to people for at least an hour. You really need some more friends than just us.

Kylan   Speaking of . . .

Kylan *leads* **Brian** *and* **Lily** *to the group with* **Cerebral** *and* **Visceral** *in it.* **Kylan** *hugs* **Cerebral**.

Kylan   Hey hey, how's it going y'all?

Cerebral   Going alright, been mostly doing a lot of philosophy reading. I was just telling V here about how Friedrich Nietzsche, despite writing extensively on nihilism, actually had a relatively positive view of life, and how the attribution of the negative connotations of the worldview . . .

Cerebral *drones on,* **Kylan** *pretends he's following.* **Lily** *notices* **Grace**, **Ciel***, and* **Jaime** *and turns to* **Brian**.

Lily   Oh my fucking god.

Brian   What?

Lily   Look who's here.

Brian   Who– ah fuck. Do you want to leave, find a different party?

Lily   I . . . um . . .

Visceral   Hey, I'm gonna go get a drink, do you want one? You look like you could REALLY use a drink right now. Like REALLY REALLY–

Lily   I'm fine. I don't drink. Thanks.

Visceral *shrugs and leaves them.*

Lily   I want to stay.

Brian   Hey. Proud of you.

Lily   Thanks. Drinks don't play well with the new meds anyway.

They hug. **Grace** *approaches without them noticing until they separate.*

Grace   Hi Lily.

Brian *gives a look to* **Lily.** *She hesitates, then nods. He goes back to the group, keeping an eye on her.*

Lily   Hi Grace.

Grace   How've you been?

Lily   Uh, good? Yeah, good.

Grace   Great.

Lily   I'm sorry.

Grace   Thank you.

Lily   I still can't be around you.

Grace   I can understand that. Same here.

Lily   Yeah.

Lily *looks to* **Ciel,** **Grace** *notices.*

Grace   They've had a rough few months.

Lily   Makes sense. Should I–

Grace   Yeah, you should. Keep yourself safe Lily.

Beat.

Lily   You too.

Lily *approaches* **Ciel.** **Jaime** *stops talking with them and goes to stand with* **Grace** *with a glare.*

Lily   Ciel?

Ciel   Lily.

Lily   Hi.

Ciel   Sorry for not responding to anything.

Lily   No, it's ok.

Ciel   You look good.

Lily   Oh, thanks. It took like four hours, I have no idea what I'm doing. I've also been going rock climbing.

Ciel   Well, it's working for you.

Lily   So . . . about the concert–

Ciel   Yeah . . . Grace told me about y'all after. I can get going crazy in that position.

Lily   Yeah, but still. I went too far.

Ciel   You did.

Beat.

Lily   I still listen to your music.

Ciel   Oh, really? God that band fell apart a bit ago. It's fine, I think I wanted to do solo stuff for a while now.

Lily   I'd love to listen to it when it comes out.

Ciel   Lily . . .

Lily   Sorry.

Ciel   No, it's ok.

Lily   Can . . . can we start over? As friends.

Ciel *looks over at* **Jamie** *and* **Grace**. **Jaime** *is watching intently.* **Grace** *is looking away.*

Ciel   I don't know if I can do that.

Lily   Ok, yeah. Totally get it.

They share a look.

Ciel   Goodbye Lily. I'm sure I'll see you around.

Lily   Bye. See you.

Ciel *walks away to join* **Jaime** *and* **Grace**. **Lily** *watches them go.* **Cerebral** *and* **Visceral** *approach her from either side,* **Visceral** *trying to give her a drink. Lily is mobbed by them, then pushes past to leave them behind. She approaches the edge of the stage.*

Lily   Hi. I'm Lily. So, what matters to you?

Lights out.

END OF PLAY

Part 2: Dance Break

Nations Made of Stars: An Introduction to *The Brunch Crowd*, by Dillon Yruegas

Sebastián Eddowes-Vargas

I

I've always asked myself what an introduction should do.
The answers are infinite.
This one is an invitation to cross a border and join the brunch crowd.

II

Who is considered part of a nation? Who *really* belongs?
And for those who don't, what do we do?
Can we build our own nations?

The Brunch Crowd is a play by Dillon Yruegas that follows a group of friends, Black and Latine, trans and enby, gathering for food and drinks. Sharing a table with your loved ones could be an everyday practice, but it becomes *something else* when you are struggling for space. Brunch with Dallas, Erik, Flor, and Q is about shared pleasure and building community. But it is also the *foundation* of a world that was not there.

To discuss the play, I think it will be useful to delve back in history.

What we call the United States of America is the continuation of the Thirteen Colonies, first stablished in 1607 by English colonizers after displacing indigenous populations. From 1619 onwards, the economy of the colonies relied heavily on the labor of enslaved Africans (The New York Times Magazine). Rooted in this colonizing process, this society has divided peoples into racial categories. According to ethnic studies scholar la paperson, this settler colonialism organizes folx into three categories: "the settler who accumulates rights, land, and property; the native whose presence on land must be extinguished; the chattel slave who must be kept landless" (paperson 2017: 8). Although paperson emphasizes that these categories do not necessarily correspond with racial identities, they did in the foundation of the United States, originally organized by the distinction between indigenous, Blacks, and whites. These categorics still structure how the country is organized, in what Latina scholar Laura E. Gómez calls "a multi-race hierarchy in which Whites continue to be dominant in terms of wealth, political power, and ideology" (Gómez 2022: 3).

Racial categories change over time. A more recent one is "Latine," for those of us with roots in Latin America. But this grouping is not always clear. Performance scholar José Esteban Muñoz states that this identity brings "the problem of being a problem," partly because the peoples it classifies "do not cohere along the lines of race, nation, language, or any other conventional demarcation of difference" (Muñoz 2020: 37-38).

Gómez claims it was produced to understand Latinos as "a racial group that is other and inferior to Whites" (Gómez 2022: 4). Some Latines are born in the United States, some are migrants. Some have migration documents, some don't. In any case, the labor of Latines (documented, undocumented or DACA-mented) is crucial to the US economy, even if the community often faces barriers to enjoy the fruits of this labor. This is rooted in the legal system and the immigration process: "in an effort to create lucrative economic gains, the United States put in place very intentional and strategic laws and regulations that led to the exploitation of immigrant labor and a limitation of the migration process" (Núñez, Rubalcava-Cuara and Tijerina Revilla 2021: 5).

Author and activist Ibram X. Kendi writes that "we are surrounded by racial inequity, as visible as the law, as hidden as our private thoughts." This is grounded in racist policies, rooted on racist ideas that "defined our society since its beginning" (Kendi 2019: 22-23). And although Latine and Black communities have different histories and experience oppression differently, there can be a shared sense of exclusion, of not belonging, even if they have been present since this country was founded, either because of the slave trade or because of the annexation of territories after the Mexican-American War (1846-1848). Furthermore, the labor and contributions to society of these communities is central to the fabric of the United States (Ortiz 2018).

How to thrive in a nation where your people is marginalized?

Can you create a nation inside this nation?

Maybe one that channels the energy of the stars? Of the universe?

I think this frame can help access the project of *The Brunch Crowd*. The play centers four friends who belong to Black and Latine communities. It begins with them having brunch, celebrating and catching up. But there is tension underneath: Erik wants to propose to Dallas and still has lots of questions. If getting to marriage is a long journey for hetero-cis folks, for us queers it can feel like rebuilding Atlantis with our bare hands. Let's start with the obvious: a few decades ago, marriage equality was not legal in the United States, and it is not an option in many countries (I'm from Perú, where queer marriage is unattainable). I write in the beginning of 2025, with fear for its future in the USA. But once it is there, it comes with questions: is marriage a reproduction of hetero-cis ideals? José Esteban Muñoz distinguished between "bucking under the pressures of dominant ideology (identification, assimilation) or attempting to break free of its inescapable sphere (counteridentification, utopianism)," asking if marginalized subjects should imitate the status quo, hoping for acceptance, or if we should create new utopias and forms of living. He will propose a third way, that he names *disidentification* (Muñoz 1999: 11). There are also practical questions for Erik and Dallas. If they do it, where will they live? Will the couple and their friends be close or will they migrate? We need a lot of answers now. You'll find them in the play, so stay tuned.

In *The Brunch Crowd*, Dillon Yruegas focuses on how the forces of neoliberalism are chasing his characters. Theater scholar Patricia A. Ybarra defines neoliberalism as

> a political and economic philosophy whose proponents espouse free markets and privatization of state enterprises as the mode by which prosperity and democracy are best reached. These policies [. . .] have also created the conditions for many of the most tumultuous events in the Americas in the last forty years.
>
> (Ybarra 2018: x)

Neoliberal policies aim to restrict the role of the state (at least, in theory), allowing the market and its laws of supply and demand to regulate social life. As Ybarra notes, this has affected the Americas tremendously, supporting the power of the wealthy and the big corporations over land and the folks who live on it. One of its consequences is gentrification, the process by which wealthier people move into low-income neighborhoods, displacing the communities living in them. This topic has been widely discussed in contemporary US theater. Yruegas' work is joining this urgent conversation.

I am thinking of *The Brunch Crowd* as a form of political theater. Historically, several pieces that frame themselves as such use the form and genre of tragedy, centering the pain of the characters, usually denying a happy ending. I think of one of my favorite plays: *The Normal Heart* (1985), by Larry Kramer. A piece about the AIDS epidemic, it stages the despair of queer communities while chronicling the effects of untreated HIV on the body. This piece is meant to be a difficult journey for the audience, witnessing the action of death by a virus that can't be traced or fought, while others make efforts to ignore the plague. This is a powerful strategy, but there are alternatives. When presenting the 2022 Latinx Theater Commons Theater Carnaval, producer Amelia Acosta Powell told the participants:

> I had been heartened and excited to see more Latine stories on stage at predominantly white institutions (PWIs), however my enthusiasm had waned as I noticed how disproportionately these PWIs favor Latine "trauma porn" that exploits the suffering of marginalized people to console or entertain the privileged and powerful [. . .] I want more comedic performance on stage for a sense of balance. Yes, our communities are facing injustice and tragedy. Yes, we should address those problems. But one of the most powerful and versatile tools that our communities use to tackle oppression is the power of humor. Laughter can soothe a broken heart, unite coalitions across differences, and even scare the shit out of a bully.
>
> (Acosta 2022)

I've been interested in narratives that use humor to address the pain we carry. José Esteban Muñoz wrote about how urgent this is: "we must dream and enact new and better pleasures, other ways of being in the world, and ultimately new worlds." (Muñoz 2009: 1) Doing otherwise may risk losing a critical approach to the status quo. I've seen recent pieces doing this wonderfully, including *Yellow Face* (2007), by David Henry Hwang; *BREACH* (2018), by Antoinette Nwandu; *Between Two Knees* (2019), by The 1491s; *White Girl in Danger* (2023) by Michael R. Jackson; *Invasive Species* (2023), by Maia Novi; *Exhaustion Arroyo* (2023) by W. Fran Astorga; or my play *Can The Peruvian Speak?* (2024) (more about this in Eddowes-Vargas 2023 and 2024). *The Brunch Crowd* can engage in this conversation. The term "comedy" is appropriate, not because these pieces make you laugh (even if they do), but because they create pleasurable experiences that reimagine societies. Instead of chronicling the collapse of social orders, centering *pathos*, comedy can build new articulations, or at least guide quests for new possible worlds.

Following this principle, Yruegas gathers his characters for brunch. Their encounters centers pleasure with company, fruit, and mimosas. But there's more. In a nation that marginalizes their communities, Dallas, Erik, Flor and Q **are founding a nation inside**

another nation, using their own sovereignty to set rules, laws, a social contract to follow. A space that, when it exists, aims to suspend neoliberal forces. They gather in the Taquería María Félix, a Tex-Mex restaurant in East Austin that owes her name to *la doña*, the one and only *María Bonita*, the Mexican actress and singer adored in both sides of the Atlantic Ocean.

If María Félix is a goddess, protecting them from above, Santa Selena guides them during their tribulations. Before Shakira and J. Lo, there was Selena Quintanilla. The Queen of Tejano Music, she revolutionized her genre and became a star. Incredibly talented, a brilliant artist, a popular fashion icon, she was tragically murdered in 1995, at 23 years old. But her voice is still with us, and you only need to hear her singing the intro of *Bidi Bidi Bom Bom* to feel your hips shaking, and be taken to a dance floor full of Latine angels. She was not queer, to our knowledge, but we adopted her. Or did she adopt us?

María and Selena protect the characters of the play as the forces of displacement push them. These forces can be silent, even subtle. They don't come with a bang. But their violence is ferocious, making living conditions impossible and sending folx to look for a life far away. This nation founded inside a taquería is devoured. Where will Dallas, Erik, Flor, and Q go now? Can they create new spaces in the future?

Candice Amich writes that "the brutality (of neoliberalism) was destructive of community everywhere" (Amich 2020: 15). Staging a nation of four, one with sovereignty to suspend neoliberal polices for a moment, becomes a strategy of resistance. Yruegas' characters remember that matter is never created or destroyed, which means our bodies are made of stars. The matter that forms the beings that we are dances with cosmic forces everywhere in the universe. The flesh of my hands writing these words could have been in a different galaxy before becoming me. What I am is in transit, boundless, uncontainable by borders. The flow of neoliberal capital becomes weak next to the cosmic forces that produced you and me.

The nation of *The Brunch Crowd* is one where we create the worlds we are hungry for, invoking forces from the universe. Bringing fire from the galaxies that made us to the land right here and now. Our nations, made of stars, are *ours*. They expand and shine with the light of a million suns, and can be founded and re-founded anywhere. When we understand this, we are ready to resist together.

III

Before you start, an invitation.
If you have access to music, find a way to listen to Selena.
Speakers or headphones are encouraged. Laptops or cellphones tend to sound somewhat mediocre.
Let her voice cover your skin, while the music gets deep into your belly.
If you can, dance.
Dance wherever you're reading. In your seat, couch, bed, bathtub, the train or the bus.
If no one is looking, let Selena guide your dance. Shake your hips, or your toes, or your knees, or your thumbs. At least move one ear.

A dance is a way of occupying space. A practice of circulating, reverberating, resonating with the air that surrounds you. Have your body transform the waves of the universe.

There is not a "correct" or "right" way to do it. You are seeking the vibration of your spine, so don't let the voices in your head tell you that, as a dancer, you are a good scholar.

Dancing on Earth restores your connection with the stars.

Think of Selena's voice as waves and of your body as a boat navigating them.

Can you sing with her?

Y se emociona. Ya no razona. Y me empieza a cantar. Me canta así.

Rene Descartes taught us to think, analyze, understand. *Cogito ergo sum.* Santa Selena teaches you to suspend your reasoning and connect with your heart, the one singing *bidi bidi bom bom.*

Love, you gotta sing with her.

Your voice connects the land with the stars.

Every time we see a show or read a play, our whole body enters another country.

If you are like me, you'll find the nation of *The Brunch Crowd*, this one made of stars, super close to yours.

Con Selena, en drag, en español y todo.

If this is not your land, that's OK. You don't need a visa. Just take your shoes off.

And remember this land is endangered. Don't take it for granted. Ever.

And remember

To nurture it

Sing to it

Porque podemos perder el suelo que ocupamos. Muches aprendimos ya a llevar nuestra tierra en los bolsillos, para que no nos deje nunca. En cualquier rato hay que meter los libros a la maleta y seguir ruta.

Prepare your body. When you're ready, turn the page.

References

Acosta Powell, Amelia. 2022. "Best Medicine: Why We Need the 2022 LTC Comedy Carnaval." *Howlround*, 9 June. https://howlround.com/best-medicine-why-we-need-2022-ltc-comedy-carnaval.

Amich, Candice. 2020. *Precarious Forms. Performing Utopia in the Neoliberal Americas.* Evanston: Northwest University Press.

Eddowes-Vargas, Sebastián. 2023. "Negotiating the Migrant Self in Maia Novi's *Invasive Species*," *Howlround*, 13 August. https://howlround.com/negotiating-migrant-self-maia-novis-invasive-species.

Eddowes-Vargas, Sebastián. 2024. "On *Between Two Knees*, or About Other Futures," *Howlround*, 17 April. https://howlround.com/between-two-knees-or-about-other-futures.

Gómez, Laura E. 2022. *Inventing Latinos.* New York: The New Press.

Kendi, Ibram X. 2019. *How To Be An Antiracist.* New York: One World.

Muñoz, José Esteban. 1999. *Disidentifications. Queers of Color and the Performance of Politics.* Minneapolis: University of Minnesota.

Muñoz, José Esteban. 2009. *Cruising Utopia. The Then and There of Queer Futurity*. New York: New York University Press.

Muñoz, José Esteban. 2020. *The Sense of Brown*. Durham and London: Duke University Press.

The New York Times Magazine. "The 1619 Project." Accessed January 20, 2025. https://www.nytimes.com/interactive/2019/08/14/magazine/1619-america-slavery.html.

Núñez, Joanna; Jasmine Rubalcava-Cuara; and Anita Tijerina Revilla. 2021. "Triunfando con o sin papeles: Muxerista y jotx historias of DACA-mentation and Activism in Las Vegas." In *Transmovimientos. Latinx Queer Migrations, Bodies, and Spaces*, ed. Ellie D. Hernández, Eddy Francisco Alvarez Jr., and Magda García. Lincoln: University of Nebraska Press.

Ortiz, Paul. 2018. *An African American and Latinx History of the United States*. Boston: Beacon Press.

paperson, la. 2017. *A Third University is Possible*. Minneapolis: University of Minnesota Press.

Ybarra, Patricia A. 2018. *Latinx Theater in the Times of Neoliberalism*. Evanston: Northwestern University Press.

The Brunch Crowd

Dillon Yruegas (he/él)

Characters

Dallas
Mid-late 20s. Trans man (he/him). POC. Speaks English.
Don't let his outward appearance fool you with his messy hair, scruffy beard, hipster glasses, and trousers covered in paint. This artist uses his medium to highlight his journey through life as a queer transman of color from big-city Texas. He also works as a bartender at a popular local dive. In a relationship with **Erik**.

Erik/La Bruja-ja
Late 20s-early 30s. Non-binary (he/they). Tejano/Mexican-American. Speaks Spanglish.
An activist by day and drag queen by night, he works for Safe House, a local non-profit that once helped them whenever he moved from the Valley. Through their drag performances, he puts their theatre degree to use with over-the-top handmade costumes. In a relationship with **Dallas**.

Flor
Mid-late 20s. Trans woman (she/her). Black Mexican-American. Speaks Spanglish.
A busily working actress in both theatre and film, this Austin native doesn't often hang out with the group due to her various rehearsal and shooting schedules. She always finds time for brunch though. Her hard work is paying off as she is already a known name in the Central Texas scene.

Q
Early-mid 20s. Non-binary (they/them). Black or Afro-latine. Speaks English.
Originally from a tiny town in the middle-of-nowhere Texas, they have a goal of becoming the next big influencer. They can actually boast a decent following and are sometimes recognized out-and-about! Even though their zodiac sign is a Leo, the animal they identify with is a peacock.

Setting

A part of East Austin that's experiencing the mid-late stages of gentrification. The group's regular brunch spot, Taqueria Maria Félix, is a traditionally decorated Tex-Mex restaurant. It is one of the last original family-owned businesses holding out against the encroaching developers.

Time

Late 2010s.

Playwright's Note:
The half scenes are texts between the group that are projected in a similar way to Q's videos. Actors/Directors: feel free to codeswitch in differing Spanish "slang" or AAVE whenever it feels necessary. I'm only well-versed with some older Tejano colloquialisms and, as a non-Black person of color, don't feel it's appropriate for me to write in AAVE. This script is not sacrosanct and can be altered to fit the language's naturalistic style at your discretion.

Scene 1

The group's regular brunch spot. **Dallas**, **Erik**, **Flor**, *and* **Q** *sit in a corner booth. All their glasses are raised, toasting the first mimosa of the morning.*

Flor   Cheers, queers!

Q   Hold it! I'm taking a pic.

Flor   Q, like you don't have hundreds of pics exactly like this.

Q   You're one to talk, Flor. I'll be awaiting a similar pic in your Insta story.

Flor   Ay, whatever. Take the damn pic. (*A beat, perhaps after at least a couple of pictures are taken.*) Wait! Let me switch hands; I want to show off my new ring I got in LA.

Erik   Ooo girl, let me see! (**Flor** *extends her hand across the table.*) That's so cute! And your nails look flawless, as always.

Flor   Thanks! My tía has her own salon in Boyle Heights.

Dallas   Is that why you weren't here last week? I must have missed it.

Flor   Yeah, it was my cousin's wedding. Her mom closed down the salon for two days so all of us could get ready. Free manis, pedis, eyebrows, y todo. Dallas, I thought you were on IG; I posted tantos fotos about it!

Dallas   Well, I—

Erik   Ay sí, but he never checks it.

Dallas   I do, too, Erik! Just because I'm not constantly scrolling through my feed, it doesn't mean I'm never on it.

Erik   True, but tell me, if you didn't need it as a "networking opportunity" for your art, would you have one at all?

Q   I can answer that: no. He barely has any social media presence outside of his art.

Dallas   That's all the presence I need. Besides, if I did, I wouldn't want to surpass you, Q: Influencer.

Q   Well, thank you for your generosity, kind sir.

Flor   Oh my goddess, did I tell you that a lot of mis primitos and their friends actually follow you?

Q   In LA? Wow, cool!

Erik   Oh, I didn't know we had a celebrity among us!

Flor   Right? They were watching your old video about *Frozen* and got all excited when I told them I knew you personally.

Dallas   You did a video about *Frozen*? Why?

Erik   I remember watching it. You said that Elsa's powers were just a magical manifestation of anxiety—

Q   —and depression. Yeah!

Dallas   Interesting. How so?

Q   Well, she's born with these powers that neither she nor her parents are willing to understand and so they live in fear of them, even of Elsa herself, right? This fear leads to isolation and loneliness and then evolves into accidental violent outbursts. As the story continues, she further isolates herself in a refusal to actually understand how her powers manifest or even to control them. Eventually, through the help of her sister, she learns ways to cope & manage her powers.

Dallas   So how do her powers translate into mental illness?

Q   It's mostly in the way they're portrayed, really. Anxiety shows itself in many ways, but mostly in debilitating fear and feelings of helplessness. Elsa was afraid of her powers and they would spiral out of control the more overwhelmed she became. That caused depression which was shown by her wanting to isolate herself from the world.

Dallas   Oh wow, I never really thought of it like that. Are you going to do a follow-up one now that *Frozen II* is finally out?

Q   Duh! I've already written and recorded it. I'm in the process of editing it. I'm addressing its Disney-fied decolonial message!

Flor   I still need to watch it, though I wasn't a huge fan of the first one.

Q   It's so much better than the first! Which is super rare for Disney/Pixar.

Flor   Yeah, that's why I've been hesitant.

Q   We should have a little watch party sometime!

Erik   Ooo yes, but as soon as I'm done producing my next Drag Bronche. That'll take up all my free time for the next few months.

Flor   Oh my goddess, I'm so excited; I can't wait! Remind me when it is again? I wanna make sure I can keep it open around my next shooting schedule.

Erik   The 23rd at 11.

Flor   Perfecto!

Q   Have you decided what you're going to perform yet?

Erik   Ay no. It's definitely going to be themed around La Reina's birthday, but I don't know which song of hers I want to perform.

Dallas   Well you do have that amazing outfit from her Houston Rodeo performance.

Erik   Pues sí pero I don't want to be that tired old queen who parks and barks *Como la flor*. As amazing and perfect and iconic as it is, gracias a Santa Selena.

They all make their own gestures/noises in praise of Selena.

Dallas   I'm sure you'll come up with something, baby.

Flor   Sí sí sí, you haven't done the disco mash-up medley thingy at that performance yet.

Erik   Ooo buen idea!

Flor   Pues claro, mi querido!

Q   Y'all, I think we're finally hitting the "speaking mostly in Spanish" level of drunk.

Flor   Pendeje, you know damn well this one little pitcher ain't doin' shit.

Q   True . . .

Erik   Yeah, not for this group of borrachos!

Erik *raises their glass to cheer and starts to dance in his seat. The rest of the group joins in for a mini dance break. Collectively, they are loud and expressive without a care as to whomever is around or blessed enough to witness this act of pure joy. Once they quiet down a bit,* **Dallas** *gets up from the booth.*

Dallas   I'm gonna load up another plate from the buffet and get us another round. Y'all need anything?

Q   Nah, I'll come with you.

Flor   Can you bring some more fruta?

Dallas   Yeah, def.

Flor   Like, a bigass plate.

Q   Oh my goddess woman, yes!

Flor   Gracias mis amores!

Dallas   Erik?

Erik   Estoy bien. (*He kisses* **Dallas** *on the cheek.*) ¡Gracias cariño!

Q (*turning to walk away*)   GAAAAAAYYY!

Dallas   Shut up . . .

They exit.

Flor   Soooo . . .

Erik   Yes . . .?

Flor   So when are you gonna do it? I've been waiting for you to bust out that gorgeous bracelet you bought since we first walked in!

Erik   Ay, I don't think I'm gonna do it today.

Flor (*almost yelling*)   Chingao pendejo, por qué no?

Erik   Oh my goddess, Florinda! ¡Cállate!

Flor   Pues dímelo!

Erik   Well I brought it up last night, just the subject of marriage in general, and he went off on one of his rants about how it's "an archaic ritual of patriarchal ownership" and "a plot to uphold inherent white supremacy." And like, he's not wrong, but it's still disheartening.

Flor   Ay, queride I'm sorry. You know he's just being a total cynical Capricorn stellium and is completely head over heels in love with you, right?

Erik   Sí yo se, pero, today's just not the right time.

Flor (*bringing them in for a hug*)   Of course, mi amor.

Q *and* **Dallas** *arrive back at the booth with a couple of plates, a carafe of mimosas, and a small tray mounded with a variety of fruits.* **Flor** *and* **Erik** *are still embracing, but break apart once the fruit tray is placed on the table.*

Q   Aw, y'all are so cute! I want in on this little love fest.

Flor (*noticing the tray*)   Ojalé, y'all! That's a ton of fruit!!

Dallas   Well you said you wanted a bigass plate so . . .

Flor   I mean yeah, but I didn't . . .how did y'all manage to get a tray?!

Dallas   Oh I just asked.

Erik   And they just gave it to you?

Dallas   Yeah—

Q (*pouring the next round of mimosas*)   Nah, this fool tried to walk away with the entire tray that was already there, but one of the staff caught his ass. Thankfully they know us so well that all he had to do was explain what he was doing and they got him a fresh tray from the back.

Erik   Oh my goddess cariño . . .

Flor   Well damn, all right!

Dallas (*shrugging*)   Hey, it worked! It's not like we're at The W where they'd ban us or something.

Q   Anyways, cheers queers! We better start working on this bigass plate of fruit.

Fade to black as they dive in and continue chatting.

Scene 1.5

Flor *texts* **Q**.

Flor   I can't believe that Erik chickened out!

Q   Chickened out from what?

Flor   OMG did they not tell you??
He wanted to propose to Dallas at brunch today!

Q   STFU NO WAY!

Flor   Sí, wey!

Q   Lol stop . . .

Flor   Never!
winking emoji
But yeah, Dallas was being his Capricorn self, disparaging the institute of marriage the night before, so that gave Erik cold feet.

Q   Oh bless his heart, poor thing.

Flor   We gotta help them out.

Q   Of course, they're meant to be!
Operation Get-Dallas'-Head-Out-Of-His-Ass is a go!

Flor   Yes, but we're choosing a different name.

Q   UGH fine lol.
Ima text the group chat!

Flor   WAIT!
What are you gonna say?

Q   I found an article with some gorgeous photos about how same-sex marriage is now legal in Nueva León.

Flor   Oooo that's perfect! Commence Operation Erik Does Dallas.

Q   *skull emoji*
Ttyl I'm gonna FT with Ashley!

Flor   Have fun!
Tell your gf that I hope she's having fun frolicking in France.

Q   *pink sparkle heart emoji*French flag emoji*baguette emoji*croissant emoji*

Scene 2

Lights up on **Q** *setting up their filming station at a desk in their bedroom. They have a desktop ring light with a phone attachment and a small lav microphone underneath it. As they sit, they check their frame in the selfie camera and adjust for various seated positions. Once they are satisfied with its placement, they go over to their bed which has a mound of clothes laid out upon it. In front of their mirror, they hold some up and try some on. These clothes showcase the array of* **Q**'*s style when it comes to their gender identity: crop tees, silky blouses, flannel shirts, dashikis, polos, dresses, tank tops, etc. They finally settle on a plain t-shirt and sit in front of their setup. They do a final look on their phone, put on the lav mic, dab away the sweat on their face, take a deep breath, and begin recording. As they do:*

Lights fade to black. Projection of **Q**'*s video.*

Q   Hey there, Q-ties! *(NOTE: pronounced "cuties.")* First off, thank you for the love on my latest *Frozen II* vid. I'm so glad that it resonated so much with so many of you and I'll be sure to catch up with my responses to you all very soon. Unfortunately, your nonbinary fave is going through a hard personal time right now so it might take me a little bit longer this time around. Don't worry, I'm fine! Well, not fine I guess, but I'll survive. I've survived worse! *(Beat.)* My college sweetheart broke up with me today. Those of you who've been around know that she's been studying abroad in France for her master's. This is coming as a bit of a shock to me. I mean, we've been together for almost two years now. I really thought we had something special, but . . . We weren't exactly sure what the future held for us once she graduated, but I thought we would figure it out together at least. Maybe she didn't think of me in her future. She does come from a relatively affluent family and they have their expectations . . . or so she says. I guess an influencer on-the-rise wasn't on the pre-approved partners list. I mean the lowkey racist thing goes without saying, but I thought that didn't matter to her. I thought she was different, could actually stand up to her family about it, me and our relationship. She already had whenever she told them she was queer and in a relationship with a very queer person! That's what hurts the most right now; it feels like she didn't fight for me. She just . . . gave in. *(More to themself, thinking out loud.)* Maybe there's someone else, some exotic Frenchman sweeping her off her feet. *(Coming back to the present recording.)* No, I can't think like that right now! Anyway I wanted to give y'all a little update so you're not worried about my lack of responses or posting. Until next time, Q-ties!

End of video.

Scene 2.5

The group chat, Bronche Babes. **Dallas** *shares* **Q**'*s video on* Frozen II.

Dallas   Wow, Q! This is such a great take!
green heart emoji

Erik   Felicidades queride!
It's already got so many views!
black heart emoji

Flor   Our baby influencer is about to blow tf up!
purple heart emoji

Erik   Hell yeah!
That YouTube partnership is just around the corner, I can feel it!

A beat. We hear the iMessage button click sound typing a message, then being erased.

Erik   Everything okay bb?

Flor   Oh, they were talking with Ashley this afternoon.

Erik   Ah well, hope y'all have a good catch up.
Again, felicidades queride!
black heart emoji

More typing. More erasing. A beat.

Q   Q loved "Again, felicidades queride!"

Scene 3

*Another brunch at their regular corner booth, but only **Dallas**, **Erik**, and **Q** are present. They are already drinking and a fourth glass awaits **Flor**'s arrival. There's a slight tension between the three as **Q** slams back their drink, refills it, downs it, and refills it again.*

Erik   Q, queride, I know you're dealing with a lot right now, but maybe you should slow down a bit. At least, until we get our food.

Q *just stares at them. A dare.*

Erik   Or not . . .

Dallas   Let them be, babe.

Q *pauses, contemplating chugging this drink too. They think better of it, take a sip, and set the drink down. An awkward pause before **Flor** enters.*

Flor   ¡Buenas mis amores! Oh, gracias for the drink; I need this.

She takes a big swig of her drink, sets it down, and notices the awkward tension.

Flor   Damn y'all, why are y'all acting like someone just told you that your dog died?

Erik   Q, did you not tell her yet?

Flor   Tell me what?

Erik   Ashley broke up with them.

Flor   ¿Qué qué? Over FaceTime?

Erik   Yes! The gall!

Flor   The audacity!

Erik   The caucacity!

Flor   Por supuesto

Flor and **Erik**   La pinche güera se—

Dallas *clears his throat to stop* **Erik** *and* **Flor** *from getting started. They are both quick to catch themselves, but another awkward pause ensues.*

Flor   Q, queride, I'm so sorry. What do you need right now?

Q   A distraction! This brunch shouldn't be about me and my drama. We're celebrating y'all's anniversary!

Flor   Of course. (*Raising her glass.*) Felicidades a Erik y Dallas! Cheers queers!

They hold up their glasses and cheers.

Flor   I know we were all there, but let's reminisce on the early years when y'all first got together.

Q   You mean when they finally decided to make it official.

Flor   Ay but for real though! Y'all took forever to do that.

Erik   I didn't want to rush him into putting a label on our relationship.

Dallas   Yeah, but like I knew we would be in each other's lives for a long time. I didn't want to scare you off with that kind of thinking too soon.

Flor   Awww qué romántico!

Q   I think one of my fave stories is the one about the rainbow bracelet.

Erik   Ugh, that trash I got that one year all the big box stores decided that it was a good idea to start investing in rainbow capitalism?

Dallas   Aw that was a lovely night though! I still have that bracelet, ya know?

Flor   Oh my goddess, that's so cute. Dímelo! I wanna hear the story again.

Erik   Ay fine, so . . . FLASHBACK: **Erik**'s *bedroom in his childhood home.* **Erik** *is finishing packing the last of their suitcases before he leaves for Connecticut in the morning.* **Dallas** *is seated on the floor next to* **Erik**'s *bed.*

Dallas   So, what else do you need to pack?

Erik   Just clothes really. I don't want to take anything that I won't use, especially because it'll get so cold there, I doubt any of my jackets will be of any use.

Dallas   Yeah, plus it'll be a good excuse to update your wardrobe to make it extra fabulous.

Erik   Exactly! You know I need to impress all the bourgeois bitches at (*pretends to flip their hair*) Yale.

Dallas   (*laughing. Perhaps they both put on an affected Northeastern US old money accent for these next few lines.*)   Of course! How ever else would you be able to earn your MFA and your MRS?

ERIK   Precisely! You know I'm going to be swimming through an ocean of modest, repressed, WASPy gay boys who are just aching to realize the full potential of their teeming sexuality.

Dallas   And how convenient that you are so wise and possess worldly experience that you may bestow upon them your sage wisdom.

Erik   It is my duty that I take very seriously.

Beat as they both dissolve into a giggle fit.

Erik   Speaking of imparting my sage wisdom, I have a surprise for you, my dear.

Dallas   Oh do you, now?

Erik   Yes, I do. (*He rummages in a bag, obviously for dramatic effect.*) It's something that I happened upon, in Target of all places, but I immediately thought of you and just had to get it.

Erik *presents a rainbow bracelet.*

Erik   Here you are, querido.

Dallas   I, wow. Thank you. This is . . . yeah, thank you.

Erik   You're welcome! And I have another surprise for you.

Dallas   Oh?

Erik (*pulling out a matching bracelet*)   I bought one for myself as well. Now we have our own special, very gay friendship bracelets.

Dallas *is speechless. He and* **Erik** *just stare at each other for a few beats.*

Dallas   I'm going to miss you so much.

Erik   Me too. So much.

Dallas   I'm so proud of you though. It's so amazing and I just love you so much.

Erik   Thank you. I love you too.

Dallas   You're going to do such wonderful things with your life. I'm so glad that I get to be a part of it.

Erik   You too, cariño. Thank goodness we live when we do because we'll still be able to keep in contact across the country.

Dallas   Right?? Thanks internet!

Eri (*after a pause, uncharacteristically vulnerable*)   We'll be fine, right?

Dallas   Yes, we most definitely will.

Erik   Good, because you're gonna be in my life por vida sabes?

Dallas   I wouldn't have it any other way.

End of flashback. Lights back up on their corner booth.

Flor   Ay, that's too damn cute. But I thought y'all didn't start seeing each other until after Erik came back?

Dallas   Oh, we totally slept together that night.

Flor   ORALE!!!

Erik   Oh my goddess, Dallas!

Dallas   What?! We did! And it was obviously so unforgettable that you just had to come back home and claim me for your own.

Flor   I thought y'all moved in together rather quickly after Erik graduated, but little did I know . . .

Erik   I hate y'all.

Dallas   Love you too, babe.

Erik   Anyways, do you want to tell these two about your good news?

Q   Nice deflection.

Dallas   No, no. We'll be nice after embarrassing his poor, delicate sensibility. I got asked to do a solo show at the Red Bird Gallery!

Flor   That's amazing!!

Dallas   Aw, thanks.

Flor   Have you thought about what your theme is going to be yet? Or are they commissioning you to do something specific?

Dallas   Um, yeah I got to choose my own actually. I know it's kinda cliché, but I've been thinking a lot about astronomy, astrology, how they've been weirdly gendered, and how it doesn't make any sense why they can't inform each other.

Flor   Honey, how is that cliché?

Dallas   Oh you know, trans masc obsessed with astrology and gender.

Erik   Querido, not at all! Tell them what you told me, how you explained it.

Dallas   Well, the way I justify my belief in astrology is that we come from stars, right? "Our bodies are made of stardust." The same elements that make up our bodies make up the planets and the stars. Also, science tells us that energy can neither be created nor destroyed; it can only be transformed or transferred from one form to another. So if our bodies come from this energy that has been reused and reworked and refined for millenia, why wouldn't our beings be influenced by the planets and the stars? Science has also proven that the phases of the moon control the tides and our bodies are a majority water, so why wouldn't the moon affect us as well? Then, when you go back far enough, the archetypes of astrology also didn't have genders, so why wouldn't we identify ourselves within them? No matter what we may look like during our time on Earth, the planets and stars, these ancient and genderless beings, are our origins. They are our home.

A beat to take this all in.

Q   Wow.

Flor   Qué mágico!

Q   Yeah, you'd've made a believer outta me if I wasn't already!

Erik   I told you so, cariño. You're brilliant and it's an amazing theme for a show that will highlight that maravilloso mind of yours.

Dallas   Thanks, y'all. You really know how to make a guy feel special.

Flor   Pues querido, you are!

Dallas   Stop, I'm getting embarrassed! I'm gonna go get another pitcher . . .

Erik   Fine, mi amor. Go be in your feels a bit and come back with tasties.

Dallas *audibly rolls his eyes and exits.*

Flor   Erik. (*They don't respond. He's too busy watching* **Dallas**' *ass.*) Erik! ERIK!

Erik (*startled*)   Chinga tu pinche madre, what?!

Flor   Damn, gurl chill.

Q   Yeah, it's not our fault you were lusting after Dallas' hot ass.

Erik   So??

Q   So! Why did I have to hear from Flor that you wanted to propose the other day at brunch?

Erik   Because I know how much of a chismose you are and how difficult it is for you to keep a secret.

Q   There is not one of us who doesn't love their chisme so don't even try that excuse with me honey.

Erik   Listen, I'm just really nervous about it, okay?

Q   Of course you are! That doesn't mean that he isn't head over heels in love with you and won't say yes.

Flor   ¿Qué te digo?

Erik   ¡Sí, yo sé! This is why I didn't wanna tell you too, Q. I knew that both of y'all would team up against me, pressure me . . .

Q   We're just trying to help you out, boo. If anyone deserves to have a cute af ceremony with a lit reception celebrating your undying love for each other, it's you and Dallas. Sometimes that means that you need your besties to keep your hopes up and that little nagging voice away. (*Quieter, more to themselves but still loud enough for the others to catch.*) And maybe knock some sense into that thick-headed boy . . .

Erik   No! Dallas cannot even have an idea that I want to propose soon.

Flor   ¿Pa' que no? It's not like y'all haven't talked about it before.

Q   Right, so where's the surprise?

Erik   Well, yeah, but it's always a "what-if" kinda thing. Like talking about the future in an abstract way. The most serious marriage talk gets is when there's an important, more immediate thing coming up like renewing our lease or planning for holidays or when our health insurance changes.

Q (*noticing that* **Dallas** *is wrapping up and about to head back*)   Listen, he's almost done so I'll just say this: Dallas loves you, probably more than he ever has loved anyone in his entire life. He talks a big game, but deep down, I think he wants nothing more than to spend the rest of his life with you and would absolutely want a fabulous party to celebrate your love.

Flor   Exactly! Even if he does act like a total pendejo sometimes.

They all laugh as **Dallas** *returns to the table.*

Dallas   Here we go. It's a good thing they like us here 'cause y'all are rowdy already.

Q   Of course they do! Between how often we come here and Erik's drag brunches, we practically keep the place afloat.

Flor   Plus we're supporting one of the last original familia places on the East Side. Did you see that they closed down Los Tacos Felizes?

Erik   Yeah, I heard they were gonna try out a taco truck instead since renting out a space is so expensive nowadays.

Q   It's a damn shame how many places are closing or downsizing because of that.

Dallas   That or because younger family members don't wanna take over the business or just want the immediate payout and sell it to developers.

Flor   It makes me sad to see so few places left.

Erik   Makes me miss the old Austin.

Flor   I know. Like there's so many new skyscrapers being built. I can hardly recognize my home anymore. (*Beat.*) BUT we can't think of that right now! Let's drink and celebrate el gran amor de mis favoritos, Erik y Dallas. Cheers queers!

They cheers and drink. As they put their drinks down and pick at the chips and salsa, there is still a melancholy air about them. Still, they try to remain jovial, enjoying each other's company. Fade to black.

Scene 3.5

Erik *sends a selfie of him and* **Dallas** *to Bronche Babes.*

Erik   Barton Springs day!
Come join us.
sun with sunglasses emoji

Q   OMG on my way!!
Wait, which side are y'all on?

Erik   The free side DUH!

Flor   Ay wish I could!
sad face emoji
Shoot day!

Flor *sends an on-set selfie.*

Erik   Cute costume though!!!

Dallas   *starry eyes emoji*

Q   OMG can you snag that top afterwards?
It would go fantastic with these new jeans I just got.

Flor   Lol I'll see what I can do . . .

Scene 4

Projection of **Q**'s *YouTube video.*

Q   Hey there, Q-ties! Listen up, y'all. I'm about to go off on something that may be a bit, okay, I mean, A LOT controversial because too many of y'all are so sensitive when it comes to this. BUT anyways, here it goes, I guess: Supreme, Off-White, A Bathing Ape, all these "hype fashion" brands (yes, even the "high end" ones like Balenciaga or Balmain) are basic and ugly and y'all are dumb af for falling for this bullshit capitalist scheme. Like, c'mon y'all! What are you doing paying as much as at least a month's, if not two month's, rent for a damn t-shirt or belt or whatever. Are you happy with these choices? Are you happy going broke for something that probably only cost a coupla dollars to make? Are you happy making your parents work that damn hard for a cheap, basic, boring t-shirt with a stolen logo on it? And for what, so you can feel special? Feel cool? Sorry not sorry, but being hella into hype fashion is not a personality trait, especially when it's something that is so directly affecting so many people's livelihoods, late-stage capitalism, and the climate crisis.

Yes, don't roll your eyes at me or try to prove me wrong. There are too many accredited studies on how horrible the fashion industry is for the planet. Please look it up, y'all.

And on the flip side, too many of you rich queers are out here cosplaying poverty. Wearing brands like Carhartt and Champion that used to be cheap af at WalMart now cost an arm and a leg at their own specialty stores. Like it's not the same damn sweatshirt made in a sweatshop or the damn duck canvas coat that Jake Gyllenhall got his bussy full of beans rocked by Heath Ledger in Brokeback Mountain. Making thrifting cool, buying up all the good clothing to resell, and leaving nothing for the actually poor folks who can only shop secondhand. Y'all out here just gentrifying everything aren't y'all?!

They take a deep breath.
Damn. All right. Anyways, that's the rant of the day. I think Mercury must be retrograde in Aries or something . . . Until next time, Q-ties!

As the screen goes dark, lights up on **Q** *and* **Flor** *in* **Q**'s *room.* **Q** *shuts their set-up off. They take a breath, look at* **Flor**, *and they both start cackling.*

Flor   I mean, DAMN! All right!

Q   Yo, I don't even know where that came from.

Flor   But for real tho! That was definitely one of your saltier rants. You dehydrated, babe?

Q   Shut up! I am perfectly seasoned.

Flor (*laughing*)   You have a great point though. I don't know how people can spend that much money on some basic-looking clothing or accessories. Like don't get me wrong, I stay up-to-date on my looks and have some high-end pieces, but ya girl didn't pay full price for them because mi mamá didn't raise no fool.

Q   Oh, you know it baby!

They both laugh a while, then **Q** *gets a serious distant look on their face.*

Flor   Ay, what is that look for?

Q   What? What look?

Flor   You know what look. That sad, spaced-out, distant, *Dondé está mi amante perdido?* look.

Q   Girl, bye. I am not in a novela.

Flor   I mean, ever since la pinche güera broke up with you—

Q   Wow . . . really? Is that how you really felt about her?

Flor   Queride, look. I know how much you cared about each other and how much this break up sucks, pero no, she wasn't my favorite person in the world.

Q   Well damn, okay then.

Flor   Ay, come on now, this is no surprise.

Q   Nah, it kinda is . . .

Flor   Honey you know how I feel about the white, the cis, especially the white AND cis.

Q   Yeah, but she's diff—

Flor   Uh uh, I'm gonna stop you right there, mi amor, and I need you to listen. You are a Black queer trans person living in a world that would rather see you die or conform to its unachievable standards than to see you thrive and be fully loved. Fuck that. You deserve to be surrounded by those who will recognize, respect, and celebrate all the beauty, kindness, and divinity in you. Little Miss was unable and unwilling to do the very basic thing of seeing you for you and not as some experimental dive into our community or as some poor wretch to be saved with her false idea of love. So she can go right on ahead and live out the rest of her boring ass life married to a boring ass man and their boring ass twice-a-year quiet missionary sex that somehow produces their boring ass two point five children. Queride, you are so much better than any of that and you deserve so much more.

Q (*quietly*)   Yeah, you're right. Thank you.

Flor   Of course, mi amor. I'm always here for you and ready to set those thoughts right. It's okay to feel sad and to grieve the loss, but I promise you that it'll pass so soon and you'll be so better off without Miss Birkenstocks and TERF bangs.

Q   OH MY GOD! She does have TERF bangs!!

Flor   Honestly, that should have been your first red flag when she got them cut as soon as she got to France.

Q   Yo but for real tho!

Flor   Come on now, we've given that Urban Outfitters reject enough time today. Let's go out to la fruteria; I'm craving a mangonada.

Q   Mmm, I want a coconut paleta.

Flor (*laughing*)   All right, nos vamos!

Fade to black as they exit.

Scene 4.5

Erik *texts the Bronche Babes.*

Erik   OMG are y'all at Bigote Elote still??
Bring me a chamoy mangonada pleeeaassseee!
black heart emoji

Q   Isn't it super close to your office?
Come meet us here!

Erik   PussInBoots.gif

Flor   Pues fiiine.

Q   But we're kidnapping you to go visit Dallas for happy hour at Thalia's.

Erik   That's a fair trade, I suppose.

Dallas *sends a selfie of him behind the bar.*

Dallas   Bring me an elote cup with extra Tajin please!
green heart emoji

Flor   *eye roll emoji*mango emoji*corn emoji*drinks emoji*purple heart emoji*

Scene 5

Another brunch at their regular corner booth, but this time only **Erik**, **Flor** *and* **Q** *are present. Again, they are already drinking and a fourth glass awaits* **Dallas'** *arrival.*

Flor   Cheers, queers!

They all raise their glasses, cheers, and drink.

Q   So is today the day?

Erik   Is today the day for what?

Q   For the proposal!

Erik   Ay no! I wasn't even thinking about it so I don't have the bracelet.

Flor   Santa Selena purísima! You're gonna give me a heart attack if you don't hurry up and propose to this boy!

Erik   Lo siento pero what's the big deal? So I forgot it!

Q   Honey, we are waiting on pins and needles for this damn proposal!

Erik   So what, y'all think I'm gonna propose every time we brunch now?

Flor and **Q**   Yes, bitch!!

Erik   Damn alright, y'all! I promise to let y'all know when I'm planning it next time.

Flor   And that next time will be . . . ?

Erik   Ay, I don't know!

Q   Oh my goddess, why don't you do it at Drag Bronche?

Flor   Yes, that's perfect!!

Erik   I don't know. Isn't that a little too public for him?

Q   Eh maybe but think about it: if you have been dropping little hints like we told you to, then he'll be expecting it to happen someplace like our brunches or any time we're out together as a family. Plus, he'll be so wrapped up in your work and the performances that he won't expect for you to share the spotlight with him. He won't expect it at all!

Flor   Es la verdad.

Erik   Okay, I'll think about it.

Q   You know I'm right. It'll be—

Dallas *enters*.

Q   There he is!

Dallas   Hey y'all. Sorry I'm late. I had a meeting with the owners of Cheer Up Charlie's. They want me to help out with updating some of the murals and signage in the new space.

Erik   No worries, cariño. I told them what you were up to.

Q   How exciting!

Flor   Yes, felicidades! Ay, but Cheer Ups hasn't been the same since it moved from its spot on the east side.

Q   I know! It's nice that it's easier to walk between there and Tuezgayz now, but that's about it. Too many random tourists and drunk bros stumbling off from Dirty Sixth.

Flor   Exactly! The only time that I-35 has been a blessing, cutting in between downtown and the east side.

Dallas   That vegan food truck is real good though!

Q   You right! I'm not even vegan, but you right!

Flor   It's been a minute since I've been to Tuezgayz.

Erik   Ay same! The Safety House folks tried to get me to go to Barbarella's on a different night the other day and that was a hard pass. I don't wanna be surrounded by unwashed crust punks crying to The Smiths.

Flor   Oh hell nah! It's Tuesdays or nothing with that trashass bar.

Q   Let's go! This week's theme is Aaliyah's birthday.

Dallas   I haven't been in a while either. I'm usually at Thalia's on Tuesdays. It might be nice to check it out.

Flor   Yesss! Nos vamos!!

Erik   I might need to call in sick the next day, partying with you borrachos!

Flor   Pero it'll be worth it!!

Erik   Speaking of birthdays celebrating artists whose lives were cut tragically short, I finalized both my costume, my number, and most of the performers for La Reina's Drag Bronche!

Flor   Fantástico! Which costume? Which number? Who else is performing?

Erik   The Houston Rodeo fit. The Disco Medley. Most of the girls from the House of Pantuflas and the reliable girls from the Court.

Q   Gurl, reliable? You mean the few former empresses who don't have a stick up their ass thinking they're better than the queens who need to work for their money just because they ain't got a rich daddy bankrolling their pet charity projects?

Flor   Out here playing Real Housewives of LG without the T.

Erik   Stoooop! The Court has helped raise a lot of money for Safety House in the past. I gotta keep in some of their good graces.

Q   Betta you than me because I cannot stand playing that fakeass shit.

Dallas   Yeah, it started as such a good idea, but they seem to be falling into the "acceptable gays" trap of respectability politics. I'm so glad you decided not to continue with them, babe.

Flor   Eso! Out here doing the real work.

Erik   Alright, alright. It's hard enough to find the money to help everyone in need. All this in-fighting and community drama doesn't help anyone. I'm just trying to do what I can with the skills and resources I have.

Q   And how!

Flor   Anyways, I'm excited to see your performance! And the other girls, I guess. Do they also have to do songs from La Reina?

Erik   Sí, I've asked them to perform anything from Selena y Los Dinos.

Flor   Perfecto! Oh my goddess, did y'all see that they're developing a Netflix series about her?!

Erik   Qué qué?! ¡No mames!

Flor   En serio! Pero it's an official family production so you know what that means . . .

Erik   Ay, I don't even wanna think about it. Let the poor girl descanse en paz.

Flor   But for real tho! We'll see how it goes.

Q   Well I'm looking forward to busting out a fire fit for Tuezgays and Drag Bronche.

Flor   Absolutely! No casual slays. We gotta look our best!

Q   We're gonna have to look our absolute best for Drag Bronche! I have a feeling that this will be one to remember forever.

Erik   Well, I'm glad that I'm set already.

Dallas   Babe, you're gonna have to help me because I have no clue.

Erik   I gotchu cariño!

Flor   Yay! (*Raising her glass.*) To all these fabulous events coming up!

Q (*raising their glass*)   Everyone won't know what hit 'em!

Flor   Cheers queers!

They cheers and drink. Fade to black.

Scene 5.5

Q sends a selfie to the Bronche Babes.

Q   Tuezgayz fit check!

One by one, the others send theirs.

Q   YAAASSSSSS!!!!
*starry eyes emoji*pink sparkle heart emoji*painting fingernails emoji*

Flor   Look at all these bad bitches!

Dallas   Erik put body glitter on me like a Twilight vampire!
Wrong kind of vampire!
QueenOfTheDamned.gif

Erik   ShineBrightLikeADiamond.gif

Q   ImAKillerBella.gif

Flor   AaliyahThatsRight.gif

Scene 6

Projection of Q's video.

Q   Hey there Q-ties! Thank you to everyone who's been liking and sharing my recent vids. Looks like the fashion one hit a little nerve with some of y'all! I'm trying to respond to as many as I can, but honestly some of you anon blank face accounts don't deserve it. Thanks for driving up my engagement though! As they used to say, all publicity is good publicity right? Anyway, I've come across quite a few other vids and accounts of other queer folks questioning their whole identity recently. So! It's your nonbinary fave coming to you with a special message. I don't know who needs to hear this right now. Hell, maybe it's me who needed to hear this when I was a little gayby growing up in middle-of-nowhere Texas. Either way, I felt compelled to share this message with y'all today. Anyway, listen up! No matter where you are on your journey in life, if you're questioning, if you're not able to be out and proud, or if you're having a difficult time right now: please know that you are not alone in your struggle. You are a divine being inhabiting a body who is in an ancient lineage of transcendent ancestors who know the fullness of humanity. I'm proud of you and I love you. Thank you for existing. Thank you for staying. Thank you for your resilience. I hope you can soon find clarity, peace, joy, and rest. If you need help, someone to listen to you vent, or to connect with various resources, please check out the link in my bio. Until next time, Q-ties!

As the screen goes dark, lights up on **Q** *and* **Flor** *in* **Q**'s *room.* **Q** *shuts their set-up off. They look at* **Flor** *and they just stare at each other a while.*

Flor   Come with me to LA.

Q   Wait, I'm sorry. What?

Flor   Ay, no seas pendeje. Come with me to LA. (*For once,* **Q** *is speechless.*) Listen, now that your YouTube partnership is coming through any day now and you're no longer pining for that güera, what do you have holding you here? And don't say Erik and Dallas because we know they'll always be here to visit, plus I know they'd be more than excited to come out to visit us, too. You always said that you moving to Austin for college was just to get you out of that tiny little nowhere town and a stepping stone to somewhere else. Why not try living anywhere other than Texas? You loved LA whenever we visited my family out there, so come with me!

Q   Even with all these new changes, I have been feeling kinda stuck lately. Like I'm not really fitting in here, other than with y'all. Do you really think LA would be any better?

Flor   I don't know queride, but for me . . . Austin hasn't felt like home lately. Sure, it's helped shape me, got me through some of my toughest times, it's where I met all y'all, and it's literally my hometown, but it's changed. I've changed. I feel like there's a bigger change coming and not for the better. I don't wanna stick around and find out what it is.

Q   Yeah, I've been feeling that too. Like I have to look over my shoulder more, make sure I have my knife on me whenever I'm out and looking more femme. These white queers will gas me up in the club, but then suddenly it's like I don't exist whenever some fucking idiot verbally harasses me on the street. It's always been bad, but it's getting worse.

Flor   Honey, why do you think I stay so booked and blessed? I don't go out unless it's for work or I'm hanging with y'all. I gotta know that I'm around people who I know got my back.

Q   So what will make LA any different?

Flor   To be honest, yo no sé. But I know that the queer scenes are different depending which part of that bigass city you're in, and there's definitely more Black and brown people that haven't been pushed out like here. That plus getting more acting gigs is all I need.

Q   I guess I don't want to romanticize it too much. That's what I did with Austin, ya know? The blue oasis in the middle of red Texas. What a crock of shit . . .

Flor   Ay, but for real though!

Q   Like yeah, it's lightyears ahead of my hometown, but it's still Texas. And then all the changes it's going through, all the fintech bros who still keep moving in and taking over . . . I don't know. I don't want to be disappointed again.

Flor   That's just our realidad. There isn't anywhere truly safe for us except for when we're all together. The four of us and even within the larger community. We keep us safe. We truly only got us. So let's get outta this town and be our own somewhere safe. Together.

Q   Together?

Flor   Siempre.

Beat.

Q   Okay, lemme think about it.

Flor   Of course! I don't know about you, but all this heavy talk really makes me want something sweet.

Q   Some fruta for my puta?

Flor   Bitch, which chingaso Instagram shitpost account did you get that from?

Q   Oh my goddess, you! It's a meme you sent the group chat. You're the chingaso shitposter.

Flor   Ay, shut up! I do want fresa con crema though.

Q   Mmm hmm!

Flor   No seas tan nasty! Get your head out of the gutter.

Q   But where else can I afford to live?

Flor   Ay ay ay, don't make me regret asking you to come with me.

Q   Whatever, you know you love it.

Flor   Yeah yeah, nos vamos . . .

Fade to black as they exit, continuing trading loving barbs back and forth.

Scene 6.5

Flor *sends a photo to the Bronche Babes of a typed flier posted on a window stating: "THANKS FOR THE LOVE EAST AUSTIN! WE'RE SAD TO CLOSE THIS LOCATION BUT CATCH US AT OUR NEW HOME IN BUDA STARTING IN MAY! <3 Bigote Elote"*

Flor   Did y'all hear about this bs?!?!
Bigote Elote is moving to Buda!!
crying emoji

Erik   W H A T ? !
NOOOOOOOO!!!!

Dallas   OMG why?

Flor   Same shit as Los Tacos Felizes.
Rent went up too much!

Erik   Of fucking course.
upside down smile emoji

Dallas   At least Buda isn't too far away.

Flor   True, but it was so easy to pop in for an elote or a mangonada or a paleta.
Now we gotta drive at least 20 mins down south!

Q   And that's without traffic.
It'll be an hour round trip at least now!

Flor   *crying emoji*crying emoji*crying emoji*

Scene 7

Another brunch at their regular corner booth.

Flor   Cheers, queers!

Q   Let me take a Boomerang real quick.

Dallas   Ugh, do we have to? You know we suck at that.

Q   Yes! You just never remember my art direction, Dallas.

Erik   Pendeje, that's because you always change it up. I told you the best way to take a Boomerang is to do it backwards.

Dallas   See, you say that and it still doesn't make sense to me.

Erik   It's just the way the loop resets. It works better if you do whatever motion you want to repeat backwards. Mira, let's try it y'all.

Q   Oh we have a new art director now, do we?

Erik   Bet. Let's do it and you'll see.

Q   Fiiiine . . .

The group lifts their glasses to the center. **Erik** *gives them either a signal or a verbal go and it doesn't work out too well. Instead of getting frustrated, they all laugh at their pendejadas and try again. After a couple of tries, success! The actors should all adlib their own sounds and/or words of reaction to these failed attempts, but keep it lighthearted and goofy. Even though they knew this would happen, they still love being silly with each other.*

Q (*through their laughter*)   Oh my goddess, finally!

Erik   You're welcome, queride.

Q   Yeah, yeah it does look good or whatever . . .

Flor   One of these days, we'll get it right the first time.

Erik   But today is not that day.

Q   But today *is* the day that your nonbinary fave officially got their YouTube partnership offer!

Flor   NO MAMES!!

Erik   BIIIIITCH!!

Flor   I'm so proud of you!

Dallas   That's so amazing! So what's next?

Q   Well I'm waiting on Twitch to add me to their partner program, which should happen any day now.

Erik   I bet they will hop on that soon since they don't want YouTube or Instagram to get all your content.

Q   Trust!

Flor   Are you gonna try for sponsorships?

Q   Of course! I really want to get new equipment so I can have a better setup and don't have to spend so much time on edits correcting color or audio.

Dallas   Your videos already look and sound so good though.

Q   Aw thank you, but I should show you the unedited versions sometime. Thank goodness I took that film editing class in college because my shit looks real profesh!

Flor   I know that's right!

Dallas   Ugh, I miss all the cheap or free supplies and software we could get as students. Sometimes I think about getting my master's just so I can update all of mine for free.

Q and **Flor** (*Singing á la Avenue Q*)   I wish I could go back to college! How do I go back to college?!

Erik   Ay pinche musical theatre nerds! Querido, I will support all your educational and artistic endeavors, but por favor do not rack up all that debt just to get free shit. It doesn't end up being free then. (*Getting up from the booth.*) Oh, I need to talk with Ramón about the final details for Drag Bronche. This might be a while and I have to get to work, so don't wait for me. I'll see y'all later. (*To* **Dallas**) Tell them the good news! Te quiero, mi amor.

Dallas   I love you too, babe.

Q and **Flor** (*singing á la Rent*)   Goodbye, love! Goodbye, love! Just came to say: Goodbye, love! Goodbye.

An exacerbated **Erik** *exits.*

Q   So what's the big news, Dallas?

Dallas   Well you know how I got that solo show at Red Bird Gallery?

Flor   Yes! I was so full and inspired y todas buenas vibras from celebrating all your brilliance.

Dallas (*blushing*)   Stop . . . anyway apparently it's already getting some buzz and I was invited to create another mural in the neighborhood.

Q   Oh okay then! Look at you!

Flor   Ay mira!

Dallas   Thanks!

Flor   Where's it gonna be?

Dallas   On the inside of Echeverrias down on Holly Street.

Q   Oh my goddess, I love that place!

Flor   Right? I love to sit there with a little cafecito surrounded by all the succulents. It's the closest thing I can have to owning one since all mine always seem to die.

Q   Isn't that ironic, with the name you chose and all?

Flor   Ay cállate pendeje.

Dallas   Also, I may have received a residency for the summer.

Q   Bitch what?! Where?

Dallas   Provincetown?

Q   You mean the queer capital of New England, Provincetown?

Dallas   Yeah!

Flor   AAHH!! ¡Felicidades querido!

Q   Oh my goddess Flor, we should visit!

Flor   Pues claro! I've never been and I wanna see what the hype is all about.

Q   I hear they have different themed weeks and drag shows every night.

Flor   Ay but isn't New England like super white?

Dallas   Yeah, but Ptown is like super artsy and a tourist destination since it's at the end of the Cape and a short ferry ride from Boston. Plus I think one of the themed weeks is around people of color?

Q   Yes! There's even a bear week!

Flor   We'll go then and get you a shirt that says, "Dip me in honey and throw me to the bears!"

Q   OMG but for real though! And we can literally do that too right?

Flor   Ay you and your suciedades . . .

Q   You love it! (*To* **Dallas**.) What about Erik? Are they gonna go with you?

Dallas (*hesitant*)   Uh, maybe? I don't know. I don't want to pressure him into it. I know they're always so busy with his work with Safety House and their drag performances. I don't want to take him away from that for too long.

Flor   Ay, pero they need a break too. A well-deserved vacation. How long is the residency?

Dallas   For all of June.

Q   Of course.

Flor   And that's one of their busiest times for events and fundraising, no?

Dallas   Exactly, so I don't know—

Flor   Querido, don't worry about it right now. You and Erik will figure out what's best for y'all. Besides, one month is nothing for how long y'all have been and will be together. Right now, we're celebrating you and your art and your achievements!

Q   Yes, honey! This is a big deal and you deserve to be happy and excited and joyful in this moment. Your art is getting the recognition it deserves and we need to celebrate that!

Dallas   Thanks, y'all. I know I need to be better about being in the present and not always let my anxieties about the future get in the way of that.

Flor   That's why you have us, querido!

Q   Always! Just don't forget us when you become this big famous artist.

Dallas   Well don't forget me whenever you become this big famous influencer. Or when you become this big famous actress.

Flor   Ay, I could never forget y'all. You're stuck with me por vida. (*Raising her glass.*) To Dallas, to his amazing art, and to his brilliant future. Cheers queers!

They all cheers and down their drinks. **Q** *and* **Flor** *hug* **Dallas** *and start to take selfies together as it fades to black.*

Scene 7.5

Dallas *sends a selfie to the Bronche Babes.*

Dallas   Work day at Echeverrias!

Erik   *heart eye emoji*

Q   I can't wait to see the finished mural!
It'll be the perfect backdrop for some new content.

Flor   Mira que purty!!

Dallas   Thanks y'all!
green heart emoji

Flor   We definitely need to have a photoshoot with all of us and your work!

Q   Yes! We should ask Shondrika to shoot it.

Flor   PERFECT!

Dallas   Y'all are too kind.

Flor   We gotta blow up your amazing work bb!
purple heart emoji

Q   Exactly! This is one of many more murals to come.
pink sparkle heart emoji

Scene 8

Lights up on **Q** *setting up their filming station at a desk in their bedroom. They go through similar motions as the first scene, but with updated equipment. Perhaps they have a lightbox or spots and a diffuser, a digital camera with a shotgun microphone, and a new/custom backdrop. They still check the frame and adjust accordingly. Once they are satisfied with its placement, they go over to their bed which again has a mound of clothes laid out upon it. Like before, they hold some up and try some on in front of their mirror. This time, however, they choose a fabulous high-femme top that would gag any basic bitch! They accessorize with necklaces and rings then add the shiniest gloss they own. Finally, they sit, do a final look in the camera, and dab away the sweat on their face. They press record with a remote, stare into the camera, take a deep breath, and:*

Lights fade to black. Projection of **Q**'*s video.*

Q   Hey there, Q-ties! Sit down with your nonbinary fave for a little storytime. Now, I'm not one to usually go to Oil Can Harry's in the downtown Fruit Loop here, but I was invited to accompany bestie Flor to a wrap party so why not? So we're at the party, drinking free drinks, schmoozing with the cast and crew, having a kiki, and a lovely time altogether! After a while, we notice that the regulars and tourists on the main dance floor start to outnumber the people from the wrap party in the side room, so we decide it's time to head out. As we step outside, we see a few friends from college walking around the corner and we stop to chat. Then out of nowhere, this neanderthal of a bro starts yelling slurs at us from across the street. Now usually this wouldn't bother me as badly, but I saw a few more neanderthal bro types walking about half a block behind him. Plus there have been a string of cis gay men being followed to their cars from the Fruit Loop and getting jumped so I wasn't taking any chances. I pulled out my knife and yelled in my deepest butch voice, "Fuck with us and I'll fuck you up." The bros thought better of it, tucked tail, and ran. Thankfully, it didn't escalate at all, but still . . . that was enough for me to steer clear of the Fruit

Loop forever now. (*Beat.*) To all you bigots out there: this is me. I do not apologize for being me. I do not apologize for expressing myself with my clothing, my jewelry, and my make-up. If you don't like it, choke. I've said it once and I'll say it a thousand times: I make these videos because it's what I needed as a little gayby growing up in middle-of-nowhere Texas and I hope to reach any other person out there who needs to see someone like me thriving. Try your damnedest, but I will always be me. I will always shine through. Until next time, Q-ties!

End of video.

Scene 8.5

Erik *sends a selfie to the Bronche Babes.*

Erik   Here's a little tease of the beat!

Q   A M A Z I N G !

Flor   YES!
I can't wait to see the rest queride!

Dallas   *heart eyes emoji*starry eyes emoji*

Q *sends a selfie.*

Q   I did this lük for a video earlier, but thinking I should keep it on for Bronche?

Erik   Yasss bitch!
That looks fabulous!!

Flor   Well shit, now I gotta up my game.

Dallas   I'm sure whatever you feel most comfortable in will look fantastic!

Q   Hell yeah, babe!
Your basic is a basic's 10.

Flor   *blushing emoji*purple heart emoji*
Thanks for gassing me up, y'all.

Scene 9

Another brunch at their regular corner booth, but this time all the different pride flags are interwoven with the already bright Mexican decor. It's busy! **Dallas**, **Flor**, *and* **Q** *enter individually, strutting to their seats like on a catwalk to show off their fabulously themed outfits. Perhaps underscore this with RuPaul's "Cover Girl: Put the Bass in Your Walk" or an equally fierce uptempo instrumental song. There is a carafe for each of them and a stack of ones for the performers easily accessible in the middle of the table.*

Flor   Cheers, queers!

Q   Let's take some pics with our carafes and our dolla dolla bills!

They pose, take tons of selfies and photos of each other.

Dallas   Wow there are so many people here.

Q   Well it is for Selena's birthday. She's just been getting more and more popular now that the 90s are back.

Flor (*making her noise or gesture from before*)   Gracias a La Reina! She deserves that and more!

Q   The other day I saw something about them trying to do a Selena-themed cruise.

Dallas   Ew, really?

Flor   Ay pobrecita, why won't people just let her rest in peace?!

Q   Right? Like I love her, but I can't imagine being stuck on a boat with hundreds of people just to "celebrate" her in such a consumerist way.

Flor   Exactly! I think events like this are such a great way to honor her memory without exploiting it.

Dallas   Yeah, I think Erik does a really good job of doing that and some of the other community events around town.

Q   Oh! Speaking of around town, how is the mural coming along?

Dallas   I'm pretty much done! I just have to add some finishing touches tomorrow.

Flor   Perfecto! I can't wait to see it in person. Is there going to be an official unveiling or anything?

Dallas   Nah, nothing formal like that. The owner is chill and not really into social media. I just gotta make sure that I have photos for my portfolio.

Q   Well lucky for you and your portfolio then because I've already got Shondrika on lock for a photoshoot!

Flor   Yesss! And just in time too.

Dallas   Just in time for what?

Q   Oh, nothing. You'll see . . .

Dallas   I'm so confused. What are you—

Lights shift drastically. We are transported to a place in our queer dreams; we are no longer in the restaurant. We hear the beginning of Selena's disco medley. Spotlight on **Erik** *as* **La Bruja-ja** *in Selena's last performance outfit at the Houston Rodeo. They perform the entire song to perfection: lip sync, dance moves, and all. If the stage permits, perhaps* **La Bruja-ja** *performs amongst the audience á la a real drag performance. After the song ends, they address everyone like an MC. To the actor playing them: Feel free to ad lib around this introduction with catching your breath. You did that! Be in the moment with it!*

Erik   Gaydies and gentlethems! Boys, girls, in-between, and neither! Bienvenides a todes mis querides! As you may know my name is La Bruja-ja, your resident host of Drag Bronche here at Taqueria Maria Félix. Today we are celebrating the fabulous yet tragically short life of La Reina de la música tejana, Selena Quintanilla-Perez! We have an amazing lineup for you today with everyone performing a song from the great Selena y Los Dinos songbook. Also, all our fantastic performers are graciously donating all their tips today to Safety House. For those of you who may not know, Safety House helps queer folks and those living with HIV/AIDS to connect with a number of resources, including safe housing and free to low-cost medical care right here in our beautiful hometown of Austin, Texas. So reach deep into your pockets to tip your performers, especially our next diva from the House of Pantuflas: Concha Rosa!

Lights shift back to the corner booth. **Erik** *joins everyone at the table where an extra carafe has magically appeared for them.*

Dallas (*kissing them*)   That was great, babe! Congrats.

Q   Yes, darling! Here is your hard-earned drink!

Flor   ¡Felicidades mi queride! Cheers queers!

They raise their carafes and cheers.

Erik   Ay yi yi! What a day trying to get this hot mess off and running.

Dallas   Ugh, who didn't show up this time?

Erik   Estrella, cómo siempre. I wouldn't be surprised if she double booked herself again.

Q   Yeah, I see that girl everywhere! She stays booked and busy.

Erik   Exactly! And I don't ever blame anyone for taking the paid gigs, but don't lie to my face like you're not gonna blow me and my work off.

Dallas   I get that, babe. So why don't you just stop asking her to join then?

Erik   I don't know. I don't want to be that asshole. There's enough catty queens in the community.

Flor   True, but you could have filled her spot with someone else.

Erik   I suppose yeah. Oh, Concha's almost done. Be right back!

They exit.

Flor   I wonder who else we're going to see tonight then.

Dallas   I know for sure that Panicka Tack and Madame Diamante are performing.

Q   Aw, those two are such sweethearts!

Flor   I know! I heard that they're heading up this year's Queer Bomb Extravaganza before the march.

Dallas   Oh too bad I'll miss that since it's during my residency.

Q   Speaking of! Flor and I are going to visit you toward the end of it to make sure we can go to the opening night of your exhibition.

Dallas   Aw, really? Thanks y'all, that means so much!

Flor   Por supuesto, querido! We're so proud of you and will always support you.

Erik *returns.*

Erik   What'd I miss?

Dallas   Flor and Q are gonna come to the opening night of my exhibition for my Ptown residency.

Erik   Y'all!! That's so sweet! Okay, I really need to plan ahead with work now so I can make it too.

Dallas   Oh, babe—

Erik   No, cariño. This is important and I want to be there for you. Plus I don't get vacation days for nothing!

Q   OMG yay! Girls trip!!

Flor   The other thing I wanted to tell y'all is that, right after coming to see you, the shoot for my next project is starting in LA.

Erik   Oh my goddess, you got the gig?!

Flor   Yes! I signed my contract today.

Erik   Felicidades querida!! I'm so excited for you! Wait, put a pin in this. I'll be right back!

They exit.

Dallas   I'm so happy that y'all are coming to Ptown. I don't know how much I'll be able to do with everyone as a group, but hopefully by then I'll know some fun places for y'all to hangout while I'm working.

Q   All I want to do is be as big and as gay and as flamboyantly me as possible.

Flor   And to also dip you in honey and throw you to the bears.

Q   Obviously that goes without question.

Flor   I really want to have at least one just beach day.

Dallas   Well I'm sure that won't be difficult to do at all.

Erik *returns.*

Erik   Ok! So, how long will you be in LA then Flor?

Flor   Well the shoot is for a few months, but I'm thinking that this would also be a good time for me to stay a little bit.

Dallas   Wait, stay as in move?

Flor   Maybe? I mean, I hope so.

Erik   Querida, that's amazing! This could absolutely be the jump-start you need. I know that you've been thinking about making a move forever now.

Flor   You really think so? I'm so nervous.

Erik   Are you nervous about the change?

Flor   Yeah, like what if I fail?

Dallas   Are you more scared about failing or of succeeding?

Flor   Oh my goddess, y'all cannot make me cry at Drag Bronche right now.

Q   True, no tears for this happy occasion! Besides, I decided to take you up on your offer.

Erik   Her offer?

Q   I'm gonna move to LA with Flor.

Dallas   Oh wow, you too?!

Q   Yeah, we talked about it the other day and I had some time to think about it. You're right, Flor. I've been feeling stuck and after that wrap party, I'm over this city. Plus, this could be a great chance to grow. Who better to take this giant next step with than my best friend?

Erik   Chingada madre now y'all are gonna make me cry. UGH I need to go introduce the next performer. BRB.

They exit.

Flor   Aw Q, I'm so excited that you want to come with me to LA. We have so much to plan!

Q   I know! Because I am not gonna be one of those broke bitch starving artists. Our life will be bad and bougie to the fullest!

Flor   I know that's right!

Dallas   Aw, I'm so happy and excited for y'all. Hopefully I'll be able to get a residency or some contacts out there so I can visit.

Q   Oh absolutely you are! Remember, you're gonna be a badass famous artist and the west coast will be fawning over you soon enough.

Erik *returns.*

Erik   Okay, so I've decided that we're gonna help y'all move, whenever that will be, with a fantastic going away Drag Bronche. I want to fundraise a bit so y'all don't have to worry too much about money when you first move out there.

Flor   Ay queride, that's too sweet of you.

Q   Thanks, friend.

Erik   It's the least I can do to set y'all up for success.

Dallas   Yeah, let us know whatever you need to help with this journey. You both deserve all the best with it.

Q   And we'll definitely be here for y'all's future together.

Dallas   Wait, what do you mean?

Q (*realizing that they almost let a secret slip*)   Oh, you know . . .

Flor   Wherever your journey takes you.

Erik   Actually, mi amor, there's something I've been meaning to ask you. Give me a second, Madame Diamante's almost done.

Instead of fully exiting, they once again address the audience as MC.

Gaydies and gentlethems! Boys, girls, in-between, and neither! How are we doing? Gracias a todes for your generous support for all these fabulous performers. They are working their asses off up here and y'all are a fantastic audience today. Before we wrap up, I'd like to shout out my lovely chosen family over there sitting in our regular corner booth. We have Flor who is an amazing actress around town. You may recognize her from her work with the Manor Road Collective or her guest spot on The Cult. We have the indomitable Q, our influencer on the rise. Be sure to follow them on all major platforms as @TheQfluence. And we have my wonderful partner, Dallas. While you may have seen him slinging drinks at Thalia's, he is a brilliant artist whose newest work can be seen at Echeverrias and at a solo exhibition at the Red Bird Gallery. Dallas, cariño, can you come up here please?

Unprepared and shocked, **Dallas** *rises from his seat with some helpful playful nudging from* **Q** *and* **Flor**.

Dallas, I love you with all my heart and soul. I can say that with confidence because you have taught me to love myself in that way. My love for you is reflected in the love you have for me. Growing up, I never thought a great, epic love was meant for me and in some ways, I was right. Your love isn't the cliché rom-com of miscommunication and wrong timing. Your love isn't the volatile and dramatic romances of telenovela divas. Your love is steadfast and warm and comforting and exciting and adventurous. It has been an honor and a privilege to share our lives these past few years. I want to continue to share mine with you because you are gonna be in mine por vida sabes.

During their speech, **Q** *and* **Flor** *move to stand by* **Erik**, *who produce a small jewelry box, and hand it to them.* **Erik** *kneels and opens the box which contains a gold chain bracelet.*

Dallas, el gran amor de mi vida, will you do the honor of marrying me?

Dallas   Yes. Yes! Absolutely, yes.

Erik *rises from their knees and embraces* **Dallas***. Once they break apart,* **Q** *and* **Flor** *rush to embrace them as well.* **Erik** *places the gold bracelet on* **Dallas'** *left wrist. They kiss as* **Q** *and* **Flor** *take tons of photos from different angles. Perhaps confetti falls from above as Selena's "I Could Fall in Love" plays. Fade to black.*

Scene 10: Epilogue

Projection of **Q***'s YouTube video. They're out on the beach.*

Q   Hey there Q-ties! It's your nonbinary fave: beach edition. But surprise! It's not the regular-degular Gulf beach that you're used to. Bestie Flor and I are literally on the other side of the country in Provincetown, gaying it up on the tip of the Cape. We're out here visiting Erik and Dallas for the week since Dallas' opening reception for his exhibition is later this weekend. What Dallas doesn't know (and I have him blocked from seeing this just in case) is that we're also here to witness their elopement! Don't worry Texas friends, they still plan on having a big party celebrating their love with all of you, but after the epic public proposal at Drag Bronche, Erik thought it would be romantic and special for Dallas to have something more intimate and lowkey. I'm gonna take a bit of a break from posting while we're here, but I can't wait to share all the fantastic professional photos and videos with all of you, especially of my fabulous fit. Until next time, Q-ties!

END OF PLAY

"I was lucky I wasn't born a man": New Orleans Second Line Parades and Transitions in *The More the Man*

Eric M. Glover

Jameson P. Murray begins *The More the Man* with the Second Line observing his protagonist's journey from a death to a rebirth. The stage directions call for audiences to hear a brass band playing off stage, and as Rachel Carrico also reminds us about the politics of pleasure in New Orleans Second Line parades, "Afro-Creole and African American New Orleanians have organized brass band processions, known as 'Second Lines,' that take hold of public spaces with rhythm and forward motion" (1). The brass band is known as the First Line and the group of people that is following is known as the Second Line. The Second Line begins as an initiation rite in late 19th-century New Orleans, where a brass band leads a parade, people celebrating and dancing behind, singing and twirling handkerchiefs in the air. People hold Second Lines on Sunday afternoons for many reasons, including rites of passage, such as celebrations of life, funerals, and weddings (Carrico 2). For example, the Second Line accompanies children born and unborn in New Orleans all year long just as the Second Line accompanies adults surviving and thriving in New Orleans against all odds. Murray suggests an analogy between Black trans men's lived experience and Second Lines as both constitute a major milestone in the circle of life. A gender transition and the Second Line are equated with each other in the play, with the suggested analogy being that in life as in death a person performs rites of passage. The Second Line mourns those dead of natural and unnatural causes and also celebrates those trans people having found peace and power in transition.

The play's setting is the post-Hurricane Katrina era in New Orleans, where the play's characters remain in states of disarray even to this day. Katrina, a category 5 hurricane at her height with 170 mph wind speeds, made landfall August 29, 2005, in the "Crescent City" and claimed 1,800 lives and $125b in damage. Parts of The Bahamas, Canada, Cuba, and surrounding areas were also hit, but none more than New Orleans, which is located below sea level. Ten inches of rain and storm surge overwhelmed the US Army Corps of Engineers levee system and left 80% of the city alongside Lakes Borgne and Pontchartrain underwater in five days' time. Katrina remains one of the costliest natural disasters in US history ever and residents of New Orleans still feel her impact long after recovery. Hip Hop Caucus and New Orleans Katrina Commemoration Foundation mark the anniversary in New Orleans yearly by organizing the Second Line with community members to call for reparations and remember storm victims.

The city's topography is divided into neighborhoods (73) and wards (17), where the play's characters work and live despite anti-Black racism and white supremacy. A trans man, King calls Algiers in the "Wank" home with his mother Tee Wa, originally from 7th Ward, who was and remains protective of her son: "Hell, you a man if I ever seen one . . . my son" (Murray 236). King's grandfather Oram, originally from 9th Ward, owns and operates a corner store in Algiers, where men and boys organize community and seek support. King's girl Ife, a beauty-school student originally from Gentilly, and King's boys Leo and Trick, "niggas" originally from Treme and Calliope Projects, respectively, form King's set in the East Bank. The actors that play Oram, Leon, and Tee Wa play figments of King's and our imagination: Chorus 1, Chorus 2, and Chorus 3, respectively. Transition comes and goes as a recurring theme throughout the whole of *The More the Man*, not only the sometimes difficult transition to manhood, but also the sometimes disorderly/violent transition into power.

bell hooks' *The Will to Change: Men, Masculinity, and Love* (2004), wherein she advises readers not to fear love, helps Murray tell his story. In her book, hooks builds on similar ideas about gender roles, identity, intimacy, masculinity, men, psychology, self-esteem, and sex roles that she established and that she worked through in *All about Love: New Visions* (2000), *Be Boy Buzz* (2002), a children's book, and *We Real Cool: Black Men and Masculinity* (2004)—arguing that anti-Black racist, white supremacist axes of gender, race, and sexuality hold men and boys captive in cis het patriarchy— and unless and until men and boys free themselves from the bonds of cis het patriarchy they can't love themselves, let alone somebody else. hooks teaches us not to use masculinity and patriarchy interchangeably and synonymously with each other because masculinity, as opposed to patriarchy, is worth salvaging. hooks, writing out of rejection from adults during her early childhood, submits that "when we love we can let our hearts speak" and when we love we live on after death (2018: xi). The ability to let one's heart speak leads King to power and the inability to let one's heart speak leads King from power conversely.

The prologue to *The More the Man* shows when and where affection, care, commitment, communication, recognition, respect, and trust take form in the play. When the full company sings and dances the Second Line in the house and also on stage, the full company invites the audience to join the Second Line across the fourth wall, which is important because Murray's stage directions encourage performers to recognize and directly address their audiences and vice versa over and against the imaginary wall of a production company's modern stage proscenium. The noun *Second Line* refers to both people at the Second Line and organizations charging people dues to be included in brass band processions. The verb *Second Line* refers to people on Sunday afternoons that chant, strut, and walk in a style that was and remains "improvised, percussive, footwork-heavy, individually executed yet collectively experienced" (Carrico 2). So enters Chorus 2 from the wings, stopping center stage to break the fourth wall, engaging the audience in preshow announcements before the show. The act of breaking the fourth wall encourages the Black people not to subscribe to anti-Black racist, white supremacist dictates of good manners but to participate in Black people's culture of call-and-response, and although the theater often fails to anticipate the presence of Black people in the audience, Murray's given circumstances are affirmative acts, his way of loving on Black people at the theater. The physical production is such that the play's venue goes back and forth between the full company on stage and the audience off stage.

Murray flips the script in the epilogue, revealing in a reversal that audiences are not attending King's funeral, but instead his father Adam's funeral, which is important because the audience, an offstage character in *The More the Man*, observes both King birthing himself at the Second Line and King leaving his father's hatred in the past. When Adam, dying of old age, returns to New Orleans attempting to make up for lost time, he coerces his son into spending space and time with him, but to no avail. Adam defines manhood based on what he can provide family members materially, never stopping to think about how love works and why love matters. When Adam warns King that no woman knows how to teach a boy to be a man, King argues that, to the contrary, his father's absence frees him and Tee Wa both. Not having a present father frees King up to define manhood on his terms as opposed to terms maintained by the cis het patriarchy. When a Black woman leads other Black people on the run to freedom from anti-Black racism, what hooks has long identified as an *imperialist white supremacist capitalist patriarchy* rears its ugly head: "Allegiance to sexist thinking about the nature of leadership creates a blind spot that effectively prevents masses of black people from making use of theories and practices of liberation when they are offered by women" (2004: xvi). Much has been made in law and public policy of absent Black fathers and single Black mothers causing poor outcomes for Black sons particularly. Since *The Negro Family: The Case for National Action* (1965), also known as the Moynihan Report, sons of absent Black fathers and single Black mothers are regarded as deficient in some way. Adam's figurative and literal absence from King's past, however, creates the conditions that do not limit King's present but leave it full of possibility. Although King disinherits Adam's biologically essentialist definition of manhood, which rewards mental and physical slavery and conquest, King inherits Tee Wa's socially constructed definition of manhood, rewarding faith, hope, joy, and love: "People are gonna see and expect things from me no matter what gender I am. But since I've grown up, nobody has asked me to keep my defenses up. That was a choice. One I don't subscribe to anymore because . . . well, Mama told me something in a dream. She said we can fight . . . or love" (Murray 271). Murray practices hooks' theories from *All about Love* and *We Real Cool*, therefore enacting King's ascendency in New Orleans as Tee Wa's heir apparent.

Different forms of Black expressive culture, including but not limited to bounce music and Umfundalai, combine to make the New Orleans of the play, therefore applying an approach to text and performance that rejects traditional categories of gender identity and narrative genre in much the same way that King continues to reject colonization of his body. When King wades in the water in the prologue à la enslaved Black people on the run, he recalls "Take Me to the Water" from Alvin Ailey American Dance Theater's *Revelations* (1960). Thomas F. DeFrantz describes Ailey, the late founder of the eponymous dance company, as the single most important Black American choreographer in modern dance history. About Ailey's *Revelations*, DeFrantz observes that, set to the Negro spiritual "Wade in the Water," a Black deaconess leads two Black initiates into a flowing river of silk-like cloth: "With focused seriousness of intention, the initiates step into the water to begin a rippling motion of the torso which builds over the course of the song into full-bodied ecstatic dancing" (10). Such choreography, at once an act by which King is initiated into manhood and by which he is overtaken during Hurricane Katrina's ten inches of rain and storm surge, is interrupted until Choruses 1, 2, and 3 perform a dream ballet with one another, depicting Adam, King, and Tee Wa's life. Trick bucks at the audience when he exits the play, after he, King,

Leon, and Oram play mack daddies and womanize many an unsuspecting sister girl beforehand. Dance, and New Orleans stomp in particular, is the language that King uses to cleanse and purge his emotions: King holds the Second Line for himself, where he cleanses and purges his fear out, mirroring people celebrating and dancing behind a brass band procession, singing and twirling handkerchiefs in the air.

Murray's *The More the Man*, unlike other contemporary plays written by Black writers, anticipates a Black audience dramaturgically through character, event, and given circumstances. Murray's contemporary play invites and encourages his audience to help the full company tell the story despite white houses policing their Black audiences and discouraging their acts of antiphony and methexis. A Black audience can react audibly to King's stomp, references to Ailey, Big Freedia, bounce music, the Second Line, and Trick's buck. Murray associates all of the above with immortality and likens them to undying New Orleans, showing each as an allegory of resurrection and life after death—ideas appealing to Hurricane Katrina's aftermath. King's stomp and Trick's buck, for example, appear as symbols of New Orleans and the symbolism remains widespread approximately one generation after the storm.

Marquis Bey, introducing Azure D. Osborne-Lee's *Crooked Parts* in *The Methuen Drama Book of Trans Plays* (2021), rejects plays about trans characters that are cathected to death, medical procedure, and medical therapy: "Trans lives in all their nuance and complexity, all their vicissitudes, are still often eclipsed by popular mythologies of extravagant balls and surgeries, skewed life chances, and death" (387). It is very much important that King, the only Black trans character in *The More the Man*, stays alive during and after the play, therefore acknowledging the affective powers of representational visibility and conveying a message to Black trans audiences, opening night cast, production staff, and others not to worry about experiencing harm at the theater. To the extent that violence takes place when King and Trick throw 'bows with each other, the violence against Black characters is not spectacularized for non-Black audiences of color and white audiences, which is important because poor outcomes, such as a decreased life expectancy, a lack of well-being, and transphobia, also overdetermine plays by cis people and about trans people in popular culture today.

Murray rewrites the stories that popular culture tells about Black trans masculinity and gives his audience new ways of meaningfully engaging Black trans men. The characters Lou Edwards, a nonbinary adolescent, in Leslie Lee's *The First Breeze of Summer* (1975) and Miss Roj, a SNAP! queen, in George C. Wolfe's *The Colored Museum* (1986) are two of US Black theater's foremost representations of explicitly living according to one's gender identity through changes to one's presentation of self in everyday life. The anti-Black racist, white supremacist mind's eye sees the Black community as homophobic and transphobic, but everybody around King from family to friends—even Leon and Trick—affirms his trans masculine identity. Leon and Trick are cis Black men, but their Black manhood does not impede their remaining very close friends with King in the play. King's grandfather Oram uses King's personal pronouns correctly and unlearns his colonization about gender expression, and King's mother Tee Wa begins to refer to King as her son and in masculine forms, which is important because, in doing so, myths about Black people being socially conservative and discriminating against, expressing an aversion to, and fearing trans people, despite evidence to the contrary, are dispelled. All Black men are not cis, all trans men are not white, and Black trans men's lived experience is made of community and support. Just as the Second Line was of significance to African Americans and Afro-Creoles before Hurricane Katrina, so too King remains of intrinsic value to his Black and trans communities after the storm.

References

Bey, Marquis. 2021. "All In and Out of the Family: A Critical Introduction to Azure Osborne-Lee's *Crooked Parts*." In *The Methuen Drama Book of Trans Plays*, edited by Leanna Keyes, Lindsey Mantoan, and Angela M. Farr Schiller, 389–95. Methuen Drama.

Carrico, Rachel. 2024. *Dancing the Politics of Pleasure at the New Orleans Second Line*. University of Illinois Press.

DeFrantz, Thomas F. 2004. *Dancing Revelations: Alvin Ailey's Embodiment of African American Culture*. Oxford University Press.

hooks, bell. 2004. *We Real Cool: Black Men and Masculinity*. Taylor and Francis.

hooks, bell. 2018. *All about Love: New Visions*. HarperCollins.

The More the Man

Jameson P. Murray

Cast of Characters

King   a black trans-man in his early 20s, a college dropout, ego-centric, trying to understand adulthood, masculinity, and love, from Algiers.

Tee Wa   a black cis-woman in her 40s, a single mother of King, heartbroken and protective of those like her, from the 7th ward, now in Algiers. (Also plays **Chorus 3**.)

Ife   a black cis-woman in her early 20s, ambitious, self-starter, finding her missing link, a lover, from Gentilly, still in Gentilly.

Oram   a black cis-man, 50s-60s, a working man, proud, stubborn, and carries a chip on his shoulder, from 9th ward, now in Algiers. (Also plays **Chorus 1 & Adam**.)

Trick   a black man in his early 20s, a menace to society, the self-proclaimed man of the block, from Calliope, now in Algiers.

Leon   a black man in his early 20s, a follower, models himself after whatever man runs his world, from Treme, now in Algiers. (Also plays **Chorus 2**.)

Adam   a black man in his 40s-50s, prideful and sick, from the 7th ward, now in California. (Also plays **Oram** and **Chorus 1**.)

CHORUS (The Dream Figures):

Chorus 1   like a father, from the sky, high and almighty, exists in King's head. (Also plays **Oram & Adam**.)

Chorus 2   like a boy on a playground, but a man, a teacher to King, exists in King's head. (Also plays **Leon**.)

Chorus 3   like a mother, from the sky, right and almighty, exists in King's head. (Also plays **Tee Wa**.)

Casting Policy

Though the characters' genders are listed in the character descriptions, gender exploration in casting is encouraged. **King** must *always* be a trans-masculine individual, but **Trick**, for example, can be cast as any gender-presenting actor who is comfortable embodying the character. This play is about the exploration of masculinity through gender expression and identity, so have fun following and breaking these.

Setting

Where

New Orleans, specifically Algiers, Gretna, and all the way across the river in Gentilly. But the majority of this takes place on the West Bank, aka the Wank, 15th ward, or the other side of the river to most. I imagine most of the play taking place in front of what used to be called "Julien's #2 Store" on Woodland Ave or in Algiers Point away from the gentrified area.

Many other neighborhoods in the city are referenced for comparison purposes. I suggest researching all these places and understanding the history behind them. The places that are not referenced much are Treme and Uptown. None of the play takes place here, but this is where the heartbeat of the city comes from. The heartbeat of the play. This is where Leon/Chorus 2 is from.

When

To me, this play exists post-Katrina, but before they started fixing up and gentrifying the West Bank. That means all the youngins in the play are Katrina babies, and everyone is displaced whether they know it or not. This is important because their displacement is another reason for their aggression. West bank vs. East bank always exists, even when East bank New Orleanians move to the Wank.

Notes from the playwright

bell hooks writes, in her book *The Will to Change,* about patriarchy and masculinity and how these two concepts are NOT the same. But she explains that the patriarchy is upheld through violence and emotional withdrawal. hooks argues that people confuse the patriarchy being upheld with exhibiting masculinity. This reminded me of Shakespeare's *Macbeth.* Some Shakespeare historians believe this play is about demons and possession. They cite a Lady Macbeth line in the play, suggesting she scolds Macbeth's cowardice and declares he will be even more the man if he kills King Duncan. She says "That I pour my spirits in thine ear, / And chastise, with valor of my tongue, / All that impedes thee from the golden round" (I.V.XXV-XXVII). And later, "When you durst do it, then you were a man; / And to be more than what you were, you would / Be so much more the man" (I.VII.LVI-LIIX). Historians believe this line is the Devil whispering into the left ear of Macbeth, pushing him to incite violence against a King. I find it interesting how alluring being "more the man" can be to men who feel emasculated. What will actually make us "more the man"? What do we do to cope instead?

All of the characters should have New Orleans accents. I suggest studying references of people from New Orleans, and not ones who standardize their accents for whiteness. Look up local New Orleanians who are musicians, like Big Freedia. Bounce artists usually have the best accent references (and each neighborhood's accent sounds a little different). If you know how we say baby, you're a third of the way there. I've also made helpful notes of words that appear in this play that may help with pronunciation and meaning.

Some' = something
Gone = going to/gonna
Yers = yours
Na = now
Wit' = with
Wit'out = without
You'n = you don't
Wan' = want to/wanna
Wazzam = what's up
Out'chere = out here
Ya 'eard me = you heard me
Allat = all that
paw paw = grandfather
maw maw = grandmother

I'on = I don't
Ya/yo = you/your
Hu = her
Hih = here
Witchu = with you
Wit'outchu = without you
Tryna = trying to
'im = him
Ole lady/Ole man = girlfriend/boyfriend
Prolly = probably
Buku = a lot
paw = father
maw = mother

Special thanks

To Julian X, River Guidry, Christian Donnerson, Keishona Weekes, Jaden Bridges, Janelle Grace, Elijah Brown, Shani Farrell, Cedric Lilly, Marc Hem Lee, Ivan Cecil Walks, Des Bennett, Maria Hendricks, Kelsey Fonise, Virchel Mack-Jackson, Jacques Matellus, Fresh Ink Theatre, Jada Saintlouis, my late paw paw Norman "Pete" Palmer Jr., and finally my mother, Lakesha.

Originally developed by Fresh Ink Theatre.

Act One

Prologue

A brass band plays off in the distance, a second-line approaching. At the same time,
Chorus 2 *runs on. He signals the show is about to begin by quieting the audience. He
delivers all pre-show announcements, then lays down in the middle of the stage. He's
the laydown man, signaling the second-line. A transition.*

Shortly after, lights down. As they come back up, the **Full Company** *enters. They
dance behind* **Chorus 2**. *Someone has a tambourine. Their words are music. They
chant them along with the music, in true second-line spirit.*

Chorus 2   Now we're here. So, what it mean to be a man?

Chorus 1   Is that how you see me?

Chorus 3   Is there anything else you'd rather me?

Trick   Me.

King   Me!

Ife   Wit' me.

King   Yeah!

Chorus 3   Wit' me . . . Wit'out me.

King   My heart.

Chorus 2   Who is King? Really?

King   I'm . . .

Chorus 1   He's my son.

Chorus 3   He's my son!

King   Me!

Chorus 2   Go like this.

Chorus 2 *does a move.* **King** *repeats.*

Trick   Look at 'im go!

Chorus 2   Na go like this!

Chorus 2 *does a more suggestive move that* **King** *repeats. The* **Men** *cheer.*

Chorus 1   Gettin' ready, gettin' ready, gettin' ready, c'mon!

Ife   Do you know what you're doing?

King   I'on really know.

Chorus 3   You can't teach somebody how to second-line.

Chorus 2   I got this. (*Brings* **King** *to his knees.*) Look inna . . . river.

Trick and **Chorus 1** *lift the river up to* **King**. *He looks in, then backs away.*

Ife   You're messing wit' the water.

King   How am I supposed to see?

Chorus 2   Don't drown in it!

The river rises higher. **King** *climbs up his house and sits on the rooftop.*

King   I can almost see!

Chorus 3   So this is him!

All but King   HE'S TRYING TO SHOW YOU: YOU AND HIM!

King   I'M TRYING TO SHOW YOU: YOU AND ME!

Chorus 1   KING!

The river shakes and overtakes **King**. *He gets swept up in the river and goes under.*

Scene One

King *sits up in his bed. He holds a letter. It is open. He carefully reseals the letter and hides it under his pillow.* **King** *eases himself back down, to sleep.* **Tee Wa** *enters, holding a leather Bible. She kisses it, and places it next to* **King**. **Chorus 1** *enters opposite. He watches* **Tee Wa** *and* **King** *with a smile.*

Tee Wa   I'm leaving out to get my hair done.

Chorus 1 *follows* **Tee Wa**, *occasionally waving in her face. She does not notice him.* **Tee Wa** *sits on the porch. Her movements go from normal to slow motion to frozen. Once she's frozen,* **Chorus 1** *runs to* **King** *and hovers over him.*

King (*from bed*)   I know you here.

Chorus 1   Damn, I thought I could surprise you.

King   I'm happy you here.

Chorus 1   Where'd we leave off yesterday?

King   It's lower than you think it is.

Chorus 1   Right! You remember that, boy.

King   There's something I gotta tell you.

Chorus 1   Don't tell me you in love or something.

King   . . . I got this girl I been jocing.

Chorus 1   How long?

King   A few months. But we go way back.

Chorus 1   I kno hu?

King   No, no, probably not.

Chorus 1   What's hu name? She cute? She thicc?

King   Hu name's Ife.

Chorus 1   She mean some' to ya?

King   I lo–

Chorus 1   Then keep it to yourself. Don't share hu wit' anybody. If she's important, ya better protect hu.

King   I wi–

Chorus 1   You mean some' to hu?

King   I th–

Chorus 1   You gotta keep her around.

King   I wanna tell hu how I feel.

Chorus 1   You can't just pop out and say "I love you." I tried so many times with your mother. Look at us now. (*Beat.*) You gotta show hu you care 'bout hu. You know how men show they care? It's all physical. Women know what all men want. That's why we spend about ninety percent of the relationship trying to convince the women to let us have it.

King   I don't think it's gone be like that with Ife.

Chorus 1   You dating a ho?

King   No! Don't call her that. It's me. I don't think I'm ready for allat.

Chorus 1   Are you sure you like her?

King   Of course I do. That's my ole lady. I love her.

On the porch, **Tee Wa** *begins to unfreeze, moving in slow motion.*

Chorus 1   Slow down on the L-word. I just told you about that! (*Beat.*) But look at my son. Becoming ya own man. Quick! Close ya eyes. I still got one surprise left in me. (**King** *closes his eyes.* **Chorus 1** *carefully picks up the leather Bible and puts it behind his back.*) Open them.

King   I thought you were gonna disappear.

Chorus 1   I come and see you every night, don't I? It's 'cause I'm always right here. (*Points to* **King's** *heart.*) Which is why I got you this Bible.

Chorus 1 *hands the Bible to* **King**. **King** *inspects the inside.*

King I got my name in it! *My* name.

Chorus 1 I put it in there. I was gonna give it to you when you left for college, but I guess it escaped me. I've never read it cover to cover. I think as the family generations go on, we read less and less. I pray you'll be better than I was.

King Anything for you, Pops.

King *pulls* **Chorus 1** *into a hug, then watches as* **Chorus 1** *exits.* **King** *takes the Bible and walks out onto the porch.* **Tee Wa** *now moves at a normal pace.*

King Oh shit! Tee Wa, when you get out hih?

Tee Wa Watch ya mouth, boy! I been out hih.

King It's a nice afternoon, huh? I thought you was gone get ya hair done?

Tee Wa I haven't left out yet. Na, why're you out hih rushing me out of my house?

King I'm doing homework.

Tee Wa Don't tell me ya slept the morning away.

King No . . .

Tee Wa You telling me a tale?

King No, Ma!

Tee Wa Mhm . . . Okay.

King If I started dating, how soon would you want to know?

Tee Wa I don't wanna know 'bout ya lil yeahs. If it's serious, then we'll talk.

King How do I know if it's serious?

Tee Wa Who the fast lil girl ya running 'round wit'?

King She my ole lady. You can't be calling ya daughter-in-law fast.

Tee Wa I'on know hu.

King I think ya just jealous. Don't worry. She ain't gone replace you. Can't nobody else be my mama.

Tee Wa And don't ya forget. I brought you into this world, boy, and . . . (*softly.*) Hell, you a man if I ever seen one . . . My son.

King (*elated*) A man? You ain't ever call me that.

Tee Wa You are. You deserve it. You worked for it.

King (*sucking his teeth*) Whatchu talkin' bout?

Tee Wa I ever tell you how proud I am of you? You in school, making some' of yourself. Whether I like ya degree or not, I say that deserves a little recognition.

King I'on know. I'm not really enjoying school.

Tee Wa   Not every man makes it through, but you . . . You're on your way to doing what ya father couldn't.

King   You ever miss 'im?

Tee Wa   Hell nah!

King   You'n ever talk about 'im.

Tee Wa   He's ya paw, you supposed to miss 'im.

King   I found his Bible.

Tee Wa   You been going through my stuff?

King   I wanna know more about 'im. He wrote my name inna Bible. *My* name. I wanna know where he is, and when he found out about me.

Tee Wa *produces a small box from under her rocking chair.*

Tee Wa   I'm sure he was gonna give you the Bible if he was hih.

King (*under his breath*)   You be trippin' sometimes, forreal.

Tee Wa   What was said?!

King   I love ya, Ma.

Tee Wa   Love you too. I'm gone make groceries on my way home.

Tee Wa *kisses* **King** *on the cheek. He tries to squirm away, but she plants it and exits with the small box.* **King** *watches her.* **Chorus 1** *enters, taking the box from* **Tee Wa**. *She is unfazed.* **Chorus 1** *returns the box back under the rocking chair,* **King** *watches.*

Scene Two

Leon *and* **Trick** *lurk on a wall outside the corner store, watching people pass them by.*

Trick   Say . . . Say . . . Say, Leon.

Leon   Wazzam, Trick?

Trick   You know who I ain't seen 'round hih in awhile?

Leon   Ife?

Trick   Why you even gotta bring hu up?

Leon   I heard she been gettin' real comfortable wit' King.

Trick   Forreal?
But they not doing nun . . .? (**Leon** *shrugs.*) Damn! I been tryna get at Ife!

Leon   That's all King, man.

King (*enters*)   What's all King?

Trick   Why ya ain't tell me ya fucking Ife?

King   She my ole lady.

Trick   So y'all fucking?

King   Nah.

Trick   So she looking for somebody to fuck.

King   You got some' ya wan' say?

Trick   You know I'm messin' witchu. Ain't that right, Leon?

Leon   It's all jokes.

King   Just leave Ife name out ya mouth.

Trick   Easy, you bucking?

King   I'm straight. Leon, when ya gonna tell ya boy to get a job? I gotchu, my paw-paw right inside. You wan' one?

Trick   I ain't working at no corner store for yo bitch ass paw-paw.

King   Easy . . . *You* bucking?

Trick *fake punches* **King**. *It was almost real. Too close for comfort.*

Leon   Trick ain't worried. He got a job. He throwin' a party 'round the corner tonight.

King   I know. I can't make it. I'm on my way na to study up wit' Ife. She's almost done wit' cosmetology school . . . That's my girl.

Leon   That's some lame ass shit.

Trick   Facts. You better hit that before somebody else take ya girl. Get all up in'ere–

Leon   -Wit' whatever ya got!

King   Shut up, son.

Trick   Go on, tell Ife to call me if she need some real dick.

King (*pounding his chest*)   Whatever, that's all me.

A Beautiful Woman, *the same actress playing* **Ife**, *struts across the stage; no face, all body.* **Trick** *and* **Leon** *watch.* **Trick** *walks to her and whispers something. The* **Woman** *laughs.* **Trick** *goes back to his post with a smile burned on. The* **Woman** *and* **King** *exit at the same time, on opposite sides of the stage.* **King**, *unlike the others, does not look.*

Leon   Damn.

Trick   Shut up. You just saying that 'cause I looked.

Leon   What'd you say?

Trick   I asked if she thought you was cute. She said yeah, so I invited hu to the party. You thought I was gonna let hu just walk by wit'out saying nun?

Leon   You lying, son.

Trick   Deadass. You better hit that too.

Leon   Nah. She prolly don't get down like that.

Trick   Guess what?

Leon   Man, what?

Trick   I heard Ife a straight freak.

Leon   You better stop playing on homie's girl.

Trick   He ain't gone do nun. Ife is a goddess of love. Add hu and a bed, and she ready to multiply.

Trick *does a suggestive motion and manages to get a chuckle out of* **Leon**.

Leon   You a fool, son! You know that?

Trick   This man shit! You know how much I would kill to get at Ife?

They both get to laughing. **Oram** *enters from inside the corner store.*

Oram   What's funny out hih?! (**Trick** *and* **Leon** *immediately shut up.*)

Leon   Nun gone on out hih.

Trick   We just playing, G.

Oram   My store ain't no playground. Ya paw ain't teach you to work?

Trick   My daddy work all day and come home to be tired. I ain't tryna be tired.

Leon   My daddy ain't believe he was the father, but he took care of me anyway, because he loved my mama. But then he left because he realized he couldn't stand my mama. Then I realized, I can't stand my mama either. So now I just stay outta the house.

Oram   And that don't motivate you to work?

Leon   Why work when we could hang out?

Oram   Get from in front my store!

Leon   Sorry, Mr. Oram. We don't mean no disrespect. (*To* **Trick**.) Leggo.

Trick   Imma catch up to ya, Leon. I gotta talk to Mr. Oram real quick.

Leon   Whatever, man. I'll see ya later.

Trick   So . . . (*Nothing.*) Sooooooo . . . (*Still nothing.*) Vreaxxx! Mr. Oram!!

Oram   Alright! Whatchu wan'?

Trick   Everybody 'round hih know you be working hard. I think ya deserve a lil break.

Oram   I'm fine.

Trick   You'n look too good. You know, ya be real lonely 'round hih. (**Oram** *goes to hit* **Trick**.) No offense. I just mean ya never get out. Ya been holding things down in Algiers, and ya deserve a break.

Oram   No time for a break. I got peoples to take care of. Nobody else out hih taking care of us.

Trick   Who is us? I just told you, ya look sad and lonely.

Oram   'Cause I work. Work doesn't leave me wit' time to sit out on the street wit' my potnas.

Trick   Is that all you think I do? I look out for our people out'chere. I bet you'n even know what King been up to?

Oram   Who's that?

Trick   Your grandson.

Oram   Huh?

Trick   Tee Wa's child.

Oram   Ohhh.

Trick   He just passed through. You missed 'im.

Oram   You know how I feel 'bout ya hanging 'round my peoples.

Trick   I ain't seen 'im since he been home, but that's more than you can say.

Oram   Go home, Trick.

Trick   You first. (*They both gear up to fight, but* **Another Beautiful Woman** *enters, same actress as* **Chorus 3**, *strutting across the stage; no face, all body.* **Oram** *and* **Trick** *watch. She stops, just before exiting.* **Oram** *averts his attention, while* **Trick** *locks in.*)

Es–cu–me-love!

Oram *watches as* **Trick** *goes over to the* **Beautiful Woman**. *He whispers in her ear. She laughs, then exits.*

Oram   What'd ya say?

Trick   I told hu to come to my party. I was gonna invite ya, but ya don't like me hanging 'round "ya peoples."

Oram   If I hurt ya feelings, say that.

Trick   I'on have feelings. Finish ya shift, so you can get home to whatever family ya got.

Oram   Same to you!

Trick *exits before hearing* **Oram's** *words.* **Oram** *exits, throwing down his broom.*

Scene Three

King's *bedroom.* **King** *and* **Ife** *sit on his bed. Her head is in the books, and he draws on a sketchpad. Both distracted. They're quite close and comfortable.*

Ife   Then go.

King   I'on wan' to.

Ife   You should if ya wan' to.

King   I wan' be witchu.

Ife   Tell the truth, shame the devil.

King   I'm deadass.

Ife   So you'd really ditch ya homeboys to be wit' me?

King   Yeah!

Ife (*Frankly*)   How much do you wan' go to that party?

King   Okay, a lil, but I really wanted to go witchu. I wan' show you off. Ayeeee.

King *does a little dance, moving closer to* **Ife**. *She backs away.*

Ife   You think I'on know what they be saying 'bout me?

King   They ain't men. Real men speak respectfully to women. Men keep promises like I made a promise I'd help you study.

Ife   Ya just been sitting and scribbling in yo notebook.

King   I'm practicing for when I draw you.

Ife   Let me see.

King   Ya really wan' to?

Ife *takes a peek at* **King's** *sketchpad.*

Ife   All you drew is a bunch of hearts.

King   It's practice. Like when you play with my hair.

Ife   I'm surprised you let me do it.

King   You gone be my go to whcn you pass that test.

Ife   King, I gotta tell you some' . . .

King   What?

Ife   . . . You can't have anybody doing ya hair.

King   I couldn't let anybody else touch me. They not you.

Ife   No? (*She gets closer to* **King**.) So I'm the only one who can touch you hih? (*She glides her fingers from* **King's** *lips to his belt. She kisses him.*) You're my man.

King   Man . . . I love the sound of that . . . Tee Wa called me a man today too.

Ife   She did? Baby, that's huge.

King   It finally feels like my life is happening the way it's supposed to.

Ife   I'm glad I get to share these moments witchu. You're kind of amazing.

King   You think so?

Ife   I know so. You're the man.

King (*Shy*)   I know.

Ife   No, say it.

King   I'm the man.

Ife   Wit' passion!

King (*Barks*)   I'm the man!

Ife   There ya go. Tee Wa raised a good man. Don't ever let anybody make you doubt it.

King   What if my Pops played some part inna man I am today?

Ife   Where's he at? You know?

King   Not sure. Only time I see 'im is in my dreams.

Ife   What does he do in the dreams?

King   He's like a dad. I don't know.

King *closes his eyes.* **Chorus 1** *enters, wearing army fatigues.* **Chorus 3** *runs on and jumps into* **Chorus 1's** *arms. They dance and separate to reveal* **Chorus 2**. **Chorus 1 and 2** *dance together as* **Chorus 3** *exits slowly, disappearing into obscurity.* **Chorus 1** *teaches a step to* **Chorus 2**, *performing it together.* **King** *starts to tear up, but hides it. He wipes it all away.*

Ife   You can cry with me, ya know. You're always safe with me.

King   It's just nice to have my dad, somewhere, teaching me how to be a man.

Ife   You ever think the stuff you know, you might have learned from women?

Chorus 1 *freezes in his step.* **Chorus 2** *tries to wake him up, but it's no use.* **King** *acknowledges the* **Chorus**.

King   Nah. It's a weird double standard. Growing up, everything I learned 'bout men came from the perspective of tryna attract one.

Ife   I know what you mean. My mama was the first person to call me fast. I wasn't even dating. I was fourteen, tryna wear hu clothes.

King   I been there too. It was always . . .

Ife & King   "No man will want you, if . . ."

King   Yeah, it was miserable and not for me. But those boys got to run the streets all day until the streetlights came on. It was everything I wanted to be. Free.

Ife   My whole life people been talking 'bout me behind my back or calling me fast because of circumstances I can't control.

King   Nobody's gonna talk 'bout you in front of me.

Ife   Don't do that. My point is, I'on care what people say, and fighting 'em on it isn't gone prove 'em right or wrong.

King   So what do you do?

Ife   Be a man.

Chorus 1 *unfreezes.*

King   I love . . .

Chorus 1   She mean some' to ya?

King   . . . that. (**Chorus 1** *exits with authority.*) What do you dream about?

Ife   I dream about being in a bigger place than the one I'm in. Somewhere with more space.

King   Like a party?

Ife *throws her book down.*

Ife   What if we just spent the night in your room? Together?

King   You want to stay the night?

Ife *kisses* **King** *on his neck.*

King   Woah.

Ife   You want me to stop?

King   No, it's just . . .

Ife   I'm stopping.

King   Wait, no. I want to.

Ife   You sure?

King *nods. He and* **Ife** *kiss and disappear under the covers. After some movement,* **King** *sneaks out of bed away from a sleeping* **Ife**. *He gets his sketchpad and draws her.*

Scene Four

Tee Wa *approaches her porch. She hums a tune.* **Oram** *enters behind her.*

Oram   Still humming that same tune, huh?

Tee Wa   Why it matter to you?

Oram   I'm just saying . . . All these years, and you ain't change.

Tee Wa   I've grown. I raised a son. Where's yers?

Oram   Working at a law firm na, but you know that. I know you still talking to his old potna.

Tee Wa   You came to make sure I'm not fucking 'im?

Oram   I didn't come hih to argue witchu. He just asks about y'all.

Tee Wa   You still haven't said why you're hih.

Oram   I came to check up on my grandchild. Deliver some news.

Tee Wa   Grand-*son*, and you came to the wrong place. He ain't hih.

Oram   Where is *he* then?

Tee Wa   *He's* doing what all the men in ya family do.

Oram   Work.

Tee Wa   Nope . . . Who even told you to stop by my house? This city ain't safe no more. You lucky I didn't grab my gun.

Oram   You ain't gone pull no gun on me.

Tee Wa   You are an uninvited guest. A weapon will be drawn.

Oram   I came hih 'cause I heard 'round by the corner store that King was getting into some trouble.

Tee Wa   Trouble? You talking 'bout that lil girl he been running 'round wit'?

Oram   Yeah, the one whose peoples from Gentilly.

Tee Wa   What about hu?

Oram   I just heard hu and King been together.

Tee Wa   Everybody inna damn neighborhood knows 'bout 'em! You just looking for an excuse to drop over hih and act all involved. You wan' to help ya grand-*son*? You should've told yer son not to leave 'im.

Oram   You right. But he made a choice, and I can't change the past. And like I said before, I ain't come hih to argue witchu.

Tee Wa   I'm not holding you up. We can sit in silence until King comes back, if you wan' to see 'im. I know how busy ya family is wit' work.

Oram *stays for a moment in silence. He shakes his head, giving up.*

Oram   And I came over hih on my break.

King *and* **Ife** *walk onto the porch from inside the house.* **Tee Wa** *and* **Oram** *stand in shock.*

King   Hey, Mama.

Tee Wa   Son.

King   There's someone I wan'chu to meet.

Oram   Where y'all going?

King   To a party. Whatchu doing here?

Tee Wa   I'm sure the party'll still be going on after dinner, right?

Ife   Yes it will. Hi, Tee Wa, it's nice to meet you. I'm Ife. King's–

King   -Girlfriend.

Oram   -Friend-, until ya married. To someone, and it doesn't have to be my grandson.

Tee Wa   -I know who you are.

King   So can we come in?

Scene Five

King, Ife, Tee Wa, *and* **Oram** *sit for dinner. Plates sit in front of them.*

Oram   You should apologize for not telling the family about your lil yeah sooner.

Ife   I have a name.

Oram   I got a name for your whole family.

Ife   King?

King   Huh?

Oram   This lil nigga got his face in the fish.

Tee Wa   Oram, you're a guest. Act like one.

Ife   That fried fish was real good, Tee Wa. Thank you.

Tee Wa   Thank you, Ife. King, you've got good taste.

King   'Cause she likes your food?

Tee Wa   'Cause she has good taste.

Ife   Mr. Oram, I didn't know you came by so often. It's nice to see you away from the corner store.

Tee Wa   He has a tendency to overstay his welcome.

Oram   King? He likes spending time with his paw paw.

King (*to* **Ife**)   If you want to leave at any time, we can.

Oram   She's doing alright. She can handle some quality time with her future in-laws.

Ife   It's fine, King. I was about to make myself another plate.

Ife *gets up and exits into the kitchen.*

Oram   Ya potnas Trick and Leon was telling me you been wit' hu for a minute.

King   Yeah.

Oram   You hit that?

Tee Wa   Stop it.

Oram   That's his lil yeah. He had hu all up in ya house while you was out. He had plenty of time to handle his business.

Tee Wa   I'm not entertaining this foolishness in my house.

Oram   He ain't have to say nun. I can see it on his face. They was knocking boots while you was gone Teewanda!

Ife *returns. The room quiets. She takes her seat. A long beat.*

Ife   Y'all were talking about me huh?

Oram   Yeah. Ya fast lil tail sleeping with my grandson?

Ife   Excuse me? King?

Oram   He can't help you. You talking to his paw paw now. What exactly are your intentions with him? Yo fast ass got any kids we don't know about?

Ife   King?! (**King** *sits quietly, like a kid caught between two worlds.*) You really gone sit there and not say anything?

Oram   The kids were a serious question. I know how your family is.

Ife *nearly knocks everything off the table getting up. She storms out and into* **King's** *bedroom.* **Tee Wa** *calmly gets up and goes after her.*

Scene Six

Ife *cries on the bed.* **Tee Wa** *enters.* **Ife** *quickly looks up, then wipes her tears, sitting up.*

Ife   I'm sorry I stormed out like that.

Tee Wa   Don't apologize to me. I understand. Those men are crazy.

Ife   Men are hysterical. It irks my nerves.

Tee Wa   You know, I'd do anything for my family?

Ife   Of course. I feel the same way.

Tee Wa   Not exactly. You see, my son is all I have, and I expect whoever he's wit' to care for 'im like family. You know what I mean?

Ife   Yes, ma'am. But are we gone talk 'bout 'im wit' 'im right outside?

Tee Wa   Do you love my son?

Ife   Yes, ma'am.

Tee Wa   You know he loves you too, right?

Ife   Of course I do. He doesn't say it. He doesn't always act like it. But I know he loves me. Somehow. Does he even know he loves me?

Tee Wa   If I knew what men thought, I'd be one. We know how we think, and I know you're thinking 'bout leaving 'im.

Ife   I know he doesn't expect me to stay with him when he can't even stand up for me. Or himself. What am I supposed to do wit' a man who can't say he loves me?

Tee Wa   Go.

Ife   So you do get it.

Tee Wa   I'm telling you to go. I love my son. He doesn't know much 'bout my relationship wit' his father, but it wasn't too different from yers. We were in love. So in love, we'd go to church together. You ever been to church wit' my son? I didn't think so. That's how in love his paw was wit' me. I knew it, but he'd never say it. He told me he didn't know how to yet. So, I got 'im this Bible. A leather one: and I marked all the verses 'bout love. Every one I could remember, find, or learn was bookmarked in that Bible. I thought maybe over time he could learn what is meant to love and that would help 'im feel comfortable saying it.

Ife   Did he?

Tee Wa   Did he? He was so comfortable. I thought God was at work, and in His own way, he was. He was so comfortable; he was spewing out I love you's like it was Christmas in Heaven. One day the I love you's went from meaning "I love you" to "I've got some' bad to tell you." Then, he was gone.

Ife   Did he tell you why he left?

Tee Wa   Yeah. King doesn't know his daddy ain't shit.

Ife   He loves his dad. He literally dreams of 'im every night. Saying his dad taught 'im what it means to be a man.

Tee Wa   I certainly didn't do any better. He just let his ignorant ass grandfather call you out ya name. Is that the love you want? Do you wan' be like me?

Ife   You're doing fine, and you raised a good man.

Tee Wa   King is my greatest accomplishment, but he was a product of my greatest shame. His father came into my life, told me he loved me, and left me. You end up like me, you'll be alone 'cause King can't leave you wit' a child.

Ife   He wouldn't. He wants to love.

Tee Wa   When he came out as King, I felt like I had been cursed. I was angry wit' men, and there he was, my mini-me, wanting to be just like his daddy. I had to learn to love a son . . . but I love 'im. I tell 'im that everyday. When he would sleep, I would read those Bible verses I had marked down to 'im in his sleep. I wanted to teach 'im everything I had learned 'bout how to love. He can wan' to love, but you can't wan' it for 'im. He has to come to his own understanding.

Ife   So I guess this is it.

Tee Wa   You seem like a great young woman for my son. I'm sorry he can't be the man you deserve right now.

Ife *ropes* **Tee Wa** *into a hug.*

Tee Wa   And I'm coming to ya salon when you open. I hope this doesn't affect my future family discount.

Scene Seven

King *sits head down at the table.* **Oram** *searches for liquor.*

Oram   You know where ya maw keep the liquor? (**King** *doesn't respond. Instead he tries to ignore as* **Chorus 2** *enters.*) You still pouting about your lil yeah?

King   You made her mad.

Oram   Nah, you did. She don't care what people say 'bout hu. She wanna know hu man got hu back. Let me teach you some'.

King   What?

Oram   Love is a business. I loved your maw maw, and she loved me. I knew she loved me because she knew I worked. She worked too, but she loved me enough to come home, cook, clean, and raise our kids. She took care of me, had my babies, and died as my loving ex-wife. I loved her enough to protect that love. That's man shit. One time, someone broke into the house we lived in Uptown, before your paw was born. At this point your uncle was ten. As soon as I heard the floorboards creak and felt ya maw maw next to me, I grabbed my gun. I stood at the doorway of the shotgun house with everyone I loved under one roof. And I shot that sucka. Someone must've been praying for him that night because the bullet was supposed to hit him square in the head. He would have been dead. That's power.

Tee Wa (*entering*)   Stop lying to my son. That story is from *Boyz N the Hood*.

King   Is Ife okay?

Tee Wa   You should go and talk to her.

King   What should I say?

Oram   Tell her to go home. It's getting late. I know hu peoples still in Gentilly.

Chorus 2 *pushes* **King** *up and out of his seat.*

King   Can you please shut up?

Oram   Who do you think you talking to, boy? (**Oram** *squares up on* **King**.) You got some' to back them words up wit'? (**King** *backs away.* **Chorus 2** *calms* **King** *down.*) That's what I thought. If you gone talk back, be ready to defend what you say. Act like a nigga, I'm gone treat you like a nigga.

Tee Wa   Oram, shut the hell up and get out of my house.

Oram   It's like that?

Tee Wa   You got to the count of three. One Two–

Oram (*jumping*)   Good night, y'all.

Oram *runs out of the house.*

Scene Eight

Ife *looks around the room. She picks up the sketchbook and sees an almost complete drawing of her. She can't help but smile.* **King** *enters.* **Ife** *throws the sketchbook down.*

King   Are you mad at me?

Ife   I'on have much to say.

King   We don't have to stay hih, we can go to ya house, and just study and forget this night ever happened.

Ife   Not right na. I really need to be alone . . . and to think.

King   But we're here. You and me. So let's talk. (**Ife** *leans in.* **King** *wraps his arms around her. A beat. She's listening.*) I'm sorry about what my paw paw said.

Ife *breaks away from* **King's** *embrace.*

Ife   I could not care less 'bout that nigga. It was me and you, King. Na, I'on really know, and you'n seem too sure either.

King (*whispering*)   I still haven't told Tee Wa I dropped out of school. I need you.

Ife   What about what I need?

King   I wan' us to be together.

Chorus 1 *lurks on the sidelines.*

Ife   Treat me like you want us to be together.

King   What can I do?

Ife   Tell me how you feel about me, King.

King   I lo–

Chorus 1   Hold onto ya pride. C'mon son.

Chorus 3 *enters opposite* **Chorus 1**.

King   I like you so much.

Ife   I wan'chu. Don't you wan' me? Don't you wan' us?

Chorus 3   Haven't you heard our cry? C'mon son.

King   I need time. I wan' us, but I'm back to square one.

Ife   Your future will be fine. Our future will be fine.

Chorus 3   She's on hu grind.

Chorus 1   C'mon son.

Chorus 3   She's tryna get ya in line.

Chorus 1   C'mon son!

Ife   Do you love me? What even are we?

Chorus 3   Your truth will set you free.

King   Ife, I- (**King** *reaches out to touch* **Ife**. **Chorus 1** *steps between them. He shakes his head at* **King**.) I care about you so much. You my girl, who I value.

Ife   "I love you" has value, when you say it and mean it. Bye, King.

Ife *exits*. **Chorus 2** *enters just to run after her.* **Chorus 1** *holds out his hand to* **King**.

Chorus 1   C'mon, son.

King *follows* **Chorus 1**'s *lead, leaving behind* **Chorus 3**.

Scene Nine

King *sits on his bed.* **Chorus 1** *messes with items in the room. Like a visitor.*

King   How did you know you wanted to be wit' mama?

Chorus 1   Oh, deep question. Uh . . . Truthfully, she pushed me. She made me wan' to get out of this city. A lot of the women I was wit' back then wanted me to stay hih and work and take care of a family until I die. Your mother pushed me to chase dreams.

King   What was ya dream?

Chorus 1   To have a son. (**King** *gives* **Chorus 1** *an unreciprocated hug.*) Your mother was a challenge, but we both wanted to be together.

King   Then why is Tee Wa still hih?

Chorus 1   She's exactly where she needs to be. For you.

King What do you mean?

Chorus 1 We come from Kings. We are descended from Divinity. We are everlasting. We only grow from the roots we know. We cannot blame souls who have been taught not to love Royalty. She won't understand that. They tell you that you aren't supposed to know ya father, but look where ya are na.

King I *don't* know you.

Chorus 1 But you love me. And that Faith keeps me alive. Do you love Ife?

King Yes, I love her. But you told me not to tell her. Do you love mama?

Chorus 1 I told her everyday that I loved her, and look where I am.

King Then come see hu. Fix this.

Chorus 1 Your mother meant something to me. She knew that, and she hurt me. I'm protecting yers. That's love, son.

King Can you protect me from Tee Wa busting my ass for dropping out of school.

Chorus 1 Son, I'm going to give you some advice that my father told me, and I'm pretty sure every man before has said: Lie.

King I'm already doing that. She's gonna find out.

Chorus 1 Keep lying?

Chorus 1 *shrugs and exits.* **Tee Wa** *enters.*

Tee Wa Look who's up.

King How long was I asleep?

Tee Wa Longer than usual.

King I got questions 'bout Pops.

Tee Wa I already said everything I feel 'bout 'im. I'm gone check on the 7-Up cake.

King This is important to me. Did he leave us? What even happened to 'im?

Tee Wa Are you ready for the truth?

The **Full Company** *enters, surrounding* **King** *and* **Tee Wa**.

Chorus 1 Are you ready for our truth?

King Yes!

Chorus 1 *takes the small box from under the rocking chair and produces a crisp piece of paper from inside. He writes.*

Tee Wa We were gonna move to California when we found out I was pregnant witchu. Na, I hate California. I was always a New York kind of woman. But, I knew Cali was his dream. We were gonna build a better life out there, like we had always wanted. He was so excited to make it real. We both were. He wouldn't go without me, but I sent 'im out there to get a job and secure a place before I had to travel, so that it'd all be less stressful on us. When I told him I was pregnant, he was gonna come back the day you were born, and . . .

King   He never did. Did he?

Tee Wa   He sent me a letter, like usual. He sent a letter every week, each saying how he loves and misses me. He would spray it wit' a little of his cologne, so I felt like he was there when I read 'em. But, this letter just smelled like ink and paper.

Chorus 1 *militantly folds the letter up, licks, and seals it. The letter is passed off from* **Chorus 1** *to each person in the* **Company** *arriving at* **Tee Wa**.

King   Do you still have it?

Tee Wa *opens the letter, and pulls out an old piece of paper. She unfolds it, and reads:*

Tee Wa   Dear Teewanda,

Chorus 1   I made it out to California safe. It's been a while since you've heard from me, but ya heart is the hardest thing I've ever had to break. I've been on this journey hih for almost 143 days.

Trick   I've found someone else. And I know what you're gone say:

Ife (*Like* **Tee Wa**)   "You done found the devil out there in California. Nobody really goes to the City of Angels to find God. You're in trouble, and you need to find Jesus, then yourself!"

Chorus 2   I love you, and I know that I wouldn't be the best father for our child. I hope you find someone better than me.

Trick   My relationships wit' the women in my life are awful, but this desert still makes me wan' to be a man of my word. I'll send money for the kid every month. Just pick a date.

Chorus 1   I hope you find someone who knows how to raise a daughter.

Tee Wa   Love . . .

Tee Wa *claws and rips the letter up to pieces. She lets out a scream she's been waiting to get out for a long time.*

King   Ma.

Tee Wa   Sorry. I haven't read that letter since I got it. Nigga shoulda just sent a postcard.

King   You should've told me he doesn't give a damn about me.

Tee Wa   Watch ya mouth. I get you're upset–

King   Damn right I'm upset! He didn't even end up having a daughter. Nobody wants me, Ma.

Tee Wa   King, don't say that.

King   I wish you told me my daddy is a piece of shit! You're a liar!

Tee Wa   I understand how you feel, but you are still speaking to your mother!

King   I walked 'round my whole life thinking my daddy must've left for some noble reason. He left 'cause he's a fucking coward, and you're a fucking coward for not–

Tee Wa   I TOLD YOU TO WATCH YA FUCKING MOUTH!

Tee Wa *grabs* **King** *by his collar, causing him to slip and almost fall as she raises her hand, ready to bat the piss outta him.*

A beat. Silence, except their heavy breaths calming.

King *gets out of* **Tee Wa's** *grip and backs away.*

King   I'm leaving. I'm going to Trick's.

Tee Wa   Oh no you not! Son, we're both just angry.

King   Yeah, I'm angry. 'Cause somehow it's still all my fault. I've been feeling like you've had a grudge against me my whole life. I thought it was because I wasn't a perfect little girl like you wanted. But nah, you hate me because of 'im.

Tee Wa   I love you as you are. You're perfect.

King   I'm not perfect. You love what I do, not who I am. I wear dresses, you love me. I graduate high school, you love me. I get angry once, and . . . You probably hate who I am. You probably think I'm just like dad. I'on know what you think, really, because you lie. You throw 'round these 'I love you's' like it's supposed to magically heal how we both feel right na. He left because of me, and you hate me for it. I'm messed up. Just say it.

Tee Wa   King, that's not true. You are nun like ya father. You're graduating school, making some' of yourself, chasing ya dreams–

King   I dropped out of school, Ma. I'm not going back there. (*A beat.* **Tee Wa** *gives the ripped up bits of letter to* **King**, *and exits toward the house.*) Ma.

Tee Wa   You're just like him.

King   I was right.

King *sits, rocking in frustration before jumping up and screaming. A deep scream, something he's been wanting to get out all his life. A roar of a lion.*

He breaks down into a step solo. The solo shifts from step to a mournful second-line, physically freeing himself from his own frustration. The **Full Company** *surrounding him do their own step routine. Their rhythm amps up his second-lining.* **Chorus 1** *takes the resealed letter from under* **King's** *pillow and puts it in* **King's** *pocket.*

The rhythm ramps up and up, until a booming STOMP. The stomp sends **King** *down to sleep. Blackout.*

End of Act One

Act Two

Scene One

A party. Not just any party. A New Orleans Party: bounce music, callouts, singing. Nothing else like it in the world. Intoxicating. The **Full Company** *enters, dancing and shaking into the audience. This party is nothing without getting the audience just as hype to DJ Jubilee as anybody else.*

All But King   The party! Ayee! Ayee!

Chorus 2   Bounce music! Bounce biggity biggity bounce!

Chorus 3   Shaking!

Chorus 1   And . . .

Trick   Trick!

Chorus 1   GIVE IT UP FOR THE MAN!

The **Chorus** *makes a bounce beat (1-2-3, 1—3, 1-2-3), on the loudest body part or closest piece of architecture.*

Trick (*rapping, bounce style*)   Everybody hih to catch a vibe tonight.
Bring ya shawties and ya niggas out from the nine.

We already inna club,
already inna cut,
already inna party
wit' the liquor and stuff.

Lowered inhibitions,
we onna mission,
we had an intermission

so don't forget, yeah
Let's get down to business.
Skip the lil shit yeah,

fuck them bitches get money.

The **Men** *all cheer, then the music slows and takes over the space, the rhythm of everyone's dancing and shaking slows with the music.* **Chorus 1** *appears and comes face to face with* **King**.

King   What are you doing hih?

Chorus 1   I came to see my son.

King   You'n even know you really had a son.

Chorus 1   I can make it up to you. Make you feel better. Give you the advice I wasn't there to give you.

King   Like what?

Chorus 1   C'mon when your paw paw was your age, he used to run through these women. Had a line around the block. You know where your maw maw was in that line? The very end. You gotta learn how to move on, son.

King   How I do that?

Chorus 1 *does a suggestive motion.* **King** *joins in, doing the same motion. They laugh. The* **Beautiful Woman** (*also* **Ife**) *walks by. The* **Men** *look.*

Chorus 1   Hu.

The dancing and music all speed up as the function returns to functioning. **Trick** *brings* **King** *in front of the crowd with him.* **Chorus 1** *watches.*

Trick   'Ight na, everybody welcome back. I bet you ain't think we throw down like this in Gretna, but we partying harder than the 'Nolia tonight.

Leon   You already knooooow!

Trick   Welcome my potna King to the party.

Full Company   Heyyyyy, King!

King (*half-heartedly*)   Hey.

Trick   Wassup, man? You 'ight? You look a lil down.

King   I'm fine.

Trick   Where you been at?

King   Home.

Leon   That's it?

Trick   Oh that's what he calling Ife's house na? "Home."

King   Nah, man. Ife ain't my ole lady no more.

Trick   You lying.

Record scratch. The whole party freezes as **Trick** *and* **King** *take a step to a corner away from the masses.*

Trick   Forreal?

King   Forreal.

Trick   Quit playing.

King   I wish I could.

Trick   Tell the truth, shame the devil.

King   Deadass.

Trick   Damn . . . don't let that get you down, man. We got buku people in hih! You'll bounce back . . . Like the ass inna party.

The party slowly moves its way back to action. A **Beautiful Woman** *passes by, played by the same actress as* **Ife**. *The* **Men** *watch.* **Trick** *and* **Chorus 1** *push* **King** *to her.*

Leon   What you doing? I thought you was jocing hu?

Trick   There are bigger things afoot. King gone go get his. And I'm getting at Ife.

Leon   How you gone do that?

Trick   I'm gone sweet talk hu up, fuck hu, and stay at hu crib 'til I find my next move.

Leon   Good luck wit' that.

Trick   It ain't like Ife hard to get at. That's what hu peoples known for.

Leon   You down bad.

Trick   I'm just a man.

The **Beautiful Woman** *exits.* **King** *watches as she does.*

Trick (*to* **King**)   Where she gone?

King   To get us a drink.

Trick   So why you pouting?

King   I told Tee Wa I dropped out of school.

Trick   Shit! And you still alive? What did she say?

King   Nun. But I know she's gonna try to talk to me 'bout it later.

Trick   Why did you drop out of school anyway?

King   It's a long story.

Trick   Whatever it is, ya better get ya story straight. (*The party fully sends back into action, but instead of shaking, they're stepping, creating a beat.*) We gone open up the floor to whoever wan' lay they voice on this beat over hih.

King   I got this.

Trick   Alright, give it up for King!

Applause.

King (*like poetry*)   Alright, Ma. Hih it goes. I was going to school, and it was all cool until . . . Well, maybe that's not exactly it, see I was easily adjusting, and then after the fall, the people who I thought were my people weren't my people at all. We all shared the space, but they were mad self-involved. I didn't wan' disappoint so I kept moving along. But more time went on, and everything I felt, they made me feel I was wrong.

Trick   Yo, are you almost done wit' this song?

King   Seriously? (*A beat.*) Just give me a drink.

The **Beautiful Woman** *brings a red cup to* **King**. *Chug, chug, chug. Once he finishes, he throws the cup to the ground, the whole party breaks down into a step routine. The* **Beautiful Woman** *now starts to resemble . . .*

King   Ife?

The step routine consists of **King** *trying to reach* **Ife**, *but being blocked and pulled back into the step.* **Ife** *turns back into the* **Beautiful Woman**. *One booming STOMP and the* **Beautiful Woman** *sends* **King** *to the ground, sleeping.*

Scene Two

Ife *holds a small box of her own.* **Tee Wa** *sits in her rocking chair.*

Tee Wa   You wan' me to deliver the message? You can't just wait until he gets home from the party?

Ife   I'on wan' see 'im.

Tee Wa   I'm not sure he wants to see me.

Ife   What happened?

Tee Wa   I tol' 'im the truth 'bout his father.

Ife   He'll get over it. He knows deep down you raised 'im to be the man he is.

Tee Wa   With how angry he was, he probably believes his father did.

Ife   He's probably hurt.

Tee Wa   Can you talk to 'im?

Ife   No. I'on wan' see 'im unless he can tell me he loves me. He shouldn't have access to me like that.

Tee Wa   I'm not gone defend 'im, because he made his choice, but this is different. I think he needs help.

Ife   He doesn't wanna grow wit' me, so why should I be the one to help 'im?

Tee Wa   Because he tells you the things he doesn't tell me . . . Like he dropped out of school.

Ife   Hear 'im out. Hear how he feels 'bout the school. Don't try to give 'im advice or tell 'im to grow thicker skin. Just listen.

Tee Wa   I can tell you love him. I'm sorry he didn't tell you he loves you.

Ife   Me too, but I've gotta move on.

Tee Wa   He's serious 'bout you.

Ife   Is that enough? Would you think that's enough?

Tee Wa   King's father told me he loved me, and he left me. Would you rather a man's words or actions?

Ife   Why should we have to pick one? Why should we decide between one bare minimum and another? What man makes a woman do that?

Tee Wa   Too many.

Ife   I'm leaving. Can you tell 'im?

Tee Wa *steps down from the porch and walks to* **Ife**. **Ife** *is a little scared at first, but* **Tee Wa** *pulls her in a hug. It's a little awkward, but* **Ife** *warms into it.*

Tee Wa   I will. You're a stronger woman than I was at ya age.

Ife   Thank you, Tee Wa. You really tryna get that discount outta me, huh.

Tee Wa   I made some stuffed bell peppers. I could make you a plate.

Ife   Oh, no thank you. I just ate. (**Tee Wa** *stares, unmoving. A beat.*) Okay, I could eat one.

Ife *and* **Tee Wa** *exit together into the house.*

Scene Three

King *awakes.* **Chorus 1** *enters, dancing from the party still. The* **Beautiful Woman** *struts across the stage, entering and exiting.* **Chorus 1** *and* **King** *watch, though* **King** *watches in disappointment.*

Chorus 1   Man, I see you. You really had a time last night, didn't you?

King   I couldn't do it. That's just not me.

Chorus 1   Boy, why not? Shoo. Did you see hu?

King   She not Ife.

Chorus 1   They got a whole lot of Ife's in this world, son.

King   Go away.

Chorus 1   If I leave, I'm not coming back.

King   I hate you.

Chorus 1   Fuck did you say?!

Chorus 1 *squares up to* **King**. **King** *backs away.*

King   I hate you for not raising me!

Chorus 1   Right. That was all Tee Wa's doing. She raised a good kid. But not a man. You think I'm the key to your manhood?

King   You talk a lot 'bout being a man instead of just acting like one.

Chorus 1   Show me then. Show me what a man does. Show me how you take that stuff every week.

King   You can be really cruel to me.

Chorus 1   I am you. Na, show me what it means to be all tough like your great uncle Archie. He was soft like you, but at least he could fight. I know *I* ain't shit, but you got to choose every bit of ain't shit you became, so how come you ain't the man you wan' to be?

King   Fuck you, man!

Chorus 1   There he is! Go get— (**King** *runs away.*) Don't run, puff your chest! Just like your uncle Archie.

Chorus 1 *goes after him, exiting,*

Scene Four

The corner store. **Trick** *hangs outside.* **Leon** *enters, dapping* **Trick** *up.*

Trick   You seen King?

Leon   Nah, man. Not since last night. Why?

Trick   Ife inna store.

Leon   Why she hanging over hih?

Trick   It surely ain't for King. Hih she come.

Ife *enters from the store, with* **Oram**.

Ife   Thank you, Mr. Oram, I can walk myself out.

Trick   You heard hu, Mr. Oram. Leave hu alone.

Oram   Shut up, Trick.

Oram *exits into the store.*

Trick   Mr. Oram been bothering you, love?

Ife   Hey Leon.

Leon   Wazzam Ife. You looking fine today.

Ife   I said hey to you 'cause I thought you were gone be the nice one.

Trick   I been tryna talk to you, Ife.

Ife   I know. I got ya text and ya call last night.

Trick   And?

Ife   It was sweet. Next time text me before midnight.

Trick   But you was up, though.

Trick *high fives* **Leon**.

Ife   Yeah, crying over ya boy.

Trick   Who King? Don't worry 'bout 'im. He's moving on fine wit'outchu.

Leon   Yep, he was wit' some shawty at the party.

Ife   And I'm moving on wit'out 'im. I'm leaving New Orleans.

Trick   Damn . . . Ya gone miss it?

Ife   Yeah. I love it out hih. This is home.

Trick   Ain't no place like NOLA. We can have one last function before ya go. I'm getting a party bus. We rolling at 9 on Saturday. Pick-up at Rouse's on Carrollton.

Leon   Man, pick-up on the eastbank?!

Trick   Leon, man.

Leon   Aight. Fuck.

Leon *exits into the store.*

Trick   So you'll come?

Ife   I'll think 'bout it. I'm leaving out early on Sunday.

Trick   C'mon, girl. For me? You can sleep on the plane, ya 'eard me.

Ife   Is King gone be there?

Trick   Not if you are. King who?

Ife   I'on think I can see 'im before I leave.

King (*entering*)   Leave where?

Ife   You haven't been home.

King   Nah, I've been out. Can we talk?

Ife   I've been crying all day and night, and you've already been wit' another woman.

King   Nun even happened. You wit' Trick na?

Ife   Really, nigga?

King   You're my world.

Trick   This corny nigga.

King (*to* **Trick**)   Since when you speaking to my ole lady?–

Ife   -I am not ya ole lady no more–

King   -Took you a day to warm up to Ife, huh Trick?

Trick   Tell ya boy to stop bucking.

King   Why you all up on my girl?

Trick   She said she ain't yers.

Ife   -I'on need anybody defending me.–

King   -You couldn't wait.

Trick   You was fucking a whole 'nother girl!

King   We ain't even do nun! Na you tryna get Ife!

Ife *exits quietly. The* **Boys** *fuss.*

Trick   You told me y'all wasn't together no more.

King   I'm ya potna! She my ole lady, bruh!

Trick   How many times somebody gotta tell you? She ain't ya ole lady.

King   She ain't yers either, so stop acting like it.

Trick   Why are you so upset? What happened to the little kid who wanted to hang wit' the big boys? This is what we do. You wanted to be like us, well you are na. You got some play. You one of us.

King   You gone stop messin' wit' me, and you gone leave Ife alone.

Trick *squares up to* **King**.

Trick   I get it. You wan' fuck Ife, but don't wan' nobody else to? You wan' be hu man, but not be hu man? What do you wan'? Make up ya mind! Then everybody can stop arguing 'bout whose got next.

Trick *stays in* **King's** *face. A beat.* **Trick** *chuckles and goes to exit into the store.* **King** *cries out and lunges at* **Trick**. *He lands a good punch, then* **Trick** *fights back. Pound for pound, everything lands, all on* **King**.

The sound brings **Leon** *and* **Oram** *out of the store. They break the fight apart.* **King** *stays on the ground, until* **Oram** *picks him up.*

Oram   Your father would be disappointed to know you lost a fight.

Leon   C'mon, Trick, let's get the hell outta hih.

Trick   Bruh, I ain't even start this shit.

Oram   Go ya ass home before I tell ya mama where ya really be hanging at.

Trick *and* **Leon** *exit.*

Oram   You 'ight?

King   I'm good.

Oram   Y'all was fighting over that girl, huh?

King   Why you so concerned?

Oram   How can I get you to talk to me? I try to be there for you. That male figure ya need in ya life.

King   Because you're sorry my dad wasn't, but that don't mean ya presence is all good.

Oram   Is that what Tee Wa tells you?

King   She didn't have to. I see you.

Oram   What more do you want from me? I work.

King   To avoid your family. You think that's love?!

Oram   I work because I lost my family! (**Oram** *cries. At first it's soft and to himself, but it grows into something hysterical. Something he's been wanting to get out his entire life.* **King** *hesitantly hugs* **Oram**. *He's surprised by the hug, but accepts it and pulls* **King** *into an even tighter hug.*) I love you.

King   I love you too?

Oram *wipes his face and calms himself. Beat.*

Oram   Sorry, I didn't mean to get emotional . . . You're my legacy, ya know. I want to be around, for you.

King   You shouldn't have to apologize for your feelings.

Oram   I should get back to work. Gotta do some man shit to make up for that outburst, huh?

King *watches, concerned, as* **Oram** *exits, still wiping his tears.*

Trick *runs up behind* **King**.

Trick   Yo, son!

Trick *throws a punch and it hits* **King** *square in his face. He falls back. The* **Remaining Company** *runs in and catches him, gently placing him on the ground. The* **Company** *and* **Trick** *exit.*

Scene Five

Tee Wa *kneels on the porch. She prays.*

Tee Wa   Dear Heavenly Father,

Everyday I thank you for every day you bless me and my son with. I thank you for the roof over our head, clothes on our backs, and food on our table. Today Father God, I ask you to watch over my son and bring him back to me. I pray you find him wherever he is and place in his heart the love that a Father like yourself would. I am always in your presence, and I'd like you to send our son a reminder of your presence. Open his eyes to acknowledge our Lord and Savior. And lastly Father God, open our hearts. The Bible says, out of the abundance of the heart, the mouth speaks, and next time I see him, I wan' us to be able to speak our hearts freely to each other. In Jesus name, Amen.

King *enters, like a call from God. He's holding his face.*

King   Ma, can we talk?

Tee Wa   What happened?

King   I got into it wit' Trick over Ife. He said some things I didn't like.

Tee Wa   So you put hands on 'im?

King   I know it was wrong. You taught me better. Na, can we talk?

Tee Wa *prepares herself. She pats the spot next to her, calling for* **King** *to sit. He does.*

Tee Wa   I'm gone listen, but first, I wan' tell you some'.

She pulls out the leather Bible from her small box.

King   That's dad's Bible right?

Tee Wa   Yes, it was his. I gave it to 'im when we were together. I wrote his name in it, and when you told me you wanted to be King, I wrote yers in it. It was a reminder that God has a plan, not me. When I wrote ya dad's name in it, I was hoping for a ring, and I got you. So, I'on care what you do, I wan' to know and love you. Na tell me why you left school. (*A beat.*) I'm listening.

King   You went to an HBCU for school. And you had me fresh out of college, so when I was a baby, I was surrounded by people who look like us. Growing up hih, I always felt being black was the normal. Most places I go hih, I could find an abundance of us. You raised me 'round culture and you taught me blackness was some' to love 'bout myself. I never knew how hard going to a PWI would be. When I got to that school, I was surviving at first. I was just going to class and trying to make friends. When I first started transitioning, that's when I made a lot of friends because my paintings were about my transition. You know, I was told I was one of the best painters?

Tee Wa   Of course ya were. That's how you got to go for free!

King   Yeah, well. I was also told I only got that much scholarship money because I'm black. Then, the further I got in my transition, the more focused I was on being the man I wanted to be, I started neglecting the person in me who just needed love. So my paintings became all about love. That's when people stopped caring. The more they saw me as a man, the more people stopped caring who I am. The only time those kids cared about what I had to say is if it benefited them. There was another black painter there too, he kind of reminded me of Trick.

Tee Wa   I hope you stayed away from him.

King   I didn't have a choice. He wanted so badly to mix with the white kids because I didn't fit what his idea of a black man was. When I did fit that idea, I was praised for it, but never praised for just being myself. Then the school offered to commission me for a few pieces.

Tee Wa   That's amazing. Why didn't you tell me?

King   They just wanted a black painter. When I gave them my ideas, they rejected it and commissioned another black painter who wanted to make a mural more to the school's liking. This past semester was when I realized that I was just so lonely. No one knew who I was. No one cared. It was like everyone had a monopoly on the space I could take up. I didn't just drop out, I was pushed out. They made me feel like I was a hostile, caged animal, all the time. And I was so tired, Tee Wa. I was so damn tired. Every day I stayed there felt like they gave more of my dreams away wit' no fair way to get 'em back. I was sick of feeling like less than what I am. So nah, I wanna do my own thing na. God made me special. I'm tryna show people.

Tee Wa   Fuck them white people!

King   Ma.

Tee Wa   I'm serious . . . But I get it. You were hurt time and time again. And you never full healed. But you have to try now. You're not in that place anymore. Don't let heartbreak get inna way of a good thing. You deserve to be loved, son.

King   I don't always feel it.

Tee Wa   You had it. Loud and clear. You have to give love as equally as you deserve it. Someone who sees you. If you want her to love you the way you need, you've gotta love her the way she needs.

King   You mean Ife.

Tee Wa   I told hu to leave you.

King   I think I get why. I wish you left dad. Maybe you would've been happier.

Tee Wa   But then you wouldn't be hih.

King   It was yer dream to go to California.

Tee Wa   He took it and shared it wit' someone else, but I got a new dream. God gave me a better one.

King   Ife's leaving town.

Tee Wa   How'd you find out?

King   How'd *you* find out?

Tee Wa   She told me, once she realized you weren't gone tell hu how you feel.

King   I gotta go take care of some'.

Tee Wa   I know, son. I'm proud of you. Always.

King *gives* **Tee Wa** *a kiss on the cheek, then exits.* **Tee Wa** *exits into the house.*

Scene Six

Trick, **Leon**, *and* **Oram**, *outside the corner store.*

Trick   He put his hands on me, and I showed 'im I'm not the one.

Leon   So you knocked his ass out?

Trick   Exactly. He ain't bouta run up, thinking he run shit.

Leon   You the man, Trick. But go like this, you got blood on your shirt.

Oram *groans.* **King** *enters.*

Leon   King's back for more.

Trick (*squaring up*)   C'mon son! Round 2, ya 'eard me!

King   Nah. I'm hih to apologize.

Leon   Apologize?

Trick   I'm listening. Gone 'head and say sorry for getting ya ass beat.

King   I'm sorry I hit you. I wasn't in a great place, and I shouldn't have done it.

Trick   Yo apology doesn't mean shit. "I wasn't inna great place." C'mon, man. I beat ya ass. Just say that.

King   Yeah, you got me.

Trick   See, y'all! I told you. He ain't shit. You gotta change ya name, 'cause King ain't it.

King   Whatever. I'on wan' no more beef.

Trick   Get outta hih. This my block, and I better not see you hih ever again.

King   We'll see. You can have the block; I got the world.

King *exits.*

Trick   What the fuck that hippie shit mean?

Leon   I think King's gonna make it out.

Trick   "I got the world" head ass.

Oram   He gone make it. He's just like his daddy . . . with obvious differences.

Trick   Where his daddy at na? Ain't hih.

Oram   California, smartass.

Leon   Mr. Oram, can I work for you? I'll take whatever job you got.

Oram   C'mon in.

Leon *exits into the store.*

Oram (*to* **Trick**)   You coming?

Trick   I'on need to work in no corner store. I'm good, man.

Oram   You gone sit out hih by yourself?

Trick   I'm good! Just gone on in.

Leon *pops his head out.*

Leon   Trick, you still the man!

Trick   Thank you Leon.

Oram *and* **Leon** *exit back into the store.*

Trick   I'on need nobody. Not Leon, not King . . . I ain't even want Ife anyway . . .
Fuck y'all niggas looking at?

Trick *bucks at the audience, then exits to the street.*

Scene Seven

Ife *does* **Tee Wa's** *hair.*

Tee Wa   I'm glad I drove all the way over here.

Ife   Y'all gone stop acting like Gentilly far. It's a 20-minute drive.

Tee Wa   That's why I was gone thank ya for the discount.

Ife   Tee Wa, when I'm done, you gone be gone out again. You gone find you a whole
new man. One that deserves you.

Tee Wa   You might be onto some' there. You good at this hair thing.

Ife   That's why I'm leaving. I'm taking my hair test when I get to California.

Tee Wa   Well, ain't that good for you. You gone be living it up, meeting new people,
and doing hair. You gone have yo own salon one day.

Ife   Watch out, world. Ife's crown got buku clients. (**Ife** *dances as* **Tee Wa** *hypes her
up.*) What about you Tee Wa? What you like to do?

Tee Wa   Me?

Ife   Yeah, you.

Tee Wa   I love cooking. I know the right food can make the unthinkable happen. I
wanted to bring seafood boils to California, before everybody and they mama was
doing it there and in Atlanta. I always had an entrepreneurial spirit. Maybe I'll think
of something once King gets back on his feet.

Ife   And you should make me a cookbook for when I leave, so I can eat more than
just mama noodles.

Tee Wa   Get me a flight to California like I'm Martha Stewart or some'. I would love to come out there and finally see it.

Ife   I will. I promise.

Tee Wa   . . . My son is looking for you.

Ife   I know.

Tee Wa   He fought that lil boy I don't like. Caught a beatdown too.

Ife   I felt like they were gone get into it. I left before I saw 'em throw hands.

King *enters.*

King   Ife.

Ife   What you wan', King? I'm working.

King   On my mama head.

Tee Wa   Business is business.

King   I came to apologize. But can we talk privately?

Tee Wa   I'll give y'all some space.

Ife   Nah, Tee Wa. You can stay. If he's got some' he wan' say, he can say it in front of his mama.

Tee Wa *settles in her seat, watching like an audience member.*

King   So you're really leaving . . .

Ife   Is that all you wanted to say?

King   I'm sorry I haven't stepped up, and I'm sorry I haven't been honest. Truth is, I been feeling like this idea of how I should love has been projected onto me. I'm a man, but I'm also King. Before you say anything, you and Tee Wa are the only ones who have made me feel like so much more. You make me feel like me, and I love that about you.

Ife   Fuck you, King. Do you love me?

King   I love you so much. Wit' you, I feel a lil less stuck, like I can do anything I set my mind to. You remind me that I'm me, and you'n let me forget it. I didn't think I deserved you. But I love you too much. Your ambition and your ability to give love to everyone, even the people you hate.

Ife   Like Trick.

King   Yeah . . . When me and you shared dreams, some of yers became mine, and some of mine became yers. I wanna see that through, share moments witchu. You've been by my side for years, and I always wanna be by yers.

Ife   Am I just supposed to get back wit' you like nun happened?

King   We could try. Ain't that what love is about? Choosing yer person?

Ife   And according to your homeboys, you moved on. I put my love into going to California.

King   I can't do what those other men do. I'm not the type to open myself up to anybody. You know that about me. I dare say, you love that about me. You were the person who helped me become the man I am today. (**Tee Wa** *clears her throat.*) And Tee Wa too. But you, Ife . . . You saw me as King before I even knew I was King. Just like I always knew you wanted to move to California.

Ife   C'mon, stop playing.

King   I did. I knew ya mama didn't want you to go, back when we was in high school. So you stayed for somebody else. (*Beat.*) I think you should really go, start fresh if that's what you want. Don't even think twice about it. Follow your dream.

Ife   I'm gone make some' of myself. Really be the Ife I always dreamed. The girl everybody calls on to do they're hair. Always riding for my people. Bringing love back to New Orleans, maybe save it from drowning. Come back and join Femme Fatale or some'.

King   Ya already on ya way.

Ife   But I also wish I didn't leave people behind so easy, like my mama, my dad, my little sisters. I give so much love, but I still wish I loved more.

King   You have so much love to give to this world. We both do. Maybe ya gotta leave to give yer love room to grow . . . And I'm definitely gone miss you.

Ife   I'm always gone be Ife from the sixth ward.

King   King from the fifthteenth.

Ife   Just say Algiers, man.

King   You're always gone have a home to come back to. (**Ife** *friendly punches* **King** *on his shoulder. He laughs and hides his face as his laughter turns into tears. He collapses to his knees.* **Ife** *gets down with him and hugs him.*) You my heart. My love.

Ife   What are you gonna do?

King   I gotta be the King that deserves love and gives it. And move outta my mama house.

Tee Wa   I might get a whole new man.

King   I gotta meet 'im first.

Tee Wa   When you moving out?

King   You already got a man?

Tee Wa   No, but I wan' know how soon I'm gone get 'im.

King   Ma.

Tee Wa   Sorry, y'all gone 'head.

Ife Then what?

King Maybe one day, I can get another chance to prove to you that I see you and love you. Can I do that?

A beat. The **Remaining Company** *enters the stage, parading through.* **Ife** *gets swept up into the second-line. The* **Company** *exits, with the second-line still heard in the distance.* **King** *and* **Tee Wa** *remain.*

Tee Wa C'mon, ya want some' to eat?

King Can you make red beans?

Tee Wa Whatever you want.

Tee Wa *joins the end of the second-line, exiting.* **King** *second-lines, but he remains on stage. He's showing himself to everyone, this is him.*

Epilogue

The second-line sounds off in the distance. **King** *picks up the letter and second-lines with it. As he does,* **Adam** *sits inside the kitchen. He scans the room around him.* **King** *joins him in the kitchen.*

Adam Not much has changed around the house since the last time I was here.

King You said that already. I don't mean to kick you out, but Tee Wa don't wanna see you when she gets back.

Adam She was always so amazing. Her love is like no other. (*A beat.*) So how are . . . you?

King I said I'm good.

Adam C'mon. I feel like you're holding back. You sound just like me.

King *plays with the letter in his hands.*

King Not really.

Adam Obviously–

King You don't look too good–

Adam I'm not well. But I don't want to talk about that. I wanted to see you. My son. You've been making some' of yourself I hear, and you look . . . like–

King A man?

Adam I could tell you don't need me. But now that you're looking more and more like me, I think it's 'bout time I start showing you the ropes.

King I needed you a long time ago, but you weren't there. I learned how to be the man I am today wit'out you. Don't you think I wanted someone to talk to about this?

Adam   I know how you feel. I did it wit'out my pops. He was always working. I wanted to be a better man than him. Comparing myself to him all the time. Isn't that stupid?

King   I used to compare myself to you, or whatever idea of you I created in my head. I even tried to be a better man than you.

Adam (*laughing*)   I don't see how you could do that. I mean, you're not a real man.

King   What it mean to be a man?

Adam   You know . . .

Adam *does a stroking movement.*

King   Sure . . . Aside from that.

Adam   It's like my paw used to say. Strong like a tide, steady like a rock, smooth as the river, and so much more.

King   My mama did all of that. What makes her so different? She did what you couldn't. And all you have to say about what it means to be a man to you is . . . a low blow.

Adam   I didn't wanna get political. I want us to reconnect. As father and child.

King   You got other kids?

Adam   No.

King   You married?

Adam   Nah. Just had a few girlfriends here or there. I pray God blesses me with more kids.

King   You lonely, huh? It feels lonely when you didn't love the people who loved you.

Adam   Sometimes men need to be alone.

King   You can go back to California, then.

Adam   C'mon, don't do me like that. How many times I gotta tell you I'm sorry?

King   Once when you say it and mean it.

Adam   You sound like a woman. Why'd you even agree for me to come?

King   I wanted to read your letter back to you. The one you sent me.

Adam   Gone 'head then.

King   "Dear," Well I'm not reading that.

"I know you have not heard from me your whole life. My name is Adam Ferguson, and I'm your father. I know you must be upset to hear from me, but I wanted to see if you were open to meeting. I have a lot of regrets and hate myself for what I have

done. Your paw paw told me what you're doing. Though I don't agree with it, I wanted to see what a son of mine would be like. You're gonna have to forgive me if this letter comes off soft. I'm not sure how to write a son that used to be a daughter. I'm proud to say now that I do have a son. Again, I'm sorry for being emotional . . ."
You apologized for two more pages.

Adam   Because I left you.

King   You never apologized for leaving. You only were sorry you felt emotions.

Adam *leaps out of his seat.*

Adam (*growls*)   What do you want me to do?! I'm not gonna sit here and keep rehashing the same thing over and over to you. I said sorry. Sorry is enough! You think this shit is easy?

King   Was leaving easy?

Adam   I needed to get away. I wasn't ready to be a father. I couldn't raise a kid. I never thought you'd . . . The hardest part was having your paw paw say what a shit man I am for not handling my responsibilities.

King   He's not wrong, but he shouldn't have pushed you like that.

Adam *cries. He quickly wipes his tears.*

Adam   I'm sorry. Don't look at me. (**Adam** *turns away.* **King** *hesitantly approaches and softly hugs him.*) I don't want you to see me like this. I'm supposed to be strong . . .

King   '. . . Strong like a tide, steady like a rock, smooth as the river, and so much more.' I know. But why you gotta be so hard all the time?

Adam   Here you go, thinking women can show a man how to be a man.

Adam *coughs.*

King   Do I look like a woman to you?

Adam   How did you manage, huh? I hear that stuff does that.

Adam *coughs more.*

King   I've always been King. Tee Wa knew that. If you stuck around maybe you could've seen that too. Maybe you could've taught me some'.

Adam   Only thing I could've taught you was how to use ya fists. Your paw paw told me about that too.

Adam *laughs. The laugh transforms into a bigger cough.*

King   Man to man: Mama told me something in a dream. She said we can fight . . . or love. People are gonna see and expect things from me no matter what. I would much rather be open to love, and being loved, than to fight my way through life.

The brass band plays. **King** *gets up, pulling out a handkerchief. He second-lines around* **Adam**, then off.

Adam *remains. He steps out onto the porch and takes one last look at the house. He reaches under the rocking chair and grabs the leather Bible.*
Blackout.

END OF PLAY

Man, Moon, and the Lorde

Stephanie Hsu

Addressing the underrepresentation of stories about trans people fighting cancer, Siena Marilyn's *Man and Moon* dares to approach an impasse in what can even be said about transness and chronic illness, an event horizon where the discourse of gendered cancer (e.g., breast) begins to disintegrate. This is the cosmology explored by Luna, the play's tweenaged philosopher and astronomy superfan, who declares that "Humans are nothing different from the Universe [. . .] You never change, you only expand. All of you is still you" (319). She has built her pulpit (literally) in a hospital waiting room, and with her mom on the other side, Luna finds herself with an audience of one—Aaron, a nonbinary trans man who is recovering from surgery and finishing chemotherapy, but who suffers all the more from existential despair and a loneliness that finds its match in this odd, precocious girl.

Transitioning and being treated for cancer at the same time, Aaron seems stung by the absurdity that the same procedure could be considered lifesaving and medically necessary for one reason and not the other. In conversations with Luna, his unfinished sentences and skipped words illustrate the difficulty of talking about body parts and their supposed biological functions at the intersection of queerness and chronic illness. This symbolic void or vacuum was first charted by Audre Lorde—Black lesbian feminist writer and activist of the late-twentieth century and one of our queer saints, reverently known as "the Lorde"—in *The Cancer Journals* (1980/2020), which records her two-year journey with breast cancer resulting in a unilateral mastectomy, and which contains core ideas that will later resound in her well-known essays.

Lorde's presence is immanent in *Man, Moon, and the Lorde*, extending its questions and deepening some of its surprises, and Siena Marilyn's play drives home the fact that living with cancer was central to the queer theory that Lorde would write for the rest of her time on earth. Luna and Aaron's cosmic search for meaning is also a search for what it means to be queer, for the source of our unique will to survive and the style of our struggle, the idiosyncrasies we recognize in each other and which somehow unite us. As Lorde's most recent biographer Alexis Pauline Gumbs puts it, "For me, Audre has always been quantum, not only because she died before I met her, not only because she shows up in the lives and actions of countless devotees across space and time, but also because her theory of energy and the way she used her lifeforce exceed a normative understanding of life" (2024: 19-20). For many of us, Lorde's writings as a cancer survivor are the first of her works we encounter, not necessarily appreciating that the source of her "lifeforce" is an intimate knowledge of death. "*For once we accept the actual existence of our dying,*" she writes during her first post-op month, the time frame during which we are introduced to Aaron, and he to Luna, "*who can ever have power over us again?*" (Lorde [1980] 2020: 45, italics in original).

Claiming Lorde as Aaron's queer ancestor helps to expand our imagination about the multiverse of intersectional possibilities and interracial ways of relating that pulse between him and Luna. His headphones and hoodie are a self-protective cocoon, simultaneously giving defiance and concealment in a way that portrays his isolated battle with disease, while also suggesting the posture of the persecuted, the shrouded image of so many young people targeted by police and state-sanctioned violence. Assailing his resistance, Luna draws Aaron into dialogues that enact the power dynamics of parent-child dyads, siblings, and romantic couples: trying to feed him by hand; questioning him about his body and speaking graphically about her own; developing a crush and trying to kiss him; asking him to meet her outside the hospital and calling him a bitch when he does not.

In her childish entitlement and aggressive optimism, Luna is not unlike the figure of the Child described by queer theory's antisocial thesis as the icon of heteronormativity; whose imagined innocence and fragility compel us with the force of "coercive universalization" to justify any inconvenience for her edification, or any violence for her supposed protection; and whose future is supposedly threated by the mere existence of queer and trans people (Edelman 2004: 11). More than twice her senior, Aaron starts to call out Luna's use of coercion but does not finish his accusation, "You *force*—" (304). With the leveling discovery of Luna's secret, revealing why she is stuck in that waiting room, the moment for confrontation has passed and something shifts between them. But how? If, like a star burning through its forms and phases, "[a]ll of you is still you" (319) then how do you ever stop being a Child?

Aaron and Luna are in different forms of crisis, but both come together in a striking observation Lorde makes about her own cancer treatment: "The pain of separation from my breast was at least as sharp as the pain of separating from my mother. But I made it once before, so I know I can make it again" ([1980] 2020: 18). Taking comfort in the notion of cycles, repetitions, and returns, Lorde comes to regard her mastectomy as a kind of rebirth. But this separation takes ongoing work, as both demonstrate when speaking about their mothers—Luna, who lies about a memory in order to veil her sick mom's embarrassment; and Aaron, who seems to talk interchangeably about a past self and a mother who also died from the disease when they admit, "Cancer is some Catholic guilt version of giving me what I want . . . Like it's killing me but it's also like killing *her* [. . .] And . . . She's still mine" (319). Aaron's guilty wish-fulfillment points to the seeming paradox that cancerous tissue removal could also be gender-affirming medical care, and he suggests that getting top surgery without being able to name it as such can feel like a murder-suicide pact when you are living under a transphobic regime.

Aaron and Luna discover some hard truths, or what they call *real lies*, as they try to survive the pain of separation, both real and symbolic. When (m)others leave us, then "[w]e can learn to mother ourselves," as Lorde will later declare in her "Eye to Eye: Black Women, Hatred, and Anger" (1984). "Mothering ourselves means learning to love what we have given birth to by giving definition to," she counsels, with her characteristic sense of consistency in thought and action, and her faith in the healing power of integrity. At the same time, it also involves the real and metaphorical powers of death, and harnessing them to create change in ourselves: "Mothering means the laying to rest of what is weak, timid, and damaged—without despisal—the protection and support of what is useful for survival and change, and our joint explorations of the difference" ([1984] 2020: 173-74). Through their bickering and banter, Aaron and Luna indeed learn to mother themselves and—crucially— they resist the urge to mother each other. When he returns to the waiting room for the last time, it is as the "unlikely" (literally, queer) adult friend who is capable of letting her take care of herself, which is perhaps the only way one ever grows up (322).

Because we can all mother ourselves, Lorde's approach to self-care has bodily autonomy at its foundation, and by demonstrating that choice about her body is vital to her survival, she also forwards a theory of queer and trans embodiment that offers liberation from the loss that Aaron carries. For instance, feeling at first betrayed by her right breast and its threat of malignancy, Lorde finds herself mourning it as a source of erotic sensation, but ultimately resolves that "I can never lose that feeling because I own it, because it comes out of myself. I can attach it anywhere I want to, because my feelings are part of me" ([1980] 2020: 79). This feeling that transcends the sexual reappears in "Uses of the Erotic: The Erotic as Power" (1980), in which she describes a lifeforce flowing through the objects and labor involved in her creative and community work, establishing an equality of being between people and things invested with her desire. After surgery, Lorde restyles her wardrobe around her beautiful asymmetry, resisting the social pressure she receives, especially from other women, to wear a prosthetic breast. Angry to learn that her personal flair and mode of victory over cancer is an affront to gender normativity, and declaring herself inspired by the fable of single-breasted Amazon warriors, she calls instead for greater visibility in the lesbian feminist movement: "Where were the dykes who had had mastectomies?" ([1980] 2020: 42).

Whether Lorde could be speaking to a nonbinary trans man such as Aaron—"across space and time," as Gumbs experiences it, or if Lorde actually knew any people of trans experience—is a question that invites us to historicize the hateful attitudes associated today with a "small but vocal minority" calling themselves trans-exclusionary radical feminists, who espouse a binary "gender-critical feminism" that can itself be traced to a small but overrepresented set of transphobic texts from the 1970s and 1980s (Sullivan 2022: 18). One such example is the text that occasioned Lorde's "Open Letter to Mary Daly" (1979), in which she holds Daly accountable for the racist exclusion of nonwhite women from her book on female symbology (except for its lurid spotlight on female genital cutting practices in the global South) but never mentions any of her transphobic claims. Lorde's "Open Letter" has nonetheless come to be read as a general denouncement of terfdom, bearing the unspoken lesson that trans exclusion is a logical extension of "racist feminism" (Koyama 2006: 702), relegating terfdom to the margin where it belongs, and keeping the faith that she could be the Lorde for us all.

When we first meet Aaron, alone and awaiting the next round of chemo, he is not yet the queer militant that Lorde will come to describe—but neither at first was she. Five years after beating breast cancer, Lorde makes a different choice to live with metastasizing liver cancer for another seven years, a decision she explains in one of her last prose works, "A Burst of Light" (1988). "If this were another breast tumor, I'd go for surgery again, because the organ comes off," she reasons, rejecting any semblance of gender essentialism and sentiment about her "organ" as before (betrayal, anger, mourning) ([1988] 2017: 46). Having learned "the whole terrible meaning of mortality as both weapon and power" the first time, she now describes a greater capacity for transforming material loss into existential gain—making the lack matter, as Luna would say—and conveying a more oppositional understanding of queer and trans embodiment: "*Caring for myself is not self-indulgence, it is self-preservation, and that is an act of political warfare*" ([1988] 2017: 45, 130, italics in original).

Without a community at his side, Aaron seems to share Lorde's existential question about her first diagnosis, "Is this pain and despair that surround me a result of cancer, or has it just been released by cancer?" because there are "abominations outside that echo the pain within" ([1980] 2020: 3). Facing a second diagnosis of the liver, Lorde is still critical of what she earlier calls the "Cancer Establishment" and "Cancer Inc.," but she does not politicize her illness as the cause of her dying, recognizing that it is her life as an activist that holds untold social value ([1980] 2020: 51, 55). In her daily visualizations, cancer takes the form of political enemies—white segregationists who retreat before Black American civil rights protesters, white apartheidists who are defeated by Black South African freedom fighters, and U.S. military interventions that must be resisted in Central America—and she is winning, or has already won, these battles ([1988] 2017: 132). More than metaphor, Lorde's notion of political survival offers us a guide to balancing the concerns of collective existence and self-care; a model for rethinking universality as that which we are all participants in, willing or not; and "a theory of energy," as Gumbs puts it, that Aaron knows he needs for his recovery, in addition to healing his body (2024: 20).

Man and Moon takes place over seven weeks and six sessions of chemotherapy, and during each transition the already liminal space of the hospital waiting room splits open, with another dimension of sound, sensation, and movement rushing in. This is not the postmodern purgatory we might otherwise imagine, and these musical interludes remind us that every patients' room is a space of profound social and personal transformation. As Aaron and Luna prepare to leave the hospital for the final time, another of Lorde's parables for queer survival comes to mind: While seeking alternative treatment for the liver cancer that will prove terminal, Lorde checks herself into a private medical clinic in the Swiss Alps for two weeks in the winter of 1985-1986, where she takes homeopathic cures derived from mistletoe and group lessons in "eurhythmics" and other physical routines following an eccentric natural healing trend known as anthroposophy. "How does an American—and a Black one at that [. . .] come to be at the Lukas Klinik in Switzerland?" she writes in her journal, noting on Christmas Eve 1985: "I feel trapped on a lonely star" ([1988] 2017: 79, 84).

Like Luna, Lorde uses the cosmic scale to convey distance in human relationships, and specifically to share what it feels like to be racialized as Black in medical settings (even "alternative" or "natural" ones) that are structured by unacknowledged histories of scientific racism, homophobia, and gender violence. Other clinic patients and visitors, provincial Europeans, assume that Lorde is a rural African or an aboriginal person from Oceania, and they pose ignorant and offensive questions; and the staff are at times "overtly racist," as a friend remembers, but Lorde "had an incredible ability to take what was useful to her and ignore the rest, and she got a great deal out of her stay" (Nissim 2015: 85). Like Aaron, Lorde has cause to feel unsafe in a place supposedly dedicated to their safety and recovery; but this is also where they learn that their capacity to heal is a power separate from and stronger so far than any antagonist's ability to do them harm.

In a time (again) of vicious and open racism, xenophobia, and transphobia in America, it seems even more important to use the knowledge our queer and trans ancestors have left us. With a ban on the very concept of "inclusion," let us hope that future queers will recognize our labored efforts to offer welcome and sanctuary to those with names we do not yet know. And as the clinic or hospital room becomes an even colder place for queers and trans people and so many others in a conservative America, may we learn from Lorde, Luna, and Aaron how a short stint in a sterile, hostile environment can prepare us afterwards to thrive.

References

Corbman, Rachel. 2024. "Ambivalent Attachments: Queer and Trans Histories of Lesbian Feminism." *Cultural Critique* 124: 185–94. dx.doi.org/10.1353/cul.2024.a926825.

Edelman, Lee. 2004. *No Future: Queer Theory and the Death Drive.* Duke University Press.

Gumbs, Alexis Pauline. 2024. *Survival is a Promise: The Eternal Life of Audre Lorde.* New York: Farrar, Straus and Giroux.

Koyama, Emi. 2006. "Whose Feminism Is It Anyway? The Unspoken Racism of the Trans Inclusion Debate." In *The Transgender Studies Reader*, ed. Susan Stryker and Stephen Whittle, 698–705. New York: Routledge.

LiveFitMagazine.com. 2023. "Interview with 'Man and Moon' Playwright Siena Marilyn Ledger." LiveFitMagazine.com. Accessed 1 December 2024. https://livefitmagazine.com/interview-man-and-moon-playwright-siena-marilyn-ledger.

Lorde, Audre. (1980) 2020. *The Cancer Journals.* New York: Penguin.

——. (1984) 2020. *Sister Outsider: Essays and Speeches.* New York: Penguin.

——. (1988) 2017. *A Burst of Light and Other Essays.* New York: Dover.

Nissim, Rina. 2015. "Audre Lorde and Her French-Speaking Readers." In *Audre Lorde's Transnational Legacies*, ed. Stella Bolaki and Sabine Broeck, 85–93. University of Massachusetts Press.

Sullivan, Mairead. 2022. *Lesbian Death: Desire and Danger Between Feminist and Queer.* University of Minnesota Press.

Man and Moon

Siena Marilyn

Characters

Aaron (28) An observer. Introverted, musically-inclined, and navigating a breast cancer diagnosis.
Luna (12) A thinker. Extroverted, obsessed with outer space, and in denial about the condition of her mother.

Casting Policy

Aaron should be played by a transman or non-binary actor.
Luna may or may not be played by an actual child actor.

Setting & Time

The waiting room of a hospital's Oncology unit, present day.

Playwright Notes

' . . . ' An ellipsis in dialogue can represent a pause, change in action or thought, or non-verbal communication.
[Transition] can explore time and space, connection and isolation.

Acknowledgments

For Kat, Chris, and my Mama

Post-Op/First Chemo

A beam illuminates **Luna***.*
Alone in her world . . .
In the future . . .
She is really in a hospital's waiting room:
Oncology unit.
Luna *has arranged the space*
to suit her speech and throughout,
the beam of light diffuses
and the focus broadens.

Luna   Thank you, thank you, thank you and welcome everyone!
I'm very excited to share with you my most recent discovery . . .
Please be quiet and pay attention:
This revolutionary discovery is . . . The theory . . . Of . . .
Year expansion and contraction by planetary time travel!
Here, what we call a year is the span of 365 days—
365 sun rises and sets. That is how long it takes
To get from this single point in space
All the way around the sun and then back again
To this same exact space.
That's a year here.
But on Venus, the revolution is much smaller.
If we were on Venus, a year would be equivalent to . . .
(*Types into a calculator.*)
224 days.
But, what if we were on Jupiter?
If we were on Jupiter . . .
(*Types into a calculator.*)
4,330 . . . Yes!
It's like *reverse* dog years.
In a sense, we could cheat the system.
And if we gain the technology, then we can:
Escape to Jupiter!
And when we go *there* we can forget time in the earthly sense.
And then we can live . . .
(*Types into the calculator*)
ELEVEN times. *Eleven* times as long as they say we ever could here.

Lights shift completely as **Aaron** *enters.*
He is wearing earphones or headphones and his hair is deep blue.
He finds a chair not in use and sits down.
Luna *disassembles her "podium."*

Luna   But it doesn't actually work that way.
Time doesn't slow down.

Not for me. And not on Jupiter.
It'd just be me. *I'd* just be moving slower.

Aaron   . . .

Luna   What are you listening to?

Aaron *doesn't make any indication that he hears this.*
Luna *grabs her backpack and moves.*
All that's between them now is one empty seat.
Luna *flips to a new section of her textbook,*
a chapter on the Solar System's planets.
She opens a pack of fruit snacks.
She takes out one examining its color: orange.
She places it on top of the seat between them.
She digs, finds a yellow one, and places it next in line.
Then she grabs a green one and places it next.
Then a red . . . She digs through the bag
and squishes three fruit snacks together
then places the mass on the seat.
She digs through to find a blue—

Aaron   . . .

Luna   This one is Uranus.

Aaron (*removes an earphone*)   What?

Luna   The planet.

Aaron   O, cool.

Luna (*offers the fruit snack pack*)   Want?

Aaron   No, thanks . . . though.

Aaron *puts an earphone back—*

Luna   WHAT ARE YOU LISTENING TO?

Aaron   Nothing . . . I wasn't listening to
Anything.

Luna   . . .

Aaron *removes both earphones.*

Luna   I'm Luna.

Aaron   Aaron.

Luna   Nice to meet you, sorry it's here.

Aaron   . . .

Luna   . . .

Aaron   Why Uranus?

Luna   Cause it's blue.

Aaron   Oh.

Luna   I like our planets.

Aaron   Cool.

Luna   I like space.

Aaron   Nice.

Luna   I'm Luna.

Aaron   Aaron.

Luna   I know.

Aaron   Right.

Luna   I'm waiting for someone.

Aaron   I'm not.

Luna   I'm not sick.

Aaron   I am.

Luna   . . .

Aaron   . . .

Luna   It gets better, honest.

Aaron   They say it gets worse.

Luna   Well, yeah . . .
But *you* get better at it.
You do, trust me.
My mom did.
She's been here—
Been coming here for 6 years.

Aaron   . . .

Luna   Just keeps coming back.

Aaron   . . .

Luna   So we just keep coming back.
Someday I think we won't.
People always eventually leave the hospital.
Some just leave dead.
But most people don't though—

Aaron   What's the book?

Luna   An astronomy textbook. Mom's copy.
From when she was getting her PhD.
So it's from the 90s and it's quite outdated.
But she gave it to me. To read.
How old are you?

Aaron   Twenty-seven— Eight. 28 . . .
How old are you?

Luna   Twelve. But
I'm turning 13 soon.
November 17th.

Luna *opens her book.*

Aaron   Looks intense.

Luna   It's *really* not. (*Shares her book.*) For instance, this is Earth.

Aaron   Looks familiar.

Luna   Yeah, it's our planet.
And that's how big it is.
And those are the significant qualities about it.
And, it is the only known planet that has ever
Successfully supported and sustained life.

Aaron   Got it.

Luna   And (*flips to another section of the book*)
That is the Huge-LQG:
The largest structure in the entire universe.
Its width spans four billion-ish light-years across
And, it's made up of around 73 individual quasars—

Aaron   Huge—

Luna   What?

Aaron   The thing . . .
The name . . .
The *huge*—

Luna   L. Q. G.

Aaron   Yeah, right. What is that?

Luna   Large Quasar Group.

Aaron   . . .

Luna   It's a quasar.

Aaron   Got it.

Luna   A *quasar*: Quasi stellar radio source. Like quasi-star.

They're known for the massive amounts of light they emit.
That's how we were able to find them. Initially,
Astronomers believed that they were just
High redshift sources of electromagnetic energy.
But really, what they are—are
these really really tight areas
in these really really big galaxies
that are orbiting these really really
BIG supermassive black holes
In space.

Aaron Quasar.

Luna Right. Anyway, I like it.

Aaron It's interesting.

Luna Pretty controversial actually.

Aaron How?

Luna Because a lot of scientists don't believe it's real.
The Huge-LQG defies all the laws.
It's too big.

Aaron But it exists?

Luna It does. But it doesn't make sense though.

Aaron Not all things that exist make sense.

Luna I like your blue hair.

Aaron Thank you.

Luna My mom had blue hair too
Right before. I'm gonna practice my presentation now.
Wanna watch?

Aaron Sure.

Luna *starts to re-assemble the chairs into her podium.*

Luna No one's gonna tell you no when your mom has cancer.
So, what's your understanding of quantum mechanics?

Aaron Very limited.

Luna How limited?

Aaron Like nothing.

Luna Oh . . . Well,
This theory will be useless to you then . . .

Aaron Oh. Sorry . . .

That you set it all up.

Luna   Quantum is the smallest anything. As small as a nothing.
But not equal to nothing, though sometimes it is . . .
A human equivalence to an eyelid flutter.
You know, someday, in the future,
it *will* be accepted as law. But for now,
It's an elaborate theory
from a new generational wave of physical understanding—

An automated machine calls "Aaron . . . Aaron . . . Aaron"

Aaron   Got it.

Luna   It does get better though, honest.

Aaron *exits through the Treatment Door.*

[Transition]

Second Chemo

Luna *is both eating fruit snacks and
Using them to work out her theories.*
Aaron *enters.*

Aaron   What?

Luna   Cool hat.

Aaron   Thanks.

Luna   I like beanie hats.
They're fun.

Aaron   Do you not go to school?

Luna   Online mostly.
I only sit in a desk with kids my age
on Mondays and Fridays.
But it's great because Mom teaches me about space
and other important things on the other days.

Aaron   . . .

Luna   We still make sense this way:
She goes in, I read
She explains things that
I don't understand later.

Aaron *grabs his earphones—*

Luna   Close your eyes.

Aaron   Why?

Luna   Just do it.

Aaron   . . .

Luna   Do it!

Aaron *closes his eyes.*
Luna *approaches* **Aaron***'s mouth*
with a fruit snack.

Aaron   Stop—

Luna   . . .

Aaron   What were you doing?

Luna   A game . . .

Aaron   Why—
Does the game require hand-feeding
a stranger?

Luna   We met last week
You're not a stranger
anymore.

Aaron   But you're still a child and—
I'm not comfortable with you hand-feeding me.

Luna   Sorry . . .

Aaron   Like . . .
We can still play it—
A different way?
Can I have my own pack?

Luna *sets a pack of fruit snacks on an empty seat.*
Aaron *takes the fruit snack packet and opens it.*

Aaron   Now what?

Luna   Watch:

Luna *closes her eyes and picks a fruit snack out of her pack.*
She holds it out for him to see and then eats it.

Luna   Red.
Now you go.

Aaron *closes his eyes. He picks a fruit snack, shows it to* **Luna**, *then eats it.*

Luna   What color is it?

Aaron   They all taste the same.

Luna   No they don't. The different colors have different flavors.

Aaron   Right but when it says"'assorted flavors" it doesn't actually mean each—

Luna   What. Flavor.

Aaron   I don't know . . . Red.

Luna   Nope.

Aaron   What was it?

Luna   My turn.

Luna *closes her eyes and eats a fruit snack.*

Luna   It could be blue . . .
But it's definitely purple.

Aaron   You cheated.
You were opening your eyes.

Luna   No I wasn't.
But fine I'll go again.
Orange duh.

Aaron   Let me try again.
Blue.

Luna   Nope.

Aaron *closes his eyes and eats a fruit snack.*

Aaron   That one's red. It has to be.

Luna   Not even close. At all.
Try one more.

Aaron *eats another fruit snack.*

Aaron   I don't know.

Luna   That one *was* red! You can
Always tell when it's red.

Aaron   No, you can't taste the difference.

Luna   You *can* . . .
You just can't.

Aaron   I shouldn't be eating these anyway,

Luna   You know a red when you taste it.

Aaron   Okay.

Luna   Okay.

Aaron *scratches his head under his beanie.*
Some hair comes out. He hides it in his hand.

Luna   I read this article.

Aaron *scratches his head again.*

Luna   Aaaand guess what? There's supposed to be a comet coming soon.

Aaron   O wow.

Luna   Yeah.

Aaron   That's cool.

Luna   I know.

Aaron   Great.

Luna   Yup—

Aaron *crumples another small tuft of blue into his fist.*

Luna   Guess what else.

Aaron   What else?

Luna   It's gonna happen on my birthday:
November 17th.
My birthday is on
November 17—

Aaron *adjusts his beanie while simultaneously scratching his head.*
A tuft of blue falls to the floor before he can catch it . . .

Aaron   Wow what are the odds.

Luna   Actually very likely.
Statistically speaking
Something spectacular happens in the sky every November
Around my birthday. But yeah . . . Not always a comet.
The last visible comet was like four years ago . . .
I watched it with my mom.
Probably gonna do it again.

Aaron   Cool.

Aaron *picks his hair up off the floor.*
Luna *points to a trash can.*
Aaron *goes to the trash can and takes off his beanie . . .*

Luna   Took my mom a while to get used to not having hair.

Aaron   It's not the hardest thing.

Luna   Know why my hair is so short?

Aaron   You cut it.

Luna   I did.
No, *I* did. Myself.
I used to have really really long hair.
Like *this* long. Then I cut it.
In my room, with kid scissors.
Like really really short.
My mom jumped when she saw me,
didn't even recognize me.
I was wearing a beanie hat like yours.
And I put all the hair in a Ziplock bag and handed it to her
To get a wig made
To wear.

Aaron   I'm sure she appreciated it.

Luna   She said thank you.
But I don't know what she did with it.
I didn't have much then. I looked like a boy.

Aaron   . . .

Luna   It's grown a bit.

Aaron   Yeah.

Luna   I just wanted to do it too.
I didn't care about it, but she did.
And then she cared about it on me too.
But neither of us had hair then.
And everything was okay.
Mine grew back.
Hers still hasn't.

Aaron   It will.

Luna   Isn't it funny how hair comes out of us dead?
What's the point?
It's just dead.
Cut it off, it's dead.
Grows back, still dead.
Hair is always dead
so what's the point?

Aaron   I don't know.

Luna   You'd think wed've evolved to a point where we didn't need it at all. Why . . .

Aaron   . . .

Luna   Why?

Aaron   What time's this comet gonna . . .
Happen?

Luna   Supposed to *pass* through our part of the sky just after sunset—
Sometimes it runs late. But,
thanks to where we are, with minimal light,
we should be able to see it pretty clearly.
Even without a telescope.
November 17th . . .
I'm gonna be 13.

Aaron   Big year.

Luna   When's your birthday going to happen?

Aaron   Already happened. April.

Luna   Well you'll have one again.

Aaron   . . .

Luna   Next year.
We both will
probably.

Aaron   Doing anything for it
Besides the comet?

Luna   I don't know.

Aaron   Well, your mom's probably got
Something planned for you.

Luna   Wanna play again but with your eyes open?

Aaron   What would be the point?

Luna   For practice.

The Automated Machine calls "Aaron . . . Aaron . . . Aaron . . . "

Aaron   Next time, I guess.

Luna *tosses him a packet of fruit snacks.*
Aaron *fumbles but still catches it.*

Luna   For practice.

Aaron *exits through the Treatment Door*
But he left his earphones on the seat.
Luna *picks them up and goes to the Treatment Door.*
She tries the handle but it is locked.
She puts the earbuds in her backpack.

[Later]

Luna *throws fruit snacks into the air and catches them in her mouth.*

Aaron *enters—sweating and breathing heavily.*
He leans against any support he can find.

Luna   Look—

Luna *throws one in the air and catches it in her mouth.*

Aaron   Um, did you see . . .
Out here—

Luna   What?

Aaron   My—
Nev'mind—

Luna   Wait watch. I've been practicing for the past hour:

Luna *does it again.*

Aaron   Sss—

As **Aaron** *moves to the door*
He throws up into his hands.
Luna *grabs the trash can, handing it to him.*
Aaron *vomits.*

Luna   Are you okay? Do you want juice?

Aaron *vomits.*
Luna *exits.*
Aaron *wipes his mouth with his beanie.*
Luna *reenters with a juice box.*

Luna   This is juice.

Aaron   Can you not be here right now?

Luna   . . .

Aaron   I mean—
Can you get a nurse?

[Transition]

Third Chemo

Aaron *and* **Luna** *are sitting.*
There is a generous space between them in chair-distance.
Aaron *has a sweatshirt on with the hood up.*
Underneath his hair is completely gone.
Luna *reads her book.*
She laughs.

Aaron   . . .

Luna   I just,
I think it's funny when they say something that isn't true anymore.
Outdated. This is the third edition.
They've since come out with the fourth and now a fifth.
But my mom hasn't gotten around to ordering it yet.

Aaron *nods.*

Luna   My mo—
I threw up in a grocery store once.

Aaron   . . .

Luna   I was six I think . . .
I . . . uh, ate a . . . bad hot dog. At the outlet mall.
Then later in the grocery store, in the cereal aisle,
My mom was asking me if I wanted the Crunch Berries or the Peanut-butter Crunch
Captain Crunch and . . . I just threw up.
No warning, right there.
And no one really did anything, they just stared.
So my mom ran to a checkout lane and took a bag boy's bag right from his hands.
And he just looked at her. Didn't really move.
Everyone else was staring or moving away quickly.
And when I was cleaned up,
we went down his checkout without buying either cereal.
Or anything else.
He didn't look up from the register.

Aaron   People are weird like that.

Luna   I just wish they hadn't looked at her like that—
Like me—
Looked at *me* like a . . .
Like a, like a piece of—

Aaron   I know.

Luna   So at, at least, you know . . .
At least you didn't do that.
Also—

Luna *hands* **Aaron** *his earphones.*

Aaron   Thanks.

Aaron *begins to put the earphones in—*

Luna   When we got home I could hear her crying even with the door closed in her
bedroom.

Aaron   Why?

Luna *doesn't make any indication that she heard this.*

Aaron   Wanna play a game?

Luna   I ate all my fruit snacks.

Aaron   A different game?

Aaron *grabs a deck of cards.*

Luna   No.

Aaron   We can bet—

Luna   . . .

Aaron   I have a dollar . . .

Luna   I only play Go Fish.

Aaron   Okay—

Luna   And I want to shuffle.

Aaron   Okay.

Aaron *hands her the deck.*
Luna *shuffles the deck many times in a row.*

Aaron   Good?

Luna   Good.

Luna *and* **Aaron** *play Go Fish.*

Luna   Tens?

Aaron   Fish. Jacks?

Luna   Fish. Four?

Aaron   Fish. Ace?

Luna   Fish. Seven?

Aaron   Fish. Six?

Luna *passes a card.*

Aaron   Do you have any twos?

Luna   Go. Fish.
Threes? Do my breasts look bigger—

Aaron   Fish.

Luna   . . .

Aaron   I don't really see you that often.

Luna   Well, they are.
32A's . . .

Aaron   Kings?

Luna *passes a card.*

Luna   Still your turn.

Aaron   Fives?

Luna   Fish . . .
Double A's . . .
The *plain* A's didn't quite feel right.
Eight?

Aaron *passes a card.*

Luna   Nines? You have breasts.

Aaron   Most people that come here
I think . . . did. Fish.

Luna   How long does it take for them to get full size?

Aaron   Well, you know it's like anything
Growing is gradual.

Luna   How big are—?

Aaron   Queens?

Luna   Or I mean how big *were*?

Aaron   Bigger. Do you have—

Luna   *How* big?

Aaron   Is it fish?

Luna   How big in planet size?

Aaron   Jupiter I guess.

Luna   Jupiter is the biggest planet you know.

Aaron   Then the next one.

Luna   Saturn minus its rings.

Aaron   Keep playing.

Luna   I wouldn't think that you would have—
Had Saturn sized breasts.
What does it feel like, like—

Aaron   The same. Queens.

Luna   . . .

Aaron   Hand it.

Luna *finally passes the card.*

Aaron   You can't lie in Go Fish.

Luna   . . .

Aaron   Jacks?

Luna   How come you're always here by yourself?

Aaron   I'm an adult.

Luna   Adult means alone?

Aaron   For me.

Luna   Why?

Aaron   Privacy.

Luna   Go fish.

Aaron   You're here by your—

Luna   Mom's inside.

Aaron   Why are you out here?

Luna   She doesn't want me to see. Twos?

Aaron *passes a card.*

Luna   Threes?

Aaron *passes a card.*

Luna   *Tens??*

Aaron *passes a card.*

Luna   No siblings?

Aaron   No.

Luna   No pets?

Aaron   No.

Luna   No fish??

Aaron   What?

Luna   Me too.

Aaron   Oh.

Luna   And your mom?

Aaron   . . .

Luna   Would you let her see?

Aaron   No.

Luna   But then who will take care of you when it gets worse?

Aaron   Why do you ask stuff about me?

Luna   Well . . . isn't that what you do with people
When they're there? Ask them things, tell them things,
And listen?

Aaron   And I thought you said it gets better?

Luna   I said you get better *at* it.

Aaron   It's still your turn.

Luna   Ace?

Aaron *passes a card.*
Luna *wins the game.*

Luna   HA, pay.

Aaron *gives a dollar to* **Luna**.

Luna   I'm gonna get some gummy worms.
Play again when I get back.
You can shuffle them *this* time.

Luna *exits.*
Aaron *shuffles the cards and then puts on an earphone.*
Luna *reenters with a pack of gummy worms between her teeth.*
In her hands are two handfuls of bras in various sizes.
She stuffs the bras into her backpack then goes to the game.

Luna   Lost and found is on the third floor. Worm?

Aaron   If I eat before I go in I get sick.

Luna   . . .

Aaron   Sorry.

Luna   Why?

Aaron   I don't know.

Luna   You're really strange.

Aaron   . . .

Luna   But I think
I'm strange too so

It's alright.
Ready?

Aaron   I'm a little tired.

Luna   It's just cards . . .
What's wrong?

Aaron   Nothing. I just . . . Don't feel like talking.

Luna   . . .

Aaron   Is that okay?

Luna *rapidly nods and eats her worms.*
Aaron *puts on both earphones.*

Luna   Wha—

Luna *goes to her book and reads.*
They sit in silence. Eventually,

Luna *exits. Then the machine calls*
"Aaron . . . Aaron . . . Aaron . . . "

[Transition]

Fourth Chemo

Aaron *is in the waiting room.*
His arms are severely bruised.
Luna *enters wearing headphones.*
She has a big cut on her leg.
She picks a chair away from **Aaron**.
The sound from her music is so loud it can
be heard by **Aaron**.

Aaron   Wha—

Luna   . . .

Aaron   HAPPENED TO YOUR LEGS?

Luna   . . .

Aaron *points to her legs.*

Luna   I FELL.

Aaron   How—

Luna   . . .

Aaron   OW.

Luna   AT SCHOOL.

Luna *unplugs her device.*

Luna   We have PE, gravity, and stairs.
What happened to your arms?

Aaron   Chemo—

Luna   Someone pushed me.

Aaron   . . .

Luna   . . .

Luna *grabs her textbook and leafs through the pages.*

Luna   It's funny how much bodies looks like the sky.
One time my mom and I were on the swings at night and
I told her that her face looked like the surface of the moon.
Because it has craters . . . She got quiet, and then we went home.
I never tried to compare her to a celestial object again after that.
But see, isn't it funny, how the bruise on your arm looks like that one?

Aaron   What does your mom look like? In there,
I sometimes look for her—

Luna   She's in a special care unit. All to herself.

Aaron   Oh.

Luna   I think she sleeps mostly anyway so.

Aaron   Wish I had a unit to myself.

Luna   No you don't.
A unit to yourself just means you're more sick.

Aaron   . . .

Luna   Are you a boy or a girl?

Aaron   . . .

Luna   Because you look like both.
And you sound like both.
And I've never really met anyone like you.

Aaron   For now I'm kind of both.

Luna   Will it change?

Aaron   Maybe.

Luna   How will you know?

Aaron   I think that a body can like . . . lie.
You know, just like a person can . . .
I'm— figuring it out.

Luna   Cool.

Aaron   Cool.

Luna   You know how stars work?

Aaron   You do.

Luna   Stars all start out the same.
All just gases and like stuff floating in space.
Hydrogen, mostly.
But as they age, they take on different forms.
Some will follow the normal sequence:
Become a red giant and planetary nebula then eventually white dwarf.
But some will supernova.
Some will grow so massive they have no choice but to explode
and create something far different, fantastic!
A neutron star or even black hole.
But what makes stars different?
What *caused* these differences?
Wasn't ever anything that space did.
Wasn't even what the star did, it didn't even change really.
The star was always what it would become.
Even in every step that it wasn't.

Aaron   . . .

Luna   Stars don't choose to become.
They just are. Always are.

Luna *re-plugs in her earphones.*
The sound is really loud again.
Aaron *smiles.*

Luna   . . .

Aaron   That was the first CD I ever bought
What you're listening to.

Luna   It's sunny.

Aaron   Yeah it is.

They listen. Something like "Just Like Heaven" by the Cure.
Aaron *starts to dance; he invites* **Luna** *to join.*
When she does, the music becomes magic transforming
the waiting room into a full-blown dance party!
Luna *runs to the bathroom.*
Aaron *keeps dancing until he loses his balance*

and reality sets back in.

[Later]

Luna   Periods suck.

Aaron   . . .

Luna   They SUCK.
Like first it's the bleeding thing.
Like I am gushing— GUSHING — blood. But . . .
Everyone acts like it's completely normal,
Nor even really cares . . .
As long as I have this disposable sponge catcher
catching all my blood droplings.
Then the cramps
AND the having to sit in this
WET disposable sponge catcher and feel it all
dribble and pool and squish up in between my legs
because sitting and because *gravity*—

Aaron   Tampons.

Luna   What?

Aaron   Tampons help that.
They make you . . . feel cleaner.

Luna   You use them?

Aaron   Used to.

Luna   I've never used one.

Aaron   Your mom can show you how to properly.

Luna   Probably . . .

Luna *takes out a box of tampons.*

Aaron   . . .

Luna   . . .

Aaron   I can't go in with you.

Luna   . . .

Aaron   . . .

Luna   Okay.

Luna *grabs the box and gets up.*
She has a period stain on her pants.

Aaron   When you . . .

Luna   . . .

Aaron *takes the box of tampons.*
He opens the box, takes one out, and opens it.
He forms a fist and points the tip
of the applicator at the center.

Aaron   Try to relax—
Breathe out and make sure
you get the plastic part up enough,
before you . . . you know? Otherwise
it will feel like it's chaffing your insides
and about to fall out.

Aaron *finishes the demonstration and hands the box back.* **Luna** *exits.*

Aaron *twirls the tampon by its string before tossing the parts into a trashcan.*
He looks at the door. As he goes to it, **Luna** *reenters.*
She waddle-squats and adjusts herself as she sits.

Aaron   Good?

Luna   . . . Good.

Aaron   Good.

Luna   Does it feel . . . the same? In you, as me?

Aaron   Yeah.

Luna   I didn't ask for this:
To grow up
And get breasts and—
All that.

Aaron   No one did.

Luna   I don't feel different.

Aaron   Because you aren't different.

Luna   Aren't I though?
Because of the bleeding.
It makes me different now.

Aaron   Doesn't have to.
Doesn't have to mean anything. For me,
It was like a monthly reminder of something
I was never ready for.
But eventually it just became
Just something that would happen
Over and over and over again.
Now that
Is this . . .

Luna   Being a girl sucks.
You're lucky . . .
Sorta.

Aaron   *You* get better at it, honest.

Luna   You always felt different?

Aaron   No, but I've always felt the *difference*.

Luna   What does the difference feel like?

Aaron   It . . . it felt—
Or it *feels* . . . sometimes to me like—
Like being . . . like having cancer.

Luna   How?

Aaron   It . . . I wouldn't have even known that I was different or whatever—
If somebody hadn't told me that what I feel isn't normal. Or,
If people just didn't like . . . notice. Or look at you weird.
It's just interesting what matters—
What people choose to give weight.

Luna   Gravity gives everything weight.
So everything matters . . .
Everything IS MATTER.

Aaron   And stars just are.

Luna   Yeah . . . but not.

Aaron   I thought you said?

Luna   Well, like they still change from one to next.

Aaron   How long does that take to change from one to next?

Luna   A *long* time. Like billions and billions and billions of years.

Aaron   I guess if it were to feel like anything
Then it would feel like that.
Like I'm a transitioning star period.
That billions and billions and billions of years.
My whole life.

Luna   Do you think I'll get cancer?

Aaron   No.

Luna   How do you know?

Aaron   I don't. I just really hope you don't.

Luna   What does it feel like?

Aaron   Like anything.
Growing is gradual.

Luna   Then why is it scary?

Aaron   Because we can't stop growing.

Luna   "Never any solutions, only what works in an instant."

Aaron   Who told you that?

Luna   Doctors . . . literally everybody.

Aaron   You don't usually like talking about it so much.

Luna   I don't . . . but I still *think* about it.
Can't help it exists.
I wish we didn't grow.
Isn't fair.

Aaron   I know.

Luna   It is better to talk about better things.

Aaron   Right.

Luna   For instance, space.

Aaron   Space is all good.

Luna   Space is all good.
What does your mom look like?

Aaron   It's been a while since I've seen her.

Luna   How long is a while?

Aaron   A while.

Luna   Well is she old or young?

Aaron   Either way she'd still look older than the last time I saw her likely.

Luna   . . .

Aaron   I don't know Luna. That's it. I don't think about it more than that.

Aaron *starts to put in earphones—*

Luna   WHAT'S WRONG?

Aaron   Nothing, Luna.

Luna   I wish you'd say more. I say lots of things. And I ask yo—

Aaron   You *force*—

Luna   . . .

Aaron   You know that feeling that happens when you realize how alone you are?
Not sudden not THERE AND GONE alone I mean r*ealize* . . .
Like when you—
You somehow—
You manage to go an entire day without speaking.
Until you go some place finally after
all this time of shifting silences—
Noises of living,
Soundtrack moments,
And then you hear your voice . . .
But suddenly it feels the thing furthest from your self?

Luna   Not really.

Aaron   That's okay . . . That's what's wrong.

Luna   . . .

Aaron   I'm—

Luna *puts on headphones.*
They sit in silence.
The machine calls "Aaron . . . Aaron . . . Aaron . . . "

[Transition]

Fifth Chemo

Luna *reads her book.*
Aaron *enters.*

Luna   Wrong.

Luna *tears out a section of the book.*

Aaron   Hi.

Luna   Hi.

Aaron   Why?

Luna   Not right anymore.

Aaron   Pluto?

Luna   No longer a planet.
But think of this:
A moon orbits Earth . . .
Moons orbit Pluto
And Earth orbits Sun
And so does Pluto
And so does Sun

It orbits somewhere.
In the middle of Milky Way . . .
Spinning— Spiraling through this galaxy . . .
That's in a Local Group every . . . Some . . . 200 million years-ish . . .
Everything is . . . Chasing something else.
Everything wants some other thing . . . And we never really touch . . .
We just . . . We're all alone in this.
All just circling forever . . . And even after all that.
A planet still orbits once it's *dead*.
I mean it . . . it . . . still keeps—
My teacher says I'm missing the point of the assignment.

Aaron   What is the assignment?

Luna   A Venn Diagram on whether Pluto is a planet or a rock.

Aaron   Both sides are true?

Luna   Who cares? There are bigger things to care about.

Aaron   Like cancer,
Or black holes.

Luna   Exactly like black holes.
But all people seem to want to talk about
is the littlest orbiting rock
on the outskirts of the Solar System
that isn't the same as its brothers.

Aaron   Are planets . . . masculine?

Luna   For now, yes.

Aaron   Cool.

Luna   . . .

Aaron   What—

Luna   . . .

Aaron   What?

Luna *shakes her head.*
Aaron *reaches in his pocket for his earphones—*

Luna   How do you tell if a boy likes you?

Aaron   He'll tell you . . .
In some way.

Luna   That's it?

Aaron   From my experience.

Luna   Yeah but you're different. No offense—
I mean you're not in like seventh grade so . . .

Aaron   Why?

Luna   Don't have a dad.

Aaron   I'm sorry.

Luna   Don't be. Mom doesn't miss him so I don't either.
Mom says she doesn't even remember him.

Aaron   . . .

Luna   This *girl*. The ***one***
that pushed me. Said:
"The reason no boys like you is because you have daddy issues."
But I said:
"No. You're. Wrong.
I *can't* have daddy issues
because I don't *have* a dad.
So, that's like saying that
Venus has lunar problems!"

Aaron   . . .

Luna   . . .

Aaron   Right.

Luna   . . .

Aaron   My dad got another family when I was like eleven.
But from what I remember we used to drive places,
And whenever he didn't wanna talk anymore,
Just done listening now,
He would turn the music up really loud,
So loud I couldn't think . . .
Till I just stopped saying things.

Luna   . . .

Aaron   But his music was always good.

Luna   . . .

Aaron   Venus doesn't have a moon.

Luna   No and Mercury doesn't either.
Planets don't need moons.
And a planet can't miss something
It never had you know?

Aaron   Your name is moon.

Luna   That's probably just cause my mom had me when she was still in like college
and the idea of the moon was still "novel" to her . . .
I bet if she had me now
She would have named me something a lot better.

Aaron   Like quasar?

Luna   Or something cooler.

Aaron   Well, the moon means things to a lot of people so,
That's cool at least . . .
I think Luna is pretty.

Luna   Thanks.

Aaron   . . .

Luna   Why's your name Aaron?

Aaron   I changed it actually—

Luna   What was it before?

Aaron   Still Aaron. But spelled with an E.

Luna   It sounds the same either way.

Aaron   I know.

Luna   You could have picked something cooler.

Aaron   Yeah I could have.

Luna   Not that your name's *not* cool but . . .
I don't know—
Names are weird anyway.

Aaron   I just wanted to sound the same . . .
But to know, I'm different.
What should my name be?

Luna   Blazar, maybe.

Aaron   Which is?

Luna   A different kind of quasar.

Aaron   Cool.

Luna   But people'd probably think you're weird if your name was Blazar.

Aaron   People already think I'm weird.

Luna   Me too.

Aaron   Don't let it bother you . . .
If it does.
Just take your time . . .

Figure *you* out
And be that.

Luna   Are you *you*?

Aaron   I was . . . I mean
I *am* but— maybe,
You never *fully*
Are . . .

Luna   Next Wednesday I'll have won a medal.

Aaron   Awesome, for what?

Luna   Participation.

Aaron   Cool.

Luna   For competing in the junior high science debates.
I'm in a special division—
Specifically for theories and ideas not tangible.
That part's supposed to be eighth graders only.
But, they made an exception
For me. Anyway, it's happening
At the end of Parents Back-to-School Night.
We each get to present what we accomplished.

Aaron   Wow, your mom must be really proud of you.

Luna   Yeah but she won't be there.
She has a surgery scheduled that morning and . . .
Can't change it, can't miss it . . .
And I don't have a dad . . .
So, I'm trying to get someone to record it on a phone for her.
So she can watch it after. So she can still see it. But . . .

Aaron   When is it?

Luna   Next Wednesday.
Six.
P.M.

Aaron   I don't think I'll be here or—

Luna   I mean *if* you want to go . . . You can. I guess.
Even though you're not a parent . . .
They don't really check.

Aaron   If you want me to—

Luna   Does your phone record video?

Aaron   Yes.

Luna   Will it be charged?

Aaron   Yes.

Luna   It will probably be mostly lame and you might—

Aaron   I want to see your presentation Luna.

Luna   Alright. Make sure your phone is charged.

Aaron   What's your presentation on?

Luna   Year Expansion and Contraction by Planetary Time Travel.

Aaron   Sounds complicated.

Luna   I'll make you an outline.

Aaron   Thanks.

Luna   Yup . . .
So . . .
How do you know
If *you* like someone?

Aaron   You'll know.
You'll start to think of them
The way *you* think
About outer space.

Luna   . . .

Aaron   Or I don't know.

Luna *attempts to kiss* **Aaron** *on the cheek.*
Aaron *pulls away.*

Luna   . . .

Aaron   . . .

Luna *runs away.*
The machine calls "Aaron . . . Aaron . . . Aaron . . ."

[Transition]

Sixth Chemo

Aaron *sits wearing both earphones.*
Luna *enters holding index cards.*

Luna   DID YOU SEE IT?

Aaron   I—

Luna   No—
No you didn't.

And so neither could my mom.
Because you didn't show up.

Aaron   . . .

Luna   AND you didn't record it.

Aaron   Okay—

Luna   Okay?

Aaron   What do you want me to say—

Luna   Keep your promises.

Aaron   I'm sorry.

Luna   . . .

Aaron   I'm sorry, Luna.

Luna   . . .

Aaron   I . . . I'm just sick okay?
Can't you under—

Luna   My mom has been sick really *really* sick. All. My. Life.
What more do I need to understand I know how being sick works—!

Aaron   Okay well you don't know me.
You don't know how I work.
You see me maybe once a week.

Luna   Scientists are talking about this star cluster called IRAS 16547-4247.
It's like, over nine thousand lightyears away but it's super interesting cause it has
formed this hourglass shape which means—

Luna *pulls out one of his earphones.*

Luna   WHAT IS SO WRONG WITH YOU?

Aaron   Last week they started putting me in a unit by myself Luna.

Luna   A star was born today.

Aaron   Cool.

Luna   A star was born today!

Aaron   *Fantastic.*

Luna   I don't understand why you are so angry.
My mom always loves it when I distract her from being sick with science—

Aaron   I'm not your mom.

Luna   . . .

Aaron   I'm not anything okay?
I'm dying. And . . .
I'm sorry but I really don't care
About something that I won't even live to see;
That anyone who is here living right now
Will ever live to see.
What matters to me is only in there:
Where the discoveries *should* happen.
Where discoveries really matter.
A new tumor was born today, probably. You know that?
And they can see it, they can touch it, and they can stare at it until their eyes hurt.
But they can't do anything about it.
Still. Still,
At some point they wash their hands of it and say,
"Sorry, moving on now, and you should too."
How is that *science*? How's that *humanity*?
Not big enough—
My wants, my problems, *my life's* not big enough
Until I'm dying . . .
Then it's too big
to care . . .
No one cares about what's right here.
People are always looking somewhere else
To hide or explain things or just . . . whatever.
Seems they're all too busy giving a— Crap
About things they will all be dead for before they . . . ever matter.
Meanwhile, I'm still alive— Barely and . . .
No one *really* cares either way.
No one. A star was born today.
But what about the rest of us.
What about your mom?

Luna *takes out her Astronomy book.*

Luna   Forty thousand.
You know Earth is an interesting one.
Not the most interesting of all,
And definitely not the biggest—
Forty thousand kilometers. But still,
It's the only one. The only planet we know
Where things like this can exist and happen where we can even breathe.
And we developed somehow out of nothing here,
Evolved and . . . here. We exist. But it doesn't—
It doesn't make sense sometimes. Bad things happen: volcanoes, hurricanes, earthquakes.
Don't know why, but we die. And
Earth lies sometimes . . . Earth made it so we could live

And then Earth kills us all like cells. Like being sick.
Everything is dying! And you all forget that. You forget it's everything and not just you.
Everything is slipping away.
But no one cries when a planet dies. Do they? No one.
Nobody even knows.
Forty thousand. That's it.
This world is so small, *so* small and it's all anyone ever thinks about.
It's all you think about.
A star was born today and you don't even care.

Luna *packs up her things.*

Luna   There is something that you have,
That no planet,
And no star, and no
Anything else bigger than us has:
Choices.
You can't just disappear and you can't give up.
You might not be a *girl* fully
But . . . You're a *bitch.*

Aaron   . . .

Luna *exits.*
Aaron *picks up index cards that* **Luna** *has left behind.*

Aaron   I wasn't always sick when I was a kid.
I would pretend I was sick sometimes . . .
So you let me stay home from school.
But you had to have known because
There were days when
You wouldn't give me cough medicine
Or anything you just
Sat with me . . .
Tell me . . .
Though my body's sick,
My mind's not sick.
It's powerful.
My mind can go anywhere.
My mind can be anything . . .
Did you mean it?
Could I really be anything?
It's Erin still.
But I'm 28 and I'm your son now.
So you know . . .
Mom I'm sick . . .
And I'm scared that I won't get better this time.

Aaron *puts on headphones.*

Something like "Boys Don't Cry" by the Cure.
The machine calls "Aaron . . . Aaron . . . Aaron . . . "

[Transition]

Seventh Chemo

Aaron *holds a guitar, a book, and* **Luna**'s *notecards.*
Luna *enters and then sits in the furthest possible seat from* **Aaron**.
She reads her book in a way that obstructs herself from seeing him, and him from seeing her.

Aaron   "In a sense, we could cheat the system. And if we gain the technology, then we can:
escape to Jupiter! And then I can live . . . Live 11 times as long as they say I ever could . . .
But I know . . . that it doesn't work. That time doesn't slow down for you or for me and not on Jupiter. No where. You are just moving slower . . . It's always only you.
Only you change."

Luna   . . .

Aaron   When I was twelve I didn't know anything about the stuff you do.

Luna   I'm almost 13.

Aaron   I didn't get science.
I liked fantasy,
I liked music,
I liked things that . . .
That didn't make sense.
I liked Peter Pan.

Luna   Used to watch it.

Aaron   Still do . . . actually.
But this is the book and like most things it's a lot better than the movie.

Aaron *gives* **Luna** *the book.*

Luna   I don't read kids' books.

Aaron   Well my mom gave me this book so . . . It's special, like yours.
I like the part when Peter loses his shadow and he's trying to catch it again.
I think just because I kind of identify with it . . .
I used to think I could remove my body like Peter could his shadow.
Then maybe if I wanted . . .

Luna   . . .

Aaron   I could pick a different one . . .
I wanted a different one . . .

Because I'm not
What my body . . .
Or I just wish, I didn't need a body at all.
Cause soon I might not have one. I don't like to think about when—
Even though there are days and places and songs and
Peter that stick and . . . I don't know if I "believe" in magic,
But I'll always believe in Peter.
He's made sense where I couldn't.
It took me over twenty years to realize that my body like,
Lied. Now I have and,
My life is mostly this place . . .
Some days all I want is to just float away.
Like Neverland.
Still leave a crack in the window and look for
The Second Star to the Right.
Maybe he'll come,
Take me away from all this.

Luna   That star's not Neverland.
It's probably Mizar.
If you were looking from the Northern Hemisphere.
The second star to the right was probably Mizar.
In the Big Dipper.

Aaron   Well . . .
That explains why he never came.

Aaron *plays his guitar.*
Luna *'s face lights up.*

Luna   Can I??

Aaron   Go for it.

Luna   Now what?

Aaron   Well you wanna put your fingers on the frets.

Aaron *moves her fingers.*
Luna *strums.*

Aaron   That's "A"-ish.
And this . . .
Use the other finger.
Is "G"—

Luna *strums.*

Aaron   The science of sound comes down to vibration of air particles
which travel to your ears from the object that is making the sound.
So the string vibrates this soundboard and that sends sound

in the form of waves out in the air.

Luna *hands back the guitar.*

Aaron   Anyway,
This song makes me think of you.

Aaron *plays something like,*
"I'll Be Seeing You" by Billie Holiday.
The music becomes magic.
Their world transcends
The walls of this hospital waiting room,
The walls of this city,
And the limits of this atmosphere.
They go beyond and out and everywhere . . .
And then the song ends.

Luna   How come you never said you could do that?

Aaron   What'd I do?

Luna   Make sound make sense.

Aaron   For a while I forgot.
You put your instrument in the closet . . .
Other things become important . . .
You get used to being what people see you as,
You get used to being what you see you as,
You get used to being one side of yourself,
You forget how to be the other when you . . .
You lose what feels like gravity.
When my mom died.

Luna   . . .

Aaron   I don't know what she'd think of me now.
So it's easier to just . . .
To just—

The Automated Machine calls "Aaron . . . Aaron . . . Aaron . . .
"Aaron . . . Aaron . . . Aaron . . . "

Aaron   But I'm Aaron. I like music.
I'm 28.
I use he/they pronouns.
And I have breast cancer.

Luna   Still Luna. Still like space.
I'm twelve but I turn 13 in . . .
16 and three-quarters of a day . . .
I think I'm she . . .
And I don't.

Aaron   Thank you.

Luna   What'd I do?

Aaron   Hold this while I'm in there?

Luna *takes the guitar and strums.*

Aaron   It's nice to meet you by the way.

Luna   You too. But you should have called yourself Peter.

Aaron   Practice.

Aaron *exits through the Treatment Door.*
Luna *puts her astronomy book in the trash can and picks up Peter Pan.*

[Later]

Aaron *reenters the waiting room.*
Peter Pan is spine-cracked face down on a seat.
Luna *still holds the guitar and strums the two chords she knows.*

Aaron   You're doing it.

Luna   I suck.

Aaron   Focus everything you got into your fingers.
It hurts at first but . . .
You get better at it . . .
Honest.

Luna   I need a break.

Aaron *takes the guitar.*
Luna *grabs Peter Pan.*

Aaron   What part?

Luna   Third read.

Aaron   Wow you like it?

Luna   Gotta read something . . . I threw away my book.

Aaron   Why?

Luna   My mom's gonna get me the new one.

Aaron   Oh, good.

Luna   Did you know that if you threw a boom-a-rang in outer space
And stayed put for the rest of time,
It would come back after reaching across all parts,
After exhausting every inch of the universe,
It would come back
And hit you in the back of the head?

Aaron   I didn't.

Luna   No air-resistance.
Nothing to pull it back.
Wouldn't be able to catch it
unless you turned around.
But you'd be dead before it got to you.
Everything would be.
It's actually an impossible theory.

Aaron   Well you know what they say . . .
What goes . . .

Luna   . . .

Aaron   Around . . . comes . . .
Comet's next week, right?

Luna   November 17th.

Aaron   Gonna watch it?

Luna   Yup.

Aaron   Cool . . . Still your birthday?

Luna   Still is . . .

Aaron   13?

Luna   Yup.

Aaron   That's exciting.

Luna   . . .

Aaron   While I was in there
I actually read an article . . .
And of course I thought of you.
It said something like:
For some time now
Astronauts have been studying tumors in space because—

Luna   Why do you believe in magic?

Aaron   I don't know if I really do,
But I'd like to.

Luna   According to my mom:
Nothing here on earth is magic.
Science can explain it. Now,
once you get really big or really small then
people start to appeal to magic.

Aaron   I take a bus here and
It's like . . . a process.

But I plug in my music so I don't have to hear
Babies screaming or scratching skin or whatever
But it doesn't always drown out your brain enough and so, I just think.
It's a strange thing coming here so much. Because, in some ways,
This is what I always wanted but—
I'm not sure how—
If I wanna let her go, completely. It almost feels like . . .
Cancer is some Catholic guilt version of giving me what I want . . .
Like it's killing me but it also's like killing *her.*
Specifically killing *her* body and . . .
The process of losing her turned out to be a lot harder than I thought.
She feels. And she wants things. And . . . She's still mine.
I don't know.
But maybe for her sake I kinda need to believe . . .
Something. Magic or—
Some place other.
Where she's okay.
So that's what the buds or headphones do.
Even if I'm not listening to anything.
They keep people from asking.
Most people.
Not you.

Luna   Wanna know my *very* first theory?

Aaron   Yeah.

Luna   Humans are nothing different from the Universe.

Aaron   Meaning?

Luna   You never change, you only expand.
All of you is still you.

Aaron   I like that one.

Luna   How did your mom die?

Aaron   She got sick.

Luna   Same as you?

Aaron   Unfortunately yeah.

Luna   How old were you?

Aaron   Three days from 20.

Luna   Were you Aaron with an A?

Aaron   No, still Erin with an E
or at least
still pretending to be . . .

Luna   What was it like?

Aaron   Like . . .
Being at the top of a roller coaster.

Luna   Like falling?

Aaron   Like stuck and waiting to fall:
Inevitable.

Luna   But specifically.
Not analogy.

Aaron   Specifically . . .
She stopped eating.
Was sleeping
A lot . . . most of the time.
Hospice said,
the last thing to go would be her hearing
so I read her favorite books, played music . . .
I couldn't tell you if she heard it most the time
So I held her hand
Toward the very end she kinda just slipped away
First her mind . . . and then
From there it was just . . . waiting
and then eventually everything stopped.

Luna   Did you like
Say anything?

Aaron   I . . .
Told her I love her.
Why?

Luna   . . .

Aaron   . . .

Luna   How many more do you have?

Aaron   This was my last one . . . For now.
I have more tests still
More waiting . . . But
They're optimistic so
I have to be too.

Luna   I guess I won't be seeing you anymore then.

Aaron   How about you?
I mean your mom.
I mean for your mom?
How many more?

Luna   Till it changes.

Aaron   I hope it changes soon.

Luna   . . .

Aaron   How old were you again?
When she got sick?

Luna   Four.

Aaron   Since you were four . . . That's . . .
But I—
I thought—
Didn't you say you've been coming here
for six years?
That would mean—

Luna   I don't . . .
really remember
anymore.

Aaron   . . .

Luna   Spend enough time here, just
starts to feel like
I've always been here . . .
Just starts to feel
more like home than
Anywhere.

Aaron   . . .

Luna   . . .

Aaron   Luna,
Is your mom—

Luna *puts on headphones and packs up her things.*

Aaron   . . .

Luna *hands back the book.*

Aaron   Keep it
Till you get a new book

Luna   I read it already.

Luna *exits.*

Aaron *puts on earphones.*
Something like "Two Coffins" by Against Me!

[Transition]

November 17th, Evening

Luna *is in the waiting room.*
Aaron *enters.*

Aaron   Happy Comet Day!

Luna   . . .

Aaron   And happy birthday.

Luna   Thanks.

Aaron   I came here because I thought the roof here might be a nice comet-viewing
spot . . .

Luna   . . .

Aaron   So . . . originally this was the present. But then,
I was able to figure out how to get the other one.
So, this is like the pre-present present.

Luna   . . .

Aaron *gives her one pound of wrapped gummies.*

Luna   Yes!

Aaron   That should hold you over what about a month?

Luna   A week-ish. Thank you.

Aaron   I was worried it wouldn't get here in time—
Or that I wouldn't see you in here before . . .
For your birthday and the comet. But it did.
And then I was worried that . . . I don't know.
I know I remember you saying that you—
And, so I—
This is the real present.
Here.

Aaron *hands* **Luna** *a poorly wrapped present.*
She opens it.

Luna   The *fifth* edition.

Aaron   The *fifth* edition.
I thought it might be useful for—
There's information about tonight's comet,
I looked it up in the index.
And I stuck a Post-It . . .
There.
There's no lights on the roof.

You'd probably be able to see really—

Luna   With my *mom*.

Aaron   Right.

Luna   Don't have to wait for me.
She's really gonna be out any minute.

Aaron   The sun is setting soon.

Luna   The sun doesn't set earth does.

Aaron   Luna are you sure you don't want—

Luna   I'm not watching the comet with *you*.

Aaron   I'll be on the roof.

Luna   . . .

Aaron *goes to exit—*

Aaron   Luna I know—

Luna *goes to the treatment door and knocks.*

Luna   Mom? Mom. Let's go. Mom? Mom. MOM!

Luna *'s knocking becomes pounding becomes kicking—*

Aaron   Luna stop!

Luna *yanks at the locked door handle.*

Aaron   Listen Luna please—

Luna   Shut up!

Aaron *reaches out to* **Luna**—

Luna   Don't touch me! I don't want you I want my mom! I want my mom I want
my mo—

Aaron   She's dead.

Luna   . . .

Aaron   She's dead isn't she?

Luna   . . .

Aaron   She isn't in there anymore.

Luna   . . .

Aaron   And you don't have to be here anymore but you are. Still.

Luna   . . .

Aaron   . . .

Luna   A body can lie.

Aaron   . . .

Luna   You told me that
a body can lie
right?

Aaron   When did it happen?

Luna   The last time there was a comet.
I was eight.

Aaron   . . .

Luna   She said we'd stay up all night for it,
all night until we saw it pass through the sky.
It was special she said
Because, maybe it would never happen again for us.
And we just waited, watching for something,
waiting for it to . . . to finally come.
She said to look closely and carefully,
cause it would happen so fast.
But I was so sleepy, it had to have been so late
So she told me that it was okay to close my eyes.
She said she'd wake me up
when it was time, when she saw the comet coming.
And so I closed my eyes, and I fell asleep.
The doctor woke me up around four.
She fell asleep too, it turned out.
The doctor carried me to a different bed
And I asked him, is the comet still coming?
"We just missed it." He said.

Aaron   . . .

Luna   BUT HE'S WRONG and I know it.
If: A *body* can lie. A *person* can lie. A *planet*. A *cell*. *ANYTHING* can lie . . .
Then she is still in there. She's still *there*.
Just her body. Just her body's . . .
Somewhere.

Luna *finally lets herself break.*
Aaron *catches her pieces in his hands.*

Aaron   Jupiter . . . Saturn . . . Not Neverland . . . The comet?

Luna   I stay with my aunt now. She's cool.
But this past summer

She got a second job
And works late a lot so . . .
I tell her I'm at Science Club . . .
Or with . . .
"friends."
But I come here
And then I take the bus back . . .
Maybe with the comet—
Sometimes I think maybe
she'll come back . . .
If I'm ready for the comet
If don't miss it
Then maybe . . .
I won't miss her.
If everything lies what is real?

Aaron   A lie, maybe.

Luna   I lie.

Aaron   So do I.

Luna   I just didn't want to be alone tonight.

They hug.

Aaron   Let's watch the comet.

Luna *nods.*

[Later]

The rooftop of the parking garage of the hospital.
They are splitting earphones listening while they wait.
Something like "Starman" by David Bowie.

Luna   How'd you find up here?

Aaron   Just looked.
No one's gonna say no.
I have cancer.
Just don't fall okay?

Luna   I wish we weren't so behind.

Aaron   Meaning?

Luna   The sky.

Aaron   Is?

Luna   Gone: all that up there is long over and changed and different.

Aaron   But we still see it.

Luna   How sick are you?

Aaron   I think the sky is the only thing that matters right now.
What will it look like?

Luna   It will look like a plane but you have to know it's not.
It might have a tail.
But it might not come.
It could just be a dust cluster.
I could be wrong about it. Or,
we may have already missed it . . .

They wait.
Something in the sky shifts.
Aaron *gets up.* **Luna** *does too.*

Aaron   Is that it?

Luna   Yes.

Aaron   Do we wish on it?

Luna   I guess if you want to.

Aaron   Okay.

Aaron *closes his eyes.*
Luna *looks at him.*
Once she is sure that he won't see
She closes her eyes too and makes a wish.
Aaron *opens his eyes.*
He looks at her and smiles.
He looks at the sky
At **it**.
Maybe a plane,
Maybe an outer space rock,
At magic or hope.
He closes his eyes again.
Luna *opens her eyes.*
She nudges him
And waits for him to join her.

Luna   Did you wish?

Aaron   Yep. Did you?

Luna   No.

Aaron   That's alright.

Luna   . . .

Aaron   . . .

Luna   Are you going to get better?

Aaron   I don't know.

Luna   Are you going to die?

Aaron   I don't want to.

Luna   I don't either.

Aaron   . . .

Luna   Or by the time I do, I hope I'm not afraid of it.

Aaron   Do stars think about what's going to happen to them?

Luna   Stars don't think.

Aaron   Then maybe we shouldn't either.

End of play.

Part 3: Waves and Water

(Extra)ordinary Heroics in Samuel Achilles's Staging of Trans Antiquity

Caitlin A. Kane

Driven by a belief that trans people—including, and perhaps *especially*, trans young people—deserve to imagine and experience themselves in spaces that are not defined by transphobia and other forms of oppressive violence, Samuel Achilles burgeoning body of dramatic work employs speculative world-building to envision the world otherwise (Achilles 2024). Using a distinctive blend of historical fiction and fantasy, Achilles depicts mythic times and places where rigid gender norms and transphobic rhetoric fade into the background, so the ordinary lived experiences and everyday desires of trans and gender-nonconforming people can take center stage. This dramaturgical strategy builds on Angela Long Chu's (2017) and B. Lee-Harrison Aultman's (2019) calls for closer and more nuanced engagement with the "trans ordinary" —the day-to-day embodied experiences of trans people that are too often overshadowed by sensationalized narratives of medical transitions—by creating theatrical worlds where trans characters and performers are the norm. Achilles's staged reimaginings of trans histories introduce audiences to factual and fictional narratives from the distant past that remind us that—despite contemporary pundits' efforts to suggest otherwise—gender plurality and fluidity have always, and will always, exist. In the play anthologized here, a dramatization of the life of Caeneus, an often-overlooked proto-trans figure from Greco-Roman mythology, Achilles transforms a Greek hero into a relatable young trans person whose presumed exceptional experiences of gender dysphoria and gender transformation are made wonderfully mundane when he finds himself surrounded by people whose experiences echo his own.

In Book Twelve of Ovid's *Metamorphoses* (8 CE), Caeneus is portrayed as an extraordinary figure. He is introduced during a truce in the Trojan War when Achilles and his men are celebrating their victory over Cycnus, a warrior whose body cannot be penetrated by weapons. King Nestor of Pylos, one of the eldest and wisest among those gathered, responds to the men's enthusiasm about Cycnus' impenetrability by regaling them with the story of an even more remarkable figure from his youth. Caeneus, like Cycnus, could not be wounded, but Nestor suggests that his imperviousness was made more notable by his having been "born female" (Ovid and McCarter 2022: line 190). Intrigued by this hero's might and origin story, Achilles presses for more information. Caeneus, Nestor explains, was once one of the most beautiful young women of Thessaly, but she refused all of her suitors until, one day, she was assaulted by the sea god, known to the Romans as Neptune and to the Greeks as Poseidon, who, after "[stealing] the joys of novel sex" from her, offered to grant her one wish (Ovid and McCarter 2022: line 214). She responded that following such an unforgivable violation the only thing that she desired was for Poseidon to "Make it impossible / for me to suffer such a thing again. / Make me not female" (Ovid and McCarter 2022: lines 217-220). Poseidon, Nestor explains, went above and beyond in granting Caeneus' wish, by not only protecting him from sexual harm through the transformation of his gender (an imperfect solution given that people of all genders can—*and do*—experience sexual violence) but by also shielding him from all other wounds.

In Achilles's eponymous restaging of this story, Caeneus is rendered as refreshingly ordinary. Instead of opening the play with the backstory given in *Metamorphoses*, Achilles begins with Caeneus directly addressing audience members, inviting us into the character's bewildering experience of transformation. Imagine, Caeneus tells us, that you encounter a god who asks you to name one thing that you want, and you— skeptical of their capacity or willingness to grant your wish—"speak into being the wildest fantasy you have," only to have them respond simply and affirmatively: "okay" (341). In this moment, and this telling, Caeneus is neither a renowned Ancient Greek hero nor a violated and vulnerable young woman seeking protection from misogynist violence. Instead, he is a young person seeking a more livable life who shares a moment of *communitas*—an instant when audience members experience "a cohesive if fleeting feeling of belonging to the group"—with any member of the audience who, however briefly, is willing to join him in daring to name a seemingly unattainable future (Dolan 2005: 11). Then, just as quickly as this moment of potentially liberatory connection arises, it collapses to the shore of Thessaly where Caeneus finds himself *physically* unchanged.

Gender Transformation Before and Beyond the Wrong-Body Narrative

It would be easy to imagine that, given *Metamorphoses*' inclusion of other fantastic transformations, including humans and gods becoming birds, bulls, and trees, Poseidon would physically change Caeneus' gender by way of shape shifting. However, Ovid does not detail how—or even, *if*—Caeneus' body was transformed. Instead, he describes the deepening of Caeneus' voice to indicate that the transformation has occurred: "the final words [of his wish] were deeper, like a man's. / And so it was [. . .] / He spen[t] his life in masculine pursuits" (Ovid and McCarter 2022: lines 221-2, 226). While this passage can be read as implying that a physical transformation has occurred, Achilles has chosen to embrace the ambiguity in the source text and to portray Caeneus' transformation as one that specifically affects others' perceptions. In so doing, Achilles models for young audiences an understanding of transness and trans acceptance that 1) is fully embodied but not necessarily predicated on a change in physical appearance and 2) is neither the result nor the cause of trauma.

Without any physical modification to his body, Achilles's Caeneus begins to be perceived as himself and is granted access to the life he wants to live. The character's reaction to this is compellingly captured in Kyle S. Roark's zine of this opening scene, which was offered as a companion to the original playbill. Portrayed as an ambiguously gendered figure with shoulder-length hair and a square jawline, Caeneus shifts rapidly through a sequence of disparate emotional responses to his unusual encounter with the divine. Kneeling on the shore with his head bowed, he reckons with the dissonance between Poseidon's promise to grant his wish and the fleshy materiality of his unchanged body. However, before he can fully give language to what has occurred, Caeneus is interrupted by a voice calling out to him: "Young man" (Roark 2018: 10). He looks out, as if searching for the young man being hailed, and then, looks down at himself, seemingly bewildered by the incongruity between his perception of his body and this stranger's. In the frames that follow, Caeneus moves from confusion to wonder

7.1 Zine Excerpt. "Caeneus." Illustrated by Kyle S. Roark. 2018.

to elation. This stranger sees Caeneus as himself: as a man. To paraphrase the play and zine, his body has not changed, but *everything else has* (341; Roark 2018: 12).

Achilles's and Roarks' portrayals of Caeneus are brimming with life-giving possibility, particularly in this moment of heightened anti-trans rhetoric, legislation, and violence, much of which has been directed at trans youth and is perversely intended to "protect" trans youth from themselves, their caregivers, and their medical care providers. Caeneus, like many trans youth (albeit for different reasons), does not have access to gender-affirming care, but his lack of access does not in this narrative—nor should it in our world—preclude him from being trans or being embraced as such. What Achilles makes clear is that Caeneus' transformation is an act of empowered self-articulation. This does not mean, however, that Caeneus unquestioningly accepts the mode of transformation chosen for him by Poseidon. Instead, he adopts what Mikey Elster describes as "a strategic, situated ambivalence" against conservatives' "insidious concern" for/about trans youth (Elster 2022: 410). For Elster, this situated ambivalence allows trans youth and their loved ones to repurpose normative language and circumvent anti-trans policies in order to carve out spaces for trans youth to live on their own terms. For Caeneus, ambivalence similarly facilitates cautious exploration of newly accessible worlds and tentative adoption of queer and trans relationalities with those around him. These changes in his life do not come easily or without risk. For instance, throughout the play, he agonizes over the possibility that Poseidon will reverse his transformation or that people from his former life, including his family, will not accept him in his new form. But as he navigates this trans reality, Caeneus finds that he does not have to confront these challenges alone.

Transformation in a Landscape of Gender Plurality

The play features five explicitly trans characters: Caeneus, Tiresias a nonbinary oracle, a Dionysian Waitress (double cast with Tiresias), and two nonbinary Priest/esses. While the remaining characters presumably understand themselves as cisgender, Achilles calls for the entire cast to be trans. In so doing, he resists the spectacularization of both the trans characters and performers and opens up the possibility for—and the likelihood of—each of the characters being read within a more expansive and productively complex landscape of gender plurality. This casting recommendation, Achilles explains, was inspired by reflections from members of the predominantly-trans cast and creative team at Hampshire College (where the work was first produced) who found that working in a creative space with an overwhelming majority of trans people "allowed different kinds of conversations to happen about transness and the story and characters" (Achilles 2024). In this way, Achilles aligns himself and his work with the kinds of institutional change that Sylvan Oswald names as necessary to create spaces of trans belonging in the theatre (Oswald 2024: 480-1). At the same time, Achilles's call for an all-trans cast allows the play to subvert the idea of an ostensibly "universal" trans narrative on multiple levels.

On the one hand, this casting creates a productive, almost Brechtian, distance between the cis or cis-adjacent characters and the people who portray them, allowing artists and audience members to critically reevaluate the gender norms that constrain cis and trans experience alike. For instance, shortly after his transformation, Caeneus meets his lifelong hero, Jason, the leader of the Argonauts, and is offered the opportunity to join the crew of the Argo. During his first conversation with Jason aboard the ship, Caeneus finds himself dismayed by Jason's arrogance, dismissiveness, and bravado. After spending years imagining sailing with Jason's crew and attempting to model himself after Jason's highly publicized heroics, Caeneus is confronted by the reality that Jason is unapologetically self-centered and markedly disinterested in both the members of his crew and his fiancée, Medea. Caeneus' disillusionment becomes an important point of connection with his love interest, Nestor, who shares in Caeneus' desire to partake in heroic adventures without accepting the gender expectations that seem to be a prerequisite for participation. Achilles refuses, however, the establishment of a simple binary between the (presumably) cisgender heterosexual characters and the characters coded as trans and/or queer by insisting on an all-trans cast. Having a trans actor portray Jason in a campy drag king style underscores the play's efforts to critique hetero-patriarchal masculinity rather than critiquing the character himself, the person portraying him, or a monolithic understanding of cis men. At the same time, Achilles gestures toward the ways in which toxic masculinity can be taken up by trans people and cautions against an uncritical acceptance of gender normativity regardless of one's gender identity.

On the other hand, the range of trans experiences and embodiments represented on stage ensures that Caeneus is not misunderstood as emblematic of all trans people. For instance, later in the play, Caeneus convinces Jason to travel to Thebes to meet with the nonbinary and gender-fluid oracle, Tiresias, a figure who Filippo Carlá-Uhink describes as "the most famous mythical transitioner [in Trans Antiquity]" (Carlá-Uhink 2017: 19). When it is his turn to speak with the oracle, Caeneus is shocked to find that Tiresias wants to talk with him about anything *other* than his gender transformation. In response to Caeneus' admission that his desire to discuss gender stems from his previously held belief that he was the only person to have undergone such a transformation, Tiresias and their posse of nonbinary Priest/esses laugh. For those gathered in the temple, gender transformation is the norm, not the exception, but they do little to welcome Caeneus into their reality. This admittedly disheartening introduction to a broader community of individuals who have experienced gender transformation, ultimately, expands Caeneus' awareness of the many possible manifestations of gender plurality and makes space for him to articulate the specificity of his identity. Unlike the Priest/esses and Tiresias, Caeneus has no desire to transform again, but by the end of the play, Caeneus recognizes how their inclination toward fluidity and his preference for constancy can coexist in relative harmony.

Speculative Trans Histories

In the introduction to their anthology, *Trans Historical: Gender Plurality before Modernity,* Greta LaFleur, Masha Raskolnikov, and Anna Klosowska persuasively advocate for continued study and engagement with histories of trans and gender non-conforming experience, stating that "One of the many goals of building collective memory about the distant past is to infuse present-day individual and collective consciousness with historical power and to support the development of thicker and more meaningful connections between resilient trans pasts and current trans lives" (LaFleur, Raskolnikov, and Klosowska 2021: 14). Samuel Achilles writing offers us one avenue for imaginatively connecting with distant trans pasts without becoming mired in the gender norms of either historical figures' times or our own. He does so (partially) by transforming extraordinary figures and narratives into remarkably relatable ones.

Each of the heroes in *Caeneus* is celebrated for what we might understand as relatively ordinary refusals of gender expectations. Caeneus' love interest, Nestor, rejects the hypermasculinity of his fellow sailors and the heroes with whom he has worked for his entire adult life, embracing instead tenderness, humility, and connection. Tiresias, who describes themself as constantly being called upon to address people's most urgent concerns only to have their advice disregarded, defends the boundaries that they have established to protect themself and their energy. Medea, after years of feigning attraction and commitment to Jason, embraces her same-gender desire and sails to Lemnos with Caeneus' sister, Dotia, where they plan to live together on an island free of men. Each of these characters frets over their choices and others' reactions to them, but they are all ultimately met with a loving enthusiasm that affirms the validity of their yearning to move through the world differently. While there is no guarantee that the young audience members reading or seeing this play will experience similarly affectionate acceptance from those around them, Achilles's writing insists on the possibility of such a reception and invites us to all work toward that reality.

References

Achilles, Samuel. 28 September 2024. Personal interview.
Carlá-Uhink, Filippo. 2017. "'Between the human and the divine': Cross-dressing and transgender dynamics in the Graeco-Roman world." In *TransAntiquity: Cross-Dressing and Gender Dynamics in the Ancient World,* eds. Domitilla Campanile, Filippo Carlà-Uhink, and Margherita Facella, 3–37. New York: Routledge.
Chu, Andrea Long. 2017. "The Wrong Wrong Body: Notes on Trans Phenomenology." *TSQ: Transgender Studies Quarterly* 4 (1): 141–152. DOI 10.1215/23289252-3711613
Dolan, Jill. 2005. *Utopia in Performance: Finding Hope at the Theatre.* Michigan: The University of Michigan Press.
Elster, Mikey. 2022. "Insidious Concern: Trans Panic and the Limits of Care." *TSQ: Transgender Studies Quarterly* 9 (3): 407–24. DOI 10.1215/23289252-9836064
LaFleur, Greta, Masha Raskolnikov, and Anna Klosowska, eds. 2021. *Trans Historical: Gender Plurality Before Modernity.* Ithaca [New York]: Cornell University Press.
Oswald, Sylvan. 2024. "Towards a Trans Theatre." In *The Methuen Drama Handbook of Gender and Theatre,* eds. Sean Metzger and Roberta Mock, 475–89. London: Bloomsbury.
Ovid and Stephanie McCarter. 2022. "Book Twelve." In *Metamorphoses.* New York: Penguin Books.
Roark, Kyle S. 2018. "Caeneus." https://kylesr.com/comics/caeneus.

Caeneus

Samuel Achilles

Cast

Caeneus   He/him. A trans man (must be played by a trans male actor), in his twenties. He was granted a wish by Poseidon, that other people's gendered perception of him be aligned with his internal reality. At the start of the play, he is withholding and closed off, and edges into spaces of expansion.

Nestor   He/him. A Sailor, not significantly older than Caeneus chronologically, but more experienced. He is the storyteller, he is (learning to be) an active listener, he is struggling with his role in the story.

Medea   She/her. A powerful witch. She is looking for power, and for something different, but keeps seeking out the same old story.

Dotia   She/her. Caeneus' sister, who is seeking understanding and similarity, but looking for it in the wrong places.

Jason   He/him. The great hero you may have heard about, but this story is not about him at all, despite what he may feel.

Tiresias   They/them. A nonbinary oracle with a large posse of followers, very showy and exciting. Has to be double cast with **Waitress/Maenad**.

Waitress/Maenad   She/they. A nonbinary Dionysian Priest/ess; double-sided, sort of mysterious, alarmingly sober. Double cast with **Tiresias**.
Theban Rep
Sailor
Priest/ess

Casting Policy

Whenever possible, all roles should be cast with trans actors; if it seems like a character "should" or "has to be" be played by a cisgender actor, challenge your own assumptions. If this is not possible, at the very least specifically trans characters (**Tiresias/Waitress/ Maenad**, **Priest/ess**, and **Caeneus**) must be cast with trans actors.

Sailor, **Theban Rep** and **Priest/ess** can be cast all with one actor or played by ensemble actors, depending on the size of the production.

Priest/ess can be one or two actors, or can be played by an entire ensemble of colorfully dressed nonbinary folks.

Setting

Caeneus takes place in an atemporal Ancient Greece. Caeneus' costumes, set design, and world should *not* be that of a period piece—the world should be obviously Ancient Greek-inspired, but should play with being out of time by having elements that are clearly contemporary or from other eras. Caeneus is, as much as possible, a fantasy world. This world should be bright, colorful, and inviting to look at, full of striking blue colors, similar to a tourist brochure for the Greek islands.

Notes

Jason works best when he is a drag king-esque role played for laughs.

Occasionally, characters tell their own stories and read their own stage directions. These directions should also be acted out as well as spoken.

Assume all characters have good intentions and are being as honest as they can be in that moment. See where it takes you.

In the first production of this play, all the actors were on stage at all times, and Dotia "reacted" throughout the first half of the play before she appears. Dotia doesn't necessarily have to be on stage the entire time if it doesn't make sense for the production, but her presence should be there before she actually is, whether it's her actual embodiment or a sound cue that follows her and reminds us of her.

Special Thanks

Ezekiel Baskin, Djola Branner, Steve Dillon, Sean French-Byrne, the entire original cast and crew of Caeneus at Hampshire, Hampshire College, Theater Between Addresses, everyone who held Caeneus in their heart and dreamed a beautiful dream with me.

Act I

Scene 1

Caeneus   Let's say you encounter a god, and it envelops you, crushes you, suffocates you.
You encounter things you never thought possible, things that rend and tear apart your soul. You feel stripped raw. And that god asks:
What do you want?
The whole world is before you. You could wish for something practical, but feeling already exposed, you speak into being the wildest fantasy you have, the one that seems impossible. And thinking he won't grant this request, thinking he'll laugh in your face, you just hear him say: Okay.
Too stunned to even speak, the tide rushes over you again and you feel like you might die from the pressure.
But you don't.
And you wash up on shore and your body is . . . the same. Completely unchanged, actually. But as you do, someone walks by and says "hello, young man."
So you're physically not changed. But everything else has transformed, because every wish the gods grant comes with an asterisk; at least you're not turning into solid gold. So maybe your body's the same, but you can still get your wish.

The tide rushes in, and obscures **Caeneus**. *When he is seen again, he is on the shore.*

Sailor   A raven approaches.

Caeneus   Hey, little guy—

Sailor (*as raven*)   Little guy?! Who are you calling little guy? That's not what I am! Look! The raven transforms in a puff of smoke!

Caeneus *looks confused, and a tad alarmed.*

Caeneus   You're a sailor?!

Sailor   No shit.

Caeneus   You were a raven just a minute ago . . . !

Sailor   Great observational skills, kid. You're a real detective. Anyway, as you can see, you're the one who's a little guy, not me.

Caeneus *visibly brightens when he hears the word "guy" used in reference to him.*

Caeneus   Wait, what did you say?

Sailor   You're a real detective . . . ?

Caeneus   No, the word you used to describe me.

Sailor   Little . . . ?

Caeneus   Just . . . what kind of person do I look like to you?

Sailor *raises their eyebrows.*

Sailor   A weird guy, that's for sure.

Caeneus *grins, and* **Sailor** *looks at* **Caeneus** *like he's just landed from another planet.*

Sailor   I don't have time to waste talking to you, kid. I gotta get to the Argo.

Caeneus   The Argo?! Like Jason's Argo? As in, the world-famous hero Jason's ship?

Sailor   Yep, and it's setting sail any minute, so I gotta get going.

Sailor *exits.*

Scene 2

Caeneus   Gods, what do I do now? I never thought I'd get this far . . .

Pause.

Caeneus   How do I make sense of this? What will I tell my family? Dotia? What if they don't see what that Sailor saw?

Pause. The whistle of the ship blows.

Jason (*from off stage*)   ALL ABOARD!!!

Caeneus *brightens; he has an idea, and he follows after the* **Sailor**, *who is just outside the ship.*

Caeneus   Excuse me—

Sailor   Ah! You again? Why are you following me, weirdo?

Caeneus   I'm not following you! I just wanted to know if the captain was hiring for this voyage.

Sailor (*sizing him up*)   A twerp like you? You ever been on a heroic ship before?

Caeneus   Well . . . no. But I've read a lot about it!

Sailor   Uh . . . huh. Ever fought a monster?

Caeneus   . . . no.

Sailor   Give me *something* to go on, here. Do you have any boating experience, at *least*?

Caeneus   A . . . little? My dad's a sailor, and he used to show me how to do some things because I wanted to be like him, but my mom didn't want him to. She thought it was "improper."

Sailor   Improper? Why? Sailing's a great skill for a young boy.

Caeneus *smiles.*

Caeneus   I completely agree.

Sailor   Honestly, you don't have a lot of experience, I don't know what the captain will—

Jason (*posing*)   Jason enters, the great hero you may have heard about.

Caeneus   Jason enters, and Caeneus recognizes him immediately! He's a little starstruck, actually. Caeneus had posters of all these great heroes on his wall growing up, and a giant shirtless poster of—

Sailor   Captain Jason! Sir.

Jason   What's the hold up?

Sailor   This kid is looking for work, but he hasn't done anything before.

Caeneus   I've done *some* things! I know the basics of sailing from my father, and I'm happy to do whatever you need me to do, captain, sir, I—

Jason   We need people with experience.

Caeneus   I'll do whatever you want, I'll scrub the decks, I'll clean the showers, I'll—

Jason   We don't need more mouths to feed.

Caeneus   Please, sir, this has been my dream since I was young—

Jason   You and every other kid in Greece.

Caeneus   I've always wanted to be a hero—

Jason   Not everyone can be.

Caeneus   I've been your fan since I was a little kid!

Pause.

Jason   Really?

Caeneus   Yes! I've been following your career for years! I even had a poster of you! Please, anything—

Jason   . . . well. I'm sure we can find something for you to do. Just stop holding up the process.

Caeneus   Wow, really?!

Jason   Sure, why not. Come aboard. There's plenty to do, and our timeline's already off.

Jason and **Sailor** *go aboard the ship.* **Caeneus** *pauses before he boards with them.*

Caeneus   And just like that, Caeneus joins the mythic Argo!

Caeneus *does some kind of excited, giddy motion (maybe a little dance) then walks aboard with them.*

Scene 3

Later. **Caeneus**, *on the Argo.* **Caeneus** *is meant to be working on the decks but gets distracted looking at the sea.* **Nestor** *approaches.*

Caeneus   Caeneus is looking down at the water, still trying to figure out how to make sense of what he's been through. It still feels a little . . . surreal, and hard to understand.

Nestor   What are you looking at?

Caeneus   Caeneus jumps, surprised by the voice. He turns and sees . . . a sailor, with kind eyes.

Nestor   Nestor sees a man he's never seen before, and he's intrigued.

There is a charge between them, and **Nestor** *smiles.* **Caeneus** *tugs at his clothes awkwardly. They pause.*

Nestor   I'm Nestor, by the way.

Caeneus   I'm Caeneus.

Nestor   Lovely to meet you.

Caeneus   Thanks. Um. I wasn't looking at anything, really.

Nestor   It looked like you were staring at the ocean?

Caeneus   Oh, yeah. Well. Um. I just find it to be . . . incredible. It feels like it'll never end, like any moment I could lean over just a little too far and be swallowed up by it. It's a little terrifying to me, actually.

Nestor   If you feel terrified by it, you've chosen the wrong profession.

Caeneus   Terrifying in a good way! Plus there's a comfort trying to control the sea by setting sail.

Nestor   Control? We could shipwreck at any time.

Caeneus   Well . . . yes. But it's a nice feeling, anyway, to think that we could try.

Nestor   It's almost like we're petitioning the gods.

Caeneus (*brightening*)   Yeah! Like we're asking a favor of some force greater than us to keep us above water.

Nestor *sees how excited* **Caeneus** *is and his affect shifts to be more open, matching* Caeneus' *energy.*

Nestor   That's a lovely way of putting it.

As they talk, **Caeneus** *and* **Nestor** *become slightly closer, in a way they are not even consciously aware of.*

Caeneus   It's like every time Poseidon could destroy us out here, but he doesn't. And whether that's by fate or a lucky break, who knows, but it feels significant. I feel like I've been given a lucky break every day since I got here.

Nestor   What do you mean?

Caeneus *suddenly realizes how close they are, almost touching, and it frightens him. He pulls away.*

Caeneus   It's just a sense, I guess.

Nestor   It just sounded like you had a story.

Caeneus   No, it was just a thought.

There is a slight awkward pause.

Nestor   Sorry, I didn't mean to pry.

Caeneus   That's alright.

Nestor   But what you said was a very nice notion.

Caeneus (*shrugs*)   Yeah.

Nestor   Nestor is aware Caeneus is pulling away, but he's unsure of how to fix it. There is an unspoken charge between them.

Caeneus   Caeneus is afraid of the charge between them.

Pause.

Caeneus   W-well, I better get going. I have a meeting with the captain.

Nestor (*sarcastically*)   Good luck with that.

Nestor exits.

Scene 4

Caeneus *goes hastily off to the captain's quarters, where the door is open and* **Medea** *is inside with* **Jason**. **Jason** *and* **Medea** *don't notice* **Caeneus** *is there.*

Medea   Where are we off to next?

Jason   The world's our oyster, babe. Where would you like to go?

Medea   I'd like to go to Lemnos at some point.

Pause.

Jason   That island where the women murdered all the men? Why?

Medea   It sounds so nasty when you say it like that. I've just always wanted to visit.

Jason   I don't think it quite fits into our plan.

Medea (*sharply*)   MAKE it fit.

Jason (*taken aback*)   I'll see what I can do, but I can't guarantee it.

Pause.

Jason   Can I have a kiss?

Medea   Sure. Medea and Jason kiss, but in a way that is chaste and passionless.

Jason   I'd love to spend more time with you, beautiful, but I'm a busy man, and my work is never done.

Medea (*sarcastically*)   I'm sure.

Jason   Goodbye, beautiful.

Medea   Goodbye, Jason.

Jason *exits.*

Scene 5

Medea *turns to leave, and notices* **Caeneus**. *She stops in her tracks.*

Medea   Who are *you?*

Caeneus   Oh, I'm sorry, I'm Caeneus, I work on the ship and—

Medea   Were you spying on us?

Caeneus   No! Not at all, I wanted to talk to the captain, I was just staying outside until you left! I'm sorry, I didn't mean to intrude . . .

Medea   Whatever. Just don't do it again.

Caeneus   I won't. Uh. I'm sorry.

Pause.

Caeneus   You're Medea, right?

Medea   I am.

Caeneus   Like, *the* Medea?

Medea (*sighs*)   Yes, *THE* Medea.

Caeneus   There was a lot of buzz when you and Jason got together; no one expected it.

Medea (*offhandedly*)   Especially not me.

Caeneus   What does that mean?

Medea   I'm sure you already know about me; everyone in the world knows about me. Tell me about yourself instead.

Caeneus   Um, I'm Caeneus.

Medea   Where are you from?

Caeneus (*uncomfortably*)   I'm from the sea.

Medea (*sarcastically*)   Like Aphrodite? Should we call you Aphroditus?

Caeneus *flinches at the name, referencing a specifically trans deity.*

Caeneus   You can call me my name, Caeneus.

Medea   Okay, Caeneus. What do you want? Why are you here?

Caeneus   You just met me, that's kind of—

Medea   I'm just making conversation.

Caeneus (*hesitantly*)   I'm trying to find somewhere new. Somewhere I can be completely different than the person I was before.

Medea (*laughs*)   I went to somewhere "completely new," and it didn't do much for me. Be careful what you wish for.

Caeneus   With Jason, you mean.

Medea   Yes, with Jason. Everyone knows the story already.

Pause.

Caeneus   It seems like the two of you are completely different.

Medea   Opposites attract, haven't you heard that?

Caeneus   I just . . . always wonder why you're together, when I read stories about you two.

Medea   Who are you to wonder about *my* life? Don't act like you know me just because you've heard rumors.

Pause.

Caeneus   You're right, I don't know you at all. I'm sorry.

Pause. **Medea** *hasn't gotten a lot of genuine apologies before, and doesn't know how to respond.*

Medea   I . . . appreciate that.

Caeneus   Can we start over? I'm Caeneus.

Medea   Medea.

There is a soft moment between them, before **Medea** *bristles again.*

Medea   Don't you have a meeting with Jason to get to?

Caeneus   Right. I should get to that.

Medea   Yes, you should.

Medea *turns to leave, but then turns back.*

Medea   Have a good meeting with Jason, Caeneus.

Medea *exits.*

Scene 6

Caeneus *enters the captain's quarters, where* **Jason** *is sitting at his desk, taking up as much space as possible and shuffling through papers, distracted the entire time he's talking to* **Caeneus**.

Caeneus   Hello, captain. Thank you for taking the time to meet with me.

Jason   Any time . . . (*squints*) Canthus?

Pause.

Caeneus   Um. Caeneus, actually.

Jason   Ohhh. Oh! Right. There are just so many Argonauts that it gets hard to keep track. Uhhh . . . why did you want to meet again?

Caeneus   I just wanted to thank you for giving me the opportunity to join your crew.

Jason   . . . that's it?

Caeneus   . . . well, yes. The other sailor didn't seem interested in letting me on, and you were willing to take a chance on me.

Jason (*dismissively*)   We needed people.

Caeneus   . . . yes, but, it's a real honor to be a part of this voyage. I always admired you, and to get a chance to actually meet you and to work with you as part of your crew, it's really indescribable, I admired you so much as a kid and I'm without words about how excited I am to be here and to—

As **Caeneus** *delivers his lines,* **Jason** *seems increasingly bored and disinterested, then interrupts once he can't take it any longer. It can be before* **Caeneus** *technically finishes his lines, according to actor and director discretion.*

Jason   Okay, okay, you're excited. Is there a point to this, or . . . ?

Caeneus   . . . I guess not. I just wanted to say how grateful I am.

Jason   I think that goes without saying.

Caeneus   What?

Jason   As in, anyone would be grateful to be a part of this crew, and to journey with a great hero.

Caeneus   . . . right, of course.

Jason   Look, I'm *always* happy to meet a fan, Canthus.

Caeneus   Caeneus.

Jason   Caeneus. But, you were there, we needed people. It's that simple.

Caeneus *says nothing, shrinks into himself.*

Pause.

Jason   Did you want to speak with me about anything else?

Caeneus   . . . no, that was it.

Jason   Okay. In that case, I'm going to get back to my work. I'm sure you have a deck to scrub somewhere.

Caeneus *exits and takes a deep breath and looks confused, unsure of how to make sense of what just happened.*

Scene 7

As **Caeneus** *is leaving, he bumps into* **Nestor** *in his confusion. He bristles, being afraid of both the sudden physical contact and the charge from earlier.*

Caeneus   Oh, I'm sorry!

Nestor   Oh, no, it's fine.

Caeneus   No, I wasn't paying attention, I—

Nestor   Don't worry about it. I'm not bothered by bumping shoulders with you.

Nestor is standing close, and the charge is there again. **Caeneus** *is unsure of what to do, and takes a couple steps back. Pause.*

Caeneus   Can I ask uh . . . what do you think of the captain?

Nestor   He's exactly what I'd expect him to be.

Caeneus   He isn't what I expected at all. Everything about him makes him sound like one of the greatest men to ever live, and he's . . .

Nestor   Rude? Selfish?

Caeneus (*surprised by* **Nestor***'s forwardness*)   . . . well, yes.

Nestor (*chuckles*)   They're always like that.

Caeneus   Who?

Nestor   Career "heroes" like Jason. I've worked with a few of them, and none of them can see beyond their own nose. (*Pause*) Is this your first mission like this ever?

Caeneus   Yes.

Pause.

Nestor   Huh, that's interesting. Explains why I haven't seen you before. I'm used to the same people. It's nice to have someone new around.

Caeneus   Thank you; I'm excited to be here.

Nestor   It's not all it's cracked up to be. It's rough work.

Caeneus   I'm sure it's rough sometimes, but we're so lucky to be able to do this. Tons of kids dream about being able to be on a ship like this - on some great quest, at the mercy of the sea.

Nestor *smiles and softens, remembering that feeling in himself.*

Nestor   I was like that.

Caeneus   Me too. I never thought I could actually do it, and now here I am. (*grins*)

Nestor   Congratulations.

Caeneus (*smiles*)   Thanks. It'd be better if Jason wasn't . . . the way that he is.

Nestor   I understand what you mean. I used to daydream about joining Hercules' crew, then I met him and realized he was just another famous egomaniac.

Caeneus   Like Jason.

Nestor   Exactly.

Caeneus (*nervously*)   To be honest, when I was growing up I had a little bit of a crush on him.

Nestor   Really?

Caeneus   Yeah. Sounds stupid to say.

Nestor   No, it's not. I felt the same way about Hercules.

Caeneus *has a moment of recognition, of realization.*

Nestor   But a guy like that . . . that's not what I want.

Caeneus   What do you want?

Nestor   Not that, I know that much.

Pause.

Nestor   What about you?

The charge is there between them again.

Caeneus   I don't know.

Caeneus *thinks about it for a moment.*

Caeneus   I want to feel . . . understood.

Nestor   Do you not feel understood?

Caeneus   Rarely.

Nestor   I'm sorry to hear that.

Caeneus   I didn't feel understood in my hometown, and talking to guys like Jason . . . I have no idea how to talk to them at all.

Nestor   Me neither.

Caeneus   Really? *You* don't?

Nestor   Gods, no.

Caeneus   But you seem so comfortable here.

Nestor   I've just learned how to talk the talk, but I don't really get it. Sometimes I'm around someone like Jason or Hercules, and I just want to connect with them, but I can't. They won't let me in.

Caeneus   Exactly! That's how I felt earlier today! It's so . . . stifling.

Nestor   That's their problem, not ours.

Caeneus   Yeah, I guess you're right.

Nestor   Doesn't have to be like that, though. There are different people, different ways of connecting . . .

Caeneus   They're close again. This time, Caeneus doesn't move away.

Nestor   They just aren't very imaginative.

Pause, with **Nestor** *and* **Caeneus** *sitting incredibly close to one another. All the unspoken charge is there, hanging in the air.*

Nestor   I find you so fascinating and mysterious.

Caeneus *reacts like an embarrassed but excited tween being noticed by his crush.*

Caeneus   Really? Oh, gosh, thanks.

Nestor   I'd love to know what your story is, if you'd like to tell it to me.

Caeneus   My story?

Nestor   Where you came from, how you got here . . .

Caeneus *pulls away again.*

Caeneus   I don't know. People keep asking me about who I am, and I don't know what to say.

Nestor   I can understand that.

Caeneus   Can you?

Nestor   Yes. Sometimes I feel sort of . . . adrift, like I'm just going with the flow.

Caeneus   Hmm . . . for me, it's more that I don't know how to say the things inside of me. I feel afraid.

Nestor   What's there to be afraid of?

Caeneus   That I'll be totally misunderstood.

Pause. **Caeneus** *pulls away even more; he feels like he's said too much.*

Caencus   Gods, it's getting really late, I better start getting to bed.

Nestor   Oh, right—me too.

Caeneus   Goodnight, Nestor.

Nestor   Goodnight, Caeneus. (*Pause*) You know, I'm always open to hear your story, if you feel comfortable telling me.

Caeneus   Thank you.

Scene 8

A sound cue plays, one that takes us back to home, back to another time, back to before all the adventure. **Dotia** *speaks.*

Dotia   I don't know why I'm writing this. I know you'll never read it, that by now you're probably long gone. Our brothers have all left; like his father, Polyphemus also took to the seas. Iskius found a wife, and moved out of town. I've decided to stay here.

Well, I don't know if "decided" is the right word. I *have* stayed here, doing the same as I've always done. I work on my weaving, sometimes, and imagine I'm a little bit like Penelope. I think I understand her more than I ever did before. When I heard that story, I thought: how sad. But, it keeps my hands and mind busy, and I certainly need that now. It keeps me from thinking about how I don't have an ending to this story, about how I feel unfinished. You just . . . vanished, and what kind of story is that? There's no horrible tragedy, no heartwarming reunion. Nothing. You're just gone.

Everyone keeps asking me if I'll marry soon. I don't have any interest in finding a husband, and it's not like I ever had any calling to be a priestess. I can stave off the questions for now, but I know as I get older, those questions will only increase. I wonder if that's part of why you ran away, too. I have so many questions, but I know I probably won't ever get answers. I pray every day to Athena for guidance, for wisdom, and most of all, I pray for her to send you back home. At least if you were here, I could cry and scream at you instead of just writing another stupid letter that I'll never send.

Love . . . no, erase. Warmly . . . no, erase.

Sincerely,
Dotia

Scene 9

Back to the present day, to the Argo, to another time. **Caeneus**, **Jason** *and* **Medea** *on the ship.*

Theban Rep *appears on the ship, in a puff of smoke, dressed in either a glamorous gown or a glamorous suit, depending on actor preference/comfortability.* **Jason** *and* **Caeneus** *look a little flummoxed.*

Theban Rep   Greetings, hero.

Jason   Oh Gods, not another one of these . . .

Caeneus   How did they get onto the ship?!

Theban Rep   Don't be alarmed. My appearance here is only an illusion; I am an automated, magical messenger from the great land of . . . THEBES.

Theban Rep *poses.* **Caeneus** *is still taken aback;* **Jason** *looks exhausted.*

Medea   Ugh, another? We get one of these every day from some sad little island or town.

Jason   I really need to get some kind of shield spell cast in here . . .

Theban Rep (*overly cheerful*)   Thebes is doing better now than ever. In fact, predictions from oracles say that Thebes will in a few decades be nearly destroyed by a terrible plague brought in by the hubris of a cursed king, so the time is ripe to enjoy our beautiful city! Come see the city where Dionysus himself was born! Surrounded on all sides by a giant magical wall built by Amphion, the son of Zeus, you will never feel safer than when you are in Thebes.

Medea   That doesn't sound appeali—

Theban Rep   In Thebes, you can see: the wall I mentioned previously, the birthplace of Dionysus, and last but certainly not least . . . the gender-bending oracle Tiresias!

Caeneus   Wait, what?

Theban Rep   Yes, Tiresias themself. Known for being granted a gift by the gods to change their gender, Tiresias has been RENOWNED as Greece's greatest oracle. Tiresias has been male, female, and everything in between and outside of that, giving them knowledge of the whole range of the human experience.

Caeneus   Their gender was transformed?!

Theban Rep   Yes indeed. Many times, in fact.

Caeneus   How come I've never heard of this?

Theban Rep (*cheerily*)   I don't know. Perhaps because you've been living under a rock?

Jason   Don't worry about it. They're just a B-list celebrity. Well-known for an oracle, but not like a *hero*.

Caeneus   They sound incredible.

Theban Rep   They are! They may not be a hero, but they've advised great heroes, such as Hercules and Perseus!

Jason (*suddenly paying attention*)   Hercules and Perseus?

Theban Rep   Indeed, they've advised the greatest heroes of our generation on their most pressing questions!

Jason   Hmm . . .

Medea   You really are convinced by this stupid advertisement?

Theban Rep   Hey! I'm not a stupid advertisement! I'm a *finely-crafted illusion.*

Caeneus   Captain, Tiresias might be able to give you some amazing advice! It might be a nice vacation for the crew!

Medea   You realize you're talking about *Thebes,* right?

Theban Rep   Hey! Thebes is doing better now than ever. In fact—

Medea (*sharply*)   We know.

Jason   I suppose if Tiresias gave me useful advice about the quest for the Golden Fleece, it'd be well worth the detour . . .

Caeneus   Yes! Exactly! You wouldn't regret it.

Jason   Hmm . . . I'll go let the other sailors know the change in our plans.

Jason exits.

Scene 10

Medea   Why are you so eager to go to Thebes? You realize they only sent that illusion because no one actually wants to go, right?

Caeneus   I want to meet with the oracle Tiresias.

Medea   Tiresias? What business do you have with them?

Caeneus   I have a pressing question.

Medea   Is it concerning the Argo?

Caeneus   It's about me. But I think going to see the oracle could be helpful for all of us.

Medea   What is it?

Caeneus   It's personal.

Medea   Can't you tell your friend?

Caeneus   We're friends?

Medea   Something like that. I talk to you more than anyone else here.

Caeneus (*thinks about it*)   Me too, actually.

Medea   What about Nestor?

Caeneus (*pause*)   That's different.

Medea   What is happening with you two? I see the way you two look at each other—lingering glances, sitting so close you're almost touching . . .

Caeneus (*flustered*)   That's beside the point!

Medea   Uh-huh.

Caeneus   Anyway, do you have something to ask Tiresias?

Medea   Yes. But if you're not going to tell me your question, I won't tell you mine.

Caeneus   Oh, come on.

Medea   It's only fair. You're so secretive, Caeneus.

Caeneus   Everyone keeps telling me that.

Medea   Sometime you've got to let people in.

Caeneus   *You* don't do that.

Medea   Sure I do! I'm an open book. Everyone knows about me.

Caeneus   They mostly know rumors.

Medea   I like to keep an air of mystery with some things.

Caeneus   I do, too.

Medea   I don't want to be someone like Jason, where what you see is exactly what you get. Nothing below the surface.

Caeneus   I'd love to be like Jason. He's an open book, and he's got nothing to be afraid of.

Medea   It'd be so boring if you were like him.

Caeneus (*laughs*)   Boring? He's a great hero.

Medea   We don't need more heroes like Jason, Caeneus.

This strikes a chord with **Caeneus**.

Caeneus   You think?

Medea   I don't think; I know. (*Pause*) So what's your question?

Caeneus   I want to know more about Tiresias.

Medea (*laughs*)   An unusual question for an oracle. Why?

Caeneus   I think it'll help me.

Medea   How so?

Caeneus *pulls away, aware he's already said too much.*

Caeneus   I just think they have a unique perspective. What about you?

Pause. **Medea** *is hesitant, but tells him.*

Medea   I want to know more about Lemnos.

Caeneus   The island where the women killed the men?

Medea   I prefer to think of it as an island of only women, but yes.

Caeneus   Why do you want to know about Lemnos?

Medea   I just think it's an interesting place.

Caeneus   I guess so. Doesn't really interest me.

Pause. **Caeneus** *and* **Medea** *both have pulled away, feeling all the unspoken things.*

Medea   Well, I hope you get your question answered.

Caeneus   Thanks. You, too.

Scene 11

It is night on the Argo, and **Caeneus** *and* **Nestor** *are completely alone together for the first time. They are in* **Caeneus**' *quarters, sitting on a bed together.*

Caeneus   You remember when you asked me to tell you my story?

Nestor   Of course.

Caeneus   I want to, but . . . I don't know how to tell it. It feels like a myth.

Nestor   If it's a myth, then tell it to me like you're a bard.

Caeneus is taken aback.

Caeneus   What do you mean?

Nestor   If it feels like a myth, then tell it to me like it is.

Caeneus   It's not interesting enough to be an actual myth.

Nestor   I'm sure it is interesting.

Caeneus   It really isn't.

Nestor   If you don't want to tell me, that's fine. But if you do want to, I'd be happy to be a guest in your story's house.

Pause. **Caeneus** *is taken back by the intensity of what* **Nestor** *just said, but tries to play it off.*

Caeneus (*chuckles*)   A guest? Are you going to get on your knees like you're petitioning me?

Nestor   Would you like me to?

Pause.

Caeneus   I was joking! But . . . if you want . . .

Nestor *kneels before* **Caeneus** *(who is sitting in this moment), wrapping his arms around his knees and looking up at him reverently. Pause in this moment.* **Caeneus** *looks down towards him with a smile.*

Nestor   Will you allow me to hear your story?

Caeneus   This is so strange—you're making me feel like a king.

Nestor   Do you want to feel like a king?

There is an electric charge between the two of them that holds for a moment or two. Afraid of this charge, **Caeneus** *laughs to break the tension.*

Caeneus   Come on, get up. This is ridiculous.

Nestor *lets go of* **Caeneus** *and rises to his feet. There is an awkward silence between the two of them; they are both aware something has happened, but are not sure what.*

Nestor   I mean it, though. If you ever want to talk, I'm happy to listen.

Caeneus   Thank you, but . . . I don't know if I'm ready.

Nestor   Maybe another time, then.

Caeneus   Yes. Um. Another time.

Pause.

Caeneus   Hey, um . . . when you acted like I was a king. I felt like there was . . . something happening.

Nestor   I was flirting with you.

Pause.

Caeneus   Wait, what?

Nestor   I've *been* flirting with you. I thought you knew? (*Pause*) Is that okay?

Caeneus   Yes! I mean . . . yes? I think so? I don't know. I didn't . . . I didn't realize you were. Um.

Pause.

Caeneus   Sorry, just no one's ever really flirted with me before. Not like this, anyway.

Nestor   What do you mean by "like this"?

Caeneus   I don't know. I'm sorry.

Nestor   Don't be. I'm sorry if I made you uncomfortable.

Caeneus   I don't really know what I'm doing.

Nestor   At least we're lost together?

Caeneus *laughs a little.*

Nestor   Sorry, that was a cheesy line.

Caeneus   No, it was sweet.

Nestor   Ha, thanks.

Pause.

Nestor   Do you want me to flirt with you?

Caeneus   Yes! Um. Yes.

Pause. The charge is there between them again; both of them are waiting for someone to make a move. After what seems like an uncomfortably long time to them both, **Nestor** *speaks.*

Nestor   Can I kiss you?

Caeneus   Absolutely.

Caeneus   Nestor and Caeneus kiss; it is gentle, sweet, but has the passion of two people who have been waiting to kiss for a long time.

They pause and smile at each other.

Caeneus   Hm.

Nestor   Is everything okay?

Caeneus   Yes. More than okay. (*pause*) I'm just realizing my imagination was more limited than I thought it was.

Nestor smiles. They kiss again.

Caeneus *steps forward, as he talks to himself and the audience.*

Caeneus   Kissing him feels like . . . settling into a warm bath. Soft and cozy and something I've been waiting for. But . . . I had never *planned* for this. I always assumed I was going to go rescue some princess; that was just what you were supposed to do as a hero. But does any of that matter now that he's here? We can be like . . . Zeus and Ganymede. (*shakes head*) No, too unbalanced. Apollo and Hyacinth? Too grim. (*pause*) Are there any of these stories that don't end with someone hurt or dying? Can I write a different ending with him?

Caeneus *sits back down next to* **Nestor**, *and looks at him as he delivers the next line.*

Caeneus   I can try.

Scene 12

Back to the deck, back to near **Jason**'s *quarters.* **Caeneus** *is wandering the ship, and runs into* **Medea** *and* **Jason** *talking.* **Jason** *and* **Medea** *kiss, and* **Medea** *looks mostly* *unenthused.* **Jason** *leaves, and* **Medea** *rolls her eyes.* **Medea** *turns and sees Caeneus watching.*

Medea   What are you looking at?

Caeneus   Nothing! I'm just still wondering . . . do you actually . . . like Jason?

Medea   That's none of your business.

Caeneus   It just doesn't seem like you do. At all, really.

Medea   I don't *dis*like him.

Caeneus   Does he make you feel warm and fuzzy?

Medea   He makes me feel . . . (*shrugs*) fine. Not everyone can have a gushy love story.

Caeneus   I guess so. (*Pause*) When you two got together, what was that like?

Medea   You don't know that story already? He came to Colchis, whisked me off my feet, said he wanted to take me with him around the world.

Caeneus   But did you talk about it?

Medea   Talk about what?

Caeneus   What you both wanted.

Medea   Not really. I was just excited for the opportunity to go somewhere else. I spent my whole life in Colchis, and I thought I'd never get the chance to leave.

Caeneus   I feel the same way about Thessaly, like I had to get away from everything I knew in order to make any progress.

Medea   We're both far from where we started.

They smile at each other.

Caeneus   But was there anything about Jason specifically that you liked?

Medea   I liked that the whole thing was easy. I didn't have to think too hard, it just all slotted into place.

Caeneus   But what about *him?*

Medea   He's . . . well . . . (*pause*) Oh, I don't know. Could *you* describe what you like about Nestor?

Caeneus   Yes, actually. He always listens, and he always asks me what I want, and being with him is like . . . feeling warm sunlight on your skin when before you only felt it through a window—

Medea   Ugh, gods, stop. You're going to give me a cavity.

Caeneus   How does Jason make you feel?

Medea   Like I have a clear road map, and I know exactly which direction to go.

Caeneus   I don't feel that way with Nestor at all. It feels like discovering whole new uncharted islands.

Medea   That sounds terrifying. With Jason, it's sort of like I'm . . . cleaning a dish.

Caeneus   Excuse me?

Medea   It's mildly unpleasant, but it's what I need to do to accomplish what I want.

Caeneus   That's . . . depressing.

Medea   It's practical.

Caeneus   Practical? How?

Medea   I can get the things I need from him. He's rich, well connected, known throughout Greece . . .

Caeneus   And a total jerk.

Medea   Not a TOTAL jerk! Everyone has their faults. Why do you care so much about me and Jason, anyways?

Caeneus   I just don't know many people in a relationship.

Medea   Are you sure you're not just being nosy?

Caeneus   No! I'm just . . . trying to figure out stuff. Relationship stuff.

Medea   Because of Nestor.

Caeneus (*flustered*)   . . . maybe. Yes. It's just . . . gotten a little more than flirty.

Medea (*eyebrow raise*)   Oh really? What happened?

Caeneus   Nothing! I mean, we might have . . . kissed a little bit. Or, well, a lot.

Pause.

Medea   Is that all?

Caeneus   . . . yes.

Medea   I was expecting something a little more serious than kissing, from the way you were acting.

Caeneus   That *is* serious!

Medea   Plenty of people kiss.

Caeneus   I don't have plenty of people kissing *me!*

Medea   Have you . . . never been kissed before?

Caeneus   Yes! Of course I have! That'd be stupid, if I was an adult and had never been kissed, who's ever even heard of *that*, like what kind of weirdo--

Medea   You definitely haven't been kissed before.

Caeneus   . . . not like . . . well . . . not at all, no.

Medea *How?*

Caeneus I don't know! I never really liked anybody before. Not anybody real, anyway. Only far away hero worship.

Medea No wonder it feels like discovering uncharted islands. (*Pause*) Why don't you ask Tiresias about all these relationship questions instead of me?

Caeneus I have more important things to ask them about.

Medea I still don't understand what you need to know about them.

Caeneus (*shrugs*) I'm just curious.

Medea I suppose you still don't want to tell me.

Caeneus considers.

Caeneus No, I don't.

Medea Fine. I'm sure it's not that interesting, anyway.

Medea exits.

Scene 13

Caeneus And so we journeyed to the great land of Thebes, the home of the famed oracle Tiresias. Jason had his own agenda, but mostly, I wanted to meet with this person who had been through the same thing as me! I had never even heard of someone who had been transformed besides me. At least, not in terms of their gender. Everyone's heard of someone who was turned into a bird or something. To be honest, I thought I was the only one in the world. Every night as we got closer to Thebes I stayed up and dreamed about what it might feel like to meet them . . .

Scene 14

Caeneus, **Nestor**, *and* **Medea** *arrive at the temple to Apollo. It is what you would imagine an Ancient Greek temple to be like: stark white with large pillars.* **Priest/ess** *waves them in.*

Priest/ess One inquiry at a time, please. And don't waste the time of the oracle; remember, you have two minutes.

Priest/ess *taps their watch (either literal or figurative).* **Caeneus** *wrings his hands, but nods.* **Caeneus** *enters first; there might be a whole group of ostentatiously dressed Priest/esses, looking a bit like colorful, strange birds.*

Caeneus Is one of you Tiresias?

Priest/ess Shh!! Don't speak. Tiresias is about to make their entrance. (*speaking like an announcer*) People come from far and wide to encounter the great oracle . . . they who have been every gender, they who have encountered Apollo himself, they who have been brought in as a consultant to settle an argument between Zeus and Hera. And now, here they are before you, to give you their great wisdom . . . Tiresias!!!

A theme plays for **Tiresias'** *entrance; try to draw this out as much as possible. The more showy and camp this is, the better.*

Tiresias (*with a dramatic flourish*)   Welcome to the temple of Apollo, traveler.

Caeneus   Thank you! This is incredible.

Tiresias   Well, style is everything, don't you agree?

Caeneus (*uncertain*)   Sure!

Tiresias   Tell me, what is your inquiry?

Tiresias *pauses, and then clutches their head before* **Caeneus** *can answer, as if they're getting some message from a faraway source.*

Tiresias   No, no, wait. I'm seeing it now . . .

Awkward pause.

Tiresias. You're in love for the first time, and don't know what to do.

Caeneus   No! . . . well, yes, but that's not what I—

Tiresias   You have problems with your sister.

Caeneus   . . . yes, that's true too, but I—

Tiresias   You don't know how to interact with the other men on your ship.

Caeneus   Yes, but—

Tiresias   The reality of being a hero doesn't match your fantasy, and you don't know what to do.

Caeneus (*becoming frustrated, but still trying to be polite*)   All of the things you're saying are true, but none of them are what I came to ask you about.

Tiresias   What was your question, then?

Caeneus   It wasn't a question exactly, more of a . . . conversation I wanted to have with you.

Tiresias   A conversation? Not many people come to me for a conversation.

Caeneus   Yes, well, it's about something that you and I have both experienced.

Tiresias   What sort of something?

Pause.

Caeneus   Well . . . we've both experienced some form of gender transformation.

Tiresias   Is that all?

Pause. **Caeneus** *is not sure how to respond.*

Tiresias   I knew *that.* I just didn't feel it was worth remarking on.

Caeneus *is a little taken aback by that remark, but chooses to ignore it.*

Caeneus   . . . well, when I heard that you had been transformed too, I just knew I had to meet you, because I had never heard of anyone else who had had this experience. I was so excited about it that I had to come here.

Tiresias   And . . . that's it?

Pause.

Caeneus   What do you mean?

Tiresias   Just, most people who come here have a *problem.* Something in their life has gone sour, they need to figure out how to overcome some great grief, they have some crossroads they've come to . . . you just wanted to talk about transformation?

Caeneus   Mostly, yes. I thought I was the only one, so I just wanted to talk to someone else with the same experience.

Tiresias   You thought you were the only one?!

Tiresias *and their posse burst into laughter.* **Caeneus** *shrinks into himself, feeling foolish.*

Tiresias   Oh, dear, I'm sorry to laugh. It's just . . . it's a bit uncommon, perhaps, but not unheard of.

Caeneus   Really?

Tiresias   Of course! Look at my priests here.

Tiresias *gestures to their posse.*

Tiresias   All have experienced some form of transformation or another, then back again, and into third and fourth and fifth genders. You think you're unique in that?

Caeneus   Back again?

Tiresias   Yes. Don't you plan on going back?

Pause.

Caeneus   Excuse me?

Tiresias   Don't you plan on changing back into a woman again, or into another gender, bringing forward the knowledge you've gained as a man?

Caeneus   Gods, no! I want to stay the same. All I ever wanted was this, why would I change back?

Tiresias   Well, most who are transformed go back and forth.

Caeneus   I don't want that at all. Is it at all possible for me to stay the same?

Tiresias *looks to their posse. They all look equally confused. Pause.*

Tiresias   I never considered staying in a transformation.

Caeneus   How have you n—

Tiresias   SILENCE! A vision is coming to me.

Caeneus   Tiresias stands, clutches their head in their hands; they move erratically, strangely, in a bizarre trance-like dance. Caeneus watches, unsure of what is happening? Everyone else seems excited?

Priest/ess   A vision!
A prophecy!

There is plenty of fanfare as the others get hyped about this vision; perhaps there is a drumroll or the banging of a tambourine. After a moment of **Caeneus** *feeling lost amongst this expectant, excited energy,* **Tiresias** *raises their hand. The whole room hushes into complete silence for an uncomfortable amount of time, until finally, Tiresias speaks.*

Tiresias   You must go . . . to the temple.

Caeneus   The temple? I'm at the temple already.

Tiresias   Not THIS temple. *THE* temple.

Caeneus   What does that mean?

Tiresias   Unfortunately, my friend, your time is up. However, I am happy to meet with you another day if you schedule with my secretary who's just outside.

Caeneus   I came all this way, I want to talk with you m—

Tiresias   Be lucky I saw you at all! I am booked incredibly far in advance, you know. And I think, upon reflection, you will find my words to have *DEEP* resonance.

The posse cheers and screams **Tiresias** *'name enthusiastically. They might try to get the audience to join in on their cheering and excitement.* **Caeneus** *is not having any of it, and is trying to mask his frustration.* **Tiresias** *takes a theatrical bow.*

Tiresias   Thank you, thank you. And now, you may leave. I have another seeker who is waiting patiently.

Caeneus   Wai—

Tiresias (*like an impatient mother, making hand motions for him to leave*)   No. No waiting. I can see it now! Your friend Medea is coming next. You wouldn't want her to be left adrift, would you?

Caeneus   I—

Caeneus *opens his mouth to speak, but* **Tiresias** *'posse are shooing him out, with increasing urgency. He starts to feel overwhelmed by all of them and leaves.*

Scene 15

Nestor *and* **Caeneus**, *outside of the temple.*

Nestor (*excitedly*)   How'd it go?

Caeneus   They . . . weren't what I expected.

Nestor   What do you mean?

Caeneus   They just seemed a little . . . self-centered.

Nestor   Really? I think they seem incredible. To have all that wisdom that comes from living in multiple ways . . .

Caeneus   Yes, and to still be centering yourself.

Nestor   Wouldn't you center yourself and talk about it all the time if you had gone through something so extraordinary?

Caeneus   No! I have been transformed, and I don't talk about it all the time.

Pause.

Nestor   What?

Caeneus (*talking fast and nervously*)   I had the same kind of transformation happen as Tiresias. I was transformed by Poseidon.

Pause.

Nestor   Why didn't you tell me?

Caeneus   I was afraid of how you might react.

Nestor   I would hope you'd know me better than that. (*Pause*) What'd it feel like, though? To get transformed?

Caeneus   Why do you ask?

Nestor   It's just interesting, that's all. I've never been through anything interesting.

Caeneus   What? You've sailed with Jason, Hercules, so many heroes—

Nestor   And I was just a side character in their stories.

Caeneus   You're not a side character to me.

Nestor *smiles at* **Caeneus** *softly.*

Caeneus   It feels sort of like . . . your most impossible dream is in front of you, and then you reach out and grab it. And then . . . you're just living it. And you try to figure out how to live in it, because you never thought this would actually be your life, and it's messier than you thought it would be, and there are parts of it you never accounted for. But you still love it enough to be afraid you'll wake up.

Nestor   Why does it have to be a dream?

Caeneus   What do you mean?

Nestor   I don't think of my life that way. I'm just . . . living it. I'm not afraid I'll wake up, because it's just my life.

Caeneus *bristles.*

Caeneus   That must be nice for you.

Nestor   Why's it not that way for you?

Caeneus   Because it's just not! You think I can just clap my hands and get rid of years of thinking what I wanted was impossible?

Pause.

Nestor   But you're here now.

Nestor *holds* **Caeneus**'*hand.* **Caeneus** *rests his head on* **Nestor**'s *shoulder. Pause in this moment.*

Nestor   You're here, and you've been through something extraordinary.

Caeneus *pulls away from him a little.*

Caeneus   Tiresias didn't seem to think it was extraordinary. They had a whole crew of people who had been transformed.

Nestor   Maybe for Tiresias, but it's . . . unlike anything I've ever heard of.

Caeneus   You don't understand. I'm realizing I might be more normal than I thought.

Nestor   You could make an entire career out of talking about this, telling others about the amazing thing you've been through—

Caeneus   I don't want to be a fascination.

Nestor   I'm just trying to help.

Caeneus   You're not helping.

Pause.

Nestor   I'm sorry.

Pause. Tension.

Nestor   What do you want to be instead of a fascination?

Caeneus   A hero.

Nestor   Like Jason?

Caeneus   No. Better. Someone who actually does something important, and not just someone who gets a lot of celebrity buzz.

Nestor   You can definitely accomplish that. Slay great monsters, save princes, and—

Caeneus   Stop telling me what I'm going to do.

Nestor   What?

Caeneus   I don't like the way you're talking to me, like you're the authority on my life.

Nestor   I don't think that.

Caeneus   Just . . . be more self-aware.

Nestor   You think I'm not?

Caeneus   No, you're not! The . . . the way you talked to me about my transformation, it just proves that you're not! You might be a side character to Jason, but sometimes you make other people feel like *they're* the side character.

Pause. **Nestor** *is unsure what to say; this cuts deep for him. Tension.*

Nestor   That's not what I want at all.

Caeneus   I know it's not. I just . . . I need to be alone right now.

Nestor   Okay. I'm sorry.

Caeneus   I know you are, but I want to be alone.

Nestor   Is there anything I could do that would—

Caeneus   Just go for now.

Nestor   Nestor pauses, trying to think of something he could say that could make it better. He can't think of anything.

Pause, before **Nestor** *leaves.*

Caeneus   We'll talk more about this later, okay? I just need time to cool off.

Nestor   Okay. It's hard for him, but Nestor exits.

Intermission.

Act II

Scene 16

Later, approaching on night. **Caeneus**, **Nestor**, *and* **Medea** *are wandering in Thebes, and arrive at a roadside diner. There is a flickering neon sign that says "TEMPLE."*

Nestor   It feels like we've been walking around Thebes forever, I'm starving.

Medea   That looks like a restaurant.

Caeneus   I don't know . . . I get a weird feeling from this place.

Nestor   I'm sure it'll be fine.

Medea (*rolls eyes*)   You're both cowards. I'm going in.

Medea *charges ahead into the diner.* **Caeneus** *and* **Nestor** *look confused.*

Caeneus   Hey, wait!

Medea *is already in the diner by the time* **Caeneus** *gets his words out.* **Caeneus** *looks irritated,* **Nestor** *looks confused. Caeneus sighs. They both walk in after her.*

The diner is almost empty, and has strange, ambient, 1950's style music playing in the background as if from a jukebox.

When they enter the diner/temple, the **Waitress** *is already there. She/they should be played by the same actor as Tiresias, but dressed very differently.*

Waitress   Table for three?

Caeneus   You look so familiar to me . . .

Waitress (*shrugs*)   I get that a lot. Mom says it's 'cause I have a common face.

Caeneus   No, I don't think that's it . . .

Waitress   So, there's three of you, right?

Medea   Yes, table for three, please.

The **Waitress** *leads them to a booth, gives them each a menu, then exits.*

Caeneus   This place feels . . . wrong.

Medea   I like it; it's oozing with magic.

Caeneus   Why does it have so much Dionysian décor? Is that the theme?

The **Waitress** *appears, seemingly out of nowhere before anyone can answer Caeneus' question. Caeneus is surprised by her/their sudden appearance.*

Waitress   What can I get you all?

Medea (*confidently*)   I'll have number four.

Nestor   I'll have a short stack of blueberry pancakes, please.

Caeneus   Just orange juice, please.

Waitress   Nothing else?

Caeneus   . . . no.

Waitress   You've had a long journey. Don't you want something to eat?

Caeneus   How do you know that?

Waitress   Oh, word gets around.

Caeneus   . . . I'm fine, thanks.

Waitress (*overly cheerful, to the point of being somewhat terrifying*)   You wouldn't want to upset the management, would you?

Pause.

Caeneus   . . . toast and orange juice, then.

Waitress   Alright, coming right up!

Waitress *exits.*

Caeneus   This is creepy.

Medea   I think it's lovely.

Waitress *comes back alarmingly fast with their food. As she/they set it down, there is a shift. The 1950s style music either cuts completely and abruptly, or a completely different musical genre starts playing. The lights flash purple. The* **Waitress**' *demeanor shifts and she/they become entirely unlike a waitress; she/they become a* **Maenad***. The distinction between the two should be clear in terms of affect, and personality.*

Maenad   Welcome to the temple of Dionysus. Let us honor this food as an offering to our great god.

Maenad *closes her/their eyes and raises her/their hands high in the air. As the characters speak the hymn, it can overlap with the other text. The poetry gets more ecstatic and erratic as it goes on.*

Maenad   Come. Raise your hands and sing for Dionysus! Dionysus I call, loud-sounding and divine, fanatic God, a two-fold shape is yours—

Medea   Your various names I sing, O first-born, thrice-begotten, Bacchic king—

Caeneus   How do you know this poem?

Maenad   Silence! Sing with us.

Medea   Rural, ineffable, two-formed—

Caeneus (*to* **Nestor**)   What are they doing?

Maenad   Obscure, two-horned, ivy crowned, pure—

Nestor   I'm . . . not sure. But it seems kind of fun.

Caeneus   No, it doesn't.

Medea   Bull-faced, and martial, bearer of the vine—

Nestor (*excitedly*)   Endured with counsel prudent and divine!

Caeneus   Nestor, what are you—

Maenad   Triennial, whom the leaves of vine adorn!

Medea   Of Zeus and Semele occultly born—

Nestor   Immortal daemon! Hear my voice!

Medea   Give me in blameless plenty to REJOICE!

Caeneus   And listen, gracious, to my mystic prayer!

The **Maenad** *laughs with ecstatic delight.*

Caeneus   I don't even know where that came from, I—

Maenad   Yes! I knew you'd get the spirit eventually! Celebrate Dionysus, celebrate the temple!

Caeneus   The temple . . . Tiresias told me I should come to the temple! Can you help m—

Maenad   Shhhh. All of that will come in time. (*slowly, deliberately*) First, eat, and be sure to saaaavor the taste in your mouth.

Maenad *exits.*

Caeneus   We need to leave this place. It's completely creepy.

Medea   It's a little . . . unusual, but the food's good, at least!

Nestor   Yes, these blueberry pancakes are incredible.

Caeneus   But, I swear I had never heard that poem before, how did I know the w—

The **Waitress** *returns, interrupting them.*

Waitress   How are you all enjoying your meal?

Caeneus   It's fine, but what was that all about earlier?

Waitress   What do you mean?

Caeneus   The stuff with your voice, and the poem, and the—

Waitress (*shrugs*)   Just having some fun, that's all.

Medea   I loved it; it was a great show of your magical talent.

Waitress   Oh, you think so? (*blushes a little*) It's just all flash, really . . .

Medea   It was lovely.

Charge between the **Medea** *and* **Waitress**.

Waitress   Thank you, dear.

Nestor   Is this really a temple? It looks more like a diner.

Medea   Wasn't that evident from the whole "temple of Dionysus" speech?

Waitress   Define "temple."

Nestor   A place to worship?

Waitress   Oh. (*smiles*) Then yes. We are here to worship Dionysus.

The lighting flashes purple again, but she/they do not go fully into her/their **Maenad** *routine. Caeneus and Nestor are alarmed by the flash of purple, but* **Medea** *and* **Waitress** *seem to treat it as normal.*

Nestor   If this place is a temple, who are you?

Medea   Isn't that evident? They're a Dionysian Priestess.

Waitress   Ooh, you're very perceptive.

The **Waitress** *does some kind of small flirtatious action here, like twirling their hair or lightly touching Medea's shoulder.*

Medea   Well, I try.

Caeneus   Why am I supposed to be here?

Waitress   Oh, I nearly forgot! There's a message here for you! From the management.

Caeneus   The . . . management? Do you mean Dionysus?

Waitress   Hold on just one second, dear.

Waitress *walks over to the counter, leans across it, and grabs what looks like an order from above the grill. She/they look at it contemplatively.*

Waitress   Hmmm.

Caeneus   What does it say?

Waitress   It says . . . (*clears throat*) "DEAL WITH UR REAL PROBLEMS & START ACTUALLY LISTENING TO ORACLES INSTEAD OF ASSUMING WHAT YR WHOLE CONVO WILL BE." Signed, D.

Caeneus *blinks a few times.*

Caeneus   Excuse me?

Medea (*laughs*)   Seems pretty clear to me.

Nestor   That was all on that little note?

Waitress (*raising her hands*)   Thank you, Dionysus, for your great knowledge!

Caeneus   What are my "real problems"? Transformation isn't a real problem?

Waitress   It's real, but not a problem. How about you deal with your issues with your boyfriend here?

Nestor (*to* **Caeneus**)   Boyfriend? Is that what we are?

Caeneus   I, uh—

Waitress   You haven't even had *that* conversation? (*shakes head*) Oof. Worse than I thought.

Caeneus (*aside to* **Nestor**)   We'll talk about it later.

Medea (*to the* **Waitress**)   They're ridiculous, huh?

Waitress   Hey, don't you talk about how ridiculous *they* are for not communicating, when you're engaged to a man you hate.

Pause. **Medea** *looks flustered.*

Medea   I don't *hate* him!

Waitress   Uh huh. (*back to Caeneus*) And what about Dotia?

Pause.

Caeneus (*icily*)   What about her?

Nestor   Who is *that?*

Caeneus   We'll talk about it later.

Waitress   You won't be able to avoid her forever.

Caeneus   I left that all behind.

Waitress   Maybe it's time to reassess.

Pause. There is a shift in the **Waitress**' *demeanor, where she/they become once again overly perky.*

Waitress   Would you all like your check?

Caeneus   Yes, *please.*

Medea   Would it be alright if I stuck around a little to talk to you about your magic?

Waitress   Oh, of course! I'd be flattered. Just one second while I grab the check for these two.

Waitress *grabs the check from behind the counter. She/they put it on the table, and instead of a traditional check, all it says is "GET OUT" in big red letters. Purple flicker again.*

Nestor   Uhhh . . . thank you?

Waitress   Of course. Come back any time. Just not too soon, alright?

Caeneus   Okthanksbye!

Scene 17

Nestor *and* **Caeneus** *quickly exit the Temple, feeling alarmed.* **Medea** *has stayed in The Temple to keep talking to* **Waitress***. There is a long pause before anyone talks; they are both still trying to process what has just happened.*

Caeneus   Hey, I think we need to talk about some of the things the waitress said.

Nestor   That's for sure. For example, who is *Dotia*?

Caeneus   Don't say it like that; it's not what you think. She's my sister.

Pause.

Nestor   You have a sister?

Caeneus   Yes. And two brothers.

Nestor   You've never mentioned a sister before.

Caeneus   We have a . . . strained relationship.

Nestor   I guess so, if you wrote her out of your story.

Caeneus   I *didn't* write her out of the story. Can you stop telling me what my story is?

Pause.

Nestor   Is this about what I said after Tiresias? I've been thinking a lot about that conversation since we had it, and . . . I shouldn't have told you how to feel.

Caeneus   Yes, you shouldn't have. Next time, just listen to me.

Nestor   I *was* listening to you. I just didn't know it'd be upsetting to you. You're not always the most direct.

Caeneus   What do you mean? Of course I'm direct.

Nestor   Like, you didn't tell me about your sister at all until JUST now, you didn't tell me about your transformation, you don't ever want to tell me about your life although I've been asking about it since we met . . . It's hard for me to know if something will upset you if you don't let me in.

Caeneus   I let you in more than I ever have anyone else.

Nestor   That doesn't mean you're being open, Caeneus. And just because I didn't understand your feelings doesn't mean I wasn't listening to you. To be honest, I was just . . . jealous.

Caeneus   *You* were jealous of *me*? Why?

Nestor   Because I've never seen a god, never had anything big happen to me . . . I've just been here, staying the course. And if I had met a god, I'd tell the whole world about it.

Pause.

Nestor   But that doesn't mean you have to feel the same way I do, and I was wrong to assume that you would.

Caeneus   Thank you, I appreciate that. And I guess you're right, I could stand to . . . maybe be more open.

Nestor   I appreciate that. In that case . . . do you want to tell me about your sister?

Caeneus *pauses for a second, uncomfortable, but pushes through.*

Caeneus   Her name is Dotia. We . . . always had problems growing up; she was always trying to get me to be something I wasn't, because she thought of us as having some kind of sisterly bond.

Nestor   That sounds difficult.

Caeneus   I used to hate her.

Nestor   Do you still?

Caeneus   I don't know. I don't even know her. It's been forever since I left, but the idea of seeing her again terrifies me . . . I hadn't even thought of her until the waitress brought her up again.

Nestor   Do you think that—

Caeneus   I don't want to talk about this anymore.

Pause. **Nestor** *sighs, a little frustrated, but lets it go.*

Nestor   We don't have to, then.

Caeneus   Thank you.

Nestor   But you do have to let me in, sometimes, if we want to have a good relationship.

Caeneus   You're right. (*Pause*) Are we in a relationship?

Nestor   Well . . . the waitress seemed to think so.

Caeneus   What did you . . . think about that?

Nestor *and* **Caeneus** *are both like awkward, nervous teenagers again as they have this conversation.*

Nestor   I liked it. How did you feel about it?

Caeneus   I liked it too. (*Pause*) Would that make me your boyfriend?

Nestor   If you want to be.

Caeneus (*grins*)   Absolutely. I've never been called that by anyone before. Feels sort of exciting.

Nestor   I think so, too.

Caeneus *and* **Nestor** *kiss.*

Caeneus   So, what does that mean to you?

Nestor   What do you mean?

Caeneus   What do you want that to look like?

Pause.

Nestor   I'm . . . not sure, actually.

Caeneus   Me neither. To be honest, I didn't think that was something I could be. Or have.

Nestor   Same here.

Caeneus   What, really?

Nestor   Not at all.

Caeneus   But what about all those stories? Zeus and Ganymede, Apollo and Hyacinth . . . at least they give you an idea it's possible. None of those characters have their gender transformed.

Nestor   Yes, but they're hardly good models. All of them end with some tragedy, just like you said before.

Pause.

Caeneus   You heard that?

Nestor   Why wouldn't I have heard that?

Caeneus   I'm not sure, I just thought I was . . . talking to myself.

Nestor   You were right, you know. We can try to write a new story. And what do you want that story to look like?

Caeneus   Well, it's important to me that I'm able to have my own life. Travel, do hero things . . .

Nestor   Of course.

Caeneus   But I want you to keep being part of it.

Nestor   Same to you.

Caeneus   What about you? What do you want?

Pause.

Nestor   . . . no one's ever asked me that question before.

Caeneus Really? You seem like you have so much relationship experience.

Nestor Experience with flings, maybe. Nah, usually when I'm with someone, I just let them make all the decisions.

Caeneus Why?

Nestor (*shrugs*) It's easier that way, to just . . . go along with whatever someone else wants.

Caeneus But what *you* want matters to me.

Pause, as **Nestor** *thinks about it.*

Nestor I want to feel . . . central.

Caeneus Not like a side character?

Nestor Exactly. And I want us to talk and work out problems we have. I want you to be open with me about what you're feeling. Sometimes you can be a little closed off—

Caeneus I'm not closed off!

Nestor We've known each other for ages, and I just found out you had a sister today.

Caeneus . . . okay, true. I'm not trying to be closed off, I'm just . . . afraid to be open sometimes.

Nestor What can I do to make you feel less afraid?

Caeneus Just . . . try not to make assumptions. Everyone's been making assumptions about who I am my whole life.

Nestor I can work on that.

Caeneus *and* **Nestor** *smile at each other.*

Caeneus Thank you, Nestor. I think we can do this.

Nestor I think we can, too.

Scene 18

Later, on the decks while **Caeneus** *is working, a raven shows up on the Argo. This raven is represented by a puppet or by raven-like body movement, and is controlled or represented by* **Tiresias**. *It has a gold band on its wing.*

Sailor A raven . . . ? (*pause*) A raven! A messenger from the god, Apollo. Captain!!

Jason *enters, confused, looking like he's just woken up from a nap.*

Jason What's going on?

Sailor There's a raven here.

Jason   Ah! A message for me, I'm sure.

Tiresias   No, actually.

Jason   What?

Tiresias   The message is for Caeneus.

Jason   Who in the depths of Tartarus is Caeneus?

Caeneus   Caeneus sheepishly raises his hand, reminding the captain—once again—of his existence.

Jason   Oh. Right. Well, good luck with your message. (*pause*) Jason turns to leave, and tries to shove down his jealousy.

Jason exits. **Caeneus** *approaches the raven, looking confused and a little frightened.*

Tiresias   Hello, traveler. I come to you as an incarnation of the great Tiresias!

Tiresias *poses, or poses as much as is possible for the raven puppet.*

Caeneus (*less excitedly*)   Oh. Them.

Tiresias   Are you not excited to hear a message from the great oracle?

Caeneus   Honestly, last time I didn't get much out of it.

Tiresias (*ruffles feathers*)   That sounds like a personal problem. You should take the waitress' advice, to listen to oracles.

Caeneus *stops and pauses.*

Caeneus   Right. I remember. But to be honest, last time I found Tiresias' advice to be . . . unhelpful. Upsetting, actually.

Tiresias   Sometimes the truth is upsetting.

Caeneus   It wasn't *that.*

Tiresias   Then what?

Caeneus   It was that you acted like I was crazy for not wanting to change back!

Tiresias   The raven looks a little taken aback; or as taken aback as a raven can look.

Pause.

Tiresias   It wasn't that I thought you were crazy, I was just . . . surprised.

Caeneus   I came all that way to see you! You could at least listen to what I wanted.

Pause.

Tiresias   I had just never thought of what you said before. For me, transformation is all about change. The magic of a shifting self! Don't you feel the same way?

Caeneus   No. I don't.

Tiresias   . . . well, it's not like you listened to my *other* advice.

Caeneus   About what?

Tiresias   I gave you plenty of messages, and you just ignored them! About being in love, about your sister, about the men on your ship. Those were all true, weren't they?

Caeneus   . . . well, yes.

Tiresias   Do you know how frustrating it is to be telling *divine truth* but have the other person not even let you finish your thought?

Caeneus   No . . .

Tiresias   Well, it's terrible. I was a little less excited to have a conversation about transformation after that. And then you called me self-centered! Do you know how much I have to focus on others *all day*, delving into their minds and soaking up all their energy for the few minutes they meet with me? Do you know how exhausting that is?

Pause.

Caeneus   No, actually.

Tiresias   I'm self-*protective*. I'm not self-*centered*.

Caeneus (*pause*)   You're right. I'm sorry. I didn't know you could hear that.

Tiresias   Never underestimate what a powerful oracle can hear! Oh, and, thanks.

Pause.

Caeneus   But you shouldn't have assumed I wanted the same things.

Tiresias   Who are you to think you know more than an oracle?

Caeneus   Who are you to think you're the expert on *me?*

Tiresias   I know all.

Caeneus   But I know *me*. Everyone's been telling me what I am my whole life, I thought you would be different.

Pause. This strikes a chord with **Tiresias**.

Tiresias   Tiresias isn't used to giving apologies. Somewhere in the world, they bite their lip and squirm, but finally spit it out.
I'm . . . sorry.

Caeneus   Thank you.

Tiresias   I think we got off on the wrong foot. I'd like to start over. If you ever find yourself in Thebes again, let's talk, and I'll try not to make any assumptions.

Caeneus   Will I have to schedule with your secretary?

Tiresias (*laughs*)   No. This'll be off the clock.

Caeneus   Thank you, Tiresias.

Pause.

Tiresias   Suddenly! The raven raises their wing, absolutely not to distract from this sentimentality, of course not, they would never do that, but because . . . a message is coming!

Caeneus   Oh no.

The raven moves erratically, mirroring **Tiresias** *from the former scene. Awkward pause, as the raven and* **Tiresias** *stay locked with their hand above their head.*

Tiresias   There are centaurs destroying Thessaly.

Caeneus   What?! That's my homet—

Tiresias   I'm aware. Soon, your captain will get an assignment to fight these centaurs, and if you choose to join him, you will get what you wish.

Caeneus   What I wish, what do you m—

Tiresias   The raven dramatically flies away!

Tiresias*, and the raven, exit.*

Caeneus (*sighs*)   They're alarmingly consistent for a shapeshifter.

Pause.

Sailor *rushes in, and knocks on the door to* **Jason***'s quarters.* **Jason** *peers out, looking unamused.*

Jason   What do you want?

Sailor   Sir, we've gotten an assignment to fight centaurs in Thessaly!

Caeneus   That was fast.

Jason   Why should I care?

Sailor   Well, there's quite a decent amount of money involved, plus plenty of heroic accolades . . .

Jason   Aha! Now I'm interested.

Scene 19

Caeneus   After that, Jason decides to go to Thessaly, just as Tiresias had predicted. Caeneus is extremely afraid to go back, to see his hometown, and most of all . . . to see his family.

Caeneus *and the crew arrive in Thessaly. This scene should visually mirror the first scene, but some things are ever so slightly and subtly different.*

Caeneus   Caeneus arrives in Thessaly, and it's . . . just as he left it. It's been years, but he can still see the houses he remembered, the temples his family used to take him to . . . All of this is the same, but everything inside of him is different. This stirs a familiar fear that this journey he's gone through won't be seen by anyone else—that others here will see him just as he was, that Poseidon's magic only works on strangers. He remembers the reason he left here in the first place.

Caeneus *pauses, takes in his surroundings, and wanders through Thessaly.*

Caeneus   After the battle with the centaurs, Caeneus goes walking through this home he left behind, and a pull that's almost magnetic takes him back to his old home. He doesn't know why; maybe part of him wants to see her.

Dotia *enters from their home.*

Caeneus   And he does. Caeneus sees Dotia, and immediately recognizes her—she's older now, but she's essentially the same sister he remembered.

Dotia   Dotia recognizes this person, but she's not sure why she does . . . he looks like family. Polyphemus?

Caeneus   No, you've got the wrong guy.

Dotia   Oh, I'm sorry. You look just like my brother.

Pause. **Caeneus** *smiles at the comparison.*

Caeneus   Really?

Dotia   Yes. It's uncanny, actually . . .

Caeneus (*laughing nervously*)   Aha, strange coincidence.

Dotia *looks at* **Caeneus** *closely, trying to place him.*

Dotia   I swear we've met before . . . What's your name?

Pause.

Caeneus   Caeneus.

Dotia   Caeneus . . . that's so close to my sister's name, Caen*is*.

Caeneus *pauses.*

Caeneus   There's a reason for that. Caenis was a name people used to call me.

Dotia *connects the dots, and she looks at* **Caeneus** *with disbelief.*

Dotia   It's you. (*pause*) I thought you were dead.

After another pause, **Dotia** *hugs* **Caeneus**, *with tears in her eyes. Pause in this moment before Dotia speaks and breaks away from him.*

Dotia   You should have been more creative with your new name.

Caeneus *laughs, and* **Dotia** *smiles.*

Caeneus   Probably.

Dotia's *soft demeanor shifts.*

Dotia   Why did you leave?

Caeneus   I felt like I had to.

Dotia   You didn't *have* to. You could have stayed here, we could have gotten used to your new name, we—

Caeneus   I lived my whole *life* here sitting by the sea, watching the sailors at work, knowing the ocean could take me somewhere else but always just staying stuck. I couldn't live like that anymore.

Dotia   You could have at least told us you were leaving!

Pause.

Caeneus   I was afraid.

Dotia   Of what?

Caeneus   That you would try to stop me.

Pause. **Dotia** *is upset, but says nothing. She knows he's right.*

Dotia   I waited for you *every day*. People had written you off as dead, but I still held out hope that you would come back. Staring out at the sea wondering where in the world you were, if you were at the bottom of the ocean . . . !

Pause. **Caeneus** *takes a deep breath.*

Caeneus   I'm sorry.

Dotia   Sorry isn't enough.

Pause in this moment, feeling all the tension between them.

Dotia   And you came back, and you're . . . you're not the person you were when you left.

Caeneus   No, I'm not, and thank the gods for that.

Dotia   I don't know how to deal with that, Caen . . .
There is a moment where she falters; she doesn't know what name ending to use.
When she says the next line, it feels strange in her mouth.
Caeneus.

Caeneus   Caeneus winces; he can feel her hesitation, and it's almost like a physical blow.

Caeneus & Dotia   There is an ocean between them.

Pause.

Caeneus   I could never be what you wanted me to be, right?

Dotia   That's not what I'm angry about.

Caeneus   You just wanted a sister—

Dotia   I just wanted you to be honest with me! If you knew this all along, why didn't you say anything?

Caeneus   I tried to, you just didn't hear.

Dotia   You could have just said 'Dotia, I don't want to be a girl, I don't want to be your sister'. Why did you lie to me?

Caeneus   I wasn't lying—

Dotia   Yes, you were. You didn't even say you were unhappy.

Caeneus   I tried to let you know in the ways I could. I was a *kid*!

Dotia   I thought I knew who you were, and now you're a stranger.

Caeneus   The person you thought I was is a stranger to me. I wasn't even a person then. I was just . . . whatever everyone told me I was. How can you even say you knew me?

Dotia   Of course I knew you—

Caeneus   You just wanted a mirror.

Dotia   Mirror? What does *that* mean?

Caeneus   You wanted to find someone like you. But we're not the same, and we never were, even before my transformation.

Dotia *is silent. Long, uncomfortable pause.*

Caeneus   I understand it. I traveled all the way to Thebes and thought I'd find someone like me, but I just got more confused.

Dotia   What?

Caeneus   Right, you don't know about that. I went and met with the oracle, Tiresias, because I heard they had been transformed.

Dotia   You met Tiresias?! That must have been incredible.

Caeneus (*laughs*)   It was something, alright.

Pause.

Caeneus   See? We can get to know each other again.

Dotia   We can, but I'm not just going to . . . instantly trust you. All that time, you could have at least written me a letter.

Caeneus   I wouldn't have even known where to start.

Dotia   At least an incomplete story would be better than *nothing*.

Caeneus   I don't know what to say except I'm sorry, Dotia. I can tell you what my life is like now, if you want.

Dotia (*sighs*)   Sure. Why not.

Scene 20

Later. **Dotia** *and* **Caeneus** *at the docks.*

Caeneus   Now, I want to tell you about the beginning, when I was transformed.

Dotia   It happened here?

Caeneus   Yes. Right there is where I saw Poseidon. He asked me what I wanted, and I made a wish to be seen as a man, and to become a hero.

Dotia   I look out here all the time, and it feels so . . . everyday. It's hard to believe that a god was here.

Caeneus   The sea's always powerful, we just don't think about it.

Dotia   I guess that's true, but I didn't know *that* was a thing it could do.

Caeneus (*laughs*)   Me neither.

Dotia   When did you decide to leave Thessaly?

Caeneus   Soon after. I landed on the shore, and a sailor told me he was going to the Argo! I didn't know when I'd ever get a chance like that again, and . . .

Dotia   And?

Caeneus   And I was afraid that the wish wouldn't work in Thessaly.

Pause. **Dotia** *is tense, but says nothing in response.*

Dotia   How do you feel, being here?

Caeneus   A little . . . afraid.

Dotia   Why?

Caeneus   I haven't been in the water since I was transformed.

Dotia   You haven't been in any water at all?

Caeneus   No.

Dotia (*wrinkling her nose*)   You've showered, right?

Caeneus   What?! Of course! I meant I haven't been *immersed* in water. I'm . . . afraid of what will happen if I am.

Dotia   What do you think would happen?

Pause. **Caeneus** *has trouble admitting this vulnerability to her.*

Caeneus   I'm afraid of being changed back.

Dotia   But you said before that you made a wish to be transformed. And this time, your wish is that you want to stay the same. So . . . why would you be changed?

Caeneus   . . . I don't know, actually. When I went to see the oracle Tiresias they said most people who are transformed go back, or transform in some way again, and I'm worried about that happening to me.

Dotia   They don't know everything.

Caeneus   They're an oracle.

Dotia   Yes, but they're still a *person.* And people can be wrong.

Caeneus   I guess so, but they seemed like they knew everything about my life.

Dotia   So what?

Caeneus   They had all this secret knowledge, they knew all these feelings I had that I hadn't told anyone—

Dotia   And they can still be wrong.

Caeneus   But they weren't wrong about anything else—

Dotia   I thought I knew everything about you, and I was wrong!

Pause. **Caeneus** *is unsure of how to react to her admitting it.*

Dotia   I was wrong. And they can be wrong, too.

Pause.

Dotia   I just wanted to find someone like me, and I was so caught up in that I couldn't see you. (*Pause*) Maybe they were doing the same thing.

Pause.

Dotia   I'm sorry, Caeneus.

Caeneus (*sighs*)   I am, too. I'm sorry you never got a sister.

Dotia (*laughs*)   Are you kidding? I have a brother who's alive. That means more to me than any imaginary sister.

Pause. This takes **Caeneus** *by surprise. It's the words he's been waiting for her to say.*

Caeneus   Thank you, Dotia.

Dotia   And this time, you're staying.

Pause.

Dotia   You are staying, right?

Caeneus   Here, in Thessaly?

Dotia   That's why you came back, isn't it?

Caeneus   . . . No, Dotia. It's not.

Pause.

Dotia   Dotia is hurt, but says nothing. Again.

Caeneus   There is a long, uncomfortable pause between the two of them. Once again, *someone* (*annoyed glance at* **Dotia**) has misinterpreted the situation.

Dotia   Long, uncomfortable pause. Once again, *someone* (*annoyed glance at* **Caeneus**) hasn't given all the information.

Caeneus   I wanted to help with the centaurs, I never intended to stay forever. I have a life outside of here now.

Dotia   I thought since you came back, you had realized it was a mistake to leave.

Caeneus   It *wasn't* a mistake to leave. It was a mistake not to tell you, but leaving wasn't a mistake.

Pause.

Dotia   It's not so terrible here, you know.

Caeneus   I know it isn't. But I spent my whole life here.

Dotia   So have I.

Caeneus   It's not the same.

Dotia   Why not?

Caeneus   Because I hated it here!

Dotia   Because people didn't see who you were. It'd be different if you lived here now, after your wish—

Caeneus   I don't care if it'd be different, I don't want to live here.

Dotia *inhales sharply. Tension.*

Caeneus   I'll write letters to you, and I'll visit. But I can't stay.

Dotia   I don't want to lose you again.

Caeneus   You won't.

Dotia   How do you know? All it takes is one terrible storm, or one false move fighting a monster, and you're dead for good.

Pause.

Caeneus   But anything could happen here, too. And I need to live my life the way I want, not the way *you* want.

Dotia (*sighs*)   Fine. Have fun on your great adventure. I look forward to getting a letter maybe once a year, if you remember.

Dotia *exits.*

Nestor *enters, and as he does, almost bumps into* **Dotia**.

Nestor   Oh, sorry.

Dotia   No, it's fine, I just have to get out of here, my brother's really—

Nestor You're Dotia.

Dotia . . . yes. And who in Tartarus are you?

Nestor I'm Nestor. I'm a sailor on Jason's ship, and I'm Caeneus' boyfriend.

Dotia Boyfriend? (*sighs and shakes her head*) Another thing he didn't tell me.

Nestor I'm not surprised. He's a little . . . withholding.

Dotia *laughs and softens a little.*

Dotia That's an understatement! And he's always been like that, too! When we were kids, he'd just sit by the docks and stare at the water, and I'd ask, what are you staring at? And he'd just say, nothing, and that'd be it. End of conversation. I just wanted him to let me in, I was so lonely all the time, and he was there, and I—sorry, I don't know you at all, I don't know why I'm telling you all this.

Nestor No, no, you're totally right. I've had almost the exact same experience, actually—water and all. The inner workings of Caeneus are an enigma.

Dotia It's like everything's about his inner angst, his Great Journey as a Hero, and there's no one else in the damn world.

Nestor It's a protective mechanism. In my opinion.

Dotia What do you mean?

Nestor Some people are lonely and seek connection anywhere they can find it—on a hero's boat, in a sibling . . . I'm like that, and I suspect from what you just said, you are, too. But when Caeneus is lonely, he just crawls up inside himself and blocks everybody out.

Dotia And then blames everyone else for things he didn't tell them.

Nestor That's the downside, yes.

Dotia I *really* thought he was going to stay in Thessaly. I'm going to be so lonely without anyone I know here. Everyone else I know has left.

Nestor You could leave, too.

Dotia No, I definitely couldn't.

Nestor You could. Ever heard of Gerenia?

Dotia Who?

Nestor (*laughs*) Exactly. It's my hometown. But, I left it years ago and haven't been back since. I write my family letters and they tell me the latest homegrown gossip, but that's about it. I left because I was stuck in a rut and kept doing the same things, kinda like you.

Dotia But there's a key difference; you're a man, and I'm not.

Nestor By a certain definition of "man," I guess. But, I see your point. What about Medea, though?

Dotia (*brightening*)   Oh my Gods, she's so incredible! Are you a fan of her, too?

Nestor   I don't know if I'd say "fan," but she's a friend of mine. Kind of . . . difficult, but nice enough.

Dotia   No way. You KNOW her?

Nestor   She's on the ship with us.

Dotia   Ohhhh my Gods.

Nestor (*unfazed*)   Yep, she's famous. But anyway, my point is, she did that, too.

Dotia   But, *I* don't have a famous fiancée to run off with.

Nestor (*sarcastically*)   Guys who like girls are a dime a dozen on Jason's ship, I'll keep an eye out for one for you.

Dotia chuckles.

Dotia   I don't think that's what I'm interested in. I'm not really into men in that way.

Something clicks for **Nestor**.

Nestor   Is that part of why you feel lonely?

Dotia   Absolutely.

Nestor   Not being interested in women was always part of why I felt lonely, too. But there's more out there in the world than what's here. Maybe you should go to that island with that . . . famous poet lady.

Dotia (*laughs*)   Oh, come on now!

Nestor   I'm serious! Why not?

Dotia   That's just not something I would do, that's all. I'm not an adventurous spirit.

Nestor   I don't feel like an adventurous spirit, either.

Dotia   You're a sailor!

Nestor   Yeah, but it's just something to do. I don't have some passionate higher calling and inner drive like Caeneus feels he does. It's what I like about him, actually, that he has such a clear sense of who he is all the time. But, being a sailor lets me meet new people, see new places, it's a steady career . . . (*shrugs*) I'm just saying, think about it.

Dotia   I'll think about it.

Pause.

Dotia   It's nice to hear you talk about what you like about Caeneus, because he really frustrates me so much. I spent so much time worried about whether he was dead or not, I forgot how grating he can be.

Nestor   Maybe it's for the best he's not staying here, then.

Dotia   I just don't want to lose him again.

Nestor   You won't. There's no way I'm going to let him forget you. Caeneus might forget there's other people in the world, but I won't.

Dotia   Thanks, Nestor. You're a sweet person.

Nestor   Nah, I just pay attention, that's all.

Dotia   I'm glad Caeneus is going to be with you, at least.

Caeneus *walks up to* **Dotia** *and* **Nestor** *on the shore.*

Caeneus   Hey, Nestor and . . . Dotia??

Nestor   Hi Caeneus! We were just talking.

Dotia (*with irritation*)   Hi, Caeneus.

Caeneus   Can I talk with you both?

Dotia   Actually, I was just leaving. Goodbye.

Dotia *exits.* **Nestor** *looks startled.* **Caeneus** *sighs.*

Scene 21

Nestor   Soooo . . . that was your sister.

Caeneus   Sure was!

Nestor   She seems . . .

Caeneus   Difficult? Bullheaded? Irritating?

Nestor   I was going to say smart, introspective . . . We had a lovely conversation, actually.

Caeneus   I'm glad YOU did. I still don't know how to talk to her, even after all these years.

Nestor   It starts with listening, just like you told me.

Caeneus   I have been listening, I just . . . she wants me to constantly be someone else!

Nestor   You both need to listen to each other. She needs to accept you need to go on your own journey, but you need to see that she feels really lonely, Caeneus, and I KNOW you have experience with that.

Caeneus *winces.*

Caeneus   I do, but . . .

Nestor   But?

Caeneus   I don't know. I never thought I'd have to deal with this again. I thought when I left here, I was starting a whole new life. That I'd never have to see anyone I knew from before ever again. That I was just Caeneus now. I didn't want to have to explain it to her, and . . . I didn't want to have to disappoint her when she saw who I am now.

Nestor   I don't know that she's disappointed by that. Maybe by you not having any contact with her since then, but—

Caeneus   Ugh, can we talk about something else? Being here is kind of overwhelming to me.

Nestor   In Thessaly?

Caeneus   No, here, on this beach. On this dock. I was telling Dotia earlier that this is where my transformation happened.

Nestor   Right here?

Caeneus   Yeah. I was talking to her about how terrified I am to go into the water here again.

Nestor   Terrified? Didn't the ocean give you a gift?

Caeneus   Yes, but . . . it's more complicated than that. I'm afraid it can take that gift away, too.

Pause.

Caeneus   And . . . it wasn't just a casual swim when I went out there. I almost drowned before I saw Poseidon. (*pause*) To be honest, part of me . . . wanted to.

Pause.

Nestor   You tried to kill yourself?

Caeneus   Not exactly? But . . . I did think as I went into the water that if I died, that wouldn't be . . . the worst thing.

Nestor (*unsure of how to respond*)   Caeneus, I—

Caeneus   I don't feel that way anymore! Just at the time.

Pause.

Nestor   Have you ever told anyone that before?

Caeneus   . . . no, actually.

Nestor   Thank you for letting me be the first to hear it.

Caeneus   You're the first to hear a lot of things.

Caeneus *and* **Nestor** *smile at each other. Some small physical affection is shared between the two of them—holding hands or a light kiss. Pause in this moment.*

Caeneus   I think I'm ready to tell you the whole story.

Nestor (*excited, and surprised*)   Really?

Caeneus   Not just bits and pieces, but the whole thing.

Nestor (*smiles*)   Let's hear it, then.

Caeneus   Nestor sits on the ground in front of Caeneus, like someone about to listen to a bard. Caeneus stands confident, for the first time.

My whole life I wanted to be something other than what people saw me as. I read all sorts of stories about heroes like Jason—

Nestor chuckles.

Caeneus   I know, I know, but I wanted to be just like him. Like all of them. Not just in terms of the incredible things they did, but how they looked, how they were looked at . . . Everyone knew exactly who they were. And I was always stuck just fantasizing, imagining, dreaming, while everyone told me I was something else. I hated it; I spent more time in my mind, in these stories, than in the world. I would just sit out here by the docks for hours and daydream about where I could go, what I could do if I was some great hero. And it got to a point where . . . I couldn't live like that anymore. Something had to move. So I walked into the water, and I thought, whatever's going to come to me is at least something new.

And I felt the water fill my lungs and enter every part of me; I could feel the pressure suffocating me, crushing me. I could feel my consciousness slipping away from me. And that was when I saw the god.

Nestor   What did he look like?

Caeneus   Not like . . . anything, really. Not anything recognizable. Not like the old man he looks like in statues. More like if the sea itself assembled into something almost human-shaped. And his voice, it echoed through every part of my body. He asked: what do you want? And I told him my most impossible dream, something I had never told anyone before. That I wanted to be seen as a man, and to be a hero.

Nestor   And he granted it.

Caeneus   He granted it, and Jason's crew was hiring. I knew I had to take this chance, and that I couldn't come back here to Thessaly. I was too afraid of what my family might say, what they might think. Plus, when was I ever gonna get a chance to be on Jason's crew again? I realized I didn't want to die at all, I just wanted to live differently. That's when you met me.

Nestor   It was that soon after you were transformed that we met?

Caeneus   Yes.

Nestor   I never knew that.

Caeneus   But . . . that's it. And you know the rest from there. Go on adventures, meet someone, fall in love . . .

Nestor *smiles, holds* **Caeneus**'*hand.*

Nestor   Thank you for telling me the rest, though.

Caeneus   I've never told the entire story to someone before.

Nestor   How do you feel after telling it?

Pause.

Caeneus   Like I want to go back in the water.

Nestor   Are you sure? You just said how afraid you were.

Caeneus   Poseidon only transformed me because I wanted it. Why would he turn me back? I am afraid, but I need to do this. (*pause*) Do you want to come with me?

Nestor   Yes, I do.

Caeneus   Caeneus and Nestor hold hands, and step into the ocean. There is a pause as they wait . . .

Long pause.

Caeneus   Nothing happens, because of course nothing happens.

Caeneus *smiles, and starts to cry a little.*

Nestor   Are you alright?

Caeneus   Never been better.

Standing there in the water, **Nestor** *and* **Caeneus** *kiss passionately.*

Scene 22

Elsewhere in Thessaly. **Dotia** *and* **Medea** *are both wandering, searching for something, although they don't know what.* **Dotia** *bumps into* **Medea**.

Medea   Hey, watch it!

Dotia   Oh, I'm sorry!

Pause. **Dotia** *recognizes her.*

Dotia   Are you Medea?

Medea   That's what they tell me.

Dotia   Oh, wow. I've always been a big fan.

Medea   Yes, everyone's a big fan of Jason.

Dotia   No, I don't care for that man. I'm a fan of you.

Pause.

Medea   Me? Why?

Dotia   I think it's inspiring that you went out on your own, and left behind all that you knew. My brother did that, too. I don't know if I could.

Medea   Why couldn't you?

Dotia (*shrugs*)   It was never bad enough to leave.

Medea   I understand that.

Dotia   It's like . . . maybe nothing really excites you about the place, but nothing really upsets you, either. So you just stay.

Medea   Yes! Exactly.

Pause. Charge between them.

Dotia   It's funny, having Caeneus back and seeing all that he's done makes me feel more adventurous, myself.

Medea   Caeneus is your brother?

Dotia   Yes.

Medea   He's a good friend of mine, actually. It's nice to meet you . . . ?

Dotia   Oh, sorry! Where are my manners. I'm Dotia.

Medea   Lovely to meet you, Dotia. (*Pause*) You said you're feeling more adventurous. Where would you like to go?

Dotia   I have no idea. I've never been anywhere, that's part of the problem.

Pause, as **Medea** *contemplates.*

Medea   I've always wanted to go to Lemnos.

Dotia   Lemnos? What's that?

Medea   An island with no men.

Dotia (*laughs*)   What? You're joking.

Medea   I'm completely serious!

Pause.

Dotia   That sounds amazing.

Medea   I think so, too.

Charge between them.

Dotia   I've been surrounded by my brothers my whole life, except . . . no, no except. (*Shakes head*) I can't imagine what it'd be like to be around only women.

Medea   Me neither.

Dotia   Huh.

Medea *and* **Dotia** *sit near each other, so close they're almost touching.*

Medea   Yeah, huh. (*pause*) I wanted to go there, but Jason didn't want to.

Dotia (*laughs*)   I could see why he wouldn't want to.

Medea   It'd be nice to have my own ship, to be able to go wherever I want, to not have to worry about him at all.

Dotia   You could have that.

Medea   Where would I get a ship?

Dotia (*shrugs*)   I'm sure you could figure it out. You could always take over the Argo.

Medea   Oh, stop. I couldn't do that.

Dotia   I'm serious! You basically run that ship anyway.

Medea   But everybody knows the story is "Jason and the Argonauts."

Dotia   So? Why can't you change it?

Medea   I just can't. The story's set. That's fate.

Dotia   My brother changed his story.

Medea   Caeneus? How?

Dotia   Yes. He was "supposed" to be my sister, but he's not.

Medea   He never told me that.

Dotia   Oh, sorry. I just assumed everyone knew. I used to call Caeneus a different name, and thought of him as my sister when he lived here, but then he was transformed.

Medea   *That's* why he wanted to meet with Tiresias.

Dotia   I assume so.

Medea   Huh. That's . . . unexpected. I wonder why he didn't tell me.

Dotia   *You* wonder why he didn't tell *you?* I knew him my whole life, and I just found out when the Argo got here.

Medea   Fair enough. He can be so secretive.

Dotia   Oh my Gods, right? I was just talking to Nestor about that! Actually, he was the one telling me how I should go on my own adventure. And I'm . . . considering it, honestly. You could do something unexpected, too, you know.

Medea   I already did. I left Colchis.

Dotia   Exactly, so you could do it again. You're "supposed" to be Jason's fiancee, but who says you have to be?

Medea   Let's see—fans, Jason, bards . . .

Dotia (*shrugs*)   And they'll learn to change the stories they tell.

Medea   What are you saying? That I should just commandeer the Argo and go to Lemnos?

Dotia   And that I could go with you.

Medea   What about Thessaly?

Dotia   What about it? I was waiting for Caeneus to come back, and he did. It's not like he's staying, so why should I?

Charge between the two of them. They are very close.

Medea   And you want to go to Lemnos.

Dotia   Yes.

Medea   With me?

Dotia   Yes.

Medea   And you're excited about that idea.

Dotia   Yes! More than anything!

Medea   And I'm going to leave Jason behind!

Dotia   Absolutely you are!

Medea   And I'm going to kiss you!

Dotia   Yes! Kiss me right now!

Medea *smiles, and they kiss, passionately. Pause.*

Dotia   Now go talk to Jason.

Medea   Oh, Gods, right. *Him.*

Dotia   You have to say something to him.

Medea   I will.

Dotia   Good!

Medea   I'll go right now!

Medea *turns to leave, then glances back.*

Medea   . . . one last kiss, before I go?

Dotia   Of course.

They kiss again.

Medea   They smile at each other, and then Medea leaves, excited and a little terrified at all the newness. She heads off to write a different ending.

Dotia   Dotia stays there, but she stays for the last time.

Scene 23

Quite some time later. **Dotia** *goes to the Argo, stepping foot in* **Caeneus'** *world for the first time. She looks around and takes it all in. Something within her has shifted; small, and imperceptible, but huge.* **Nestor** *is at the front of the ship.*

Nestor   Oh, hey, Dotia.

Dotia   Hey, Nestor. Is my brother here?

Nestor   Yeah, I'll go get him.

Sound of a door closing. Door open as **Nestor** *reenters with* **Caeneus***.*

Caeneus   Dotia? I thought you'd never want to talk to me again.

Dotia   What? I'd never . . . you're my brother.

Caeneus   I'm glad to see you.

Dotia   I'm glad to see you, too. (*Pause, then quietly so the sailors don't hear*) I've decided to go to Lemnos with Medea.

Pause. **Dotia** *is excited about her new revelation;* **Caeneus** *is confused.*

Caeneus   Lemnos? The island where they killed all the men?

Dotia   Yes! Isn't that exciting?

Caeneus   I'd never want to go there.

Dotia   Well, I'd never want to BE a man.

Caeneus   Okay, fair. Will you send me a postcard at least?

Dotia   I will. And I'll hear from you too, right?

Caeneus   Yes. This time, I definitely will. I hope you have a wonderful journey, just like I have.

Dotia   You're so supportive. That's why you've always been my favorite brother.

Caeneus (*laughs*)   Just don't tell Polyphemus that!

Caeneus *and* **Dotia** *hug, sweetly.*

Dotia   Promise I'll see you again.

Caeneus   I promise.

Dotia   Good. And if you and the Argonauts are ever going by Lemnos, be sure to stop for me.

Caeneus (*laughs*)   You think they'll let us in?

Dotia   I'll make sure they do. I'll say "hey, my brother's on that ship!"

Caeneus   Have a wonderful adventure, Dotia.

Dotia   You, too.

Dotia *and* **Caeneus** *hold hands, and smile at each other.*

This gentle sibling moment is interrupted by the sound of commotion, a fight on the ship, general bedlam. **Sailor** *drops to the ground, asleep.* **Nestor** *and* **Caeneus** *look at each other with confusion.* **Dotia** *is grinning.* **Medea** *enters, grinning from ear to ear.*

Medea   Meet your new captain!

Caeneus   What happened to Jason?!

Medea   Fast asleep. He'll wake up sometime this century, I imagine. A little trick the maenad taught me. We're headed for Lemnos now!

Dotia *cheers with excitement.* **Caeneus** *and* **Nestor** *look at each other.*

Caeneus   I . . . think this is your adventure, Medea.

Medea   But what will you do if you're not on the Argo?

Dotia   You and Nestor can take our father's ship, Caeneus. No one's using it now.

Caeneus (*sincerely, tenderly, as though accepting a dear and unexpected gift*)   Thank you, Dotia.

Nestor   Safe travels.

Medea   Safe travels, Caeneus. I'll be sure to write.

They linger there for a moment, smiling at each other, and then part ways.

Nestor *walks up to* **Caeneus** *and smiles.*

Nestor   So you told me the beginning of your story, but tell me the end.

Caeneus   I don't know how to tell it yet. In fact, I don't think stories end at all. They just keep going, as long as someone remembers.

Somewhere else, **Tiresias** *is talking to their posse, telling the story.* **Nestor** *is older, now, as he recalls.*

Tiresias   . . . and that was the first time I met Caeneus . . .

Nestor   Nothing is more firmly in my mind than the story of him, the most handsome man I had ever seen . . .

Dotia & Nestor   He was the greatest hero who ever lived—

Medea   He was much better than Jason or Hercules—

Dotia   My brother.

Nestor   My love.

Medea & Tiresias   My friend.

All   Caeneus.

Caeneus   Onto other adventures.

THE END, *or maybe not the end. Maybe the play starts again and just keeps on going.*

The "Ruhls" of Play: Mythical and Real Currents in Tyler Rocio Ecoña's *Unfair Advantage*

Joshua Bastian Cole-Kurz

Tyler Rocio Ecoña engages with complex themes of identity, intersectionality, and systemic injustice, weaving these into narratives that blend poetic theatricality with rich cultural specificity. Despite having a modest online footprint as an emerging playwright, their work has sparked significant discourse. A pointed example is a TERF tweet by someone named "Karen Orlando," dismissing *Unfair Advantage* as "anti-woman garbage." This comment unintentionally encapsulates the fearful, self-justified hostility Ecoña critiques in the play. The name itself—Karen Orlando—feels almost too fitting, with "Karen" signifying not just entitlement and privilege but also a certain brand of aggressive, vocal self-interest and performative victimhood. Meanwhile, "Orlando" conjures themes of transformation and fluidity, reminiscent of Sarah Ruhl's adaptation of Virginia Woolf's 1928 novel. *Orlando* follows a young Elizabethan nobleman who inexplicably transforms into a woman, navigating centuries of societal change without significant aging, offering a rich interplay of identity and time.

This inadvertent evocation of *Orlando* is a serendipitous connection, as Ecoña's theatrical style shares much with Ruhl's, particularly in its embrace of the surreal and mythic to explore transformation and identity. Ruhl's characters inhabit what she calls "the real world and also a suspended state" (Lahr 2008). Ecoña similarly bridges the mundane and the extraordinary, infusing their narratives with elements of Quechua folklore and the traditional Andean cosmology central to their Native heritage. In *Unfair Advantage*, they reimagine mythic traditions within the modern context of systemic oppression faced by trans athletes. The Sea Witch character exemplifies this synthesis, blending Western mythologies—such as a childhood fascination with *The Little Mermaid*—with the animistic spirit world of the Andes, where the natural and supernatural merge into an inseparable worldview. This grounding in Andean spirituality contrasts with the classical Western myths Ruhl sometimes explores, creating a unique cultural and geographic framework—a deeply localized, yet equally profound engagement with the metaphysical, emphasizing the fluid interconnectedness of the natural and spiritual realms in Quechua traditions.

Ecoña's narratives integrate folkloric elements and poetic structures to critique societal norms while offering spaces for empowerment and self-invention. Their work reflects themes of resilience and transformation, establishing Ecoña as a vital voice in contemporary theater, extending the legacy of playwrights like Ruhl while forging a distinct path shaped by their own identity. Like Ruhl's complex female characters who defy traditional gender roles, Ecoña crafts nuanced, diverse characters challenging societal expectations. Skillfully blending realism and fantasy, Ecoña can be seen as a Peruvian-American counterpart to Ruhl, exploring similar themes through a fresh, contemporary lens.

Unfair Advantage engages with longstanding debates about trans inclusion in sports while offering a sharp critique of the conditions that create the struggles trans athletes face today. By examining the intersections of identity, gender, and competition— particularly in the context of NCAA swimming—the play underscores both the historical persistence of these issues and their pressing relevance. It highlights the urgent implications in the current discourse on fairness, representation, and inclusion in athletics, offering a theatrical lens through which to address contemporary debates, which are often quite densely litigious.

While leaning heavily into fantastical visual elements, the play's plot and dialogue are only loosely fictionalized. The story centers on Mia Jonas, a trans woman competing for an unnamed Ivy League school—clearly inspired by the real-life Lia Thomas, a former swimmer for Penn and the first openly trans athlete to win an NCAA Division I National Championship for women's swimming, before being barred from the sport by World Aquatics. Mia, like Lia, faces the intense challenges of navigating a cisnormative, hyper-competitive collegiate sports environment, all while being relentlessly targeted by TERF competitors who claim to be defending the sanctity of "women's space" in the name of fairness.

Although revolving around Mia and her dilemma, the play shifts focus to the lives of other individuals who are influenced by the ongoing public gender policing surrounding her eligibility to compete. The narrative critiques systemic barriers in sports—particularly transphobia—while delving into themes of belonging, resilience, safety, and self-discovery. Key characters include Jamie, Mia's primary rival both in competition and as an outspoken anti-trans "real" women's sports advocate, and Bell, a Black cis woman who has been Jamie's friend since childhood. Another subplot features Jamie's nonbinary sibling, Ash, and their best friend Iguana, who create a safe space in an online gaming environment. Ash, who has a growing fascination with Mia, reflects on what they could have become as an athlete had they not left a girls' soccer team.

What's particularly effective about the dynamic between Ash and Mia is not simply their shared experience as trans people facing transphobic resistance from those around them, including family and teammates, but the striking lack of progress over the years. While the play highlights Mia as a target, focusing on the specific challenges she faces in women's NCAA swimming, it's important to note that Lia Thomas, though the first openly trans woman in women's NCAA swimming, was not the first or only openly trans athlete. Many others came before or alongside her, competing in high school, NCAA, and even professional sports, all of them igniting debates about fairness in gender-segregated events. Preceding Thomas, Schuyler Bailar made waves in 2015 at Harvard as the first openly transgender Division I athlete to compete on a men's swim team. Five years before Bailar, Kye Allums became one of the first openly transgender NCAA athletes, playing basketball at George Washington University. While Thomas was competing, Andraya Yearwood gained attention in high school track, Mack Beggs made headlines in high school wrestling, CeCé Telfer won an NCAA Division II title, Patricio Manuel was the first openly transgender man to compete in professional boxing, and Chris Mosier, a triathlete and advocate, was the first openly transgender man to represent Team USA.

Over the last fifteen years, the visibility of trans athletes has made significant strides. However, nearly thirty years ago, when I too was an NCAA Division I trans athlete, there were no clear precedents for openly trans competitors. It would be another decade and a half before people like Allums or Mosier entered the scene. I competed in a gender-segregated sport, fencing, where the saber event was initially only offered for men. Many women pursued saber regardless and competed on men's teams until it became officially recognized as a women's sport. While the event was added to the Olympic Games in 2004, it had been gaining momentum earlier, with the first Women's World Championship in saber held in 1999. At my university, which only offered a women's fencing program despite its Division I status, I became the captain of the school's inaugural women's saber team. Yet, like Ash in *Unfair Advantage*, I ultimately didn't want to be part of a women's team at all. I walked away from competitive athletics, and it wasn't until 15 years later that I saw someone share an experience like mine.

The number of openly transgender athletes competing in the NCAA remains very small, making up less than 0.002% of all college athletes (Buzinski 2024). Currently, there are only approximately ten, reflecting a continued underrepresentation in collegiate sports. Policy changes have shifted recently, with the NCAA updating its guidelines in 2022 to delegate eligibility criteria to the governing bodies of individual sports. This shift allows each sport to determine how transgender athletes can participate. These developments exist within a broader context of state laws and federal litigation. Some states have implemented restrictions that require athletes to compete based on their sex assigned at birth, as was the case with Mack Beggs in Texas, where he was mandated to compete in the girls' wrestling division. In contrast, other states have enacted policies that allow athletes to participate in sports consistent with their gender identity. Federal rules regarding transgender athletes and Title IX protections are still being debated and are expected to face legal challenges before finalization.

Although the number of trans athletes remains as small today as it was during my own experience three decades ago, Ecoña's *Unfair Advantage* doesn't limit itself to depicting a singular narrative of one trans athlete enduring targeted oppression. Instead, the play delves into the larger dynamics at work, critiquing TERF aggression while examining the underlying motivations for such hostility—though never legitimizing or empathizing with it. Jamie, Mia's primary antagonist, is given a backstory that is referred to but not explicitly depicted, involving a traumatic assault during her middle school years. While enough time has passed to provide some distance from the event, it lingers as a source of recurring triggers. Similar to high-profile TERFs like J.K. Rowling, Jamie conflates her personal trauma with the presence of assigned male bodies in spaces she deems safe. Ecoña juxtaposes this with Mia's own sense of vulnerability—both characters feel unsafe almost constantly, but they navigate their displacement and trauma in markedly different ways. Jamie weaponizes her fear, directing it outward against those with less power, while Mia channels hers into advocacy, stating, "I shaped it into patience, but it wore me down [. . .] smooth into seaglass (436).

Mia, like many real-life trans athletes thrust into the public eye, feels a moral obligation to advocate—not just for herself but for those who might follow. Ecoña uses this narrative as a dual critique, simultaneously addressing and clarifying the contentious debates surrounding trans inclusion in athletics while exposing them as bad-faith arguments designed to undermine the legitimacy of trans people. Through Ash, Ecoña delivers a striking message to both Mia and the audience: while advocacy is essential, it is unsustainable if driven solely by relentless self-sacrifice. Mia expresses repeatedly that she is only able to continue her advocacy because she has become desensitized to the pain of being hurt, describing the feeling as "like a dead nerve" (426). In one pivotal moment, Ash confronts Mia, demanding, "is this ALL YOU DO?" (436).

Ecoña further enriches the play with a visually and emotionally evocative portrayal of the internet and social media landscapes that many trans people navigate daily. This is shown through Mia's advocacy on social media and Ash's and Iguana's use of fantasy gaming as forms of trans world-building and affirmation. The stage directions offer designers expansive opportunities to imagine online gaming spaces as vibrant arenas for self-expression and trans identity. Like Sarah Ruhl's stagecraft, which allows for poetic interpretation and abstraction, Ecoña invites fluidity in how these virtual worlds are rendered. In this way, the online world becomes both a narrative device and a metaphorical escape, offering sanctuaries for trans and non-binary people like Ash and Iguana. Ecoña emphasizes the potential of digital spaces as empowering, immersive environments where individuals can express their authentic selves in ways often denied in the physical world.

Gaming, with its limitless avatar creation and communal interaction, serves as a medium for exploring identity and agency, while social media—specifically its notorious comment sections—plays a crucial role in online advocacy. This mirrors real-world experiences like those of Chris Mosier, who regularly uses his platform to respond to hate mail. While Mosier's resilience is admirable, it's exhausting to witness, and Ecoña captures this duality through Ash's perspective in the play. Early in my process of writing this piece, I considered reaching out to trans athletes like Mosier to gain insight into professional and collegiate sports. I also briefly explored connecting with Schuyler Bailar through a mutual contact. I mentioned that this project was inspired by Lia Thomas, focusing on NCAA/Ivy League swimming, but my contact warned me about the overwhelming number of similar requests Bailar receives: "If you DM him, he may never see it." Ultimately, I abandoned the idea, understanding Bailar's burden and resonating with Ash's sentiment toward Mia: "Do you ever rest?" (436).

This exhaustion also surfaces in the play's focus on Bell, a Black cisgender athlete whose journey becomes central to the emotional and political stakes. Torn between loyalty to her team and a deep sense of justice, Bell hesitates to publicly support Mia, a decision that places her at the heart of the play's main conflict. The pivotal moment comes when the NCAA implements mandatory blood tests to measure testosterone levels, aiming to impose an "acceptable" standard. Bell's disqualification following the revelation of elevated testosterone levels poignantly underscores the racialized biases inherent in the TERF-driven ideal of the "perfect biological woman." As Bell recognizes, she is 'not the first Black female athlete this has happened to' (432). This moment sharply exposes the systemic discrimination that disproportionately harms Black women in sports, making Bell the unintended casualty of this ideological "turf war."

While the weight of this systemic oppression hangs over Bell's journey, Ecoña infuses the play with moments of surreal beauty, blending documentary realism with Ruhlian theatricality. This is exemplified in the penultimate scene, a striking underwater nightmare that intensifies Jamie's emotional journey with, or as, the Sea Witch. Both surreal and disturbing, the nightmare sequence propels the play into a hopeful epilogue, one set in a grounded, realistic space where trans athletes—especially youth—are fully embraced. In this inclusive realm, Ecoña offers the solace and affirmation that marginalized athletes have long been denied in the "real" world. However, the juxtaposition between this hopeful conclusion and the fantastical nightmare it follows highlights the necessity of such created spaces in response to exclusionary practices masquerading as fairness. The warmth of the epilogue underscores this bittersweet reality: the need to invent spaces where difference is celebrated, such as an all-inclusive kids' sports team, reveals the failures of existing structures to accommodate or affirm diverse identities.

This theme of creating alternative realities is central to the play, and like Ash and Iguana's collaborative online game, it acts as a metaphor for constructing new spaces in which marginalized identities can thrive. Ecoña's abstract theatrical framework echoes this act of creation, positioning the play itself as a constructed world where possibilities previously denied to these characters can be explored. This final juxtaposition between the imagined and the actual world encapsulates both the resilience of trans athletes and the profound inequities they navigate. Ultimately, the play challenges us to reflect on the importance of building inclusive environments in the real world—spaces where humanity is valued, and differences are celebrated. Ecoña's work, like the game(s) within it, insists on the necessity of such spaces, even as it mourns the fact that, in our current reality, such inclusion remains largely aspirational.

References

Buzinski, Jim. 2024. "There are 510,000 NCAA Athletes. Less than 0.002% are Trans." *OutSports*, December 18. https://www.outsports.com/2024/12/18/24105317/ncaa-trans-athletes-hearing-charlie-baker-richard-durbin/.

"Folkslore: Breaking the Binary." 2023. Philadelphia Women's Theatre Festival. https://www.phillywomenstheatrefest.org/festival2023.

Jamieson, Carlos. 2022. "The Current Landscape for Transgender Student Athletes." Education Commission of the States, October 11. https://www.ecs.org/the-current-landscape-for-transgender-student-athletes/.

Lahr, John. 2008. "Surreal Life." *New Yorker*, March 10. https://www.newyorker.com/magazine/2008/03/17/surreal-life.

McEwan, Gordon F. 2008. *The Incas: New Perspectives*. New York: W.W. Norton.

Orlando, Karen. 2024. X Post. June 5, 10:00 AM. https://x.com/KarenFOrlando/status/1798354270036910218.

Passantino, Fiona. 2020. "Inca Creation Myth." *YouTube*, June 22. https://youtu.be/rr8pFiL1F WI?si=eQ977FcLxjwPMm0j

"The Religion of the Quechua " *Overview Of World Religions*. PHILTAR. http://www.philtar.ac.uk/encyclopedia/latam/quech.html.

"Tyler Rocio Ecoña." *New Play Exchange*. https://newplayexchange.org/users/72379/tyler-rocio-econa.

Webb, Karleigh. 2024. "Trans Women Are Still Eligible to Compete in All NCAA College Sports. For Now." *OutSports*, December 16. https://www.outsports.com/2024/12/16/24105154/trans-athletes-women-ncaa-college-sports-rules/.

Unfair Advantage

Tyler Rocio Ecoña

Cast

Mia   she/her, 20, white trans woman making history competing on an Ivy League women's swim team. Bell's teammate.

Jamie   she/her, 21, non-Black POC, cis woman. Mia's opponent and a legacy student from a different Ivy League.

Ash   they/them, 18, non-Black POC, AFAB nonbinary student, Jamie's sibling who lives a double life on the Internet. Iguana's best friend.

Bell   she/her, 21, Black cis woman on athletic scholarship at Mia's school. Technically Jamie's opponent, but also her close childhood friend.

Michelle   she/her, 40s-50s, non-Black POC, cis woman. Jamie & Ash's mother.

Iguana   they/them, 19, nonbinary BIPOC, Ash's best Internet friend.

Doubling

Bell / Reporter / Nurse
Michelle / TERF / User 1
Jamie / User 2
Ash / User 3 / Coach
Iguana / Announcer / Swimmer / User 4
Sea Witch could be played by either **Jamie** or **Michelle**. Collaborators are encouraged to play with the thematic implications of each option.

Setting

A world much like ours, around Spring of 2023

Notes

[quoted words and phrases] represent things implied or thought, but not spoken.
/ indicates dialogue interrupted by another character
TERF stands for Trans Exclusionary Radical Feminist

There is room for creativity when representing swim sequences, as well as characters using the Internet. Digital planets as home. Swimming as dance, or an act of transformation. Water as a medium: surrounding, propelling forward, freeing from the pull of gravity.

Special thanks to Savannah Reich, the UArts community, and everyone at the Philadelphia Women's Theatre Festival for their encouragement and loving support of this work in its earliest, most vulnerable iterations.

1.

A tournament pool at a collegiate swim competition. Cheers and chants from a crowd in the background.

Announcer   And here come our swimmers for the women's final collegiate 500-yard freestyle! Jamie Landon's held the championship record for five years straight now, but three-time Ivy League champion Mia Jonas was the top qualifier in the preliminaries and she's bound to make history today . . .

*Swimmers **Mia** and **Jamie** by the pool. **Mia** is visibly nervous. **Jamie**, confident, takes it all in.*

A whistle blows. They kneel at the edge of the pool.

Three, two, one-

BUZZER.

Swimmers dive in and freestyle for their lives.

It's visceral. Energizing.

Announcer   Looks like Jamie's in the lead, but Mia's just behind . . . and here we go, another lap!

*As they swim, **Mia** and **Jamie** inch just ahead of each other every now and then.*

*From the bleachers emerges an angry **TERF** holding up a banner that reads "Keep Men out of Women's Sports"*

Announcer   Regardless of which side you're on, you can really feel the tension in the room . . . Some protestors from this morning have even taken to the stands.

The race is in its final laps. They gulp for air, ration breaths, keep moving

Announcer   AAANDDD we're in the last lap!

*As everyone reaches the end of the pool, **Mia** swims out before **Jamie** again.*

Mia *touches the ledge first.*

Announcer   And it's Jonas in the lead! Mia Jonas, winner of this year's 500-yard freestyle!

The race is over. Everyone resurfaces.

*From the audience, as **Mia** reaches to shake her opponents' hands: a loud, resounding "BOOOOOO"*

2.

*A different pool. **Jamie** swims laps and laps. **Bell** stands above her, stopwatch in hand, whistle in her mouth. **Jamie** swims with a furiousness. Barely breathes. Feels the strain and keeps pushing.*

Eventually, **Bell** *taps the watch and blows the whistle.* **Jamie** *comes up for air, heaving*

Bell (*showing her the watch*)   Wow! New personal best!

Jamie   I guess it's fine.

Bell   "It's fine"? You just beat your own record twice!

Jamie   Championship selections are in a month. I need to get faster.

Bell   You've <u>been</u> getting faster

Jamie   Stop. It's not good enough. So stop.

Bell *puts two and two together*

Bell   You're trying to beat <u>her</u> personal best?

Jamie   Shut up.

Bell   Alright, I wanna get my laps in too.

She takes off her watch and whistle and dangles them in front of **Jamie**, *who won't let go of her mood.*

Bell   Jamie.

Jamie   You don't get it.

Bell   ???

Jamie (*doing pronoun mental gymnastics*)   You're on [his team]
You're on the same team as [him]
Mia
You don't think the whole thing's unfair?

Bell   If I said yes would you time my laps for me

Jamie   Could you be serious for like <u>one</u> second please?

Bell   Sure. If Mia's so illegitimate, why are you even bothered? Focus on your own personal best. That's the one thing you're completely in control of.

Jamie   If your teammate didn't have the highest personal best out of everyone here, I wouldn't have to push myself to the brink to try and beat it.

Bell   . . .

Jamie   There's a reason men's and women's sports were separated in the first place. It's biology.

Bell   Okay. Maybe you're right, maybe they made the wrong call letting Mia compete. But it doesn't change much now, does it? We can still improve ourselves (*teasing, in an old friend way*)
Stop being such a sore loser and appreciate how far you've come!

Jamie (*indeed sore*)   My sportsmanship is <u>not</u> the problem here Bell.

Bell   Okay, I was kidding? But really, what else can we do about it?

Jamie   Not much . . . I guess

She accepts defeat. They switch off, with **Bell** *in the pool and* **Jamie** *timing her.*

3.

Mia *sits for an interview with a* **Reporter**.

Reporter   Now, Mia, you've been setting record times this season! You've come out as number one in women's swim consistently. But back in the day, as a man, you were ranked in the 400s. How does it feel to have switched over from men's swimming to women's?

Mia   Well, it's great to be out and participating as my most authentic self. Back then it was a very awkward experience, being a woman in a men's competition . . . in men's locker rooms, surrounded by men, knowing I was different but inevitably compared to them . . . it was uncomfortable. I started withdrawing. Can you blame me for not doing my best?

Reporter   Some people might think going from #400 in men's to #1 in women's is a bit telling.

Mia   My highest rank before transition was #11. Plenty of cis girls go from a hundreds-place to top 10 in the span of a few years and no one calls that unfair. They call it getting good.

Reporter   . . .

Mia   Transitioning has been amazing for my mental health. I'm feeling confident in my swimming and my personal relationships. So yeah, I'm doing better sports-wise. But not for the reasons everyone thinks.

Reporter   So, you aren't worried about any unfair advantage over biological women?

Mia   Well, I play by the rules. I've transitioned with two years and counting of hormone replacement therapy, testosterone blockers. The NCAA approves. I'm in compliance, so I'm allowed to compete.

Reporter   And what do you have to say to all your critics out there?

Mia   I try not to pay attention to transphobes. I don't feel like proving my worth to people who don't see my humanity

Reporter   Right, thank you Mia. (*To the camera*) More at eight.

Commercial break.

Reporter   Alright, you can leave.

The interview disappears. **Mia** *wanders for a bit.*

She sees something on the horizon. A tinge of blue-green.

The distant cry of a gull. It's beautiful . . . she gazes into it.

Then a car speeds by, almost knocking her over.

She snaps out of it; the far-away land disappears.

Mia *exits.*

4.

Michelle *sets food on a dining table. Silverware is laid out already. She squints at a certain fork and tries to straighten it out. Not quite right. She tries again. Not quite right. She swats at it. The fork clatters to the floor.*

Michelle   ASHLEY!

Ash   WHAAT

Michelle   COME HELP SET THE DINNER TABLE.

Ash   UGGGHHHHHHH

Loud, heavy stomping from upstairs, all the way down. **Ash** *appears before her.*

Ash   What.

Michelle   Fix your attitude. I asked you to arrange these forks neatly and you made a mess. Look!

Ash   That wasn't me!

Michelle   If you hadn't arranged them all crooked it wouldn't have fallen like that.

Ash   What the fuck? I literally HEARD you chuck it onto the floor–

Michelle   Stop CURSING and help me set this table for your sister

Ash   FINE

They get another fork and haphazardly toss it towards the table. Just go with wherever it lands.

Michelle   Ashley!

Ash   My name is Ash. How many times do I have to–

Michelle   Dear Lord, will you GROW UP?

Ash I told you I'm not fucking hungry, I don't wanna sit down for this stupid little pity party for my loser sister	**Michelle** What kind of behavior is this? You're eighteen years old! Your sister trained for years just to lose to a <u>man</u> in a dress

Ash   Ohhh. That's what this is about. God, you are such a

A knock on the door.

Michelle   You better zip it and behave tonight.

Ash *rolls their eyes.* **Michelle** *opens the door.* **Jamie** *enters carrying a bottle of . . . something.*

Michelle   Jamieeeee! It's so good to see you sweetie!

Jamie   Hi. I brought (*looks at the label*) whatever this is.

They all sit down to eat.

Michelle   So, how's school?

Jamie   It's fine.

Michelle   Did you see my text about your midterm grades

Jamie   No

Michelle   You never answer your messages. What would happen if the house burned down and someone messaged you about it? Would you answer that?

Jamie   Probably not. Is Dad still in France? On that retreat with

Ash   With his "work buddies", which is code for his secretary? Yes.

Michelle *kicks* **Ash** *under the table.* **Ash** *rolls their eyes and gets up.*

Michelle   Where do you think you're going?

Ash   I'm getting water.

Jamie   What, is the drink I brought not gluten free and woke enough for you?

Ash   This is why I don't bring people over.

While getting water, **Ash** *spots an envelope on the counter under a stack of papers.*

Ash   What's this?

Michelle   Oh, I was just saving it.

Ash   It's addressed to me. You were hiding my mail?

Jamie   Somehow that's unsurprising

Ash *begins to open the envelope.*

Michelle   What is it?

Ash   None of your business.

Michelle (*snatching it*)   As long as you live here, your business is my business.

Ash   Ma!

Michelle   No business at the dinner table. You'll get it back later.

They settle down. Forks and knives clatter.

Jamie   I think I'm gonna quit swim.

Michelle   What?!

Ash   Oh my god here goes.

Michelle   Why would you say that? What about your scholarship!

Jamie   Who cares? Dad has money. He even offered to loan me some.

Michelle   Oh so you answer **his** messages then?

Ash   Jamie, stop trying to give her a heart attack, it's not funny.

Jamie   I'm not joking.

Silence.

Jamie   I'm not doing a bit to see her reaction. I'm serious.

Ash   . . . Just cause you lost this one tournament?

Jamie   It's not that

Michelle   She didn't lose, she got second place.

Ash   Can't be perfect so why bother! Wow, that's the most privileged thing I've ever heard.

Jamie   It's not that

Michelle   Why would you throw away all your hard work?

Ash   What, are you gonna move back here and work at Subway with me?

Michelle (*to* **Ash**)   I told you to quit that nasty wage job.

Jamie   I had to change with a MAN in the locker room and no one seemed to give a SHIT.

Jamie *dissolves into tears, which becomes panic.* **Michelle** *fawns over her.* **Ash** *seizes the opportunity, snatches their letter back and retreats upstairs.*

Jamie   Ma, you <u>know</u> what I've been through to get this far. You saw me go through it.
I mean, not to mention how many hours I've spent in that pool working my ass off to even qualify for this scholarship. Of course I don't want to quit. I just need to.

Michelle   Why?

Jamie   My nightmares are back.

Michelle   But your medicine, I thought–

Jamie   It doesn't work anymore. I'm just too stressed.

Michelle   There has to be another way. And you know I always hated pills. These Western doctors just pump you full of chemicals instead of treating what's actually wrong. Listen, your auntie has this traditional healer

Jamie   No, I've made up my mind.

He's in there so often during competitions. In the locker rooms. The showers.
And the feeling of being watched just
it brings back too much. I just can't be in that environment anymore, I'm sorry.

Michelle   You can't be the only one who's uncomfortable. You're going to give up
like that, without even a fight?

Jamie   I'm already fighting just to stay afloat! To keep my grades up, to even get a
good night's fucking sleep! I'm tired, Ma.

. . .

Swimming was the one thing in my life afterwards that made me feel whole. I could
focus on my strength, and my girls cheered me on and I could finally just let
everything go. Out of all places, I thought an all-girls team would be my safest
place.

Michelle   There has to be <u>something</u> you could do

Jamie   It's TOO FUCKING LATE. That space is gone now! It's just- gone.

She feels her world shrink. **Michelle** *attempts to comfort her.*

Michelle   Jamie. I can't stand by and watch this happen again. You aren't the one
that needs to go. And you shouldn't be forced to.

A thought emerges.

Michelle   I can make it better. Just let me try. Ok?

5.

Ash *in their room, on a Discord call with friends. The Internet is an ocean teeming
with life. Links and messages sparkle in saltwater. In this realm, they're allowed to
take up space.*

Ash   Iguana!

Iguana   Ash! You're finally on. Everyone's wondering where you've been.

Ash   Just dealing with stuff. It's fine. What'd I miss lately?

Iguana   Oh you're gonna freak when you see this.

Iguana *sends a link.* **Ash** *clicks it.*

Ash   No way. They updated Siren Call?! UNANNOUNCED???

Iguana   Yes dude, hop on right now!!

Ash *immediately logs into a nautical-themed game server.* **Iguana**'*s character greets
them.*

Ash   No fucking way. THE NEW SKINS ARE CUSTOMIZABLE?! Holy shit I'm
doing mine right now.

A dazzling array of clothing and accessory options float down from the heavens, surrounding them. Mermaid tails, sailor getups, fancy hats and boots.

Ash (*marveling*)   They removed the boundaries between male and female styles.

Iguana   Ahh I forgot about that part. Here I was, excited about the actual story updates

Ash   Okay but this is huge! Before this, most clothing and hairstyles were restricted to one of two genders- now I can wear whatever I want!

Iguana   But the mermaid characters already had a gender-neutral option, didn't they?

Ash   But this is different. Mine is human.

. . .

Remember that one show where that alien came to Earth and fell in love and was all like "I don't subscribe to your male-or-female concepts of gender, cause I'm inhuman and unnatural and not from this planet!" and the human love interest was like "how could I possibly love such a monstrous creature that isn't a man or a woman?!"

Iguana   Yeah, which one?

Ash   Exactly! That's like, so often the case! But this . . .

They have chosen their character's outfit. Stylish. Euphoric. They are transformed.

Ash   In this realm, no one confuses me for something I'm not. My character is human and outside the binary.

Iguana (*showing off their outfit*)   Mine is a two-spirit healer. You know we had trans medicine people in like every Pre-Columbian tribal nation?

From the outside world, **Jamie**'s *muffled yelling.*

Jamie   Yeah well TOO FUCKING LATE.

Iguana   You still there Ash?

Ash   Yeah, sorry. My sister lost this huge competition so she and my mom are like screaming downstairs

Iguana   Hmm. I feel a 'your mom' joke coming on here but I think I'm gonna let it go. Sorry.

Ash   Alright, enough dress-up. I'm stuck on this level, help me beat it?

Iguana   OF COURSE

The two of them gear up for a monstrous boss battle.

Meanwhile, downstairs:

6.

Michelle *is on the phone.*

Michelle   Hey, Jackson! How have you been? How are the kids? And the wife! Ah, it's been a minute since I've seen Barbara.
. . .
Yes, yes we should absolutely get together soon. Mhm. Yeah.
. . .
I'm doing fine. Just fine. The girls are <u>fine</u>. How are things over at Harvard? Yes, I heard about your recent promotion, congratulations!
. . .
Wonderful. You know, I always found you to be a man of <u>science</u>. So well-read.
. . .
Listen
I've been doing some reading myself. About collegiate swim guidelines.
It's just been on my mind ever since that big race. Nothing personal. I'm concerned about <u>fairness</u>. You know I want everyone to have a fighting chance.

I was reading this article the other day, and it got me thinking about the science behind it all- why are the guidelines for transgender athletes so vague? All it says is "one year of testosterone-suppressing medication" if they want to compete in women's sport. Nothing else. But are you even measuring actual levels? Wouldn't that be more accurate? You don't even know what testosterone levels these athletes have and they're just allowed free reign?
. . .
What if that's the only reason this "Mia" person is suddenly at the top of the ranks? What if their testosterone is off the charts and you don't even know it? All you have is a slip of paper claiming they've been taking these meds.
I'm just saying.
I just want it to be <u>fair.</u>
. . .
Yeah. I agree, the Board would benefit from hearing my concern. Thank you for listening.

7.

Mia *online, doing a Q&A event.*

Mia   Hello! I'm Mia Jonas, the first trans girl to be on a collegiate women's sports team . . . ever. I'll be answering select questions posted to this thread for the next 2 hours. Ask me anything!

She waits for a bit, scrolls. Comments and questions pop up instantly. She selects a few to read out loud.

User 1   Mia, what do you think about the current state of America, knowing there's doctors allowing kids to be permanently "transed" before they can even–

Mia *clicks away. The question disappears.*

User 2   How do you feel knowing you're single handedly destroying women's spaces and setting us back 100 years of suffrage—

She clicks away again. Another question pops up.

User 3   Hello Ms. Jonas. Casual sports fan here. I mean no disrespect, I'm just curious. What was your motivation to transition in the middle of your college career? Did you really feel so trapped in your natural body that you had to?

Mia   Oh we're getting right into it! Okay then.

She thinks.

Mia   I've never enjoyed the expression 'trapped in your body'. Cis people just eat up that Hollywood tearjerker drama and trans kids grow up with that narrative over our heads. I've trained too hard to hate my body at all! As an athlete, you learn to care for yourself with determination.
I loved myself enough to transition. Trans bodies as a site of love. That's the wave I want to start.

She hits send. Reply posted! Next question.

Mia (*scrolling through the comments*)   Alright, next question.

User 4   Hi Mia! HUGE fan. Dumb question but here goes. What piece of media do you attribute to your queer awakening?

Mia   Ooh that's a fun one. Well . . . my friends go on and on about the one about the girl in Feudal China who dresses up as a soldier and goes to war in place of her father. But that one just didn't do it for me.
I think mine was the one about the Mermaid.
Y'know?

The far-away place approaches. **Mia** *floats. Everything is chlorine blue.*

Mia   It was just something about seeing this graceful girl sing about not fitting in anywhere, magically transforming her body and happily navigating a brand- new world that made little-kid me go crazyy for a while. Never thought I'd actually get there. That I'd be just like her.

It becomes an ocean, agleam with life. Fish and coral, waves and birds. **Mia** *relishes in a dream realized.*

Mia   Mia Jonas, professional fucking mermaid.

Meanwhile, in a different corner of the internet, **Ash** *and* **Iguana** *play their video game together. Their characters battle an evil* **Sea Witch***: the ultra-powerful final boss of the game. This could be a fight scene, a dance sequence, or something else entirely.*

Sea Witch   Impersonators! How DARE you ransack the house of Triton?!

She casts curses, spills magic ink, and bewitches the energy out of both of them.

Ash *and* **Iguana** *fight back diligently, dodging blows and dealing damage.*

Ash   FUUUCK! She's gaining XP back with her final form, Iguana back me up here!

Iguana   I GOTCHU BRO! I MEAN SIBLING!

Ash   Take THAT! And THAT!

They fight hard, but the **Sea Witch** *redirects and overcomes* **Iguana**'s **character instead.**

Ash   NOOOO!!!

Iguana   OHH GOD SHE'S GOT ME

Ash   DON'T GIVE UP YET!

Iguana   GAHHH I DON'T KNOW IF I'M GONNA MAKE IT! HERE, TAKE MY LOOT . . .

Ash *scrambles to do something, anything, as* **Iguana**'s *character dies dramatically.*

Ash   It's over, she's too strong . . . I can't do it without you, dude.

Sea Witch   Giving up, are we? Well then. You must face the next quest on your own.
. . .
Open the letter.

An envelope lands before **Ash**'s *feet. They pick it up.*

Sea Witch   No way out of this one.

They try to throw the envelope, but it floats, suspended in mid-water. **Ash** *sinks like a heavy seashell.* **Mia** *notices and swims over. She holds out her hand, but it's too late. The fantasy has shattered.*

7.5

Ash, *alone in their room, envelope in hand. Frustrated.*

Ash   It's so boring and basic to be nervous about this.
If everyone had a feeling anyways, why bother worrying?
. . . .
Your life can't start until then.
No matter what this says

Ash *has made up their mind: they will come out to their family tonight.*

They open the envelope and read the letter.

Ash   Oh my God. I got in.

. . .

I'm going to college.

A quiet hope.

8.

Mia, **Bell**, *and* **Jamie** *on different sides of the stage. Separate conversations happening simultaneously, but apart.*

Announcer   Miss Landon, how do you feel about the NCAA's new guidelines for transgender swimmers?

Light up on **Jamie***, perhaps standing at a podium or surrounded by mics.*

Jamie   I'm so glad you asked. I think fairness is key, and any unfair advantage should be closely monitored and ultimately, eliminated.

Bell   My comments can be anonymous right? (*Re: a yes*) Okay. Well. I don't particularly enjoy the idea of / signing

Mia   Signing away my privacy rights and submitting hormone levels to the committee? But "Only for trans athletes", so you mean me. Because I'm the only one.

Jamie   I know so many real girls who have worked so hard to get where they are today. They train endlessly, without thanks, sometimes even sacrificing friendships to be able to compete to their fullest potential . . . imagine being someone like this, then being told you're going lose your spot on the roster to a [man] — trans person. I just think it defeats the purpose of women's sports.

Bell   If we're being honest . . . when we're together it's like "oh my gosh, you're the best, go Mia!" but I feel like everyone at some point has spoken to the coaches about not liking it.

Announcer   How do you think this will affect the future of women's swim?

Jamie   I think this is really good news for women's sports in general. Especially with Championships coming up. We should protect our own at all costs.

A chair floats by; **Jamie** *takes a seat. Then, a* **Nurse** *wearing an odd combination of scrubs and scuba gear approaches* **Mia**. *She draws* **Mia***'s blood into a vial, slaps a bandage on her and swims away.*

A **Reporter***'s segment in the distance:*

Reporter   The NCAA says that "due to issues of fairness," **all** athletes on women's teams must be subject to the same testosterone testing as was previously ruled for transgender athletes. It is unclear whether or not this practice will remain in place for the foreseeable future, but sources state that the committee is in the process of updating eligibility standards for the upcoming season.

Bell *appears underwater as well, lining up to get poked by the same nurse.*

Brine and blood dissolve together.

9.

Enter the **Sea Witch***, presenting the anatomy of two oysters to us.*

Sea Witch   I know this isn't normally the content you all are used to, but with the platform I have, as ruler of the depths and daughter of the House of Triton and all, I am driven to spread awareness. So you see, this oyster on the left is <u>clearly</u> a biologically natural oyster. You can tell by the crevices in its shell and the folds of its muscles. Now, notice these scrapes in the shell on the right. If you look closely you can see . . . the surgery scars. Power-hungry mermen want to deceive the laws of nature by which we <u>all</u> abide. One can only imagine their disgusting motives.

The sea grows cold, but water boils nonetheless.

Sea Witch   To usurp our struggle, to claim weakness and fragility?
To rise the ranks of merkind and become ungovernable?
. . .
Imitation oysters. Isn't that horrific? Aren't you afraid?

10.

The empty pool locker room an hour before practice. **Jamie** *has just finished changing.*

Enter **Bell**. **Jamie** *jumps.*

Bell   Hey

Jamie   What are you doing here so early

Bell   My bus only comes once an hour so I kinda had no choice. You?

Jamie   Thought I'd get a few laps in beforehand.

Bell   That's what practice is for?

Jamie   I don't like changing with [him] — anyone else in here.

Quiet. **Bell** *realizes what she means. She chooses to ignore it.*

Bell   Listen, I'm sorry for calling you a sore loser the other day. That was mean.

Jamie   Thank you.

Bell   I texted you a few days ago.

Jamie   You're not the only one.

Bell   I just . . . are you good?

Jamie   Welllll, I really was about to quit for good, but then I realized I'd be proving you right about the "sore loser" thing. So that's off the table.

Bell   Cause you'd rather die than let me win an argument?

Jamie   Pretty much yeah.

A shared moment. Once the humor passes:

Bell   I've been thinking about what you said. How Mia has the highest personal best out of everyone. Maybe you're right. The biological stuff . . . maybe it is a benefit.

Jamie (*lightly*)   I was wondering when you'd get your common sense back.

Jamie *offers a gesture of security: a hand over her shoulder or a scoot closer.*

Bell   You forgive me?

Jamie   Duh. You know I can't stay mad at you.

Relief.

Bell   You still wanna practice laps together? I've still never recorded my personal best. I wanna try and get there today.

Jamie   Sure.

They help each other up and out.

11.

Ash, in their room on Discord. In a separate room, **Michelle**, *on the phone with a friend.*

Iguana   So did you do it?

Ash   I tried. I came out to my mom, kinda. She didn't like immediately kick me to the streets. Obviously. But she doesn't understand, to say the least.

Michelle   I feel like I should be more surprised. My daughter thinks she's transgender.

Ash   Tried to explain the concept of nonbinary without losing my shit.

Michelle   I think it's because of the separation. I told you we're thinking about divorce? I read somewhere that problems at home make kids wanna rebel.

Ash   Having to put aside your emotions to be a patient, forgiving, impartial teacher about something that is so gut-wrenchingly, heart-crushingly personal— I mean, not to brag, but I think most Olympians would fold.

Michelle   I just never anticipated how deep it could go. She started talking about hormones and testosterone, injecting herself . . . it's just horrifying. I was like, how did these ideas even get into her head?

Ash   So of course, instead of paying attention to anything I'm saying, she blames the Internet and my phone and we've all heard this a million times.

Michelle   Neither of them even talk to me anymore. It's like I don't even know her. I've resorted to stealing mail and guessing phone passwords to even get a glimpse into her life! It's not like that- listen, if she's dead-set on me being bad cop, I'm done trying to fight it.

Ash   What she doesn't know, what I think I'll take to my grave, is that she's right. The Internet gave me the language for this. I found myself faster. I can't count the years of dysphoric confusion it saved me.

Michelle   Of course I think about that. Every free minute I have, my mind combs through the past few years. I think . . . maybe it was the moment my husband had something to hide. Or the day I found out. It changed us all, the space between us, before we could even talk about it.

Ash   Like yeah, where <u>do</u> you go when you can't express yourself physically, when no adult has made it safe for you? Your kid comes out and your first reaction is "It's because of that damn phone"? I think you're telling on yourself a little.

Michelle   I tried to tell her there's different ways to be a woman. You can be masculine, sure, but you can't run from what you were born with. Biology sets us apart. Denying that, trying so hard to believe you can— doesn't that sound like a symptom of something?

Ash   But when I tried explaining dysphoria, I didn't do it in the best way. She was all "Oh, you're just depressed, you're not getting enough exercise and sunlight, you need to get back into your sports like you used to do" but the entire reason I quit my soccer team was because of dysphoria! I didn't wanna play on the women's team anymore, I hated when the coach called us "girls" collectively, I was insecure and anxious in the locker room. It's this giant snake, going in circles, eating its own tail.

Michelle   How could she hate herself so much? How could I set such a bad example?

Ash   "So you wanna be a boy then? In the real world you're gonna have to choose." As if I don't already know the real world. In one ear and out the other.

Michelle   One daughter with a man in her locker room and another who wants to be one. I've never called myself a feminist, but these days I'm starting to regret that.

Ash   A friend of mine at school, when she came out to her family they were concerned for her safety more than anything. They wanted to read all the books and blogs and materials to make sure letting her go on blockers was the right decision. (*Imagining*) If I'm being honest, no matter how much I educate her . . . I have a feeling she'll always just see me as her fucked up little daughter.
. . .
It was just not the greatest.

Iguana   Does your sister know?

Ash (*scoffing*)   No. She's even more transphobic than our mom. God, I just need to move out and transition and never talk to either of them again.

Iguana   Wait, Ash, you said your sister just lost a huge competition? I feel like you've mentioned swimming before. Isn't she a swimmer?

Ash   Yeah, what about it?

Iguana   Listen, don't freak out. I think I just saw her on TV like fully advocating for a ban on trans athletes.

Ash   I know . . . I've seen clips. I've been trying to tune it out by playing video games all week.

Iguana   Damn, all this because she lost to that one girl? Jones something?

Ash   Mia Jonas. The first trans women in the US to compete on the collegiate level. Yeah. God, I can't believe we're actually going to be— (*They pause, hold up the envelope*) Actually. Um. I guess now would be a good time to announce I got an acceptance letter.

Iguana   WHERE?!

Ash   The same school Mia's at.

Iguana   TO AN IVY?! ARE YOU SERIOUS?

Ash   As a heart attack.

Iguana   Congrats! Holy shit!

Ash   Thanks. I honestly don't know why I'm not more excited. I guess it's just not real yet.

Iguana   Dude, you're only like one degree of separation from knowing Mia Jonas! That's crazy! People say she'd be heading to the Olympics soon if it weren't for . . . you know.

Ash   Yeah . . . . well, I quit sports ages ago. Not like I was going anywhere anyways. (*Looking at the envelope*) But I guess that's too bad.

Iguana   Actually, speaking of . . . your campus is in the city, isn't it?

Ash   Yeah, why?

Iguana   I guess now would be a good time to tell you I'm moving.

Ash   From Ohio? HERE?

Iguana   I'm kind of in the same boat, with my parents and all. And I've always kinda wanted that city life. I thought if I could move out by the summer, it'd be easier. If you're gonna be in the area for school . . . and I'm looking for a roommate . . . maybe we could even split rent?

Ash   Oh my God yes? Moving in with my best friend is that even a question Iguana yes of course!

Iguana   Let's make it happen. I'm so happy for you, Ash. Damn, an Ivy League!

Ash   I'm happy for you! US! Man, I already want to start looking at apartments.

Iguana   We could. You want me to screenshare a few I saved?

Ash   Absolutely.

Iguana *pulls up some rental listings. They dream together.*

12.

Bell *and* **Mia***'s team in the locker room packing up after practice.*

Coach   Good work today everyone! Don't forget, the NCAA will be doing another round of blood tests next week after the first results arrive. And Bell, a moment please?

Bell *and* **Coach** *alone.*

Bell   What's up?

Coach   Here's the deal. I know you girls have raised some . . . concerns. Specifically dealing with locker room use. So, a few <u>anonymous</u> team members drew up this petition.

He retrieves a paper and pen.

Coach   All I'm gonna say is the first draft was a blatant Title IX violation. But I worked the terms around. If this gets more than half the team's signatures, <u>all</u> team-members agree to change in the stalls, privately, instead of out in the open. Sign a pseudonym if you want, at the end it's just a tally. If you disagree, do not sign. Alright?

Bell   I mean . . . okay.

Coach   Now I'm gonna turn around and you can make your decision.

Coach *hands her the pen and paper and turns around.* **Bell** *studies the signatures, all pseudonyms.*

A sudden shift in atmosphere: the ocean draws close.

The **Sea Witch** *approaches from the shadows, looming over her shoulder.*

Bell *signs the petition, then hands it back.*

Darkness swallows her up.

13.

Ash*'s video game character in their battle attire. They've been doomscrolling at the bottom of the sea. Different headlines from several newscasters, a game score or nautical ballad may accompany.*

Reporter   The transgender community in Florida faces heavy burdens as lawmakers restrict

Ash   GRAAAAH

They destroy the headline with their weapon.

Announcer   A Texas bill would make it difficult for trans teens to access

Another strike from **Ash***.*

Reporter   Requiring schools to report kids using preferred names

Punch. Kick. Swing. Slice.

Announcer   A "healthcare ban"

Reporter   "Bathroom bills"

Announcer   "Drag queen story hour"

Bam, bam, bam. The music stops. **Ash** *puts the weapon away.*

Ash   Get blocked, idiots. This is MY corner of the ocean and I decide what I see.

They scroll towards brighter waters.

Eventually, **Bell** *emerges, in that same far- away place that revealed itself to her teammate. Algae and starfish and sun.*

Ash   Local pride collective? Awesome. A drag performer. A lesbian activist. A member of my— our— college team.

Enter **Mia***, in her own corner of the Web.* **Ash** *stops to marvel.*

Ash   The first trans athlete to win an NCAA Division I national championship, in any sport.

Mia *takes a picture and shares it with her followers.* **Ash** *swims into the comments.*

Ash   You look great.

Mia   Thank you!

Ash   Oh my God she replied.

They compose another message.

Ash   Hey, I know there's a lot of controversy right now— no that sounds stupid, delete that. I think you're a real inspiration to— no that's weird. Why am I even commenting on this picture? DM? It's weird to DM a stranger. But I'm just a fan, that's normal fan behavior! What if I just—

The message sends on accident. Onstage, they're compelled to say it.

Ash   Sometimes I wonder if I had kept going with soccer, if I could've been like you.

Mia   . . .

Ash   OH NO SHE'S TYPING. Hi! Sorry. You don't know me. My name's Ash. As a kid I used to play soccer, but I don't anymore. I quit cause I was trans and I just felt like an alien on the team and like there was no place for me but I saw your account and thought, wow! That's good. There are people like me out there, achieving things. Good for you. For us. Thank you. Send message.

Mia   Oh! That's really sweet. Thank you for reaching out. I'm really happy that my story gives other trans folks hope.

Ash   I don't wanna be too forward. But one day I'd like to pursue sports again. Maybe. Just . . . how do you tune out all the hate?

Mia   Well, I touch grass, first of all. There's a lot to me that I keep private just because I value my sanity. I have frequent "no-phone" days.

Ash   That's probably smart. I need to build up the willpower to do one of those, heh . . .

Mia   I mean, during practice, I mostly keep to myself. Let everything float past. I just focus on myself, my time. I train hard. And obviously it's paying off.

Ash   I'm glad it is. And everyone can tell. You're really great, I mean.

Mia   It's just now that I'm winning that's a problem. Like, sure you can be an honorary part of the team so you don't sue us for discrimination, just as long as you don't win, cause then you're taking opportunities from cis women.

Ash   You know it's really— oh she's typing again.

Mia   Honestly, my advice? Just tune it all out. Erase all notions that you're always taking someone else's spot. That I, *we,* can't earn something through hard work alone.

Ash   I really admire you, Mia.

Mia   . . .

Ash   Okay that's enough direct interaction for one day. What about her profile? Who's commenting on her photos? I wonder if . . .

Ash *dips out of DMs and, out of curiosity, opens the comment section to one of* **Mia***'s posts.*

It is a wretched sight. Horrific and explicit hate comments. **Ash** *cannot look away.*

Enter the **Sea Witch***. Her mere presence corrupts tranquility. She approaches* **Ash***, an anglerfish luring its prey.*

Mia *and* **Bell** *fade away, until the* **Sea Witch** *is the only source of light.*

Eventually, **Ash** *gives in. Darkness.*

SPLASH.

Ash*, human and back in their bedroom. They get up from their desk, disoriented.*

Their laptop is absolutely soaked with water.

It flickers a bit, then shuts down entirely.

Ash   Oh no.

They hurry to clean up the water. Soak it up with an old shirt, tilt it sideways to drain the ports, trying desperately to turn it back on.

It doesn't.

Ash   Noo no no this can't be happening. Fuck!

They pace the room, try not to cry . . . then pull it together and haul the laptop downstairs.

14.

The kitchen. **Jamie**'*s having a snack. Enter* **Ash** *with the soaking wet laptop.*

Jamie   What are you doing?

Ash   None of your business.

Ash *rummages for a huge bag of rice and the absolute largest bowl in the house.*

Jamie   What, are you housing soldiers in your quarters or something?

Ash *pours as much rice into the bowl as possible, then submerges the laptop.*

Jamie   That's against the 3rd amendment.

Ash   What?

Jamie   Never mind.

Ash *waits for something to happen. Adds a few more rice grains for good measure. Nothing happens.*

Jamie (*realizing*)   Ohhh shit

Ash   DO NOT tell / Mom

Jamie (*gleefully*)   Mom's gonna be piiiiissed

Ash   I SWEAR I will murder you if you breathe a word.

Jamie   Relax. I have nothing to gain anyways

Ash   Good.
. . .
Psycho.

Jamie   Freak.

Ash *flips her off and leaves.*

Alone somewhere, **Ash** *retrieves their phone and starts a call.*

Ringing . . .

Iguana   Hello?

Ash   Iguana I fucked up. I fucked up so bad oh my God everything is falling apart

Iguana   Woah woah slow down, just breathe.

Ash   My computer won't turn on.

Iguana   What happened?

Ash   Water damage. (*Breath*) Iguana, my name change forms are on there. And the rental stuff you were sending me and the bank account I just opened by myself and all my research on HRT— I can't retrieve any of it. It's all gone. I don't have any hard copies or passwords saved— oh my God it's all gone

Iguana   Did / you

Ash   YES I PUT IT IN RICE!

Iguana   I was gonna ask if you went to the bank about your account. You put a computer in rice?

Ash   I don't know, what else was I supposed to do? Fuck, it's never gonna turn back on.

Iguana   Alright. I know it seems bad, but we can get through this. Okay?

Ash   Okay. Yeah, you're right.

Iguana   Maybe go to the bank first and tell them about this? Secure your money first.

Ash   That's a good idea. Thank you.

They hang up, grab a bag, and leave the house.

Back in the kitchen, **Jamie** *finishes her snack and eyes the huge bowl. She checks to make sure Ash is gone, then approaches it.*

Jamie (*sigh*)   You are so fucking weird.

She digs the laptop out of the rice, examines it.

Touches a key or two..

. . .

A CHIME rings out as the laptop turns back on.

A moment of sheer surprise, then:

Jamie   Ah. Lockscreen. Right. (*Typing*) P-A-S-S-W-O-R-D.

That's incorrect.

Jamie   Worth a try. (*Thinking*) Pet names . . . old beta fish? (*Typing*) S-P-A-R-K-L-E.

Still not it.

Hmmm . . .

Jamie (*an idea*)   Oh.

She types in "SIRENCALL"

The computer unlocks.

Jamie *learns everything.*

15.

Bell *in the locker rooms, seemingly alone.* **Mia** *exits from a bathroom stall.*

Bell   Oh. Hey.

Mia   Sorry! I didn't know anyone was still here.

Bell   I was just killing time, since the bus— it doesn't really matter

Mia   No I get it. I don't have a car either.

Bell   Yeah.

A pause.

Mia   Okay, well, I better get going.

Bell   Yeah. See you tomorrow.

She walks away veryyyyy slowly, pretending not to notice **Bell** *lingering.*

Mia   Nope. Okay. We're doing this.

She summons all her good-trans-spokesperson patience and turns back around.

Mia   You can just ask, you know.

Bell (*caught*)   What do you mean

Mia (*sitting next to her*)   Let me guess. There's a curiosity you've been rolling around in your head because Google isn't giving you the answer. Or it's politically incorrect, but it's still biting at you. Or you think, maybe if you just catch me at the right angle and glimpse hard enough you could figure it out?
. . .
Am I close?

Bell   I just wanted to [apologize] — I don't know. Sorry, I don't mean to be rude.

Mia   Oh, don't worry. I was queer in high school, my feelings are entirely incapable of hurt.

Bell   Is that what you tell people?

Mia   It's true. Like a dead nerve.

Bell   I'm sorry.

Mia   Huh?

Bell   That just doesn't sound pleasant.

Mia   What, is there some sort of rumor?

Bell (*dodging*)   No.

Mia   Then what's up?

Bell (*making something up*)   Sometimes I wonder . . . why jump through all the hoops, all the red tape, just to fit in here? Why not just, I don't know, have a trans-only team?

Mia   Ah. I mean, besides all the other implications of separating teams that way, there also aren't many of us. Team Mia, population: one?

Bell   Yeah. That's what I figured.

Mia   Maybe someday it could happen though. Maybe a . . . campus collective, or something, for trans athletes who get barred from the mainstream. I'd do it myself, if my situation was a little less . . . I don't know, I made my bed and now I gotta lay in it, right?

Bell   I feel you.

Mia   But that wasn't really your question.

Bell (*clocked*)   You really don't mind people up in your business like this?

Mia   What about this: for every question I answer, you have to answer one too.

Bell   Fine. Yours first though.

Mia   All right. (*Thinking*) When's the last time you felt proud of something? Like really proud. Besides getting in here, I mean. Too easy of an answer.

Bell   Wow, creative. Okay. (*Also thinking*) I don't know, let me see . . .

She lands on a memory.

Bell   It was one of the first races I ever won on this campus. I'd been going through this rough patch with a certain professor— I wasn't sure if I wanted to stay at this school, actually. But it was also competition season y'know, the pressure was on, and that was a good outlet.

As she recalls the following, an azure tint creeps up behind her, elusive but comforting.

Bell   So when the race came, I had all this pent-up energy and it kinda fueled me— I won first by a lot. Beat my personal best, too. Afterwards, as everyone is getting ready to leave, this little Black girl comes up to me. She's with her mom, she can't be more than fourteen. And she hands me this piece of printer paper, stuck in a sheet protector to keep it from getting wet — it's a picture of me. Then she goes: "I can't believe I get to meet you. I'm a swimmer too. Can I have your autograph?"

The far-away place rescinds.

Bell   And I really had to keep myself from bawling on the spot cause PHEWW.

Mia   Awww!

Bell   That's when I knew I had to stay. Cause when I think about it, it's not just me in that pool.

Mia   I get what you mean.

A shared moment.

The weight of a thousand minds: young, dreaming, watching.

Mia   You next. Ask me something.

Bell   What was it like to switch teams here?

Mia   I don't know. It was a lot. On the men's team, it was like I was just different. *Soft* in the way everyone clocks immediately. Luckily, I was able to kinda fade into the background. Part of the team officially, but not in the groupchats or after-practice hangs or anything.

Bell   I will say, if there is an unofficial groupchat for our team, I don't have an invite either.

Mia   Funny how that happens to some more than others.

Bell   Yeah

Mia   The thing is that, usually, men will confront someone they don't like. They'll single the queerness out of you before everyone in broad daylight. But women are sneakier.

Bell   Yeah. Welcome to womanhood . . . they'll be fake to your face, give you a smile or whatever, then behind your back they're saying the most twisted shit you've ever heard.

Pause. **Mia** *thinks for a second.*

Mia   Well there you go. My turn.

Bell   Fair enough, hit me.

Mia   What do the others . . . say about me?

Bell   OH no, I was just speaking, like, generally, that's how girls are in social settings and stuff, I wasn't trying to throw shade

Mia   Do they use my deadname?

Bell   No. Well, if they are, at least I'm not around for it.

Mia   "He" pronouns?

Bell   No.

Mia   I don't buy it.

Bell   The team spirit is just . . . a little artificial, that's all.

Mia   Alright.

BUZZ. Mia checks her phone.

Mia   I gotta go.

They both get up to leave. **Bell** *collects her things.* **Mia** *turns around one last time.*

Mia   You know, I probably wouldn't despair about exclusion from a team groupchat. I have a feeling if you were in it, you'd have a lot more to feel guilty about.

Bell   Yeah.

Mia   See you around?

Bell   See you.

16.

Back at the house. Enter **Ash***, returning from the bank.*

Jamie *stands before them, holding their laptop.*

Ash (*startled*)   AH! Fuck, Jamie, were you just standing there the whole time?

They notice the computer. Her face says it all.

Ash   No.

Jamie   A video game as your password, really?

Ash   Give it back!

They lunge for it. She dodges. This can go back-and-forth for a bit.

Jamie   Where were you just now? If you say "none of your business", I'm going straight to mom with the contents of this.

Ash   Why are you like this?

Jamie   Just tell me where you were.

Ash   . . .

Jamie   Okay. You have 30 seconds til I scream.

Ash   You're fucking obsessed. You plot and scheme and move in silence like a goddamn villain. I saw you on the news the other day! "We should protect our own at all costs?" Jesus, how alt-right brainwashed are you?

Jamie   Oh that's RICH coming from you. "Non-binary," come on. Meanwhile men are using that label to creep on women and self-proclaimed feminists celebrate it as equality.

Ash   Okay, you need to stop. You are so out of your depth you have no idea.

Jamie (*a bit too genuine*)   Why would you move out without telling anyone?

Ash   It's been proven time and again that I'm not safe here.

Jamie   There's no one coming to get you, Ashley. No one's putting their hands on you, or yelling at you to accept Jesus or whatever.

Ash   There's no one supporting me either.

The fact sits for a moment

Jamie   You feel <u>unsafe</u>. So like, not sleeping? Always looking over your shoulder? Scared. Yeah?

. . .

That's how I felt constantly, in that locker room.

Ash   There's a difference, Jamie. You're constructing a danger that isn't there, hanging onto trauma that has nothing to do / with the situation

Jamie   Jesus, I've had enough victim blaming to last a lifetime. You do not get to tell me what is and isn't dangerous.

Ash   I think your credibility relies on it. You need to convince everyone Mia Jonas is a pervert, or a cheater, or something, cause otherwise you're just a transphobe with no shot at winning gold.

Jamie   . . . HEY MOM?

Michelle (*unseen*)   YES?

Ash   Whatever. Go ahead, show her all my private shit. There's nothing stopping me from telling her about your boyfriend.

Jamie   I was going to tell her anyways. (*to Michelle*) COULD YOU COME DOWN HERE FOR A SEC?

Slow footsteps down the stairs.

Ash   Or maybe I'll come out publicly as your transgender sibling.

Pause. This is a real threat.

Ash   Bet the media would love that. And all your conservative brand sponsors . . .

They stare each other down as **Michelle** *appears before them.*

Michelle   What is it?

Jamie   Have you seen my water bottle? I can't find it anywhere and I really need it for the gym.

Michelle   Ah, you're always losing things. Look for it yourself!

As **Michelle** *walks away,* **Ash** *grabs their computer back and leaves immediately.*

17.

The locker rooms before a meet. Soft sounds of the pool just outside. Lively energy as team-members walk to and from the bathroom stalls in various states of dress.

Bell *changes inside a stall as a* **Swimmer** *pounds on the door.*

Bell   I'm almost done!

Swimmer   Please hurry, I need to pee. (*Under her breath*) I hate this.

Bell   Sorry, just a sec!

Stall door opens. **Swimmer** *and* **Bell** *swap places just as* **Mia** *enters the locker room.*

Bell (*waving*)   Hey Mia!

Mia *only glares back, beelining to a stall with her clothes in hand.* **Bell** *deflates.*

Enter **Coach** *with a handful of envelopes.*

Coach   All right girls, results are in for both teams. Let's get this over with.

Everyone gathers single-file. **Jamie**'s *up first.*

Coach (*offering*)   There you go.

Jamie   Oh, I'd rather hear mine out loud. I don't mind.

Coach   Yeah okay (*Opening it, reading*) Congratulations Jamie, your testosterone levels were found to be acceptable. As expected for . . .

Jamie   A normal, natural woman. I figured.

Coach   You will be allowed at the Championship tournament this season.

Jamie   Thank you.

She exits, content. **Mia** *steps forward.*

Coach   Ok, Mia . . . (unfolding her test results) Congratulations, you will be able to compete in the championships this season.

A quiet celebration.

Mia *exits and* **Bell** *steps forward.*

18.

Bell *in her apartment, blasting some loud music. A knock on the door.*

Bell   It's OPEN

Enter **Jamie**, *shielding her eardrums.*

Jamie   I GOT YOUR TEXT

Bell   HUH?

Jamie   YOU TEXTED ME

Bell   I DID WHAT

Jamie   COULD YOU TURN IT DOWN

Bell   NO :) YOU WANT SOME?

She pulls out some weed. **Jamie** *is utterly flabbergasted.* **Bell** *goes to light it;* **Jamie** *smacks it out of her hands.*

Bell   HEY, WHAT THE FUCK?

Jamie *turns the music down while* **Bell** *collects the scattered remnants.*

Jamie   What is wrong with you?!

Bell   What's wrong with YOU! You spilled it everywhere!

Jamie   You're doing pot right before championships?!

Bell   I'm not "doing pot," I'm smoking weed.

She lights up. **Jamie** *dodges the smoke like it's mustard gas, maybe finds a rag to breathe into.*

Bell   Anyways, I'm not going to championships.

Jamie   What?

Bell   You heard me. I'm. Not. Going.

Jamie   Please put that out.

Bell   Fuck you.

Jamie   ???

Bell   My test results came back. They said, "elevated levels of testosterone." Above the acceptable limit. I'm not allowed to compete.

Jamie   What? How is that possible?

Bell   It's just the way I'm built apparently. At first, I was surprised too. Then I learned I'm not the first Black female athlete this has happened to.

Jamie   Oh . . .

Bell   Was your media campaign worth it?

Jamie   I never meant for this / to happen

Bell   You were trying to equate womanhood to test results, and look who came out the wrong end.

Jamie   I'm sorry, Bell.

Bell   But it's fine for you, right? One less competitor.

Jamie   You think I wanted this? That I had some huge plan to ban you from competing all along?

Bell   No. I just think you took advantage of a system where these things intertwine.

Jamie   What are you talking about?

Bell   You passed 9th grade history. Look me in the eyes and remind me exactly where the idea of the perfect biological woman came from.

Jamie   <u>No</u>. No, Bell, my priority has always been sportsmanship. I saw a women's space in danger, in need of preservation, and I have fought like hell to protect it.

Bell   So what, you'll just find another way to weed her out, casualties aside?

Jamie   You aren't just a casualty to me. I mean it. But I've had so many survivors reach out to me with support, telling me what I'm doing is desperately needed in this day and age. Meanwhile, I haven't slept more than 3 or 4 hours a night since I don't know when. I'm always looking over my shoulder during practice, in the locker rooms. I'm <u>afraid,</u> Bell, you don't see that?

Bell   You ever wondered if that's how Mia felt, on the men's team? Or how I feel now as the only Black girl? That feeling isn't unique, you aren't / alone

Jamie   That (*choosing words carefully*) <u>Person</u>. Will <u>never</u> understand what it's like to be a woman who's been hurt by a man.

Bell   How do you know that?

Jamie   Bell, look at me. You see someone who's re-traumatized out of her mind because there's suddenly a male presence in the place where she undresses every week, and your first thought is really "that other person must've had such a hard life"?

Bell   Empathy isn't some finite resource that needs to be rationed.

Jamie   Don't some people deserve it more than others?

Bell   Sure. What about me?

Jamie (*sigh*)   You do. And I really am sorry, Bell. Your body is perfect the way it is; I regret that this happened. You're my friend.

Bell   But?

Jamie   Letting [Deadname] <u>Mia</u> — compete on a women's team, alongside girls who are half that height, weight, speed . . . it sets a precedent for our future. If the NCAA keeps allowing it, what's stopping any man from just declaring himself to be a woman to win gold at a women's championship?

Bell   No one's like that in real life. Come on.

Jamie   But they <u>could,</u> if we let it continue. It's about precedent, Bell. And to me it's also about safety. If girls don't feel safe here, what's even the point?

Bell   I think you and I have different definitions of safe.

Jamie *opens her mouth, but backs down.*

Bell   Do you remember the day we met?

Jamie (*begrudgingly*)   Swim tryouts in third grade? Yeah.

Bell   I was late cause of transit and bombed <u>so</u> hard that the other girls teased me til I cried. And I just stood there, taking it. But then you came up and told them off, / like

Jamie   "At least Bell never peed herself in front of the lifeguard."

The two of them wade in the memory. Blazing sun, pool floaties, a shriek of laughter.

Bell   Right. Then your mom drove both of us to the pool each week til the next round of tryouts. And that was that.

Eventually, it circles the drain.

Bell   I was so proud of myself when I finally made the team, but I could never shake off that shyness. You made it better. It was like, as long as you were around, I could belong. It was easier if there was someone fighting for me. Even through middle school, when you were absent, I wouldn't say a word for the whole meet. But I'm not a kid anymore. I know I've earned my right to be here.

Jamie   Bell . . .

Bell   What digs at me the most is that, despite everything, I still <u>crave</u> that approval. Like a knife needs blood. So I stayed neutral on this for longer than I should've. Chipped away pieces of myself til that was left was . . . this. (*Motioning between them*) This.

Jamie   So now what?

Bell   You know, I thought maybe if I sued you, or the NCAA, it'd make it too expensive for anyone to pull something like this ever again. Maybe then I'd be doing something for the greater good. Then I realized . . . I'm tired. I fought twice as hard as every white girl, every rich legacy kid on my team to be here. And in the end, you all still found a way to eliminate me. I'm just tired of fighting.

Jamie   "You all"?

Bell   You know what I mean.

Jamie   No, I really don't. I thought our friendship was built on solidarity. Navigating a system that wasn't made for women / like us

Bell   Oh please. I've seen your house— families like yours ARE the system. You can't even see the fucked-up standards right in front of you because you've spent your life contorting yourself to fit them.

Jamie (*hardening*)   I am not a bad person. I'm just speaking my truth. And I've come to learn the truth just offends people who can't face its consequences.

Bell   You were my best friend, Jamie. I would've done anything to keep you.

Jamie   Except support me in a way that matters.

Bell   . . .

Jamie   Ok. I'm done.

Jamie *moves towards the door. On her way out:*

Bell   There are cis women with Mia's wingspan! There are women at <u>her</u> height, women at <u>her</u> weight, women at <u>her</u> muscle mass! And she's got the same amount of testosterone as YOU! No matter how you test her, she's eligible to compete! So what am I? What does that make me, huh?

The door slams. **Bell** *is alone.*

19.

Back in **Ash**'s *personal corner of the Internet. Elements of their fantasy character are present.*

Ash   In this realm, anything is possible. I could be anything. I could talk to anyone. Even . . . my mom.

*Mermaid-***Michelle** *appears on command.*

Ash   And . . . my sister.

*Mermaid-***Jamie** *appears beside her. They both retain elements of the* **Sea Witch**.

Ash   I can do it over again. I can explain everything better. If everyone was just able to say exactly how they felt, nothing more, nothing less.

*Mermaid-***Mia** *appears next to them.*

*Mer-***Jamie** *snaps into a default dialogue with her.*

Jamie   And you know the worst part? Not one person who disagrees with me can put up a single scientific argument. They just resort to name-calling. Suddenly I'm a "bigot" or a "transphobe," when those words are just as empty as their thought processes.

Mia   You want a scientific argument? What about the Olympian with all those mutations that make him better at swimming? Extra-wide arms, hypermobility, and huge tail fins, but no one dares eliminate <u>him</u>. It's just luck for this natural-born merman. But when Black and trans women excel, our bodies are wrong and we have to forfeit?

Ash   Hey, Mia?

Jamie   Mermen are biologically stronger than mermaids. It's just a fact. It's nature and hard science. That's why our sports are separate.

Ash   Jamie?

Mia   You're a feminist, but you also believe you're biologically inferior? What happened to "women can do anything men can do"? Nature isn't as binary as you'd like it to be.

Ash   HEY, ENOUGH! NO MORE OF THIS STUPID FUCKING ARGUMENT! WHEN WILL WE STOP HAVING TO LEGITIMIZE OUR EXISTENCE TO EVERYONE ON EARTH?

They both stop and stare at **Ash**.

Ash   Mia, you are my superhero, you truly have no idea how much I look up to you, but is this ALL YOU DO?

Mia   No, / I don't think so

Ash   Do you ever <u>rest</u>?

Mia   . . .

Ash   Is that what our future looks like? A debate for my life each time I post a picture, or win an award, or use the bathroom?

Mia   Of course not. For you, at least, I <u>hope</u> not. I'm just in the spotlight. I have to advocate for us. I mean, who else is going to do it?

Ash   Is this what advocacy really is? Putting up with people who don't understand you, and probably never will? Who hate you regardless?

Mia   I do it so you don't have to.

Ash   We shouldn't have to at all.

Mia   I used to have the kind of rage you do. I shaped it into patience, but it wore me down . . . smooth into seaglass.

The fantasy begins to crumble.

Mia   Take your rage and use it for something. Make something beautiful.

Ash   I don't want to make it beautiful. I just want them to understand.

*Mermaid-***Bell** *and Game character-***Iguana** *emerge from the darkness.*

A sequence of movement: boundaries and breakthroughs as the push and pull of a tide. Merpeople shed layers to become human, meeting each other where they are.

Bell *and* **Jamie**, *a history.*

Iguana *and* **Ash**, *a beginning.*

Michelle, **Jamie**, *and* **Ash**, *a family— and so forth. All characters interact somehow.*

Then, **Ash** *steps out to leave a note.* **Michelle** *watches.*

Ash   Mom, I need to leave. I don't know when we'll speak next. I'm just looking for some peace. I was accepted into . . . well. "As long as I live here, my business is your business." And you go through my mail, so . . . you already know.

A breath. **Ash** *prepares to dive.*

Darkness.

Splash.

20.

The locker rooms. **Mia** *and* **Bell** *alone.*

Bell   I wanted to apologize.

Mia   Oh. Hey, Bell.

Bell   I just figured, it might be a while til we see each other again. Since you're . . .

Mia   Disqualified too, now? Yeah. I was just packing up.

Bell   I'm sorry. For everything. My conscience has been eating away at me for months knowing I wasn't standing by you when I should've. But I had my own shit going on and it was just a little / overwhelming

Mia   Hey, it's all right. I honestly never expected to get this far, but I had a good run. And it's definitely not your fault.

Bell   I should have stood by you from the beginning. It shouldn't have taken disqualification for me to see that.

Mia   I mean, I know you and Jamie were close.

Bell   We're not anymore.

Mia   That must've been really difficult.

Bell   God damn it, are you always this understanding? You can be angry at me, you know, for my complacency. I actually think I'd prefer that.

Mia (*a little laugh*)   Would it absolve you of your guilt faster?

Bell   Yes. Yes it would.

Mia *tries something she's never tried before.*

Mia   Hm . . . not . . . my job?

Bell   Yeah. That's a little better.

Mia   Oh hush.

Bell   What are your plans now that you're out?

Mia   Oh, I'm taking a longgggg nap and then deleting all my social media. Maybe I'll remake some private accounts. See some friends out West. You?

Bell   I think I need to go to the beach. Get back in touch with why I chose swimming in the first place.

Mia   Why's that?

Bell   That first time I went into the water, I must've been five or six . . . there was this feeling. Like I'd found a part of me I didn't know was missing. A part that had gills.
It's like I <u>become</u> water.

Measuring breath, flexing muscle, moving so fast
I feel strong
and focused
and changed.
For me it was never about the scores or the ranks. It was about that zen.   .
Plus, it's the only sport where it's impossible to get sweaty. So that's a plus. You ever felt like that?

Mia   Sweaty?

Bell   No, like everything I just said!

Mia   I'm kidding. Of course I do. I just wish trans kids were allowed to explore that feeling without having their bodies policed. I think that's why I held out for so long, just that hope . . .

Bell   "Maybe I could change something."

Mia   Right. Maybe I could've.

Bell   Maybe you still can.

They dream together.

21.

Finally, the tournament pool. The lack of a crowd makes the echoes louder.

In the corner, **Michelle** *holds up another banner: "Woman = Adult Human Female."*

Reporter   The big day has finally come, and we've got an interesting round in this evening's tournament . . . After a controversial number of pre-qualifier blood tests, measurements, and other factors, Jamie Landon seems to be the only one left standing. Out of everyone, she's the only swimmer meeting all qualifications to swim in the women's championship tournaments this year.

Jamie *stands at the edge of the pool, a ghost of herself.*

Reporter   According to official tests, she's the perfect biological woman with a fertile egg count of 150k. She's also got a beautiful muscle-to-fat ratio of 16% and a perfect BMI score, with just the right amounts of testosterone and estrogen for the average female— and of course when we mean average, we mean Caucasian. Not to mention her perfectly working uterus, for which she takes no birth control, like we discovered in some other opponents . . . apparently the last eligible woman had a hysterectomy! What a shame. Anyways, there she is, ready to beat her own best time and set a new record again!

A whistle blows. **Jamie**, *not wearing a swim cap or goggles, kneels at the edge of the pool, then looks up at the crowd. No one is there except her mother, holding the banner.*

Three, two, one- BUZZER.

Jamie *dives in. She relishes the feeling of submersion.*

As she progresses through the water, her movement shifts from elegant to erratic. Her breast-stroke is super fast. Bit by bit, it becomes more unsettling. She gets delirious, pulls at her hair, flails her limbs.

*A nightmare sequence into the depths of the **Sea Witch**'s lair.*

Then, finally, she emerges—

Hair dripping wet.

Eyes red with chlorine, spitting up water.

She wins first place.

22.

An epilogue.

A team of trans/queer kids on an all-inclusive sports team. All available actors play kids donning soccer-type jerseys. **Mia** *and* **Bell** *both wear something distinguishing them as coaches. Rainbow banners or pride flags above; this is a space in which joy is abundant and shame is forgotten.*

Mia   All right friends, we've got a tough round waiting for us tonight, but I know we can do it. We've been through a lot to get where we are, but our fans are counting on us.

Bell   And we reached a milestone on Instagram the other day. Isn't that amazing? Thousands of people all over the country and the world are cheering us on to the field today. People just like you. There's so much good energy here. Think about that today on the field.

Mia   I'm so proud of everyone.

Bell   Okay, hands in.

They put their hands in. They chant their team chant.

The whistle blows—

And they're off.

End of play.

What We Leave & What We Carry in Eliana Rubin's *Tides*

Fig Lefevre

There are 14 non-work safari tabs open on my computer when I download the latest draft of *Tides*. 8 are about identity documents. An ACLU announcement warning trans people not to try to update any ID documents at this time. A Dot Gov page reminding readers that my home state does not and will not make changes to anyone's sex on their birth certificate. A close reading of the executive orders from January 2025, with my notes and highlights. A handful of tabs of forms for the passport I am so desperately trying to get. And a privately shared google doc with a trans travel advisory—where it is and is not safe to go right now. The page is full of red annotations from previous visitors warning: *Not Safe. Don't Come Here.* None of them say what to do if you are already there.

I open the play, and instead of being transported elsewhere—some fantastical imagining one might expect from a play set in the future—I am home. Not in the heart-filling, satisfied, old worn chair feeling of home. But the "this is so familiar to me that I know it in my bones" kind of home. I've been here. I am here. Despite playwright Eliana Rubin initially writing Part I ("May, June, July") back in 2019, this Part may as well be set in May of 2025 (3 months away at the time of this writing) for all that it speaks to the current political, legal, and social anxieties trans people are facing.

But Rubin doesn't leave us in this place forever. Like the moon, she pulls the water from beneath our feet, ripping it out to sea.
"The
        tide
              comes
                    in
                         and
                  the
            tide
   goes
out,"
Rubin tells me when she meets me on zoom to discuss the play. She repeats it, rhythmically brushing her hand through the air.

If the familiar immersion of the opening scene is high tide, then Scenes 3 & 4 are a riptide, with the Part ending in the strange new world of low tide. In low tide, the remnants of the ocean are left on the bare sand, uncovered, like exposed nerves. In *Tides*, our exposed nerves are our attachments: to each other, to our homes, to our grudges. And Rubin aims to make us choose. Before the uncertainty of high tide comes back, what will we rescue? What will we preserve? And what will we sacrifice? When our safety is snatched from us, will we hold fast to our chosen family or run away with our lovers? When our rights are at risk, will we stay and fight or seek refuge elsewhere? What are we willing to let go of if it means keeping ourselves safe? If we get the chance for change, will we recreate the pain we felt or can we imagine something new? Rubin's characters each make disparate choices, forcing us to ask who can ever know what the right answer is—what the right choice is, and if there even is one.

". . . the tide comes in and the tide goes out . . ."

If low tide in Part I exposed our nerves, Part II ("The Shepherd") brings them into hyper-focus. With the rest of the world zoomed out, this Part seemingly offers a clarity to our query: that anything is excusable in the name of safety. That beyond freedom, what oppressed people really desire is to see our oppressors suffer the same fates we have. That this destruction is brought most simply through the re-appropriation of their own tools of oppression. Rubin tells me she wanted to explore the idea that "hurt people hurt people," but to also trouble the notion that violence is never the answer. "Why are these people trying to tell me what's best for me—what's safest for me?" she asks, frustrated with marginalized communities being told to respond to our own oppression with gentle call-ins and polite educating. I tell her that it reminds me of my attachment to the film version of the Marvel character Magneto (*X-Men* franchise, 2000-). Growing up watching Ian McKellen, a gay man, made a villain for wanting mutants to not hide or be "cured," but instead to thrive, sparked something in me that was never comfortable with the drive for homonormativity, cisnormativity, and assimilationism I saw in many LGBTQ+ narratives. Something that felt queer attachments to other anti-heroes like Erik Killmonger (*Black Panther*, 2018), Carrie White (*Carrie*, 1976), and Jennifer Check (*Jennifer's Body*, 2009), something that cheered for them as they took their revenge and wished for a world where their characters lived at the end. And when they lived, like Angela Baker (*Sleepaway Camp*, 1983) and The Girl (*A Girl Walks Home Alone at Night*, 2014), I wondered if they could ever be seen as something less monstrous. But maybe to thrive in a world that wishes your death is monstrous in its miraculousness.

In Part II, this figure (the titular Shepherd) is Elizabeth Abbott, a Black trans woman who has run for president under the false platform of reinforcing the already terrible conditions for queer and trans people, only to reveal her plan to do the opposite once she's been elected. It's every transphobe's worst fear. An unclocked trans woman. She's in your (White) house, she's influencing your children, she's taking away your rights. It's as if Rubin took the adage "when you are accustomed to privilege, equality feels like oppression," and hyperbolized every worst-case scenario anti-LGBTQ+ activists have ever spun. In an essay about their play *An American Animal* (2023), non-binary playwright Katherine Gwynn perfectly encapsulates the way persecution experiences get reclaimed by those in power: "It's really about American Fear: marginalized people's reality of being hunted in this country and the fabricated instinct America has fostered that makes white cisgender straight Americans feel hunted" (Gwynn 2023). In *Tides*, Rubin makes this fear real and visceral. It's a persecution reversal trope I've seen played out before in queer media for comedic effect (like the play *Zanna, Don't!*, 2002), for sociopolitical critique (such as the film *Love is All You Need?*, 2016), and even for self-actualization (as in the movie *Almost Normal*, 2005).

As the middle Part of *Tides*, the persecution reversal also acts as a revenge fantasy, evoking punk band G.L.O.S.S.'s album *TRANS DAY OF REVENGE* with lyrics such as "When peace is just another word for death/it's our turn to give violence a chance" (G.L.O.S.S. 2016). It's giving gay superhero Rage from the *Rage* comics from the TV show *Queer as Folk* (2000-2005) defending the city of Gayopolis from homophobes. It's Bubbles, Pinky, and Rachel on a rampage against their attackers in *Ticked-Off Trannies with Knives* (2010). It's equal parts cathartic and terrifying.

"Death before detransition. But not my death."

—*trans proverb, original source unknown*

But tides will always change, mirroring "the ways in which people, our society, politics, our acceptance shift and flow in cycles," Rubin says, the only constant being transition. And with the third Part, Rubin pulls the water in around us, waters that might feel and look a lot like that of Part I, but with the next generation of queer found family at the center. It seems queer family is what we carry from the first page to the last. In Part I Sasha is taken in by Tanya, and in turn helps Ross with his houseful of youth in Part III. After their fraught conversation in Part II, Elizabeth funds Ross and his found family in Part III. By the end of the play, Kai considers taking on the same role for the next generation. Despite the differing intersectional identities that impact their path to safety, each of these characters is grounded and connected by this web of queer kinship. Each of these characters finds and makes their own family, fighting for them in the way they believe best. "What makes me, me," Tanya explains in Part I, "is my love for the three of you" (xx).

Queer kinship is an integral part of so many trans narratives in theater—like the group rallying around Zodiac in *The Interrobangers* by M Sloth Levine (also in this volume), Colt, Kaysar, and Zara quite literally building a home together in *Close to Home* by Sharifa Yazmeen (*Methuen Drama Book of Trans Plays, Vol 2)*, or Rue, Oxalis, and the community they build and support in the Ambulatory in *Doctor Voynich and Her Children* by Leanna Keyes (*Methuen Drama Book of Trans Plays, Vol 1*), and so many more. Queer kinships stories amplify the necessity of these relationships and spaces. Queer kinship spaces become our main source of learning our histories and remembering our ancestors, but also for learning to recognize each other in the present. Moments in *Tides*, like Tanya seeing Maddie for the first time, hint at the link between queer kinship and queer recognition, or a queer gaze. As the titular characters from *The Faggots & Their Friends Between Revolutions* (2023 stage musical, adapted from the 1977 book of the same name by Larry Mitchell) sing, "their bodies have secret methods to recognize each other" (Venables and Huffman 2023: 2). For so many of us, it's queer coded gestures, words, or accessories that help us recognize one another. But even without those codes, under all the masks of cisheteronormativty, Ross and Elizabeth still seem to recognize each other. There is an undercurrent of *knowing* across the generations of characters.

This *knowing* does little for *understanding*, however. For the characters in *Tides*, kinship is fraught from the start. Characters are asked to choose between safety and family, romantic bonds and platonic bonds. They fight over beliefs about safety, family, and violence. But they also find ways to connect and build community under extreme circumstances. They invest in the future of their community. Moments like Tanya shoving Sasha and the arguments between Kai and Ross exemplify the messiness of queer kinship, of attachments so impactful that they become our families, our elders, our ancestors. They pass on lessons and histories and music. For queer people in both the world of the play and the one I am in, our biological and legal bonds rarely are where we inherit queer cultural knowledge. Unlike other forms of cultural socialization, queerness is learned usually outside the first home, in spaces of queer kinship. This is our queer inheritance.

Queer inheritance has become a widespread topic for queer artists of many media. Aditya Vikram's collected writings called *A Queer Inheritance: Borrowed & Stolen*

(2021) speak to the complexity of queer inherited knowledges interwoven with those inherited from our biological & legal families. Textile artist Max Adrian's *A Constellation of Queer Inheritance* (2021) investigates how the artist continues to be impacted by queer elders and generations past. For queer people in this play, elders are central to kinship and survival. Even after their death, the specters of Tanya and Elizabeth haunt those left behind. Photographer Todd J Danforth explored the depth and power of our relationships with queer elders through his interview and portrait series, *Queer Inheritance* (2022), explaining,

> Elders are not just storytellers and teachers, but guardians of cultural heritage and stewards of spirituality. The elders in my biological family passed mostly in my teenage years, taking with them their stories, lived knowledge, and guidance. I've felt cheated out of that historical inheritance, attempting over the years to salvage what's left–the pursuit of which evolved into a thirteen-year portrait project centered on my family. I hadn't realized during those thirteen years what I was searching for might only be found in queer chosen family, an understanding that my biological elders would likely be incapable of nurturing my gay identity.
>
> (Danforth 2022)

Danforth's project radiates a longing for queer ancestry, a deeply felt absence I can feel slowly filled by each of his portrait subjects.

I have long believed that since we can choose our families, we can choose our ancestors. It's why so many queer and trans people feel kinship with Sylvia Rivera, Marsha P Johnson, Lou Sullivan, and other trans ancestors who blazed this path for us. It's why Kai's journey echoes Ross's and Tanya's before them. It's why Ross and Sasha fight with Kai to listen to the elders' stories before making up her mind. To be queer is to be in relation to an ocean of queerness. To be queer is to carry the weight of that ocean with you, always. For the characters in *Tides*, as in our world, to be queer is to be a small part inextricable from the larger story of queerness. And as *The Faggots & Their Friends Between Revolutions* sing, we "tell each other these stories over and over so that the past is never lost. And so that the ones who came before them are never forgotten" (Venables and Huffman 2023: 5).

Outside the world of the play, our high tide has come in, thrusting us into dangerous, though not unfamiliar waters. You saw how Rubin's characters chose to face three cycles of these waters. Now how will you face them? What will you fight for? Who will you hold tight against the undercurrent?

A Spell to Invoke the Ancestors, Living & Dead:

Lay down a scrap of fabric – something you have worn or used. This will be your altar cloth

Light a candle on your altar

As it burns, swirl its smoke in the air around yourself

Pour an offering into a small bowl—something sweet, something spicy, or something strong

Dip your finger into the offering and with the liquid write the name of your ancestor(s) on your cloth—see their face in your mind, imagine their smell, their warmth, their joy

Drip your candle atop each name and press your finger into the wax as it cools
Say "I am here and you are with me" each time
When you are satisfied that your chosen ancestors have been invoked, now is the time
to chat
to Kiki
to Spill Tea
What Have You
Maybe
Ask them for help with your mother
Tell them about that boy
Or
Apologize for not calling sooner
But, listen
Listen to how they fought, how they survived
Listen, because that time will come again
And when you are done
Tear a small slip of paper and write a word. A sign. A signal. Something that will help
your ancestors to guide you
An orange sunset
Bright blue hair
The right song coming on your boombox
Or a fresh tomato
Write it on your paper and burn that paper
Don't burn yourself
When it is burnt, let the ashes fall on your cloth
Snuff the candle
Bury the cloth somewhere you'd like to sit and talk with your ancestors
Or somewhere that feels like home
And remember
You are Here
And They are With You

References

Eliana Rubin, personal correspondence with the author. February 18, 2025.

G.L.O.S.S. "Give Violence a Chance." *TRANS DAY OF REVENGE.* Prodced by Total Negativity (US). Released June 13, 2016.

Gwynn, Katherine. "On Wolves, Queer and Trans Life, and American Fascism." *Howlround Theatre Commons,* June 28, 2023. https://howlround.com/wolves-queer-and-trans-life-and-american-fascism

Todd J Danforth personal website. "Projects - Queer Inheritance." Accessed 15 February 2025. https://www.toddjdanforth.com/projects/queer-inheritance

Venables, Philip and Ted Huffman. *The Faggots and Their Friends Between Revolutions.* Ricordi, 2023. https://issuu.com/casaricordi/docs/00_venables_faggotsandtheirfriends_fs_2023_08_22?ff

Tides

Part I: May, June, July
Part II: The Shepherd
Part III: Ripe

Eliana Rubin

List of Characters

Tanya (she/her). Person of Color. Late 30s. Motherly. Protective.
Elizabeth (she/her). Black. 40s/50s. Powerhouse. Calculating.
Sasha (they/them). Any race. Early 20s and early 30s. Brash. Passionate.
Henry (he/him). Any race. 20. Simultaneously childish and mature.
Kai (any pronouns). Black. 18. Angry. Growing.
Taylor (she/her). Any race. 19. Innocent. Lovestruck.
Brigitte (she/her). Any race. Tweens. Whimsical. Loves tomatoes.
Ross (he/him). White. Mid to late 20s. A bit meek. Curious.
Michael (he/him). White. 20s. Never grew out of his frat days.
Marty (any pronouns). Any race. Teenager. Smart. A good sibling.
Trevor (they/them). Any race. 19. Playful. Hopeful.
River (she/he/they). Any race. Teenager. Brooding. Kind.

Where

The United States of America.
Specifically, a backyard; Washington, D.C.; and a mansion.

When

Too close to our present.

Part I

May, June, July

Scene 1

June 30.

A backyard. Late afternoon. Blue skies turning to orange. Sun blazing. Green grass (turf?), lawn chairs, maybe a kiddie pool. A barbecue with burgers on the grill, and a table next to it with burger fixings and a map. Music plays softly.

Tanya, Henry, wearing sunglasses and reading a magazine, and Taylor are in the backyard. Tanya is on grill duty. Henry and Taylor lounge. Taylor is in the middle of a story.

Taylor . . . and I didn't even know she was there. But I kept talking about how cute I thought she was, and the girls at the bar were trying to signal that she was RIGHT behind me, it was like a movie . . . but I didn't get it. So I keep going and going, until I feel someone tap me on the shoulder, so I stop talking, and my face goes hot, and I slowly turn around, and she's RIGHT THERE, and I just kinda stare at her, and she smiles at me, and she asks me if I want to dance, and then we dance, for, like, three songs!!

Henry lowers his sunglasses.

Henry Did you make out?

Taylor A bit.

Tanya What's her name?

Taylor Jasmine. She's so sweet, and nice, and beautiful, oh my God, Tanya, her eyes were like . . . gorgeous. The greenest eyes I've ever seen.

Henry Did you get her number?

Taylor Yeah.

Henry Then text her! Or call her or something.

Taylor I don't want to mess it up. I read in a magazine that you're supposed to wait two days before calling the person up again.

Henry Rules are meant to be broken.

Tanya Not always.

Henry Do you even have two days?

Tanya Henry.

Henry What? It's just a question.

Taylor   She lives across town. So, if I can get over there, then yeah.

Henry   Across town? Babe, it might be a while until / you see her—what?!

Tanya   Henry! (*Beat.*) You know what.

Taylor   I wish I could see her again.

Tanya   I know, sweetheart.

Henry   I'm not gonna be able to see Trevor for eleven months.

Taylor   Oh—sorry.

Henry   I'm not saying it to make you feel bad. It's just a fact.

Taylor   Yeah, but it must be hard, right?

Henry   Not any harder than this.

Taylor   I guess.

Henry   Also, you met her last night?

Taylor   Yeah.

Henry   Then you've got nothing to lose. At the very least, text her.

Taylor (*getting her phone out to text Jasmine*)   Tanya, did you ever have someone special?

Tanya   Quite a few.

Taylor   But, like, did you ever have *the one*.

Tanya   Yeah, there was *some*one.

Taylor   What was their name?

Tanya   Maddie. We met six years ago at the Parade downtown. I was wearing my hair down, back when it was still long, and I was in this outfit that I loved, hanging on the sidelines with some friends . . . And then I saw her, across the street. She was radiant. I don't know what came over me, I walked through the Parade to ask for her name. Maddie. I couldn't stop smiling. She woke something up in me. That feeling of . . . well, almost love, but not quite there yet.

Taylor (*lost in the story*)   Hmmmm.

Tanya   Thank goodness the Parade happens on the 1st as opposed to the 30th, otherwise . . . Anyway, we spent every waking minute together. We had ice cream every day.
When the 30th rolled around, I asked her to stay with me, but she went back to her family. We said we'd keep in touch, but . . .

A pause. **Tanya** *has plated all of the burgers.*

Tanya   Burgers are ready.

Taylor   I'm sure she still thinks about you.

Tanya   Maybe.

Taylor   I hope Jasmine and I see each other again. I want to be in love.

Henry   It's not all roses.

Taylor   At least you have someone.

Tanya   You'll find your person soon enough.

Taylor   You think?

Tanya   I know.

Taylor *smiles.* **Henry**'*s phone buzzes.*

Henry   Oh! Trevor's gonna call me soon.

Tanya   During the barbecue?

Henry   Is that a problem?

Tanya   . . . Not necessarily. We just have to cover some info before. Shouldn't take long.

Taylor   I think it's great you're still together.

Henry   What do you mean?

Taylor   Just that, like, I don't know, you've made it through a whole year! You're an inspiration.

Henry   Oh, go on.

Taylor   I wish they could've stayed with us a bit longer. He's so . . . good. Like, a genuinely good person.

Tanya   Remind me who they're with?

Henry   A group of faeries in Oregon.

Tanya   I'm happy he found a community.

Taylor   Do you know when you'll—

CRASH!!! The backdoor is kicked open. **Sasha**, *with brightly colored hair, walks out holding a boom box, causing the soft music to reach an almost unbearable loudness.*

Sasha   Woohoo! Let's fucking party!!

Tanya (*over the music*)   Sasha!

Sasha *turns the music down.*

Tanya   You know the rules.

Sasha   Rules, schmooles.

Henry   Dude, that's so 1996.

Sasha   Suck my dick. It's our last day of freedom for eleven months. I should be able to play my music as loud as I want.

Tanya   We can't become a target. I'm sorry, Sasha, but you have to keep it at the regulated volume.

They have a stare down, but we already know the winner. **Sasha** *puts the boom box down and starts back inside.*

Tanya   Where are you / going?

Sasha (*exiting*)   Drinks!

Taylor   Are they gonna be okay?

Tanya   Well, it's Sasha. They're about to lay low for a long time, and they're not going down without a fight.

Henry   Wouldn't wanna be on the receiving end of that punch.

Tanya   No one is punching anyone.

Sasha *comes back out with a tray of drinks. They put them on the table.*

Sasha   End of the rainbow. Vodka, tequila, rum, and some orange Kool-Aid.

Taylor   . . . yum?

Everyone gets a drink.

Tanya   Cheers.

They drink.

Tanya   Oh, Sasha, this is strong!

Sasha   Happy last night of freedom.

Henry   Here's to hoping.

Henry *and* **Sasha** *clink their glasses. A brief silence.*

Tanya   How about we all go around and say one of our favorite memories from this past month?

Taylor (*at same time*)   Ooh!

Sasha (*at same time*)   Fuck.

Henry (*at same time*)   Uhhhh—

Taylor   I'll go first. I loved getting to go to the park two weeks ago. For the picnic? Remember? Anyways, I really liked the sundress I wore. And it was so beautiful outside! Also, just getting to, like, exist in a public place. I had forgotten what that felt like.

Tanya   Thanks for sharing. Henry?

Henry   I liked getting railed by Trevor.

Tanya (*at same time*)   Henry!

Taylor (*at same time*)   Wow, uh . . .

Sasha (*laughing, at same time*)   Oh my God.

Tanya   Try again.

Henry   I liked getting to spend time with them. It was cool to actually, like, touch each other. And not always like that, but, like, holding hands, too.

Tanya   Sasha?

Sasha   I liked getting to fuck shit up at the concert last week.

Henry (*shouting with no melody*)   I'M NOT HERE FOR SELF-CONTROL

Sasha/Henry   WHEN THEY SAY STOP IS WHEN WE GO
SHIVERS DOWN MY SPINE IS WHEN YOU KNOW
YOU'RE DOING ALL THE RIGHT THINGS, BABY

Sasha   Ohmygod, it totally made me straight-soothe too!!

Henry   I still can't believe you survived reeducation.

Sasha   Nothing will make me like those cishet normies! (*Doing a specific physical motion, mocking.*) I am cis, I am straight, I am normal, it is great!

Henry   Dude, you should totally put that in a song.

Sasha   Fuck yeah, let's do it—

Tanya   Okay, hold on! We've gotta go over logistics.

Sasha   Right now?

Tanya   Yes, right now. I know that as soon as we're done with our barbecue, you're going to run right back into the world to soak up as much freedom as you can until midnight.

Taylor   Eleven fifty-nine.

Tanya (*sighs*)   Yes, Taylor. Technically one minute before midnight.

Sasha   So, what's the plan?

Tanya   Well . . . things are changing.

Sasha   Well, duh, they always do. Remember last year's rule? "No more power walking down the street." The fuck was that?

Tanya   This time it's . . . more.

Henry   What do you mean?

Tanya   According to the info we have, they're not happy with how loud (*she glances at* **Sasha**) we've been. Not just us—everyone. Apparently we don't know how to "be proud appropriately."

Sasha   What the hell does that mean?

Henry   The fuck?!

Tanya   I know, I know. So, they're tightening parameters.

Taylor   Can they do that?

Henry (*to* **Taylor**)   Does it matter? (*to* **Tanya**) How tight?

Tanya *crosses out a section of the map.*

Tanya   The town square is off limits for / us now. For NOW.

Taylor   What?!

Henry   FUCK that.

Sasha   Are you serious?

Taylor   We can't even go to the movies? Or the mall?

Tanya   We're lucky we get to leave our homes. There are people across the country who aren't allowed to step foot off their front porch.

Sasha   Oh, I'm so grateful. I'm so glad I get the honor and privilege to walk an extra three miles to go to the grocery store! Who needs cars anyway?!

Henry   "What if they use them as weapons? We've got to ban them!"

Sasha   You're Goddamn RIGHT I'd use it as a weapon. Or at the very least, get out of this shit hole!

Tanya   Sasha—

Sasha   We're sitting ducks! Jesus, we're going to DIE in this town!

Henry's *phone rings. He looks at it.*

Henry   Trevor.

Tanya   I'd prefer if you stayed with us—

Henry   Tanya, please?

Another stare down, softer this time. **Tanya** *waves her hand at* **Henry**. "*Go ahead.*" *He answers the phone.*

Henry (*exiting*)   Hey. I miss you too . . .

He's in the house.

Taylor   Sasha, do you want to hear about this girl I met?

Sasha   No.

Taylor   Okay.

Beat.

Tanya   Sasha . . . I think it's time.

Sasha   For what? Oh. Oh, fuck. No. Come on, / Tanya.

Tanya   You knew this going into it.

Sasha   Tanya, please, please let me / keep it—

Tanya   We had a deal. I don't want this anymore than you do.

Sasha   Tanya . . .

Pause. **Sasha** *goes inside.*

Taylor   I hate this day.

Tanya   Me too.

A heavy pause.

Sasha *reenters the backyard with a pair of hair clippers. They slump into a chair.* **Tanya** *turns the clippers on and silently shaves* **Sasha**'*s head.* **Sasha** *keeps their eyes closed the entire time. When* **Tanya** *finishes, she dusts hair off of* **Sasha**'*s shoulders.*

Tanya   There. Done.

Sasha *opens their eyes. They feel their buzzcut.*

Sasha   I want to die!

Tanya   Sasha—

Sasha   What? Is it so wrong to express my wants? You're the one who always tells us to be honest.

Tanya   I also tell you to stay strong—

Sasha   You don't think there's strength in honesty?

Tanya   Of course I do. Don't twist my words.

Taylor   It'll be okay—

Sasha   Shut the FUCK up, Taylor! We live in literal hell! I can't be myself at all except for thirty days out of the year, and then July 1st comes around, and I have to close all of my doors and windows, and lock them, and load the gun, and sit in the corner of my room and pray to a God that doesn't exist to make sure I don't get murdered! I haven't felt free EVER!

Taylor   Tanya says we're lucky—

Sasha   Do you really believe that?

Taylor   I mean, I don't, I don't know—

Sasha   Do you know how I realized I was different? It wasn't some fucking cutesy love story with a girl or seeing myself on tv or whatever. I saw someone one day on the street, and they had bright blue hair and were walking with a girl, and they were holding hands, and I thought to myself, "that! That's me!" And then these two guys showed up and beat the shit out of them. I was eleven. And then the two guys saw me, and you know what they did?

Taylor   N-no.

Sasha   They asked me if I wanted to join. They asked me if I wanted to kick these freaky faggots in the stomach. I just ran. I ran as fast as I could, back to my house, and I was sobbing, and my mom asked me what was wrong, and I told her, and she— fuck, she looked me right in the eyes and said, "join in next time." Right there I realized I could never be myself around her. When I ran away, I wrote my mom a note letting her know I was leaving, but I didn't say why. And I wish I could've told her the truth in some way. But every time I pick up the phone, I think to myself, "she's going to HATE me," and who fucking knows! Maybe she'll send someone to where I am to shoot me in the fucking skull.

Henry *has reentered the backyard at some point.* **Sasha** *storms into the house.* **Tanya** *starts to clean up.*

Henry   Maybe I shouldn't go out—

Tanya   No, it's okay. I'm gonna stay here for the night. Just be back by eleven fifty-nine.

Taylor *'s phone buzzes.*

Taylor   It's Jasmine! She wants to meet and go for a walk. I'm gonna go get my shoes on—

Tanya   Wait, hold on. Henry, you're going too.

Henry   What?? But tonight's "buy one get one free" night at the bar—

Tanya   You've got to stick together.

Henry (*huffs*)   Fine. (*to* **Taylor**) Just don't make out in front of me.

Taylor   No promises!

She runs inside.

Tanya (*to* **Taylor**)   Make sure to have your phone on you!

Taylor (*o/s*)   Okay!

Henry   You sure you're alright?

Tanya   Yeah. You go enjoy your night.

Henry *exits.* **Tanya** *looks up.*

Blackout.

Scene 2

Night. **Tanya** *paces in the backyard. She checks her watch and phone, a bit frantically. A siren rings. The* **Announcer** *is robotic, cold.*

Announcer   Attention please, attention please. The date and time is now July 1st at midnight. Pride Month has ended. All Pride Month festivities must cease. Everyone who is not heterosexual and cisgender must return home. The rules of July through May are now in effect.

Tanya   Shit.

Blackout.

Scene 3

July 1st. Afternoon.

Sasha *lays in the backyard. They lounge, peel through a magazine. They take their phone and call someone. No answer. Again.*

Sasha   C'mon, dude. Pick up.

Tanya *enters the backyard.*

Tanya   Any word?

Sasha   No, not yet.

Tanya   I hope they're okay.

Sasha   I'm sure they're fine. It's Henry. He wouldn't let anything happen to Taylor.

Tanya   Yeah, but what about himself?

Sasha   They're fine.

Beat.

Tanya   This fucking blows.

Sasha   Whoa. Where did that come from?

Tanya   What do you mean? The world we live in—it fucking blows.

Sasha   Well, yeah, duh. I've just never heard you talk like that?

Tanya   Surprise! I hate this too. (*Beat.*) There's gotta be someone we can call.

Sasha   Who?

Tanya   What about your friends?

Sasha   They took a trip across the country.

Tanya   Oh.

Sasha   You suggested I don't go.

Tanya   What? No I didn't.

Sasha   Yeah, you did. "Sasha, the world is so scary." "Oh, Sasha, you're so much safer here." "Sasha, help me set the table while I tell you about the DANGERS of tornadoes."

Tanya   Tornadoes are terrifying!!

Sasha   I just . . . I wish I could see the world. You know? My hometown is only a three-hour drive away. Not far. I've never even been in a plane.

Tanya   Oh, they're not that exciting.

Sasha   What're you talking about? We literally superseded God to build a flying machine that takes us around the world. That's not exciting to you?

Tanya   Alright, fair enough.

Sasha   Wait, when were you on a plane?

Tanya   My family and I used to take trips every so often. We went to Disneyland once.

Sasha   What?!

Tanya   Mhmm. It was pretty great.

Sasha   Oh my God, did you meet Mickey? Did you have dole whip? / What was your favorite ride?

Tanya   Yes. Yes. Space Mountain. It was all lit up inside and we were in a rocket ship flying through the planets and stars.

Sasha   And you say planes aren't interesting.

Tanya   Spaceships are different from planes.

Sasha (*smiling*)   Yeah, whatever. (*Beat.*) What made you want to do this, anyway?

Tanya   Do what?

Sasha   Take us in. I mean, I've been with you for a year now. Henry came a few weeks later, and Taylor's been here, what? Six months?

Tanya   Five.

Sasha   She's so young.

Tanya   You're telling me. Running away from home at 17 . . .

Sasha   Her birthday party was fun.

Tanya   At least they lowered the drinking age to 18.

Sasha   Probably to kill us sooner.

Tanya   Don't talk like that.

Sasha   You know it's true. (*Beat*) But seriously. Why do you do this?

Tanya   Why the sudden curiosity?

Sasha   I dunno. I guess I just never asked. So I am now.

Tanya   You're not one to normally care about these sorts of things.

Sasha   I just—don't want to think about Henry and Taylor right now. So.

Tanya *thinks for a moment.*

Tanya   I wanted someone to do the same for me. When I came out . . . it was—it was different. I didn't have to hide myself as much as we do now.

Sasha   Yeah, but it still sucked. Right?

Tanya   My mom—one day I came home from school, I was 16 or 17, and my mom was sitting in the living room, and she called me in and gave me a book.

Sasha   Oh, yeah?

Tanya   It was some young adult novel where two girls fall in love.

Sasha   Cute.

Tanya   It was more than cute. It meant that she had to go to the bookstore and find it, maybe even ask someone for help, and buy it. She spent real money on that book. For me. The story was cheesy, and the characters were way too stereotypical, but . . . it meant the world that she did that.

Sasha   Must be nice to have a mom that accepts you.

Tanya   My mom died when I was 22. She was killed by—someone I knew who hated the fact that I was gay, but I was away at school, so he killed the next best thing.

Sasha   Oh. Fuck, I'm so sorry.

Tanya   It was hard. Harder than it is now. When I found out, I became really depressed. I made it through my final semester of college, but after I graduated, I was lost. I couldn't go back home. So, I wandered for a bit. Ended up here. I found a group of traveling queer folk that were trying to get to Maine. They said if they could make it to the tip of the States, they might be able to make it out.

Sasha   Did they?

Tanya   I don't know. I got off early. When the new rules started to be put into place, I had already gotten a job as a server at a restaurant. This house was actually for sale at a super discounted price because a gay couple had lived here before. "Untouchable property," the realtor had said. So, I bought it. Then I found you. I had empty bedrooms, and I was getting lonely.

Sasha   I was too.

Tanya   Then with Henry and Taylor . . . we've got a rag-tag team going.

Sasha   Yeah.

Tanya   I hope they're okay.

Sasha   I'm sure they are.

Beat.

Sasha *begins to walk into the house.*

Tanya   What're you doin——

Sasha   Shots!

They go into the house.

Tanya (*shouting to o/s*)   Sasha! (*Beat.*) I don't know if we should be drinking right now——

Sasha *reenters with two shot glasses. They thrust a shot glass at* **Tanya**. *She sighs, then takes it. They clink glasses and take the shot.* **Tanya** *gags.*

Tanya   Oh, jeez, Sasha, what is this?

Sasha   It's just vodka.

Tanya   Remind me to never take a shot from you again.

Sasha *pours both another shot.* **Tanya** *gives them a look, but they both take it.*

Sasha   Do you ever wish you weren't queer?

Tanya   No.

Sasha   Oh.

Tanya   Why?

Sasha   I dunno. (*Pause.*) Because then we'd be free. We'd get to live our lives to the fullest, we wouldn't have to follow these stupid rules, we could travel the world in as many airplanes as we wanted to.

Tanya   But then I wouldn't be me.

Sasha   Yeah you would, you'd just be a straight version of you.

Tanya   And that's not the me that I know.

Sasha   But—

Tanya   I'm not here to play by someone else's rules. At least, as much as I can help it. I like being queer. I like being different. I feel like it's a superpower, like when I'm around my queer Justice League, I can do anything.

Sasha   But you can't.

Tanya   Neither can straight people!

Sasha   They can do a hell of a lot more than we can!

Tanya   So what? I knew straight people who had as much drive in them as I do in my left big toe. These parts of us don't speak to how passionate we are about our job, or our will to survive. If anything, being queer's helped me see what's really important. And that isn't traveling, or breaking rules, or getting to stay out past sunset. Sure, I'd love to do all of that, but what makes me, me, is my love for the three of you. It's my choice to do what I can to keep us all safe, and healthy, and happy. It's my decision to say, "screw you!" to the world we live in. Because that's just the fact. That's our world. And I want to make it as good as I can for me. For us.

Tanya *pours herself another shot, takes it.*

Tanya   All that being said, though . . . I would love to have my freedom back. Those two things can live at once.

Sasha   What two things?

Tanya   Making the best of the world I have, and wishing it wasn't the world we have.

Sasha   Yeah.

Tanya   Also, just, like, going out dancing. I miss moving to a beat with strangers.

Sasha   We can dance right now if you wanna.

Tanya   No, no.

Sasha   Come on! It'll be fun.

Tanya   I lost my ballet slippers in the war!

But **Sasha** *has already started the boom box. They put on a song with a good beat.* **Sasha** *starts to dance.*

Sasha   Come on! Don't be such a pussy.

Tanya   Hey now, don't use that language with me.

Sasha   Take a chill pill, *grandma.*

Tanya   Grandma?? Okay, now I sense a challenge.

Tanya *starts dancing. The two dance for a while. Perhaps* **Tanya** *twirls* **Sasha**. *It is free, wild, rejuvenating.*

Tanya   Whooo, I need to sit down.

Sasha (*still dancing*)   Oh, come on! This is the best part of the song.

Tanya   Nah, that booze is hitting me a little harder now.

Sasha   Whatever. I'm used to dancing by myself.

Sasha *continues to dance.* **Tanya** *stares up at the sky. Her phone rings, she answers it.*

Tanya   Hello? Taylor?

Sasha *turns the music down.*

Tanya   Where are you? . . . You're what? You're breaking up . . . Who's coming? . . . He went where??? . . . Come home, right now— . . . Taylor? Taylor, hello?? FUCK!!

Sasha   What??

Tanya   She—they were attacked. Last night. Apparently Henry convinced Taylor and Jasmine to go to the club, they were about to leave but—I think they lost track of time? Henry tried to fight back, he ran off, said he's going to go find Trevor, oh my god, he left her, he left Taylor, I'm going to kill him—

Sasha   Okay, deep breaths.

Tanya   This is EXACTLY why I didn't want you all to go out!!

Sasha   Where's Taylor?

Tanya   I don't know, she was cutting out, I couldn't tell if she was on her way back, or what. She might still be with Jasmine. God, I'm so stupid. Why did I let them go?

Sasha   They're going to be fine.

Tanya   You don't know that.

Sasha   They're smart, Henry wouldn't have run off if he didn't think it would help—

Tanya   My ONE rule for him was that he stay with her.

Sasha   I'm sure it's going to be—

An explosion in the distance.

Tanya   What was that?

Sasha   I don't know—

Another explosion, a bit closer now.

Tanya   Get inside. The sun's going down, people could be coming from anywhere—

A siren rings. More explosions. Shouts. **Tanya** *and* **Sasha** *freeze. The* **Announcer***'s voice comes on. Explosions are heard throughout this text.*

Announcer   Attention please, attention please. A word from our president.

Static. Then:

The President   My fellow citizens of America. We have a crisis on our hands. As I'm sure many of you know, uprisings have started across the country. The attackers are those who have refused quarantine. When we implemented The New Pride Month, we held expectations for those who fell inside its parameters. We also explained the consequences. To those that chose not to listen this year, I have a message for you: You are not the first to rebel. You will not be the first to succeed.

We are a strong nation, with an army that exceeds all power you think you hold. We will fight back using any means necessary. You do not get to live above the law. To those in quarantine: I thank you for your cooperation. Remain in your spaces. Stay there. It's where you're safest, and where you belong.

To those able to move freely: I recommend you get inside as quickly as possible. We want to keep all normal casualties to a minimum.

God blesses those who deserve it. You know who you are. You know who you aren't.

Static. Silence. A pause. **Tanya** *gets up. She moves into the house with purpose.*

Sasha   What are you doing? . . . Tanya?

Tanya *returns holding a gun.*

Sasha   Holy fuck, why do you have / a gun?

Tanya   I'm going out there.

Sasha   What??

Tanya   I have to / find Taylor–

Sasha   You're just going to leave me here?

Tanya   You're tough. You'll be fine. Taylor's innocent, she can't survive on her own.

Sasha   I'm coming with you.

Tanya   No, you're not.

Sasha *starts to go inside.* **Tanya** *grabs them.*

Sasha (*struggling*)   Let go of me!

Tanya   You have to stay here!!

Sasha   Fuck that, fuck you!! I'm coming with you!!

Tanya   No, you're NOT!!

She pushes **Sasha** *to the ground.*

A dizzying silence.

Tanya *gets down on the ground next to* **Sasha**.

Tanya   I can't lose you too. Please.

An explosion much closer than before.

Sasha   It's not safe here either—

Tanya   Call me if you need me. I'll be back soon.

Before **Sasha** *has time to say anything,* **Tanya** *runs out.* **Sasha** *slowly moves back to a chair and sits down. They look up at the sky.*

Blackout.

Scene 4

That night.

Sasha *is wide awake in the chair. They haven't gone inside. It is well past the two hours that* **Tanya** *said she'd be back by.* **Sasha** *called many times, to no avail. They try again. The call goes straight to voicemail for the first time.*

They turn the news on again from their boombox. They've been listening on and off.

News Anchor   —hundreds of deaths thus far. The riots currently show no sign of backing down. The National Guard has been called in, and we're not sure what weapons they're planning on using. The mall and movie theater are safe havens for those with the gray dot sticker on their forms of ID, identifying them as heterosexual and cisgender. Members of the Disowned have been ordered to return to quarantine, or risk facing death—

They turn the news off. Eventually, **Sasha** *gets up and goes into the house. We hear the front door open and slam shut.*

Blackout.

Scene 5

May 31st of the next year. A forest in Oregon. **Henry** *sits in a very out-of-place lounge chair next to a tent. A gas-powered stove is lit, cooking a stew.*

Trevor *returns with some vegetables.* **Henry** *looks over.*

Trevor   Hey hey, I brought some zucchini.

Henry   Ugh, I hate zucchini.

Trevor   But you love me!

They put the vegetables in the stew. The two of them remain in silence for a moment.

Trevor   How're you doing?

Henry   Fine.

Trevor   Good.

Beat.

Trevor   I saw Samantha at the gathering spot.

Henry   How is she?

Trevor   She's okay. Caroline is coming back soon.

Henry   That'll be good for her.

Trevor   Yeah.

Beat.

Trevor   Stew's ready.

They pour some into two bowls and bring one to **Henry**.

Henry   Thanks. (*He takes a bite.*) It's really good.

Trevor   You think? I tried something new—

Henry   Yeah, tastes great.

Trevor   Thanks.

Beat.

Henry   Taylor called me today.

Trevor   She did?? Oh, fuck. What did she say? How is she?

Henry   She's fine. Her and Jasmine are still going cross country.

Trevor   That's so dangerous.

Henry   I mean, look at us.

Trevor   Yeah, but we're not out in the open, and we're with a group.

Henry   I'm sure they'll find us eventually.

Trevor   Henry . . .

Henry   Whatever. They're coming to Oregon.

Trevor   Oh, really?

Henry   Yeah. They were wondering if they could visit. I told them we live in a forest, they said they live in their van. They should be here in a few days.

Trevor   Cool! I'm excited to see her again.

Henry   I miss them.

Trevor   Yeah.

Henry   I'm glad Taylor is still in touch, but . . . I don't know. I just want some closure with Sasha, you know? They're not talking to me. When they told me about Tanya . . .

Trevor   I remember.

Henry   But—I guess I gotta give them time.

Trevor *comes up behind* **Henry** *and wraps his arms around him.*

Trevor   Sasha's tough. Smart, too. I'm sure they're fighting against the villainous cishets of the world.

Henry   It's not the same as knowing.

Trevor   I know. (*Beat.*) I'm excited to take Taylor and Jasmine to the beach.

Henry (*chuckling*)   What?

Trevor   The beach! Tomorrow's the first and we can go to the beach every day for the next month!

Henry   Yeah. It'll be nice.

Trevor   What do you want to do?

Henry   Oh, I don't know. Grab an ice cream cone and sit in the park. Go to the movies. Have an orgy.

Trevor (*laughing*)   Shut up.

Henry   I just wanna get out of this forest.

Trevor   Yeah. And just like, not shower at the gym.

Henry   Where else can we shower?

Trevor   The ocean.

Henry   We won't get clean!

Trevor   Who needs to be clean when you have FREEDOM!!!

They run around. **Henry** *laughs.* **Trevor** *pulls* **Henry** *up to play. They eventually hold each other.*

Trevor   I'm so glad you came here.

Henry   Yeah. Me too.

Trevor *looks up at the sky.*

Trevor   Not much longer now.

Henry   Hmm?

Trevor   The sun. It's going down.

Henry *looks up. They look at the sky together.*

Blackout.

End of Part 1.

Part II

The Shepard

Scene 1

A video appears projected onto the back wall. It's of a commercial for a politician.

Elizabeth (*voiceover*)   The world we live in needs to change. I can be that change for you.

Shots of people laughing, smiling, talking with one another.

Elizabeth (*voiceover*)   The United States of America has gone through many changes throughout history. Many of us have worked to make it safer. Cleaner. More accessible.

Shots of queer and trans people, tinted red.

Elizabeth (*voiceover*)   Others have worked to make it worse. Dirtier. Pushing agendas left and right.

Shots of scared people.

Elizabeth (*voiceover*)   Over the past 12 years, riots have overtaken our country. The Disowned need to learn who's in control.

Slo-mo shots of a woman standing in front of a herd of sheep, arms wide, eyes closed.

Elizabeth (*voiceover*)   We need to get back onto the right path.

Elizabeth *comes onscreen. She wears a red pantsuit. She is the epitome of powerful.*

Elizabeth   Let me be your shepherd. My name is Elizabeth Abbott. And I'm running to be your next president.

Blackout.

Scene 2

Elizabeth'*s office.* **Elizabeth** *sits at her desk. The desk has paperwork and a landline telephone. A fresh young aide,* **Ross** *sits opposite of her, on his phone.*

It's election day. Tensions are high.

Ross   Polls are looking good.

Elizabeth   I know.

Ross   How're you feeling?

Elizabeth   Great.

Ross   Good. We've sent out a press release to The Right Way News, they'll be reading it in an hour or so. We've also got to get you to headquarters for the rally and results in a bit—

Elizabeth   Ross. Calm down. I'm gonna win. We're gonna win.

Ross   I know, I know, it's just, with Whitmore's smear campaign—

Elizabeth   That bitch of a Speaker? Please. She's got nothing on me.

Ross   I'm just nervous because both the house and senate are democrat-led, even if you do win—

Elizabeth   Ross! Don't let your nerves get the best of you. We've got the white vote, we've got the normal vote, we've even got some of the Disowned vote, for Christ's sake. We can't lose.

Ross   I—yeah. You're right.

Elizabeth   Where is Michael?

Ross   He's finishing up an interview with The Right Way—

Elizabeth   I know that. How long could an interview with a VP take?? He's not the president.

Ross   No, of course, sorry—

Elizabeth   Jesus, just go get me a Perrier.

Ross   Uh—sure. Just a sec.

He leaves. **Elizabeth** *takes out her phone and calls someone.*

Elizabeth (*on phone*)   Hi . . . Yeah, I'm good, we should win . . . Don't be nervous! Even if we do lose, we have plans in place, you know this, that's why we're in this together. Right?. . .yeah, exactly.

Ross *reenters the room, holding a bottle of Perrier.*

Elizabeth (*on phone*)   Okay, I've got to go . . . Yeah, me too. Bye.

Ross (*handing her the bottle*)   Who was that?

Elizabeth (*opening the bottle*)   Michael. He was asking what gerrymandering was again. Fucking idiot.

Beat.

Elizabeth   Ross, what brought you to politics?

Ross   Hmm?

Elizabeth   What brought you to politics?

Ross   Oh, uh, why do you want to know?

Elizabeth   Just making conversation.

Ross   I wanted to change the world for the better.

Elizabeth   You wanted to change the world for the better. (*Beat.*) Do you feel like you've accomplished that?

Ross   I, uh, feel like I'm doing it, especially working for you—

Elizabeth   Oh, please. Don't give me that. Do you feel like you've changed the world for the better? (*Beat.*) You're, what? 30?

Ross   28, actually—

Elizabeth   28, 30, what's the difference. You're *young*. (*Beat*) What brought you to work on preserving our country's safety? To work against the Disowned?

Ross   Um. Well, it wasn't one thing, really. My parents just brought me up with these values and morals, and I agreed with them—

Elizabeth   Have you ever questioned them?

Ross   Questioned them?

Elizabeth   Yes. Or do you just agree with anything that's brought forth to you?

Ross   Uh . . . I'm not sure.

Elizabeth   You're an aide. To someone who's going to win the presidency. And you don't have any morals or values of your own?

Ross   Well, I do—

Elizabeth   Tell me one.

Ross   I care about people.

Elizabeth   You care about people.

Ross   Yes.

Elizabeth   Which people?

Ross   The people that matter.

Elizabeth   Who matters?

Ross   Normal people.

Elizabeth   And who decides that?

Ross   We do.

Elizabeth   Who's "we"?

Ross   I'm sorry, I'm not sure why you're asking me all of this—

Elizabeth   Because being a politician means being very acutely aware of what you believe in, why you believe it, and who it affects. It means being able to stand up against those shitheads who disagree with you by any means necessary, but doing so in a way that appeases everyone. Being a politician means knowing how to answer any question, at any time, with minimal damage to your party, your constituents, and your brand.

So. I ask you again. Who's "we"?

Ross   We are the ones who are in the right. The ones who know what's best. The ones who can enact tangible change for everyone, even those who don't know what's best for them.

Elizabeth   Good.

Ross   Yeah?

Elizabeth   Don't grovel for approval, Ross.

Ross *goes quiet for a moment.*

Ross   What brought *you* to politics?

Elizabeth   I really hope you know the answer to this question.

Ross   Well, yeah, of course, but like, what *happened*? You talked a lot on your campaign trail about wanting to protect the innocence of children and families because of what you saw when you were growing up. What did you see?

Pause.

Elizabeth   What did I see.

Ross   Yeah.

Elizabeth   Hmm.

I saw pain. I saw anxiety. I saw parents trying desperately to protect their children and failing to do so. I saw . . . people causing chaos, violence, tragedy against those who have never deserved it because of ruthless lies.

Ross   Anything in specific?

Elizabeth   You're very curious, aren't you?

Ross   It's just a question.

Elizabeth   I was young. My parents came home one day with . . . another child. A boy. Who became my brother. I was never asked if I wanted a brother. I never found out why they didn't just have another child the way people are supposed to. But . . . that child, my "brother," was one of the most stereotypical little homos I've ever met. I hate him.

Ross   Why did they do that?

Elizabeth   Because they could.

I won't let anyone hurt the way I did. I won't let anyone bring another . . . member of the Disowned into their lives or the world again.

Ross   Oh. I'm sorry.

Elizabeth   It is what it is.

Ross   My, um, uncle was bi.

Pause.

Elizabeth   Okay.

Ross   It was really hard for my dad to accept.

Pause.

Elizabeth   Great.

Ross   He was really hurting—

Elizabeth   Ross, this isn't a competition.

Ross   I was just trying to relate–

Elizabeth   Well, don't. You can't.

Elizabeth *works on paperwork.* **Ross** *gets a text.*

Ross   Shit.

Elizabeth   What?

Ross   Michael was caught with another sex worker.

Elizabeth   What?? Again?? Who??

Ross   Doesn't say.

Elizabeth   God fucking damn it, and on election day!

Ross   It'll be fine—

Elizabeth   Shut up.

Beat.

Ross   Can I ask you a question—

Elizabeth (*visibly stressed*)   I mean, that's all you've been doing, so.

Ross   Why did you bring him on? He's new to the world of politics, he's young.

Elizabeth   Exactly. He pulls the young vote. And the female vote.

Ross   The female vote?

Elizabeth   Yeah. He's conventionally attractive. Women love him.

Ross   I guess.

Elizabeth   I don't even know why he pays for sex. Any woman with a pulse wants to fuck him.

Ross *does a very brief straight-soothing motion.*

Elizabeth   Uh—

Ross   What?

Elizabeth   You just—

Ross   No I didn't.

Beat.

Elizabeth   Ross, have you ever been in a relationship?

Ross (*going to exit*)   Hey, The Right Way wants an interview with you—

Elizabeth   Answer the question or you're fired.

Ross   Wow, um. No. I haven't.

Elizabeth   Why not?

Ross   This feels a bit personal to talk about—

Elizabeth   I'm your boss.

Ross   Technically, your campaign manager is my boss—

Elizabeth   And I'm his boss, so I'm yours. Answer me.

Ross   I just. Haven't, um. Found anyone I want to be with.

Elizabeth   No? There's plenty of young women around who would love to go out with you.

Ross   I don't find any of them attractive.

Elizabeth   Really? Not even Beth? Her tits are huge.

Ross   Wow, that's not—

Elizabeth   Or what about Tiffany? She'll sleep with any guy with a pulse.

Ross   Can we not—

Elizabeth   There's always Matilda. I'm pretty sure she's asked about you—

Ross   Stop, okay! I don't want to date any of them.

Elizabeth (*locked and loaded*)   And why not?

Ross (*straight-soothing*)   I just don't, can we drop it?

Elizabeth   There.

Ross (*stumbling over words*)   No, I just, look—

Elizabeth   I know what that was.

Pause.

Ross Look. I'm good. Okay?

Elizabeth You're good.

Ross . . . . Yes. I'm . . . normal.

A very tense beat.

Elizabeth You should leave.

Ross What?

Elizabeth You should leave. Now.

Ross Look, I'm sorry—

Elizabeth Ross.

Ross *looks at her, deeper than before.*

Elizabeth Go.

Michael *saunters in.*

Michael Hey hey hey! How's my favorite lady?

He sees **Elizabeth** *and* **Ross***.*

Michael Am I interrupting something—

Elizabeth I've just fired Ross. He's too incompetent.

Michael (*with power*) Oh?

Elizabeth Goodbye, Ross.

Ross *looks at her, then* **Michael***, then stands up and walks to the door.*

Ross *turns around. He makes eye contact with* **Elizabeth***.*

He leaves.

Michael What was that all about?

Elizabeth Another prostitute?

Michael Oh, come on, Liz, it's no big thing.

Elizabeth What did I say about calling me Liz.

Michael Sorry. (*Back on track.*) Anywho, polls are looking good! We're gonna win.

Elizabeth Yep.

Michael*'s phone rings. He answers it.*

Michael (*on phone*) Bro, what's up!. . .Yeah, just chilling with Liz.

She gives him a dirty look.

Michael (*on phone*) Dude, Matilda was totally into me last weekend at the bar . . . Mhmm, she wants a one-way ticket to pound town, I can tell.

Elizabeth   Michael.

Michael (*on phone*)   One sec. (*To* **Elizabeth**.) What's up?

Elizabeth   Off.

Michael (*on phone*)   Sorry man, gotta go. I'll chat once I'm VP.

He hangs up.

Elizabeth   Is this a joke to you?

Michael   What?

Elizabeth   This race. Your position. Is this just one big game?

Michael   A game? Nah, this isn't a game. But if it was, we'd totally be winning.

Elizabeth *takes a moment, then walks over to* **Michael**.

Michael   What's up?

Elizabeth (*toying with his hair*)   I just . . . think you're doing great work.

Michael   Yeah?

Elizabeth   Mhmm. And . . . thinking about you and Matilda gets me kinda . . . jealous.

Michael (*getting excited*)   Yeah??

Elizabeth   Yeah. I don't want you to be with her.

Michael   Yeah???

Elizabeth   I want you all to myself.

She leans in for a kiss, then knees him in the groin.

Michael   Ow! Fuck!

Elizabeth   Don't you EVER talk about my staff like that again. Got it?

Michael (*in pain*)   Yes ma'am.

His phone pings. He looks at it.

Michael (*looking at his phone*)   Oh, shit.

Elizabeth   What now?

Michael   Ohhhh, you're not gonna like this.

Elizabeth   What?!

Michael *passes* **Elizabeth** *his phone.*

Elizabeth   Are you *fucking* kidding me? Two rallies???

Michael   I know, it makes / no sense–

Elizabeth   I'm going to murder that dismal excuse for a press secretary.

Michael   What're you gonna do?

Elizabeth (*after a microsecond of thought*)   You're going to go in my place to the one in Virginia.

Michael (*with great responsibility*)   I am?

Elizabeth   You are.

Michael   Oh, wow. (*Puffs chest out.*) Looks like the Mikester is ready for action.

Elizabeth (*unphased*)   Michael.

He turns to face her.

Elizabeth   If you fuck this up in any way, you're dead.

Michael *chuckles, but when he sees* **Elizabeth** *remain firm, he stops.*

Michael   Oh, come on, Elizabeth. We make a great team.

Elizabeth   Right. Team. Sure.

Michael'*s phone pings.*

Michael (*reading from phone*)   The car is here. That was fast. Says I'll be briefed on the way.

He begins to leave.

Michael (*while leaving*)   Don't worry Liz, everything will / go according to plan!

Elizabeth   Stop calling me that!!

But he's already out the door.

Elizabeth *sighs into her hands, then calls someone on her cell phone.*

Elizabeth (*on phone*)   Hi . . . Yeah, he's on his way. You did your end of the deal, right? . . . Good.

Her phone pings.

Elizabeth (*on phone*) Oh, babe, one sec.

She checks it.

Elizabeth (*on phone*)   Baby, I gotta go to my rally downtown . . . Mhmm . . . You and I, together forever. See you on the other side.

She hangs up and leaves.

Blackout.

Scene 3

Over black.

Announcer (*voiceover*)   And with 97 percent of the votes being counted, it's official, Elizabeth Abbott is our next president of the United States, and our first female president.

Scene 4

The day of **Elizabeth***'s inauguration.*

LIGHTS UP on **Elizabeth** *sitting at her desk in the oval office.*

Elizabeth   My fellow Americans. As I said during my inauguration, I am honored to serve as your president. Now that I've been elected, I'm able to tell you a few truths that I've been waiting to share. All of my actions, from my campaign announcement up until this very moment, have been heavily calculated to the point that nothing could go wrong. And nothing did. So now, the truths.
First. My name is Elizabeth Abbott. But it has not always been Elizabeth Abbott, and I was assigned male at birth. I am a transgender woman.

Second. I am not a conservative. I am a liberal. Specifically, what many of you would call a "left wing extremist." I am everything you were voting to annihilate. And I am going to annihilate you.

Third. You may be wondering where Vice President Walters is. Vice President Walters is dead. Because of such, our Speaker of the House, Sasha Whitmore, becomes our new Vice President.

Finally, I speak to the queer and trans communities. Our time has come. Do not hide in fear any longer. Create it instead.

And. I speak to the cishet, the new Disowned, community. I am your shepherd. You are my sheep. And I will slaughter anyone who gets in my way.

Sounds of chaos surround her, but she is the eye of the hurricane. As people are arrested, as champagne bottles are popped, as orders are shouted, she sits. Smiles. She has won.

Blackout.

End of Part II.

Part III

Ripe

Scene 1.

Four years after Part II.

We're in a ridiculously nice house.

Kai, **Marty**, **River**, *and* **Brigitte** *sit and play cards.*

Kai Got any fours, River?

River Go fish.

Kai *draws a card.*

Brigitte Hmm . . . Hey Kai, got any fours?

Kai (*handing his cards over*) Ughhhhhh.

Brigitte Heheheheheh. (*To* **Marty**.) Marty, got any queens?

Marty *gestures to himself. The group laughs.*

Marty (*handing his cards over*) Brigitte, you're good at this!

Brigitte (*taking the cards*) What can I say? I'm a natural.

Ross, *a bit older now, enters with a snack platter.*

Ross Who's hungry?

Brigitte *gets up quickly and races over, scattering the deck in the process. All the other kids groan at her.*

River Come on, dude!

Brigitte (*mouth full of food*) There is HUMMUS, Riv. Do not get mad at me when there is HUMMUS. (*Maybe in a bad British accent.*) Thank you for the food, papa!

Kai (*joining in*) Yes, thank you so much!

Ross (*joining in*) Of course, anything for my precious children!

River You all are so weird.

Brigitte Maybe YOU'RE the weird one!

River Yeah, right.

Marty's *phone pings. He checks it.*

Marty Oh oh oh! Ross!

Ross (*matching* **Marty***'s excitement*)   Marty!

Marty   You gotta come with me to the comic store this weekend!! The author of *The Non-Binary Bandit* is going to be there!

Ross   No way! Do you think they'll sign comics?

Marty   Duh!

Ross   I'm in!

Brigitte   Wait, if Ross is going with you to the comic bookstore, then I want Ross to go with me to the park! You said we could get ice cream, too!

River   Will you go with me to the sports store? I wanna get a new basketball.

Kai   Didn't you get one, like, last week?

River   Yeah, but this one is SPARKLY.

Ross   We'll get you a new basketball. (*To* **Brigitte**.) And ice cream. (*To* **Marty**.) *And* we'll get your comic signed.

Marty, **River**, *and* **Brigitte** *cheer.* **Marty***'s phone pings again. He checks it.*

Marty   Ohmigod!!! Taylor's livestreaming!!

Brigitte   WHAT?!? With Jasmine?!

Marty   Yes!!!

River   We gotta watch! She's so cool!

The three start to race out of the room.

Brigitte   Are you coming, Kai?

Kai (*pointed, with love*)   Nah, I'm gonna hang with Ross for a bit, help him *clean up.*

Brigitte   Hah! Nerd.

She races out of the room. **Kai** *shakes his head.*

Kai   She's a lot.

Ross   Hey, she's happy being herself, which is all I want. You've all been through enough.

Kai   Yeah. (*Beat*) Do you think you should talk with them about President Abbott?

Ross   Where'd that come from?

Kai   I dunno, just thinking.

Ross   What about?

Kai   Her partner.

Ross   Oh. Yeah.

A gloomy beat.

Kai (*trying to lighten the mood*)   Can I have twenty bucks?

Ross (*chuckling*)   What?

Kai   If Marty gets a basketball, I should get twenty bucks.

Ross   That doesn't make any sense–

Kai   ¯_(ツ)_/¯

Ross   Fair enough.

Ross *gets his wallet out. A picture falls out of it.*

Ross (*going to get it*)   Oh, oops—

Kai *gets it first. They stare at it.*

Kai   Wait, is this—is this you and President Abbott?

Ross   . . . Yes. (*Beat.*) I, uh . . . used to work for her.

Kai   You WHAT?

Ross   Yeah—

Kai   You never mentioned that!!

Ross   I was on her first campaign as an aide. This was before she came out. She didn't let anyone know about her true identity. There was so much violence, specifically against our community, she couldn't risk telling anyone.

Kai   Except for President Whitmore.

Ross   Yeah.

Kai   I hope they're doing okay.

Ross   They're in mourning. We all are. Elizabeth was a trailblazer for our communities. And to go out in such a terrible way . . .

Kai   These people are so fucking sick.

Ross   Language—

Kai   This just really pisses me off!! The Disowned / think they can just take the power back.

Ross   Cishet. (*After* **Kai** *finishes.*) I mean, it can't be easy for them. Having parameters for where they can stay? Only having one month out of the year to be free?

Kai   You're *sympathizing* with them??

Ross   All I'm saying is, it must be hard.

Kai   It was hard when Brigitte got her head stuck in the banister and we had to get her out. Our lives were awful because of them. I'm glad the Disowned are getting what they deserve.

Ross   That's intense, Kai.

Kai   They can't take away the trauma they caused for hundreds of thousands of people. They can't take away **your** trauma—

Ross   I know, but violence doesn't solve anything—

Kai   We wouldn't have rights if it weren't for violence.

Ross   But the rights of others were taken away—

Kai   No! All of my friends from my message boards agree with me. / We have to keep fighting back.

Ross   I thought I asked you to stop going onto those boards—

Kai   They're the only ones who get it. And they have such good ideas! They're not afraid to fight.

Brigitte (*offstage*)   Rossssssssssss!!

Brigitte *rushes in, trailed by* **Marty** *and* **River**.

Brigitte   We're gonna go for an adventure in the garden!! Wanna come??? Kai, you should come too!! Oh my god, Kai, can I ride on your back????? OH MY GOD DO YOU THINK THE TOMATOES ARE READY—

Kai   We're busy.

Brigitte   Okay, party pooper, your loss! (*To* **Marty**.) Come on, my trusty steed!

Marty   I am not a HORSE.

Brigitte   All in favor of Marty being a person?

Silence.

Brigitte   All opposed?

River   Neigh!

Brigitte (*running out*)   Weeeee!

Marty (*following*)   Really?

River (*following*)   Heh.

They're gone.

Kai   She can be so LOUD sometimes.

Ross   Well, yeah, she's a kid.

Kai   It's just so obnoxious—

Ross   You used to be loud.

Kai   I used to be a child.

Ross   And now you're all grown up, at eighteen?

Kai   I'm *mature.*

Ross   Do your friends on the message board tell you that?

Kai   Shut up, Ross.

Ross   Excuse me?

Kai   You just don't know what it's like, being young.

Ross   You do know I used to be young, right?

Kai   Well, yeah, but life SUCKS sometimes.

Ross   Kai, we live in a beautiful home, we never go hungry, and we're *safe.*

Kai (*under his breath*)   Whatever.

Ross   What was that?

Kai (*in* **Ross**'*face*)   WHATEVER. God!

Ross   Go to your room!

Kai   I don't have to listen to you!

Ross   I'm getting angry. I need a breather.

He leaves.

After a moment, the other three kids run in. **Brigitte**'*s shirt is stained red.*

Brigitte   Kai, Kai! I've been attacked by a killer llama! Oh, help me!

She pretends to fall to the ground, dead. It's a very dramatic performance. After a moment:

Brigitte   Nah, I'm just kidding, it's tomato juice. Want one?

She presents a tomato to **Kai** *in the palm of her hand. She takes it.*

Marty   Dude, you okay?

Silence.

River   Wanna talk about it?

Kai   I'm just so tired of fighting.

Brigitte   Fighting what? Dragons? Monsters? Tax increases?

The three give her a look.

Brigitte   I heard it on TV. I don't even know what a tax is!

Kai   Fighting *people.* Arguing. It like, doesn't even feel good when I do it.

River   When're you arguing with people?

Kai   Just like, online and stuff.

River   Oh. Yeah, those people never get you anywhere.

Brigitte   Also! Remember what Ross says. It's okay to be sad. (*In a very zen voice.*) You gotta let yourself feel the feelings, MAN.

River   Straight up.

They high five without making eye contact.

Kai   I just hate how much this world can suck sometimes.

Brigitte   Well, duh. We live in the same world as tax increases!!

Kai   And like, you're all still so young, you've got so much to look forward to.

River   You're eighteen.

Marty   Yeah, dude. You can't even be President yet. Or rent a car.

Brigitte   At least you don't have to worry about tax increases!

River   Brigitte—

Brigitte   Heheheheheh.

Ross *reenters, a bit sheepishly.*

Brigitte   Ross! Tomato!

Brigitte *throws a tomato at him. He eats it.*

Ross   Delicious! I know what's going in the salad tonight. Will y'all go collect some more for me?

Brigitte (*running out the door*)   DIBS ON THE BASKET!

River (*running after her*)   No fair, you got it last time!

Marty *and* **Kai** *share a look. Based on* **Kai***'s reaction,* **Marty** *feels good enough to leave.*

A slightly awkward pause.

Ross   Did you know I was scared when I took you all in? (*Beat.*) It's true. I was a mid-30s asexual single guy who had just randomly inherited a mansion. My dinners consisted of takeout or microwavable meals. Throw four new humans into the mix? I was terrified. But it was also the best thing I've ever done. (*Beat.*) I didn't have anyone to look to when I was younger. When I was working for Elizabeth, I was so deep in my reeducation that I genuinely thought she was right. But the day I got fired, I came back into myself almost fully. And after I left, I had this moment of, 'how the hell did I get here?' And I wanted to do my best to make sure no one else would have those moments. I think you have moments like that. Right?

Kai *shrugs.*

Ross   Well, if you do, I'm glad you can do it in a *safe place.* (*Beat.*) I want to welcome more into this house. We still have tons of room. Now that there's more accessibility for queer and trans kids to find people who want to care for them instead of the people they were born to . . . I dunno. I might do it.

Kai *considers this for a long moment.*

Kai   You really did change our lives. I mean, Brigitte was a wreck when she was placed here.

Brigitte *peeks in from the kitchen, holding a basket of tomatoes.*

Brigitte   I heard that!

Kai   Go collect your tomatoes!

Brigitte   Okay, MOM.

She goes back outside.

Kai   I know I've only been here for a few months, but you made me feel like . . . like I belong here. I want to help others find that feeling.

A moment.

Kai   I'm gonna go help with tomatoes.

They start to leave.

Ross   Kai?

Kai *turns around.*

Ross   If you need help, financially . . .

Kai   Thanks.

She goes. **Ross** *looks around at this big, big house.*

A knock at the door. **Ross** *goes to answer it. He opens the door.*

Sasha *stands on the other side. They're more put together, less angry from when we last saw them. Hair still wild. Two secret service agents stand behind her.*

Ross   Oh my god.

Sasha   Ross?

Ross   President Whitmore—

Sasha   Call me Sasha, please. May I come in?

Ross *(taken aback)*   Uh—yes, of course.

Sasha *(looking around)*   You have a lovely home.

Ross   Um. Thank you. What are you doing here?

Sasha   I'm sorry I didn't call first, I just wanted to come for a quick visit.

Brigitte *(entering, run-on sentence)*   Ross, I found a really cool bug but then I ate it—(*Seeing* **Sasha**) Your hair is so cool, oh my god!!!

Sasha   Thank you!

Marty (*entering*)   Oh my god, you're—

River (*finishing the thought*)   President Whitmore!

Brigitte   President? Wait, like, the PRESIDENT President??? (*She salutes.*) Brigitte McWilliams, at your service, your majesty!

Sasha   At ease.

Marty   What're you doing here?

Sasha   I came to talk with Ross.

Brigitte   Wanna stay for dinner? We're having tomatoes!

River   Among other things.

Marty   Speaking of, we gotta help Kai with cooking.

Sasha   I'm afraid I can't stay for long.

Brigitte   That's okay! Come back tomorrow! More tomatoes!

She runs back to the kitchen. **Marty** *and* **River** *follow.*

Ross   I'm sorry, but, um, what're you—

Sasha   I'm actually here on behalf of Liz.

Ross   Behalf of . . . oh!

Sasha   Before she . . . well, you know. Before, we were talking about our checks and / we wanted to—

Ross   Your checks—wait, has my money been coming from you?!

Sasha   Yes.

Ross   I need to sit down.

He sits in a chair. **Sasha** *sits beside him.*

Sasha   You alright?

Ross   Yeah, just . . . keep going. Sorry.

Sasha   I know it's a lot to take in. I just wanted to see how things were going. Liz really cared about you.

Ross   She did . . .?

Sasha   Yes! You know why she fired you, right? To protect you.

Ross   I guessed as much.

Kai (*entering*)   Ross, where's the olive oil—

They stop short when they see **Sasha**.

Kai   Oh, wow.

Sasha   Hi. I'm Sasha.

Kai   President Whitmore, it's an—

Sasha   Call me Sasha, please.

Kai   President Whitmore, it's an honor.

Sasha   The honor is all mine. I like your hair.

Kai   Oh, thank you.

Ross   Sasha and . . . Elizabeth have been funding our lives. Monetarily.

Kai   Monetarily . . . no fucking way.

Ross   Language!

Sasha   Yes, the money has come from us and our foundation. We kept it anonymous to ensure that it stayed in the right hands.

Kai   You've, like, truly changed our lives for the better. Thank you.

Sasha   Of course. That's actually why I'm here. Now that Liz is gone . . . Sorry. I just, I've been doing a lot of thinking over the past month. About what I want to do now.

Kai   Aren't you going to run for president?

Sasha   I . . . don't think I am. Working in the presidency has been incredibly fruitful for a number of reasons, but it's not for me in the long run.

Kai   Why not?

Sasha   So much arguing. I'd rather use my energy and resources to enact tangible change for those that need it. So, that brings me to you.

Ross   How so?

Sasha   I'm going to open another foster home, just a few towns over. With all of the policy changes Liz enacted, queer and trans people are in a safer place, and our other candidate, Trevor Rivera, is definitely a good person to take over the presidency. Their partner is actually a good friend of mine. I want to use my resources to help them out. And frankly, I don't think their opponent stands a chance against them. So I'm wondering. Would you like to open this new home with me? I'd like to welcome in around fifteen to twenty kids.

Ross   Wow. That's . . . I'm honored you'd ask me. (*Beat.*) What about Kai?

Kai   What *about* Kai?

Ross   I think it would be great for her to take on a responsibility like this on her own. Maybe they could help you, Sasha.

Kai   Whoa, whoa, what?

Sasha   Kai? Would you like to?

Kai   Ross, that's not what I meant when I was talking about helping others feel safe.

Sasha   How do you want to help people, Kai?

Kai   Well, some friends on these message boards / and I have been talking about protecting the rights the Disowned are fighting for. We're just worried they're going to take our rights away from us again, we just want to protect queer and trans people!

Ross   Kai—!

Sasha (*after Kai finishes*)   Kai, I know it's difficult seeing those that once harmed you trying to get their footing back—

Kai   No, President Whitmore, don't do that, don't defend them.

Ross   KAI.

Kai   What?! I've read their interviews, I know what it was like to have boundaries for them, / we can't let that happen—

Sasha   No. No you don't. What I faced, what Ross faced, is NOTHING like what the cishet community faces. People are *safe*.

Kai   No they're not!! Queer and trans people live in constant fear that the Disowned / are just going to take over again!

Ross   Stop calling them that and go to your room.

Sasha   We both know that's not going to happen.

Kai   Fuck this. I'm out.

Sasha   If you just listen, I can tell you more—

Kai *stomps off to his room.*

Ross   President Whitmore, I am so, so sorry—

Sasha   It's . . . it's fine. She's angry. I was angry once. I get it.

Brigitte (*running in*)   TOMATOES ARE READY!!!

Marty   Among other foods.

Brigitte (*to herself*)   I freaking LOVE tomatoes.

Sasha   I need to go.

Brigitte   No tomatoes?

Sasha   Another time, I promise.

River   It was nice meeting you.

Sasha   You too. Ross . . . (*they hand Ross a business card*) let me know if you need anything.

Ross (*Taking it.*)   Thank you, Sasha.

Sasha   Thank you, too. Goodbye.

They're out the door.

Marty   Hey, where's Kai?

Ross   They'll be down in a bit. Will you go help set the table?

Brigitte   Gosh, we have to do all the work!

Ross   I'll be on cleaning duty.

Brigitte (*going to the kitchen*)   Oooo! Come on, let's go make a MESS.

Marty (*going to the kitchen*)   Woo!

River (*going to the kitchen*)   Alrighty . . .

Ross *takes a breather and goes to the kitchen.*

Blackout.

Scene 2

That night.

Ross *is standing outside of a door. He holds a plate of food, including tomatoes.*

Ross   Kai? (*he knocks*) Kai, we missed you at dinner. I brought you up a plate. (*beat*) Look, I know you're upset, but President Whitmore and I just want you to feel safe. I know it doesn't seem like it, but the way America is . . . that's what's best for you right now. (*beat*) Brigitte made these tomatoes especially for you . . . (*beat*) Alright missy, I'm coming in.

Ross *enters* **Kai**'s *bedroom. It's empty. The window is open and clothes are strewn about.* **Ross** *places the plate down somewhere. He walks in, slowly. He sees a note on the bed. He picks it up, reads it.*

Blackout.

Scene 3

The next morning. **Ross** *is sitting, exhausted. He picks up his phone and dials. After a moment:*

Ross   Kai, it's me again, please just let me know that you're safe or something, I just. Please let me know. Love you.

He hangs up. **Brigitte** *comes into the room with a big ol' yawn.*

Brigitte   Goooooood morning, Ross! Pancakes with tomatoes for breakfast? (*beat*) Look at those bags under your eyes! Are they designer? (*beat*) I heard that on a talk show once. What's a designer bag?

Ross   Just sleepy.

River *and* **Marty** *come into the room, a bit frantically.*

River   Ross?? Kai wasn't in her room this morning.

Ross   I know, River.

Marty   Where are they??

Ross   I don't know, Marty.

Brigitte   We should find him—!

Ross   I KNOW!!

(*Beat.*)

Brigitte (*small*)   Sorry, Ross.

Ross (*exhales*)   I'm sorry, Brigitte. I shouldn't yell, that's not fair. I'm just exhausted. Why don't the three of you go make some pancakes?

They hesitate before going.

Ross   I'll be in soon.

Marty   I'll make some coffee.

Brigitte   Can I have some?

Ross   You know the answer to that, young lady.

Brigitte (*with a smile creeping in*)   Yeeeeeeeeessssss?

Ross (*returning the smile*)   Go on, now.

The three kids go to the kitchen. **Ross** *puts his head in his hands.*

The front door opens. **Kai** *walks in. He's got a black eye forming.*

Ross   Kai!

Kai *just stands.*

Ross   Are you okay?

Kai *doesn't move. After a beat:*

Kai   I joined a protest last night. Got socked in the face.

Ross   Let me get you some ice—

Kai   My friends from—the people from the forum, we went to a protest in the town square to stop a bill that would allow cishets play in sports again. It was awesome at first. Lots of chants, I was surrounded by queer and trans people. But then someone said there was a cishet in the crowd with a knife. I don't know what happened, someone elbowed me in the face, but suddenly I was running, and Samantha—that's the name of the girl who I'm close with on the boards—I mean, I thought I was, turns out she's like in her 40s but whatever, she took my hand to run with her and when I asked where we were going, all she said was, we have to get weapons, we have to go back to her house to get guns and shit, and I just looked at her. Like, yeah, guns can be helpful I guess, but I don't know if I want to be close to a gun!! And then I started to psych myself out and I got scared and I thought about what this bill was trying to do, and I was like, why the fuck do I care? I don't even play sports! I've never hit a touchdown in my life!

Ross I don't think that's—

Kai So I came back here.

Beat.

Ross *pulls* **Kai** *into a hug.*

Kai Do you hate me?

Ross I could never hate you, Kai.

Kai I just, I don't know what to think!!

Ross I've always taught you that violence never solves anything—

Kai Yeah, but that's what *you* think. *I* don't know what *I* think.

Ross You just said that you don't want to be close to a gun. Guns are violent things that only hurt people—

Kai Ugh, I do *not* need a lecture right now.

Ross Then I don't know what to tell you.

Beat.

Kai I made a complete ass of myself in front of President Whitmore yesterday.

Ross Yes. Yes, you did.

Kai I need to apologize.

Ross *takes a second, then pulls out the card* **President Whitmore** *gave him.*

Ross Here. Call them. I'm going to go help the kids.

Ross *starts to leave.*

Kai I'm sorry.

Beat.

Ross *pauses for a moment, then heads into the kitchen. We hear the four of them talking, laughing.* **Kai** *looks at the kitchen, then the front door, then the card. They think. Take out their phone. Calls the number. After a moment:*

Kai   Hi, President Whitmore, it's um, it's Kai, we met yesterday with Ross? I wanted to apologize for my behavior yesterday. I wasn't thinking. Or like, I was, but I wasn't thinking clearly, I guess. Um. Anyways. I went to a protest last night. It was . . . weird. I'd really like to talk with you about it, if that's okay. And like, about other stuff. Um. Let me know. Thanks. Bye.

They hang up. They take a second before going into the kitchen. The kids are ecstatic that **Kai** *is back. Maybe* **Brigitte** *brings up her black eye.*

Fade to black.

End of Part III.

End of Play.